Innovation in English Language Teaching

Innovation in English Language Teaching provides both theoretical perspectives and practical tools for analysing, developing and evaluating English language teaching curricula. It presents English language teaching in a variety of specific institutional, geographic and cultural contexts.

This Reader focuses particularly on curriculum change in context. The articles – which include both classic and specially commissioned pieces – have been selected and edited to highlight the debates, discussions and current issues from different parts of the English-speaking and English-using world.

Academics and teachers from around the world examine the role and influence not just of language teachers and students, but of parents, teacher-trainers, the local community, the press, politicians, and all who have an interest in what goes on in the language classroom. Issues are illustrated and discussed in different contexts, including: teaching migrants in English speaking countries; teaching large classes in developing countries; teaching English for academic purposes; using information technology in the classroom.

Articles by: Michael P. Breen; Kimberley Brown; Christopher N. Candlin; David R. Carless; Ronald Carter; Guy Cook; Susan Feez; Kevin Germaine; Kathleen Graves; David R. Hall; Ann Hewings; Martin Hewings; Adrian Holliday; Gary M. Jones; Clarice Lamb; Joan Lesikin; Michael Lewis; Defeng Li; Numa Markee; Michael McCarthy; David Nunan; Pauline Rea-Dickins; Zakia Sarwar; William Savage; Simon Sergeant; Graeme Storer

David R. Hall is Head of the Department of Linguistics at Macquarie University, Sydney, Australia. **Ann Hewings** is a lecturer in the Centre for Language and Communications at the Open University, UK.

Teaching English Language Worldwide

Companion volumes

The companion volumes in this series are:

Analysing English Language in a Global Context, edited by Anne Burns and Caroline Coffin

English Language Teaching in its Social Context edited by Christopher N. Candlin and Neil Mercer

These three readers are part of a scheme of study jointly developed by Macquarie University, Sydney, Australia, and the Open University, United Kingdom. At the Open University, the three readers are part of a single course, *Teaching English to Speakers of Other Languages Worldwide,* which forms part of the Open University MA in Education (Applied Linguistics) and Advanced Diploma in Teaching English to Speakers of Other Languages. At Macquarie University, the three readers are each attached to single study units, which form part of the Postgraduate Diploma and Master of Applied Linguistics programmes.

The Open University MA in Education is now established as the most popular postgraduate degree for UK education professionals, with over 3,500 students registering each year. From 2001 it will also be available worldwide. The MA in Education is designed particularly for those with experience in teaching, educational administration or allied fields. The MA is a modular degree and students are free to select, from a range of options, the programme that best fits in with their interests and professional goals. The MA in Education programme provides great flexibility. Students study at their own pace and in their own time. They receive specially prepared study materials, and are supported by a personal tutor. (Successful completion of the MA in Education (Applied Linguistics) entitles students to apply for entry to the Open University Doctorate in Education (Ed.D.) programme.)

The Professional Development in Education prospectus contains further information and application forms. To find out more about the Open University and request your copy please write to the Course Reservations and Sales Centre, The Open University, PO Box 724, Walton Hall, Milton Keynes MK7 6ZW, or e-mail ces-gen@open.ac.uk, or telephone +44 (0) 01908 653231 or visit the website *www.open.ac.uk.* For more information on the MA in Education (Applied Linguistics), visit *www.open.ac.uk/applied-linguistics.*

Macquarie University introduced distance versions of its influential on-campus degrees in 1994 and now has students in over thirty countries. Both the Postgraduate Diploma and the Master's are offered in three versions: Applied Linguistics, Applied Linguistics (TESOL) and Applied Linguistics (Literacy). Credits are freely transferable between the Diploma and the Master's and between the three versions, and students may change between distance and on-campus modes or mix modes if desired. Students study at their own pace, with specially developed materials and with support and feedback provided directly from lecturers in the Linguistics Department through e-mail, web, fax, phone and post. A special-ised library service is provided through the Resources Centre of the National Centre for English Language Teaching and Research (NCELTR). External doctoral programmes are also available.

Information about the Macquarie programmes and application forms are available on *www.ling.mq.edu.au* or by writing to the Linguistics Postgraduate Office, Macquarie University, NSW 2109, Australia tel.: +61 2 9850 9243; fax +61 2 9850 9352; e-mail: lingdl@ling.mq.edu.au).

Innovation in English Language Teaching

'This volume brings to the fore diverse, fundamental issues about the processes and politics of curriculum change and improvement, new technologies, and concepts of language use, communication, and instruction vital to guiding the organization and practices of teaching English internationally.' *Alister Cumming, Ontario Institute for Studies in Education, University of Toronto*

Teaching English Language Worldwide

A selection of readers' comments on the series:

'This three-part series offers a map to ELT research and practice . . . it represents the best that ELT, as an Anglo-Saxon institution, has developed over the last thirty years for the teaching of English around the world . . . Readers will find in this series the Who's Who guide to this dynamic and expanding community.' *Claire Kramsch, University of California, Berkeley, California*

'Experienced English language instructors seeking to deepen their knowledge and abilities will find this series forms a coherent basis to develop their understanding of current trends, sociocultural diversity, and topical interests in teaching English as a second or foreign language around the world. All three volumes provide ample flexibility for discussion, interpretation, and adaptation in local settings.' *Alister Cumming, Ontario Institute for Studies in Education, University of Toronto*

'This series provides a collection of essential readings which will not only provide the TEFL/TESOL student and teacher with access to the most up-to-date thinking and approaches to the subject but will give any person interested in the subject an overview of the phenomenon of the use and usage of English in the modern world. Perhaps more importantly, this series will be crucial to those students who do not have available to them articles that provide both a wide spectrum of information and the necessary analytical tools to investigate the language further.' *Joseph A. Foley, Southeast Asia Ministers of Education Organisation, Regional Language Centre, Singapore*

'The strong representation of the seminal Anglo-Australian development of the European functional tradition in the study of language and language education makes this a refreshingly bracing series, which should be widely used in teacher education for English language teaching.' *Euan Reid, Institute of Education, University of London*

'In a principled and accessible manner, these three volumes bring together major writings on essential topics in the study of English language teaching. They provide broad coverage of current thinking and debate on major issues, providing an invaluable resource for the contemporary postgraduate student.' *Guy Cook, University of Reading*

Innovation in English Language Teaching

A Reader

Edited by

David R. Hall and Ann Hewings

London and New York
in association with Macquarie University
and The Open University

For my parents, Ron and Anne Hall

First published 2001
by Routledge
2 Park Square, Milton Park, Abingdon, Oxon, OX14 4RN

Simultaneously published in the USA and Canada
by Routledge
270 Madison Ave, New York, NY 10016

Reprinted 2003, 2005

Routledge is an imprint of the Taylor & Francis Group

Typeset in Perpetua and Bell Gothic by Keystroke, Jacaranda Lodge, Wolverhampton
Printed and bound in Great Britain by TJ International Ltd, Padstow, Cornwall

British Library Cataloguing in Publication Data
A catalogue record for this book is available from the British Library

Library of Congress Cataloging in Publication Data
Innovation in English language teaching : a reader / edited by David Hall and
Ann Hewings.
    p. cm. — (Teaching English language worldwide)
  Includes bibliographical references and index.
  1. English language—Study and teaching—Foreign speakers. I. Hall, David, 1947– .
II. Hewings, Ann. III. Series.
  PE1128.A2 I54 2000
  428′.007—dc21   00-059194

ISBN 0–415–24123–5 (hbk)
ISBN 0–415–24124–3 (pbk)

Contents

PART TWO
Political and institutional constraints in curriculum development

PART THREE
Planning and implementing curriculum change

PART FOUR
Evaluating curriculum change

Illustrations

Figures

Tables

Acknowledgements

The editors and publishers would like to thank the following for permission to use copyright material:

Kimberley Brown and Blackwell Publishers Ltd for 'World Englishes in TESOL programs: an infusion model of curricular innovation' in *World Englishes*, Vol. 12:1, 1993.

Michael P. Breen and Christopher N. Candlin for 'The essentials of a communicative curriculum in language teaching' in *Applied Linguistics*, 1980. Reprinted by permission of Oxford University Press.

David Carless for 'A case study of curriculum implementation in Hong Kong'. Reprinted from *System*, Vol. 26, 1998, with permission from Elsevier Science.

Ronald Carter and Michael McCarthy for material from *Language as Discourse: Perspectives for Language Teaching* (Longman Group UK Limited 1990.) Reprinted by permission of Pearson Education Limited.

Ronald Carter and Taylor & Francis Books Ltd for 'Politics and knowledge about language' in *Investigating English Discourse*, 1997.

Guy Cook for 'The uses of reality: a reply to Ronald Carter' in *ELT Journal*, Vol. 52, No. 1, 1998. Reprinted by permission of *ELT Journal* and Oxford University Press.

Kevin Germaine and Pauline Rea-Dickins for 'Purposes for evaluation'. Reproduced by permission of Oxford University Press from *Evaluation* by Pauline Rea-Dickins and Kevin Germaine (Oxford University Press 1992.)

Kathleen Graves and Cambridge University Press for 'A framework of course development processes' in K. Graves (ed.) *Teachers as Course Developers*, 1996.

David Hall and SEAMEO Regional Language Centre for 'Material production: theory and practice' in A.C. Hidalgo, D. Hall and G.M. Jacobs (eds) *Getting Started: Materials Writers on Materials Writing*, 1995.

Adrian Holliday for 'Achieving cultural continuity in curriculum innovation' in C. Kennedy (ed.) *Innovation and Best Practice* (Pearson Education Limited 1999). Reprinted by permission of Pearson Education Limited.

Gary M. Jones and Multilingual Matters for 'Bilingual education and syllabus design: towards a workable blueprint' in *Journal of Multilingual and Multicultural Development*, Vol. 17: 2–4, 1996.

Joan Lesikin and College ESL for 'Determining social prominence: a methodology for uncovering gender bias in ESL textbooks' in *College ESL*, Vol. 8, No. 1, 1998.

Michael Lewis and Language Teaching Publications (LTP) for 'Lexis in the syllabus' in *The Lexical Approach: The State of ELT and a Way Forward*, 1993.

Defeng Li and TESOL for 'It's always more difficult than you plan and imagine: teachers' perceived difficulties in introducing the communicative approach in South Korea' in *TESOL Quarterly*, Vol. 32, No. 4, 1998.

Numa Markee and Cambridge University Press for 'The diffusion model of innovation in language teaching' in *Annual Review of Applied Linguistics*, 13, 1993.

David Nunan for 'Action research in language education' in J. Edge and K. Richards (eds) *Teachers Develop Teacher Research Papers on Classroom Research and Teacher Development*, 1993. Reprinted by permission of Macmillan Press Ltd. Includes table: 'Types of information required in a learner-centered system' from G. Brindley *Needs Analysis and Objective Setting in the Adult Migrant Program*, 1984, reproduced by permission of NSW Adult Migrant Education Service. Includes material from table: 'Three alternative ways of grouping learners' from *ESL Curriculum Guidelines*, South Australian Education Department, 1990, reproduced by permission of The Department of Education, Training and Employment (SA). Includes material from table: 'Three alternative ways of grouping learners' from K. Willing, *Learning Styles in Adult Migrant Education*, 1998, reproduced by permission of NCELTR.

David Nunan, Clarice Lamb, and Cambridge University Press for material from *The Self-Directed Teacher: Managing the Learning Process*, 1996.

William Savage and Graeme Storer for 'An emergent language program framework: actively involving learners in needs analysis' reprinted from *System*, Vol. 20, No. 2, 1992 with permission from Elsevier Science.

Simon Sergeant for 'CALL innovation in the ELT curriculum' in C. Kennedy, P. Doyle and C. Goh (eds) *Exploring Change in English Language Teaching*, 1999. Reprinted by permission of Macmillan Press Ltd.

Zakia Sharwar and English Teaching Forum for 'Adapting individualisation techniques for large classes' in *English Teaching Forum*, April 1991.

While the publishers and editors have made every effort to contact authors and copyright holders of works reprinted in *Innovation in English Language Teaching*, this has not been possible in every case. They would welcome correspondence from individuals or companies they have been unable to trace.

We would like to thank the authors who contributed their chapters, as well as colleagues within and outside The Open University and Macquarie University who gave advice on the contents. Special thanks are due to the following people for their assistance in the production of this book:

Helen Boyce (course manager)
Freda Barnfield, Pam Burns and Libby Brill (course secretaries)
Liz Freeman (Copublishing)
Nanette Reynolds, Frances Wilson and the staff of the Resource Centre of the National Centre for English Language Teaching and Research, Macquarie University.

Critical readers

Professor Vijay K. Bhatia (Dept of English, City University, Hong Kong)
Geoff Thompson (Applied English Language Studies Unit, Liverpool University, UK)
Professor Leo van Lier (Educational Linguistics, University of Monterey, USA)

External assessor

Professor Ronald Carter (Dept of English Studies, Nottingham University, UK)

Developmental testers

Ilona Cziraky (Italy)
Eladyr Maria Norberto da Silva (Brazil)
Chitrita Mukerjee (Australia)
Dorien Gonzales (UK)
Patricia Williams (Denmark)

We have reproduced all original papers and chapters as faithfully as we have been able to, given the inevitable restrictions of space and the need to produce a coherent and readable collection for readers worldwide. Where we have had to shorten original material substantially, these chapters are marked as adapted. Ellipses within square brackets indicate where text has been omitted from the original. Individual referencing styles have been retained as in the original texts.

Introduction

David R. Hall and Ann Hewings

WHEN MACQUARIE UNIVERSITY IN SYDNEY, Australia, and The Open University in the UK decided to collaborate on the development of new curriculum materials for study at Masters level, the partnership brought together the considerable experience and expertise of the two universities in open and distance learning, applied linguistics and language education. The collection of essays in this book and the two companion volumes is a result of that collaboration. While the edited collections have been designed as one part of an overall study programme, they stand alone as extensive yet focused collections of essays which address key contemporary issues in English language teaching and applied linguistics.

A major concern in editing these three volumes has been the desire to present English language teaching (ELT) in a variety of specific institutional, geographical and cultural contexts. Hence, as far as possible across the three volumes, we have attempted to highlight debate, discussion and illustration of current issues from different parts of the English-speaking and English-using world, including those where English is not learnt as a first language. In doing this we recognise that English language teaching comprises a global community of teachers and learners in a range of social contexts.

The chapters in this volume address issues relating to curriculum change in context, and all three terms in this noun phrase are important. The essays deal with the different ways in which actual classroom practices change, whether at an individual or a system level. Recognising that language teaching does not take place in a neutral or value-free environment, they look at the choices that have to be made within institutional or cultural constraints when designing curricula and evaluating their success. They examine the role and influence of all the stakeholders who might have an interest in what goes on in the language classroom: not just language teachers and students, but parents, teacher-trainers, the local community, the press, politicians, and so on.

The titles of all four parts of the volume contain the word 'curriculum'. The different usages in the literature of words such as 'curriculum', 'syllabus' and 'programme' (or 'program') are evidence that precise definitions of these terms are hard to pin down. In some cases the words are differentiated while in others they are used almost interchangeably, and you will notice different meanings attached to the terminology by different authors in this volume. Here, we intend the term 'language curriculum' in its widest sense, covering all the issues relating to the planning, implementation and evaluation of a series of language-learning events conceived as a coherent whole with a specified purpose.

The first part, 'Directions in curriculum change', raises some issues underlying curriculum design by examining the theoretical underpinnings of a number of recent approaches. This does not attempt, of course, to cover all the different ways of specifying a curriculum, and is not meant to be a historical survey (but see the Feez article in part 3 for a contextualised account of the development of language teaching practices). The assumption underlying our choice of essays for part 1 is the view which few people in language curriculum design would now argue with that content and classroom practice must be considered together: a curriculum is not simply a list of items to be taught. The first chapter by Breen and Candlin, covering work done at Lancaster University on communicative language teaching (CLT), was extremely influential in bringing this view into language teaching, although the focus on the process of learning rather than just the product is consistent with a much older tradition in general education.

CLT is not a monolithic packaged set of procedures, despite frequent talk in the literature of the 'communicative method'. All of the authors of essays in part 1 would no doubt place themselves in the communicative tradition. Where CLT has been introduced or encouraged or advocated in specific contexts around the world it has often been in the form of a package, introduced top-down as a great and reified new idea rather than arising from and devised within the classroom and the needs and problems of particular teachers and learners. As the name of CLT has been invoked as a justification for a process of change taking place in specific geographical, cultural and temporal contexts, some of its underlying principles and practices have been contested or reinterpreted, as will be seen in later chapters in this volume. Its influence is such, however, that anyone putting forward an alternative paradigm has to define it in relation to CLT.

The essays by Nunan and Lamb and by Lewis both place themselves in the communicative tradition by emphasising the centrality of the learner and the learning process. The first explores task-based learning. Although the word 'task' is overused in many published textbooks to the extent that it is often little more than a synonym for 'exercise', and although it is certainly possible to devise context- and communication-free 'tasks' in this sense, the proponents of a task-based syllabus have something more specific in mind. They take tasks to be the interactive learning procedures through which learners both in and out of the classroom learn to understand each other and to make themselves understood, so gaining confidence and experience in using the target language. The links to Lewis's proposal to replace the traditional Present-Practise-Produce teaching procedure with Observe-Hypothesise-Experiment are clear. The observing, hypothesising and experimenting are all being undertaken by the learner in actually using the target language. The emphasis is on the learner, and the teacher's role changes from 'presenter' to something more like 'collaborator' or 'facilitator'.

Breen (1984: 53) claims for CLT that its 'greater concern with capacity for communication rather than repertoire of communication, with the activity of learning a language itself, and with a focus upon means rather than predetermined objectives, all indicate priority of process over content'. We emphasise that this does not say 'process to the exclusion of content', although some have seen CLT as a methodology that rejects the teaching of formal aspects of the language altogether. There are parallels here with arguments that have been used about whole-word teaching of reading as opposed to phonics-based methods, and about process writing as opposed to the teaching of sentence-grammar, spelling and punctuation. The differing roles assigned to process, product, content and form still constitute a major site of struggle within language curriculum development.

This struggle underlies much of the argument between the Cook essay and that by McCarthy and Carter. McCarthy and Carter argue that the curriculum must take account of variation and of context, and this means that learners' interaction with texts must take account of the 'dynamism inherent in linguistic contexts'. The understanding of the dynamism of language and contextual variation is reinforced in McCarthy and Carter's own work on language corpora, large collections of actual texts stored on computer and accessible for quantifiable linguistic analysis. To an extent, then, they may be seen as advocating teaching programmes based on quantitative data, an argument that dates back many years (see, for example, West's General Service List of English Words, based on word counts, and first published in 1936). Cook argues that language teaching should not be a slave to language description, that the processes of learning and teaching are not coincident with the records of language behaviour evidenced through corpora. The argument comes back, as many times before in the history of language pedagogy, to the role played by formal language description in helping teachers to teach and learners to learn.

No linguist would dispute the ubiquity and importance of language variation over time, space, context, purpose, etc. The essay by Hewings and Hewings, which ends part 1 and provides a link with the first chapter of part 2, deals with the variation in language use between academic disciplines. Particularly when applied to the teaching of English for Specific Purposes, this is an area which is attracting growing attention, with increasing levels of research being undertaken around the world (see, for example, the essays in Candlin and Hyland, 1999). The capacity of computers to store large and specialised corpora of language as it is actually used is, whatever we may think of the Cook argument, beginning to revolutionise the way we see language. Where corpora are sufficiently specialised, they underline differences in lexical patterns, word meanings, grammatical patterns and textual cohesion in a way that was possible only in a limited and largely intuition-based way before the corpus databases were created. This development has already had an influence on fields such as lexicography, forensic linguistics, English for academic purposes and curriculum and syllabus design. The approaches taken by Hewings and Hewings and by McCarthy and Carter are illustrative of these last two. Further developments in these areas may serve to inform and/or challenge both learners and teachers in the future.

The incorporation of variation into language curricula is not, at present, a widespread practice, and the essay by Carter which opens part 2 gives some indication of why it is not. In fact, all of the essays in part 2 deal in one way or another with the political and institutional constraints in curriculum development. Language, as an intimate component of individual and national identity, is a particularly emotional issue, and curriculum developers tamper with 'the way things have always been done around here' at their own risk. Carter was branded in some sections of the press as a revolutionary traitor to the nation for his emphasis on knowledge about language and how it functions. Even at a local level, teachers working by themselves in individual classrooms and taking what seem like innocent decisions about the day's activities can easily find themselves the subject of parents' or the school principal's ire.

All but one of the seven chapters in part 2 deal with attempts to change curricula in specific contexts. The exception is the essay by Markee, which presents a framework for the introduction of innovations. As might be expected from an examination of Markee's categories and criteria, none of the projects reported could be judged unequivocally as a failure or a success. He deals with issues such as: At what point can an innovation be judged as satisfactory? What is the critical mass which determines whether an innovation has been adopted by the population for which it was intended? Each of the other essays in this section could be examined in the light of Markee's criteria and followed up to see what has happened in the period since the first publication of the essay. Have the innovations discussed by Carter, Jones, Brown, Sarwar, Savage and Storer, and Li actually had any lasting effect? Have, for example, Carter's ideas set out in the LINC project influenced British teachers' views on language? Has the mix of Malay and English in the Brunei school system actually been modified following the publication of Jones's essay? Has Kimberley Brown managed to persuade American libraries to stock more world-English titles? Has Zakia Sarwar convinced her colleagues to introduce similar methods in their classes, or transferred what she was doing to the mainstream, official curriculum? Have the needs analysis procedures of Savage and Storer been extended to other contexts? And have Defeng Li's Korean teachers adapted, adopted or rejected a communicative approach? These would be interesting questions to follow up, and sometimes they can be pursued through publications in journals (see, for example, Storer and Savage, 1999, for further extensions of their own work) and increasingly through internet discussion lists.

Part 3 examines both the planning and the implementation of curriculum change. Many curriculum development textbooks treat these two aspects separately, but it is clear that the processes involved are circular rather than linear, and that both need to involve or at least take into consideration all of the stakeholders. This part, then, continues the theme of curriculum development in its social and institutional context.

All the essays in this part examine the ways in which change is brought about. They also raise the question of whether change is always desirable, particularly in cases where successful models from one context are imported into new contexts. This is currently a much-disputed point in language teaching in relation to the recent insistence in some circles on learner autonomy as a necessary condition for successful language learning. The chapters by Sarwar and Savage and Storer in part 2 both deal with the introduction of autonomous approaches. In the first essay in part 3, however, Holliday presents a rather different and provocative view of learner-centredness. For Holliday, 'learner-centredness' has become a short-hand way of referring not to individuals but to the skills and competencies we can equip them with and the evaluative mechanisms that can be used to test how effective we as teachers have been. This teacher-centred interpretation of learner-centredness is a highly contentious position, with those advocating learner-centredness strongly disputing this understanding of their approach (see, for example, Savage, 1997). Clearly, there are complex and sometimes contradictory arguments involved here, with both sides claiming to hold the moral high ground. The relationships between different stakeholders – between donors and recipients, policy-makers and practitioners, native and non-native speakers, teachers and learners, insiders and outsiders, experts and novices – are delicate and involve many more issues than how to teach language, as we see again and again in these essays. While Holliday assumes a top-down model (which he attacks), the chapters by Graves and by Nunan both look at ways in which innovation can be instigated by the teacher or by teachers and others working together. Feez gives examples of this collaborative approach when she describes in some detail the ways in which curriculum change has taken place within a large system. Although systemic innovation necessarily involves some form of imposition, it will be seen that through consultation and workshops, teachers at all levels have been involved in the various reformulations of the curriculum. Hall describes four different curriculum-development projects and examines them in the light of their capacity for helping the learners to learn. Hall's introduction of the importance of defining what you are trying to do in developing curricular innovations leads on to the final chapter in this part, in which Sergeant analyses the various uses made of computers in the language classroom and the motivations attached to those uses. He makes a valuable distinction between 'change' brought about by computer-assisted language learning (CALL), which he sees as a superficial addition to the curriculum, and 'innovation' using CALL, which is embedded in the curriculum and encourages new ways of teaching and learning. This separation of superficial versus embedded, change versus innovation is applicable to all areas of the curriculum, not just CALL.

Part 4 focuses on evaluating curriculum change, placing this as an integral component of the planning and implementation cycle. While evaluation is an essential element underpinning all the essays in the volume, this section looks in some detail at different kinds of evaluative processes. Rea-Dickins and Germaine, in answer to the question of why we might need to evaluate at all, provide an overview of the different purposes for which evaluation is conducted. The kind of evaluation exemplified in the Carless essay is one of a growing number of research projects using qualitative methods. His case-study approach, involving what is sometimes called a 'thick' description, turns a microscope on one specific event in one specific context. As a research methodology, it may not yet have the academic cachet of quantitative and controlled research methods, and may not be able to uphold claims to generalisability in the same way as quantitative methods do, but it can reveal much more about why ideas that seem fine in theory work rather differently, if at all, in real life. In the longer term, as more and more small-scale context-embedded research projects are reported, it may be that these stories will constitute the most valuable resource for the teacher and curriculum developer.

The final chapter, by Lesikin, provides a framework for evaluating and analysing language-teaching materials. Using the tools of systemic-functional grammatical analysis she uncovers systematic gender bias in a published textbook. Lesikin's procedures are very much in the tradition of critical discourse analysis, and it is clear that they could be used in contexts other than that outlined here.

The essays in this collection are designed as a source of thought-provoking ideas for all students of language teaching, language teachers, teacher-trainers, curriculum developers and educational administrators. They exemplify a range of work by academics with wide experience in different parts of the world and by teachers who are still very close to the chalk-face. They make the link between theory and the actual circumstances in which language learning takes place or fails to take place. This volume is not a handbook, and has no predetermined answers to the problem of finding appropriate ways of putting together language curricula so that learners can learn. Instead, it provides a series of conceptual frameworks within which such a quest can be undertaken.

References

Breen, M. P. 1984. 'Process syllabuses for the language classroom', in C. Brumfit (ed.) *General English Syllabus Design: Curriculum and Syllabus Design for the General English Classroom*, ELT Documents 118. Oxford: British Council and Pergamon Press.

Candlin, C. N. and Hyland, K. (eds) 1999. *Writing: Texts, Processes, and Practices*. Harlow: Longman.

Savage, W. 1997. 'Language and development', In B. Kenny and W. Savage (eds) *Language and Development*. Harlow: Longman, 283–325.

Storer, G. and Savage, W. 1999. 'Extending an emergent framework to other contexts', *System*, 27, 3: 421–5.

PART ONE

Directions in curriculum change

Chapter 1

Michael P. Breen and Christopher N. Candlin

THE ESSENTIALS OF A COMMUNICATIVE CURRICULUM IN LANGUAGE TEACHING

Introduction

AT A TIME WHEN THERE IS A RECOGNISED NEED in language teaching to give adequate attention to language use as well as language form, various 'notional-functional' or so-called 'communicative approaches' to language teaching are being advocated. In this context, the present paper is offered as a set of proposals in an effort to define the nature of communicative language teaching.

Any teaching curriculum is designed in answer to three interrelated questions: What is to be learned? How is the learning to be undertaken and achieved? To what extent is the former appropriate and the latter effective? A communicative curriculum will place language teaching within the framework of this relationship between some specified purposes, the methodology which will be the means towards the achievement of those purposes, and the evaluation procedures which will assess the appropriateness of the initial purposes and the effectiveness of the methodology.

This chapter presents the potential characteristics of communicative language teaching in terms of such a curriculum framework. It also proposes a set of principles on which particular curriculum designs can be based for implementation in particular situations and circumstances. Figure 1.1 summarises the main areas with which this chapter will deal. In discussing the purposes of language teaching, we will consider (1) communication as a general purpose, (2) the underlying demands on the learner that such a purpose may imply, and (3) the initial contributions which learners may bring to the curriculum. In discussing the potential methodology of a communicative curriculum, we will consider (4) the process of teaching and learning, (5) the roles of teacher and learners, and (6) the role of content within the teaching and learning. Finally (7) we will discuss the place of evaluation of learner progress and evaluation of the curriculum itself from a communicative point of view.[1]

Inevitably, any statement about the components of the curriculum runs the risk of presenting in linear form a framework which is, in fact, characterised by interdependence and overlap among the components. In taking purposes, methodology, and evaluation in turn, therefore, we ask readers to bear in mind the actual interdependence between them.

What follows is a consideration of those minimal requirements on communicative language learning and teaching which, in our view, must now be taken into account in curriculum design and implementation.

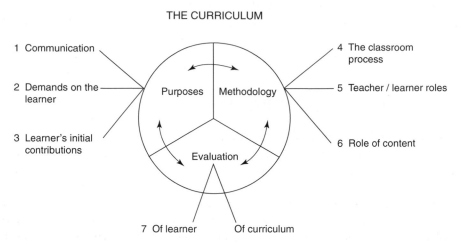

Figure 1.1 The curriculum

1   What is the purpose of the curriculum?

The communicative curriculum defines language learning as learning how to communicate as a member of a particular socio-cultural group. The social conventions governing language form and behaviour within the group are, therefore, central to the process of language learning. In any communicative event, individual participants bring with them prior knowledge of meaning and prior knowledge of how such meaning can be realised through the conventions of language form and behaviour. Since communication is primarily inter-personal, these conventions are subject to variation while they are being used. In exploring shared knowledge, participants will be modifying that knowledge. They typically exploit a tension between the conventions that are established and the opportunity to modify these conventions for their particular communicative purposes. Communicating is not merely a matter of following conventions but also of negotiating through and about the conventions themselves. It is a convention-creating as well as a convention-following activity.

In communication, speakers and hearers (and writers and readers) are most often engaged in the work of sharing meanings which are both dependent on the conventions of interpersonal behaviour and created by such behaviour. Similarly, the ideas or concepts which are communicated about contain different potential meanings, and such potential meanings are expressed through and derived from the formal system of text during the process of communication. To understand the conventions which underlie communication, therefore, we not only have to understand a system of ideas or concepts and a system of interpersonal behaviour, we have to understand how these ideas and this interpersonal behaviour can be realised in language – in connected texts. Mastering this unity of ideational, interpersonal and textual knowledge allows us to participate in a creative meaning-making process and to express or interpret the potential meanings within spoken or written text (Halliday, 1973).

There is an additional characteristic of this unified system of knowledge. The social or interpersonal nature of communication guarantees that it is permeated by personal and socio-cultural attitudes, values and emotions. These different *affects* will determine what we choose to communicate about and how we communicate. The conventions governing ideas or concepts, interpersonal behaviour, and their realisation in texts all serve and create attitudes, judgements and feelings. Just as communication cannot be affectively neutral, learning to communicate implies that the learner will come to terms with the new learning to the extent that his own affects will be engaged. At that point, the learner's affects become further involved in a process of negotiation with those affects which are embodied within the communicative performance of the target community. So, affective involvement is both the driving-force for learning, and also the motivation behind much everyday communication and the inspiration for the recreation of the conventions which govern such communication.

Communication in everyday life synthesises ideational, interpersonal, and textual knowledge – and the affects which are part of such knowledge. But it is also related to and integrated with other forms of human behaviour. In learning how to communicate in a new language, the learner is not confronted by a task which is easily separable from his other psychological and social experiences. The sharing and negotiating of potential meanings in a new language implies the use and refinement of perceptions, concepts and affects. Furthermore, learning the conventions governing communication within a new social group involves the refinement and use of the social roles and the social identity expected by that group of its members. Thus, learning to communicate is a socialisation process. [. . .] Therefore, it makes sense for the teacher to see the overall purpose of language teaching as the *development* of the learner's communicative knowledge in the context of personal and social development.

2   What underlies the ultimate demands on the learner?

A language teaching curriculum, from a communicative point of view, will specify its purposes in terms of a particular target repertoire (Gumperz, 1964). Different curricula will hopefully select their own particular repertoires from a pool of communicative performance on the basis of a sociolinguistic analysis of the target situation. This does not imply that any one curriculum will be necessarily entirely distinctive in the target repertoire to which it is devoted. At the surface there will be inevitable overlap among different repertoires. However, underlying any selected target repertoire there will be an implicit target competence. It is this target competence which we may define as the capacity for actual use of the language in the target situation. So, in specifying the purposes of the curriculum, a requirement for the communicative approach would be to make an initial distinction between the target repertoire ultimately demanded of the learner and the target competence which will underlie and generate such a repertoire.

How can we characterise this target competence? We have already proposed that learning to communicate involves acquiring a *knowledge* of the conventions which govern communicative performance. In addition, we have proposed that such communicative knowledge can be seen as a unified system of ideational, interpersonal, and textual knowledge, which incorporates a range of affects.

We have also suggested that communication and learning how to communicate involve the participants in the sharing and negotiating of meanings and conventions. Such sharing and negotiating implies the existence of particular communicative *abilities* as an essential part of competence. Therefore, we may identify within competence both the knowledge systems and the abilities which call upon and act upon that knowledge. These abilities can be distinguished within competence more precisely. In order to share meaning, the individual participant needs to be able to interpret the meanings of others and to express his own meanings. However, such interpretation and expression will most often take place in the context of interpersonal and personal negotiation. The ability to negotiate operates between participants in communication and within the mind of the individual participant

– the latter negotiation is perhaps more conscious during new learning. More obviously, participants in communication negotiate with one another. But, in endeavouring to interpret and express with a new language, the learner will himself negotiate between the communicative competence he already possesses and that which underlies the new learning.[2]

We suggest, therefore, that the communicative abilities of interpretation, expression, and negotiation are the essential or 'primary' abilities within any target competence. It is also likely that these three abilities continually interrelate with one another during communicative performance and that they are complex in nature. They will involve psychological processes for the handling of rich and variable data – the attention and memory processes, for example – and they may contain within them a range of secondary abilities such as 'coding', 'code substituting' and 'style-shifting' (Bernstein, 1971, Hymes, 1971, Labov, 1970).

The use of these communicative abilities is manifested in communicative performance through a set of skills. Speaking, listening, reading and writing skills can be seen to serve and depend upon the underlying abilities of interpretation, expression and negotiation. In this way we are suggesting that the skills represent or realise underlying communicative abilities. The skills are the meeting point between underlying communicative competence and observable communicative performance; they are the means through which knowledge and abilities are translated into performance, and vice versa.

In selecting any target repertoire, therefore, a communicative curriculum also distinguishes and specifies the target competence on which the performance of such a repertoire depends and through which it is achieved. This specification would indicate the ideational, interpersonal and textual conventions – and the affective aspects of such conventions – as a related and underlying system of knowledge which is shared and developed within the target community. The specification would also indicate the demands upon the learner's communicative abilities of interpretation, expression, and negotiation similarly underlying communicative performance in the target community – and the range of skills which manifest these abilities. Such a specification would account for what the learner needs to know, and how the learner needs to be able to use such knowledge. The ultimate demands on the learner in terms of some specific target repertoire will, in our view, derive from and depend upon this underlying competence of communicative knowledge and communicative abilities.

3   What are the learner's initial contributions?

[. . .] A communicative specification of purposes supports the principle that the roots of our objectives can already be discovered in our learners – however beneath the surface of the actual target repertoire these roots may be. We need to try to recognise what the learner knows and can do in communicative performance with the first language and not assume that the learner's ignorance of the target repertoire implies that the learner is a naïve communicator or someone who evaluates communication in only a superficial way.

This principle, which seems to require us to credit the learner with a highly relevant initial competence of communicative knowledge and abilities, has often been overlooked or only partially applied in language teaching. In the past, it has seemed easier to somehow separate the learner from the knowledge to be learned – to 'objectify' the target language as something completely unfamiliar to the learner. This objectification of the language in relation to the learner has perhaps been encouraged by a narrow definition of what the object of learning actually is, and by an incomplete view of what the learner has to offer. We have tended to see the target only in terms of 'linguistic competence' or textual knowledge, and we have limited such knowledge to the level of syntax without reference to structure above the sentence. Thus, ideational and interpersonal knowledge, which continually interact with textual knowledge and from which textual knowledge evolves, have tended to be overlooked or neutralised. We have often seen the learner primarily in terms of the first language, and we have often assigned to it 'interference' value alone – again taking a narrow textual knowledge as our criterion. More recently, due to developments within sociolinguistics, we have recognised the significance of 'sociolinguistic competence' and also of the 'functional' aspect of language. However, a partial and knowledge-based view of learner competence seems to remain with us and the learner's communicative abilities underlying the initial repertoire still need to be more thoroughly exploited. Rather than just allowing the use of the first language in the classroom, we should perhaps be more concerned with activating that which underlies the initial repertoire of the learner, and to evoke and engage what we may describe as the learner's ongoing or *process competence*.[3] Once we define the object of learning as communication, then we are enabled to perceive the learner in a new light. His initial textual knowledge is placed in its proper perspective – it is merely the tip of the iceberg. Language teaching need no longer be primarily concerned with 'linguistic competence'. We can begin with the assumption that text is the surface realisation of communicative knowledge and abilities and that text is used and created – and learned – on the basis of them. The communicative curriculum seeks to facilitate – even guarantee – the involvement of the learner's communicative knowledge and abilities from the outset rather than overlook them for the sake of some apparent 'fluency' with text. [. . .] However, learners not only contribute prior knowledge and abilities, they also have expectations about the learning of a language. What the curriculum seeks to achieve in terms of any specified purposes must be balanced by what the learner personally expects of the curriculum. Perhaps the current interest in teaching language for 'special purposes' may eventually reveal the challenge to curriculum designers: that all learners regard themselves as learning a language for some special purpose.

We can identify several types of learner expectations and these may, of course, influence one another. We can ask: What is the learner's own view of the nature of language? What is the learner's view of learning a language? (The answers to these questions may lie in the learner's previous formal education, and how he reacted to that experience.) We can also distinguish between, first, how the learner defines his own language learning needs; secondly, what is likely to interest the learner both within the target repertoire and the learning process; and, third, what the learner's motivations are for learning the target repertoire. All these initial expectations are distinct and need to be discovered in some way so that areas of potential match and mismatch between learner expectations and the selected target repertoire and its underlying competence can be best anticipated.

Two important problems need to be identified here in accounting for learner expectations. These expectations are inevitably various and – more significantly – they are subject to change over time. So, the curriculum will need to accommodate and allow for a heterogeneity of learner expectations. It will also need to allow for changes in different learners' perceptions of their needs, in what interests different learners, and in the motivations of different learners. In this way, curriculum purposes should account for initial expectations of learners and anticipate changes in expectations during the learning–teaching process. Such an account and such anticipation may appear to be an impracticable dream when confronted with the variety and fluctuation in the real expectations of learners. That we should try to account for and anticipate these is a further motivation for a communicative curriculum, and – more particularly – for a communicative methodology (see sections 4ff). However, there is a second important aspect of learner expectations: expectations can be educated. For this to happen, learners need to be enabled to express their own expectations;

to explore them and the sources from which they derive. They also need to be enabled to interpret the expectations which the specific purposes of the curriculum make upon them as learners. They need to interpret – at the start of the learning–teaching process and throughout this process – what the target repertoire and its underlying competence demands of them. However vague a learner's initial interpretation may be, he is not going to learn anything unless he has an idea of what he is trying to achieve. Therefore, a process of negotiation between the learner's contributions – including expectations – and the target repertoire, and the means by which these two are brought together, is likely to be characteristic of a communicative methodology. Curriculum purposes inform and guide methodology, and an account of learner expectations within purposes can enable methodology to involve these subjective contributions of the learner and, thereby, call upon the genuine *inter*subjective responsibility of that learner.

4   How are the curriculum purposes to be achieved?

4.1   Methodology as a communicative process

Language learning within a communicative curriculum is most appropriately seen as communicative interaction involving all the participants in the learning and including the various material resources on which the learning is exercised. Therefore, language learning may be seen as a process which grows out of the interaction between learners, teachers, texts and activities.

This communicative interaction is likely to engage the abilities within the learner's developing competence in an arena of cooperative negotiation, joint interpretation, and the sharing of expression. The communicative classroom can serve as a forum characterised by the activation of these abilities upon the learners' new and developing knowledge. This activation will depend on the provision of a range of different text-types in different media – spoken, written, visual and audio-visual – which the participants can make use of to develop their competence through a variety of activities and tasks. The presence of a range of text-types acknowledges that the use of communicative abilities is not restricted to any one medium of communication. The earlier distinction we saw between underlying abilities and the set of skills which serve and depend on such abilities enables us to perceive that the learner may exploit *any* selected skill or combination of skills to develop and refine his interpretation, expression and negotiation. The learner need not be restricted to the particular skills performance laid down by the target repertoire. Because communicative abilities permeate each of the skills, they can be seen to underlie speaking, hearing, reading and writing and to be independent of any prescribed selection or combination of these skills. Similarly, just as no single communicative ability can really develop independently of the other abilities, so the development of any single skill may well depend on the appropriate development of the other skills. In other words, a refinement of interpretation will contribute to the refinement of expression, and vice-versa; just as a refinement of the skill of reading, for example, will contribute to the refinement of the skill of speaking and vice-versa.

Classroom procedures and activities can involve participants in both communicating and metacommunicating. We have referred to the characteristics of communicating in section 1 of this paper. By metacommunicating we imply the learner's activity in analysing, monitoring and evaluating those knowledge systems implicit within the various text-types confronting him during learning. Such metacommunication occurs within the communicative performance of the classroom as a sociolinguistic activity in its own right.

Through this ongoing communication and metacommunication, learners not only become participants in the procedures and activities, they may also become critically sensitised to the potential and richness of the unified system of knowledge, affects and abilities upon which their communication depends. [. . .] In particular, the involvement of all the participants in a process of communicating through texts and activities, and meta-communicating about texts, is likely to exploit the productive relationship between using the language and learning the language.

4.2 Methodology as a differentiated process

The emphasis given in the previous section to the interactive nature of the communicative curriculum suggests, in turn, the need for a communicative curriculum to be differentiated. A communicative curriculum begins with the principle that we should differentiate within purposes between the target repertoire and the communicative knowledge and abilities which underlie it. A second principle is that the learner's process competence needs to be differentiated from the target competence, and that different learners may exploit different process competences as the means towards some particular target. These kinds of distinctions involve differentiation at the curriculum level between purposes and the methodology adopted to achieve such purposes.

Within methodology, differentiation is a principle which can be applied to the participants in the learning, the activities they attempt, the text-types with which they choose to work, and the ways they use their abilities. It is worth considering differentiation within these areas in more detail:

(a) Learners' contributions

Individual learners bring individual contributions to the language learning process in terms of their initial competence, their various expectations about language learning, and their changing needs, interests and motivations prior to and throughout the language learning process. We can recognise that, even in the achievement of some common target competence, different learners through their changing process competence may well adopt different means in attempting to achieve such competence.

(b) Routes

The emphasis within a communicative curriculum on the communicative process of language learning, with the consequent emphasis on cooperative learner activities, offers a natural means for differentiation. Different learners need the opportunity of following different routes to the accomplishment of some individual or common group objective. Such variation in choice of route typically involves selection among alternative skills or combinations of skills, and hence the choice of alternative media. The variation may be motivated by the need to work at a different pace from other learners, or by the desire to pursue alternative content. This selection among routes can itself be open to joint interpretation, the sharing of expression and cooperative negotiation.

(c) Media

In order to allow for differences in personal interest and ease of access, or to permit the search for alternative perspectives on the content, learners should be offered the possibility of working with one or more of a range of media. We mean by this that learners would be expected to act upon text-types in the appropriate medium: written texts would be read, spoken ones listened to, visual ones seen. Just as communication is governed by conventions, so we can see that the different media represent and obey conventions specific to themselves. Learning dialogue by reading, for example, may neutralise the authentic conventions of spoken discourse, and we may be asking the learner to become involved in using and applying knowledge in a distorted way.

(d) Abilities

Whatever the route chosen or the media and text-types selected for communicative learning, different learners will have differentiated ways of making use of the abilities within their communicative competence, and will therefore adopt different learning strategies. Such heterogeneity is often seen as problematic for the teacher, but a communicative methodology would take advantage of this differentiation among learning strategies, rather than insisting that all learners exploit the same kinds of strategy.

These four illustrations of the principle of differentiation within a communicative methodology imply more than merely offering to individual learners opportunities for differential communication and learning, or acknowledging differences between performance repertoires and the developing competences underlying them. Differentiation demands and authenticates communication in the classroom. The various perspectives offered by alternative media, the accomplishment of shared objectives through a variety of routes, and the opportunities for exploiting different learning strategies, all facilitate the conditions for authentic communication among the participants in the learning. Differentiation also enables the learner to authenticate his own learning and thereby become involved in genuine communication as a means towards it. Further, if we confront learners with texts and text-types which are also authentic, this obliges us to allow for different interpretations and differences in how learners will themselves negotiate with texts.

4.3 Methodology exploits the communicative potential of the learning–teaching context

We are easily tempted to excuse the classroom as an artificial or synthetic language learning context – as distinct from some natural or authentic environment. The communicative curriculum seeks to exploit the classroom in terms of what it *can* realistically offer as a resource for learning. This would not necessarily mean changing or disguising the classroom in the hope that it will momentarily serve as some kind of 'communicative situation' resembling situations in the outside world. The classroom itself is a unique social environment with its own human activities and its own conventions governing these activities. It is an environment where a particular social-psychological and cultural reality is constructed. This uniqueness and this reality implies a communicative potential to be exploited, rather than constraints which have to be overcome or compensated for. Experimentation within the prior constraints of any communicative situation is, as we have seen, typical of the nature of communication itself, and the prior constraints of classroom communication need be no exception.

We can make a distinction between the different contributions offered to learning by, on the one hand, the 'formal' language learning contexts of the classroom and, on the other, the 'informal' learning which takes place at any time, anywhere. The classroom can be characterised by the kinds of learning which are best generated in a group context, while 'informal' learning undertaken beyond the classroom is often an individual commitment, especially in the context of foreign language learning. Thus the 'formal' context is one where the interpersonal relationships of the classroom group have their own potential contribution to make to the overall task. Within the communicative curriculum, the classroom – and the procedures and activities it allows – can serve as the focal point of the learning-teaching process. In adopting a methodology characterised by learning and teaching as a communicative and differentiated process, the classroom no longer needs to be seen as a pale representation of some outside communicative reality. It can become the meeting-place for realistically motivated communication-as-learning, communication about learning, and metacommunication. It can be a forum where knowledge may be jointly offered and sought, reflected upon, and acted upon. The classroom can also crucially serve as the source of feedback on, and refinement of, the individual learner's own process competence. And it can serve as a springboard for the learner's 'personal curriculum' which may be undertaken and developed 'informally' outside the classroom. As a coparticipant in the classroom group, the learner's own progress can be both monitored and potentially sustained by himself on the basis of others' feedback and by others within some shared undertaking.

To ensure that the special and differing contributions offered by both 'formal' and 'informal' contexts of learning can be fully exploited, a communicative methodology has to try to relate the two. The classroom can deal with and explore phenomena which are significant in the experienced 'outside world' of the learner, and it can become an observatory of communication as everyday human behaviour. As well as looking outwards, the classroom has a reflexive role as a laboratory where observations can become the means for the discovery of new knowledge and the development of abilities.

A communicative methodology will therefore exploit the classroom as a resource with its own communicative potential. The classroom is only one resource in language teaching, but it is also the meeting-place of all other resources – learners, teachers, and texts. Each of these has sufficiently heterogeneous characteristics to make classroom-based negotiation a necessary undertaking. [. . .] The authenticity of the classroom lies in its dual role of observatory and laboratory during a communicative learning-teaching process.

5 What are the roles of the teacher and the learners within a communicative methodology?

5.1 The teacher

Within a communicative methodology the teacher has two main roles. The first role is to facilitate the communicative process between all participants in the classroom, and between these participants and the various activities and texts. The second role is to act as an *interdependent* participant within the learning-teaching groups. This latter role is closely related to the objective of the first role and it arises from it. These roles imply a set of secondary roles for the teacher: first, as an organiser of resources and as a resource himself. Second, as a guide within the classroom procedures and activities. In this role the teacher endeavours to make clear to the learners what they need to do in order to achieve some specific activity or task, if they indicate that such guidance is necessary. This guidance role is ongoing and largely unpredictable, so the teacher needs to share it with other learners. Related to this, the teacher – and other learners – can offer and seek feedback at appropriate moments in learning-teaching activities. In guiding and monitoring the teacher needs to be a 'seer of potential' with the aim of facilitating and shaping individual and group knowledge and exploitation of abilities during learning. In this way the teacher will be concentrating on the process competences of the learners.

A third role for the teacher is that of researcher and learner – with much to contribute in terms of appropriate knowledge and abilities, actual and observed experience of the nature of learning, and organisational capabilities. As a participant-observer, the teacher has the opportunity to 'step back' and monitor the communicative process of learning-teaching.

As an interdependent participant in the process, the teacher needs to actively share the responsibility for learning and teaching with the learners. This sharing can provide the basis for joint negotiation which itself releases the teacher to become a co-participant. Perceiving the learners as having important contributions to make – in terms of initial competence and a range of various and changing expectations – can enable the teacher to continually seek potential and exploit it. A requirement on the teacher must be that he distinguish between learning and the performance of what is being learned. The teacher must assume that the performance within any target repertoire is separable from the means to the achievement of that repertoire. Also, he must assume that learners are capable of arriving at a particular objective through diverse routes. The teacher needs to recognise learning as an interpersonal undertaking over which no single person can have full control, and that there will be differences between ongoing learning processes. The teacher has to accept that different learners learn different things in different ways at different times, and he needs to be patiently aware that some learners, for example, will enter periods when it seems that little or no progress is being made and that, sometimes, learning is typified by silent reflection.

5.2 The learner

Regardless of the curriculum in which they work and regardless of whether or not they are being taught, all learners of a language are confronted by the task of discovering *how to learn* the language. All learners will start with differing expectations about the actual learning, but each individual learner will be required to adapt and continually readapt in the process of relating himself to what is being learned. The knowledge will be redefined as the learner uncovers it, and, in constructing and reconstructing his own curriculum, the learner may discover that earlier strategies in the use of his abilities need to be replaced by other strategies. Thus, all learners – in their own ways – have to adopt the role of negotiation between themselves, their learning process, and the gradually revealed object of learning.

A communicative methodology is characterised by making this negotiative role – this learning how to learn – a public as well as a private undertaking. Within the context of the classroom group, this role is shared and, thereby, made interpersonal. If we recognise that any knowledge which we ourselves have mastered is always shared knowledge and that we always seek confirmation that we 'know' something by communicating with other people, we have to conclude that knowledge of anything and the learning of anything is an inter-personal matter. Also, if we recognise that real knowledge is always set in a context and this context is both psychological and social – what is known will always be contextualised with other knowledge in our minds and will always carry with it elements of the social context in which it was experienced – then we also have to conclude that a significant part of our learning is, in fact, socially constructed. These justifications for a genuinely interpersonal methodology are quite independent of the nature of what is to be learned. If the object of learning is itself communication, then the motivation to enable the learner to adopt an interpersonal means to that learning is doubly justified. Quite simply, in order to learn to communicate within a selected target repertoire, the learner must be encouraged to communicate – to communicate about the learning process, and to communicate about the changing object of learning on the basis of accepting that 'learning how to learn' is a problem shared, and solved, by other learners.

Within a communicative methodology, the role of learner as negotiator – between the self, the learning process, and the object of learning – emerges from and interacts with the role of joint negotiator within the group and within the classroom procedures and activities which the group undertakes. The implication for the learner is that he should contribute as much as he gains, and thereby learn in an interdependent way. The learner can achieve interdependence by recognising responsibility for his own learning and by sharing that responsibility with other learners and the teacher. This commitment can be initiated and supported by a milieu in which the learner's own contributions – interpretations, expressions, and efforts to negotiate – are recognised as valid and valuable. Such a context would be typified by the acceptance of ongoing success *and failure* as necessary prerequisites towards some ultimate achievement, where it is assumed that learners inevitably bring with them 'mixed abilities' and that such a 'mixture' is, in fact, positively useful to the group as a whole. Commitment to communication on the learner's part need not be regarded as something unattainable or threatening – even for the 'beginning' learner – because he is expected to rely on and develop that which is familiar: his own process competence and experience of communication.

As an interdependent participant in a cooperative milieu where the learner's contributions are valued and used, the individual learner is potentially rewarded by having his own subjective expectations and decisions informed and guided by others. In a context where different contributions and differential learning are positively encouraged, the learner is allowed to depend on other learners and on the teacher when the need arises, and also enabled to be independent at appropriate moments of the learning. He can feel free to exploit independent strategies in order to learn, to maintain and develop personal affective motivations for learning, and to decide on different routes and means which become available during learning. The paradox here, of course, is that genuine independence arises only to the extent that it is interdependently granted *and* interdependently accepted. Learning seen as totally a personal and subjective matter is seeing learning in a vacuum; indeed we may wonder whether such learning is ever possible.

Learners also have an important monitoring role in addition to the degree of monitoring which they may apply subjectively to their own learning. The learner can be a provider of feedback to others concerning his own interpretation of the specific purposes of the curriculum, and the appropriateness of methodology to his own learning experiences and achievements. In expression and negotiation, the learner adopts the dual role of being, first, a potential teacher for other learners and, second, an informant to the teacher concerning his own learning progress. In this latter role, the learner can offer the teacher and other learners a source for new directions in the learning-teaching process of the group. Essentially, a communicative methodology would allow both the teacher and the learner to be interdependent participants in a communicative process of learning and teaching.

6 What is the role of content within a communicative methodology?

Language teaching curricula have often been traditionally defined by their content. Such content has itself been derived from a target repertoire in terms of some selected inventories of items analysed prior to the commencement of the teaching-learning process and often acting as predeterminants of it. Similarly, sets of formal items taken from an analytic grammar of the language, or sets of 'functions' taken from some list of semantic categories, have been linked to themes and topics deemed in advance to be appropriate to the expectations of the particular learners.

Communicative curricula, on the other hand, do not look exclusively to a selected target repertoire as a specifier of curriculum content, for a number of reasons. First, the emphasis on the process of bringing certain basic abilities to bear on the dynamic conventions of communication precludes any specification of content in terms of a static inventory of language items – grammatical or 'functional' – to be learned in some prescribed way. Second, the central concern for the development and refinement of underlying competence as a basis for a selected target repertoire requires a distinction between that target and *any* content which could be used as a potential means towards it. Third, the importance of the curriculum as a means for the activation and refinement of the process competences of different learners presupposes differentiation, ongoing change, and only short-term predictability in what may be appropriate content.

The communicative curriculum would place content within methodology and provide it with the role of servant to the learning-teaching process. Thus, content would not necessarily be prescribed by purposes but selected and organised *within* the communicative and differentiated process by learners and teachers as participants in that process. Therefore, the learner would use the content of the curriculum as the 'carrier' of his process competence and as the provider of opportunities for communicative experiences through which personal routes may be selected and explored as a means to the ultimate target competence.

From this concern with means rather than ends – with the process of learning-teaching rather than with the product – the communicative curriculum will adopt criteria for the selection and organisation of content which will be subject to, and defined by, communicative learning and teaching. The content of any curriculum can be selected and organised on the basis of some adopted criteria, and these criteria will influence five basic aspects of the content: its focus, its sequence, its subdivision (or breakdown), its continuity, and its direction (or routing). What are the criteria for the selection and organisation of content within the communicative curriculum?

(a) Focus

Content within communicative methodology is likely to focus upon knowledge – both cognitive and affective – which is personally significant to the learner. Such knowledge would be placed in an interpersonal context which can motivate personal and joint negotiation through the provision of authentic and problem-posing texts. If content is to be sensitive to the process of learning and to the interpersonal concerns of the group, it needs to reflect and support the integration of language with other forms of human experience and behaviour.

(b) Sequence

If we accept that the communicative process requires that we deal with dynamic and creative conventions, we cannot assume that any step-by-step or cumulative sequence of content will necessarily be appropriate. In learning, the various and changing routes of the learners crucially affect any ordering of content, so that sequencing derives from *the state of the learners* rather than from the implicit 'logic' of the content itself. It may be naïve to assume that what may be 'simple' for any one learner is likely to be 'simple' for all learners. Sequencing in communicative content is therefore likely to be a cyclic process where learners are continually developing related frameworks or aggregations of knowledge and ability use, rather than accumulating separable blocks of 'static' knowledge or a sequence of ordered skills. Thus, content becomes something which learners move into and out from, and to which they return in a process of finer analysis and refined synthesis. Curriculum designers cannot, therefore, predict with any certainty the 'levels' of content on which learners will decide to evolve their own sequencing in learning. [. . .]

(c) Subdivision

Traditionally content has been subdivided into serialised categories of structures or 'functions'. A communicative view of content precludes this fragmentation and argues for subdivision in terms of whole frameworks wherein there is interaction between all the various components of the knowledge system – ideational, interpersonal and textual – and all the abilities involved in using such knowledge. Content would be subdivided or broken down in terms of activities and tasks to be undertaken, wherein both knowledge and abilities would be engaged in the learners' communication and metacommunication. The various activities and tasks would be related by sharing a holistic 'core' of knowledge and abilities. So, we would not be concerned with 'units' of content, but with 'units' of activity which generate communication and metacommunication.

(d) Continuity

The need to provide continuity for the learner has, in the past, been based upon content. Within a communicative methodology, continuity can be identified within at least four areas. First, continuity can reside in the activities and the tasks within each activity; and from one activity to another and from one task to another. Second, continuity potentially resides within communicative acts during the learning and teaching: either at the 'macro' level in terms of the whole lesson and its 'micro' sequences of negotiation, or within the structure of discourse in terms of the 'macro' communicative act with its own coherent sequence of utterances. Third, continuity is provided through the ideational system. At the 'macro' level the learner may have access to continuity of theme, while at the 'micro' level the learner can have access to conceptual or notional continuity. Ideational continuity is realised through a refinement of textual knowledge – the refinement of a concept, for example, can imply a refinement of its linguistic expression, and vice-versa. Fourth, and finally, continuity can reside within a skills repertoire or a cycle of skill-use during an activity. For example, there could be a progression from reading to note-taking to speaking for the achievement of a particular activity. A communicative methodology would exploit each of these areas of continuity as clusters of potential continuities, rather than exploit any one alone. All can be inherent in a single activity. These kinds of continuity offer two important advantages. They can serve the full process competences of learners – knowledge systems and abilities – and they can allow for differentiation. Learners need to be enabled to seek and achieve their own continuity and, therefore, the criteria for their own progress. In the process of accomplishing some immediate activity, learners will impose their own personal and interpersonal order and continuity upon that activity, the communication which the activity generates, the interpersonal, ideational and textual data which they act upon, and on the skills they need to use in the activity's achievement. As a result, the progressive refinement of the learner's own process competence can provide an overall *learning* continuity. Once the teacher can accept that each of these areas provides potential continuity for different learners, it ceases to be a problem if different learners pursue several routes or progress at different rates.

(e) Direction

Traditionally, learners have been expected to follow the direction implicit in some prescribed content. Typically an emphasis on content led the learner from the beginning, through the middle, to the end. From what has been indicated so far, a communicative methodology would not exploit content as some pre-determined route with specific entry and exit points. In a communicative methodology, content ceases to become some external control over learning-teaching procedures. Choosing directions becomes a part of the curriculum itself, and involves negotiation between learners and learners, learners and teachers, and learners and text. Who or what directs content becomes a justification for communication about the selection and organisation of content with methodology, and about the various routes to be adopted by the learners through any agreed content. Content can be predicted within methodology only to the extent that it serves the communicative learning process of the participants in the group. It might well be that the teacher, in negotiation with learners, will propose the adoption of aspects of the target repertoire as appropriate content. However, the teacher would recognise that the central objective of developing underlying communicative knowledge and abilities can be achieved through a range of alternative content, *not necessarily* including aspects of the target repertoire. Such 'carrier' content can be as diverse as the different routes learners may take towards a common target: perhaps content can be more various and more variable. Also, the teacher would remain free to build upon the contributions of learners – their initial competences and expectations – and exploit the inevitably different ways in which learners may attain the ultimate target. [. . .]

7 How is the curriculum process to be evaluated?

The communicative curriculum insists that evaluation is a highly significant part of communicative interaction itself. We judge 'grammaticality', 'appropriateness', 'intelligibility', and 'coherence' in communicative performance on the basis of shared, negotiated, and changing conventions. Evaluation within the curriculum can exploit this 'judging' element of everyday communicative behaviour in the assessment of learners' communication and metacommunication. The highly evaluative aspect of communication can be adopted as the evaluation procedure of the curriculum. If so, the essentially intersubjective nature of evaluation can be seen as a strong point rather than, possibly, a weakness.

How might we evaluate learner progress? Evaluation of oneself, evaluation of others, and evaluation of self by others is intersubjective. In this way, evaluation need not be regarded as external to the purposes of the curriculum or external to the actual process of learning and teaching. In recognising that relative success or failure in the sharing of meaning, or in the achievement of some particular task, is most often an intersubjective matter, the communicative curriculum would rely on shared and negotiated evaluation. Criteria for eventual success – in some particular task – could be initially negotiated, achievement of the task could be related to these agreed criteria, and degrees of success or failure could be themselves further negotiated on the basis of the original criteria. Evaluative criteria, therefore, would be established and applied in a three-stage process: (i) What might 'success' mean? (ii) Is the learner's performance of the task successful? (iii) If so, how successful is it? Each stage would be a matter for communication. Instead of the teacher being obliged to teach towards some externally imposed criteria – manifested most often by some external examination or standardised test – he can exploit the interpretation of these external or standardised criteria as part of the joint negotiation within the classroom. The group's discovery of the criteria inherent in such end-of-course or summative assessment would be one means for the establishment of the group's own negotiated criteria and, crucially, for the sharing of responsibilities during the learning-teaching process.

In a communicative curriculum we are dealing with an interdependence of the curriculum components of purposes, methodology, and evaluation. It follows that any evaluation within the curriculum also involves an evaluation of the curriculum itself. Any joint negotiation among the various participants within the curriculum may obviously deal with the initial purposes and ongoing methodology which have been adopted. Indeed, communicative evaluation may well lead to adaptation of initial purposes, of methodology, and of the agreed criteria of evaluation themselves. Evaluation within and of the curriculum can be a powerful and guiding force. Judgements are a crucial part of knowledge, learning, and any educational process. By applying judgements to the curriculum itself, evaluation by the users of that curriculum can be brought into the classroom in an immediate and practical sense. Once within the classroom, evaluation can be made to serve as a basis for new directions in the process of teaching and learning.

A genuinely communicative use of evaluation will lead towards an emphasis on *formative* or ongoing evaluation, rather than summative or end-of-course evaluation which may be based on some prescribed criteria. That is, it can shape and guide learning and guide decisions within the curriculum process. Any shared and negotiated evaluation within the classroom will generate potentially formative feedback for and between learners and between learners and the teacher. Formative evaluation may not only indicate the relative successes and failures of both learner and curriculum, it can also indicate new and different directions in which both can move and develop. [. . .]

This placing of evaluation within the communicative process as a formative activity in itself does not necessarily invalidate the place of summative evaluation. Summative evaluation becomes valuable if it can reveal the learners' relative achievement of a particular target repertoire. However, we have already proposed that any target repertoire needs to be seen as the tip of an iceberg. Therefore, an essential requirement on any summative evaluation would be that it can adequately account for the learner's progress in the refinement of a particular underlying competence – the communicative knowledge and abilities which provide the *capacity* for the use of a target repertoire. Summative evaluation, in other words, needs to be sensitive to differential competences which may underlie some common target. As such, summative evaluation within a communicative curriculum needs to focus on the assessment of the learner's developing communicative knowledge and abilities as well as on his actual performance within the target repertoire. [. . .]

Therefore, the essential characteristics of evaluation within a communicative curriculum would be that such evaluation is itself incorporated within the communicative process of teaching and learning, that it serves the dual role of evaluating learner progress and the ongoing curriculum, and that it is likely to be formative in the achievement of this dual role.

8   Achieving communicative language teaching

We emphasised at the outset of this paper that any curriculum framework for language teaching and learning necessarily involves designers, materials writers, teachers and learners in a process of relating the three components of purpose, methodology and evaluation. Even so, we need to acknowledge that any curriculum – including a communicative curriculum – cannot strictly be designed as a whole from the start. We can only deduce and propose the principles on which a variety of communicative curricula may be based. Any curriculum is a personal and social arena. A communicative curriculum in particular, with its emphasis on the learning and teaching of communication, highlights a communicative process whereby the interrelating curriculum components are themselves open to negotiation and change.

From this it follows that the communicative curriculum – no more than any other – can never be one uniquely identifiable language teaching curriculum. In a real sense there can be no such thing as an ideal and uniquely applicable language teaching curriculum since any realisation of the curriculum must reflect a realistic analysis of the *actual situation* within which the language teaching will take place. To cope with this requirement of appropriateness to situation, the communicative curriculum has to be proposed as a flexible and practical set of basic principles which underlie a whole range of potential communicative curricula. It is this set of principles which we have tried to present in this paper, in the knowledge that such proposals need to be translated into action in the classroom in order to test their own validity. This is, after all, the only means by which curriculum theory and practice can develop. Even though the curriculum designer may have taken account of the actual language teaching situation, he has to recognise that from design to implementation is itself a communicative process. J. M. Stephens (1967) identified this process when he said:

> The curricular reforms emanating from the conference room will be effective only insofar as they become incorporated into the concerns that the teacher is led to express. Any statements or decisions coming from the curriculum committee will not be transported intact into the lives of pupils. Such statements must work through a complex chain of interactions. The original statements of the committee will act as stimuli for one set of people such as subject-matter supervisors. These people, in turn, will react to the stimuli, possibly merely mirroring what they receive, more likely, incorporating much of themselves into the reaction. Their reactions will then act as stimuli for a second set of people who will also react in their own way. After a number of such intermediary transactions someone, the teacher, will apply some stimuli to the pupil himself.
>
> (pp. 12–13)

While Stephens, in talking about stimuli, does not emphasise transactions as a two-way process, he clearly implies that the translation from principles through design to implementation is most often a process of reinterpretation of the curriculum, and a process of negotiation between the curriculum and its users. If adopted within the design and implementation procedure, the conditions or minimal requirements on any communicative curriculum must take account of those situational constraints which are unchangeable. However, such minimal requirements should also serve as the general criteria against which any situational constraints will be tested in order to assess whether or not the constraint is genuinely immutable or whether it may be overcome.

If a curriculum based upon the principles which we have examined here is not implementable within a particular situation, then it may be that a genuinely communicative curriculum is simply not viable. It may be the case that curriculum designers and teachers in such a situation need to consider whether the achievement of language learning *as communication* is appropriate.

Communicative curricula need – through time and according to situation – to be open and subject to ongoing developments in theory, research, and practical classroom experience. Communicative curricula are essentially the means of capturing variability. Variability will exist in selected purposes, methods, and evaluation procedures, but variability must also be seen as inherent in human communication and in the ways it is variously achieved by different learners and teachers. The classroom – its social-psychological reality, its procedures and activities – is potentially a communicative environ-ment where the effort to pull together such variability is undertaken. The learning-teaching process in the classroom is the meeting-point of all curriculum components and it is the place where their coherence is continually tested. The learning-teaching process in the classroom is also the catalyst for the development and refinement of those minimal requirements which will underlie future curricula.

Notes

1 'Curriculum' can be distinguished from 'syllabus' in that a syllabus is typically a specification of the content of the teaching and learning and the organisation and sequencing of the content. Content and its organisation is subsumed within a curriculum as part of methodology (Section 6 of this paper). A syllabus is therefore only part of the overall curriculum within which it operates. For interesting discussions of curriculum theory and design see, *inter alia*, Lawton, 1973; Stenhouse, 1975; Golby *et al.*, 1975.

2 This negotiative interaction within the learner between prior knowledge and the new learning has been a concern within psychology for many years. See, for example, Piaget (1953), Bruner (1973), and Neisser (1976).

3 This 'process competence' is the learner's changing and developing communicative knowledge and abilities as the learner moves from initial competence towards the target competence. It is partly revealed through a series of 'Interlanguages' (Selinker, 1972, Tarone, 1977, Corder, 1978).

References

Bernstein, B., 1971. *Class, Codes and Control*, Volume 1: *Theoretical Studies towards a Sociology of Language*. London: Routledge and Kegan Paul.

Bruner, J. S., 1973. *Beyond the Information Given*. London: George Allen & Unwin.

Bruner, J. S., Olver, R. and Greenfield, P., 1966. *Studies in Cognitive Growth*. New York: John Wiley & Sons.

Corder, S. P., 1978. 'Error analysis, interlanguage and second language acquisition' in Kinsella, V. (ed.) *Language Teaching and Linguistics: Surveys*. Cambridge University Press.

Golby, M., Greenwald, J. and West, R. (eds.) 1975. *Curriculum Design*. London: Croom Helm in association with the Open University Press.

Gumperz, J. J., 1964. 'Linguistic and social interaction in two communities' in Gumperz, J. J. and Hymes, D. (eds.) *American Anthropologist* 66 (6 ii): 1964.

Halliday, M. A. K., 1973. 'The functional basis of language' in Bernstein, B. (ed.) *Class, Codes and Control*, Volume 2: *Applied Studies towards a Sociology of Language*. London: Routledge and Kegan Paul.

Hymes, D., 1971. 'On communicative competence' in Pride, J. and Holmes, J. (eds.) *Sociolinguistics*. Harmondsworth: Penguin Books, 1972.

Labov, W., 1970. 'The study of language in its social context'. *Studium Generale* 23, 1970.

Lawton, D., 1973. *Social Change, Educational Theory and Curriculum Planning*. London: University of London Press.

Neisser, U., 1976. *Cognition and Reality*. San Francisco: W. H. Freeman & Co.

Piaget, J., 1953. *The Origins of Intelligence in the Child*. London: Routledge and Kegan Paul.

Selinker, L., 1972. 'Interlanguage'. *IRAL* 10: 3, 1972.

Stenhouse, L., 1975. *An Introduction to Curriculum Research and Development*. London: Heinemann.

Stephens, J. M., 1967. *The Process of Schooling: A Psychological Examination*. New York: Holt, Rinehart & Winston.
Tarone, E., 1977. 'Conscious communication strategies in inter-language: a progress report'. Paper presented at the 11th TESOL Convention, Miami, Fl. 1977.

Chapter 2

David Nunan and Clarice Lamb

MANAGING THE LEARNING PROCESS

"I dunno," Jimmy said, "I forget what I was taught. I only remember what I've learnt."
(Patrick White)

You are given the experiences you need to understand the world.
(Paulo Coelho)

Introduction

T HE DECISIONS THAT TEACHERS ARE REQUIRED to make during the instructional process are all driven by the nature of the program, the goals of instruction, and the needs of the individual learners. It is therefore critical for us to consider these issues before turning to the management of the learning process in the classroom. [. . .]

In this chapter we cover the following issues and concepts:

— *Setting the context and defining terms* key terms defined are "learner-centeredness," "experiential learning," "humanism," "learning-centeredness," "communicative language teaching," "high-structure and low-structure teaching"
— *Curriculum processes* the scope of curriculum development and the importance of curriculum development for the management of learning
— *Needs analysis* definition and examples of needs analysis
— *Setting goals and objectives* from learner needs to learning goals, illustration of goals and objectives, how clearly stated goals and objectives provide a sound basis for managing the learning process

Setting the context and defining terms

[. . .]

Learner-centeredness

The concept of learner-centeredness has been invoked with increasing frequency in recent years. What does the term mean? Like many widely used terms, it probably means rather different things to different people (Nunan and Brindley 1986). For us, learner-centered classrooms are those in which learners are actively involved in their own learning processes.

The extent to which it is possible or desirable for learners to be involved in their own learning will obviously vary from context to context (and, indeed, from learner to learner). If learners are to learn anything at all, however, ultimately they have to do the learning for themselves. Thus it is a truism to say that they should be involved in their own learning. In an ideal learning-centered context, not only will decisions about what to learn and how to learn be made with reference to the learners, but the learners themselves will be involved in the decision-making process. Each element in the curriculum process will involve the learner, as Table 2.1 shows.

Table 2.1 Learner roles in a learner-centered curriculum

Curriculum stage	Role of learner
Planning	Learners are consulted on what they want to learn and how they want to go about learning. An extensive process of needs analysis facilitates this process. Learners are involved in setting, monitoring, and modifying the goals and objectives of the programs being designed for them.
Implementation	Learners' language skills develop through the learners actively using and reflecting on the language inside and outside the classroom. They are also involved in modifying and creating their own learning tasks and language data.
Assessment and evaluation	Learners monitor and assess their own progress. They are also actively involved in the evaluation and modification of teaching and learning during the course and after it has been completed.

The philosophy of learner-centeredness has strong links with experiential learning, humanistic psychology and task-based language teaching. These links are evident in the following quotes:

> [A learner-centered] curriculum will contain similar elements to those contained in traditional curriculum development, that is, planning (including needs analysis, goal and objective setting), implementation (including methodology and materials development) and evaluation (see for example Hunkins 1980). However, the key difference between learner-centred and traditional curriculum development is that, in the former, the curriculum is a collaborative effort between teachers and learners, since learners are closely involved in the decision-making process regarding the content of the curriculum and how it is taught. This change in orientation has major practical implications for the entire curriculum process, since a negotiated curriculum cannot be introduced and managed in the same way as one which is prescribed by the teacher or teaching institutions. In particular, it places the burden for all aspects of curriculum development on the teacher.
>
> (Nunan 1988: 2)

The proponents of humanistic education have broadened our concept of learning by emphasizing that meaningful learning has to be self-initiated. Even if the stimulus comes from outside, the sense of discovery, however, and the motivation which that brings has to come from inside driven by the basic human desire for self-realization, well-being and growth. . . . [I]n terms of personal and interpersonal competence the process-oriented classroom revolves around issues of risk and security, cooperation and competition, self-directedness and other-directedness; and meaningful and meaningless activities. We have also tried to make clear that "teachers who claim it is not their job to take these phenomena into account may miss out on some of the most essential ingredients in the management of successful learning" (Underhill 1989, p. 252).

(Legutke and Thomas 1991: 269)

We can see from these extracts that learner-centeredness is strongly rooted in traditions derived from general education. Our view is that language pedagogy needs to draw on its general educational roots for sustenance, which it has not not always done. In fact, some language programs seem to have suffered an "educational bypass."

Learning-centeredness

Table 2.1, which sets out the role of the learner in relation to curriculum planning, implementation and evaluation, represents the ideal. As teachers and course designers, we have been in relatively few situations in which learners from an early stage in the learning process have been able to make critically informed decisions about what to learn and how to learn. In our experience, learners need to be systematically taught the skills needed to implement a learner-centered approach to pedagogy. In other words, language programs should have twin goals: language content goals and learning process goals. Such a program we would characterize as being "learning centered." By systematically educating learners about what it means to be a learner, learners reach a point where they are able to make informed decisions about what they want to learn and how they want to learn. It is at this point that a truly learner-centered curriculum can be implemented. Learning-centeredness is thus designed to lead to learner-centeredness.

The previous discussion underlines the fact that learner-centeredness is not an all-or-nothing process. Rather it is a continuum from relatively less to relatively more learner-centered. Nunan (1995b) has captured this continuum in the following tables, which show that learner-centeredness can be implemented at a number of different levels. The tables also illustrate some of the practical steps that can be taken in implementing a learner-oriented approach to instruction.

Table 2.2 relates to the experiential content domain. It demonstrates that, all other things being equal, a classroom in which learners are made aware of the pedagogical goals and content of instruction is more learner-centered than one in which goals and content are left implicit. We would argue that all learners should, in the first instance, be alerted to goals and content. In collecting data for this book we were surprised at how infrequently this step happened. However, we would go further, and argue that it is just a first step along a path that, given the appropriate context and types of learners, could take the learners through a gradual learning process in which they made selections from a range of alternatives, modified and adapted goals and content, created their own goals and selected their own experiential content areas and finally moved beyond the classroom itself. (For practical descriptions and illustrations of these processes, see Nunan 1995b.) How far one chooses to move along the continuum depends on one's learners and the context and environment of the instructional process.

Table 2.3 shows how the continuum can apply to the learning process domain. Once again, we see that learner-centeredness is not an all-or-nothing process, but can be implemented in a series of gradual steps.

Table 2.2 Learner-centeredness in the experiential content domain

Level	Learner action	Gloss
1	Awareness	Learners are made aware of the pedagogical goals and content of the course.
2	Involvement	Learners are involved in selecting their own goals and objectives from a range of alternatives on offer.
3	Intervention	Learners are involved in modifying and adapting the goals and content of the learning program.
4	Creation	Learners create their own goals and objectives.
5	Transcendence	Learners go beyond the classroom and make links between the content of the classroom and the world beyond the classroom.

Table 2.3 Learner-centeredness in the learning process domain

Level	Learner action	Gloss
1	Awareness	Learners identify strategy implications of pedagogical tasks and identify their own preferred learning styles/strategies.
2	Involvement	Learners make choices among a range of options.
3	Intervention	Learners modify/adapt tasks.
4	Creation	Learners create their own tasks.
5	Transcendence	Learners become teachers and researchers.

Communicative language teaching

Communicative language teaching emerged from a number of disparate sources. During the 1970s and 1980s applied linguists and language educators began to re-evaluate pedagogical practice in the light of changed views on the nature of language and learning, and the role of teachers and learners in the light of these changing views. The contrast between what for want of better terms we have called "traditionalism," and communicative language teaching (CLT), is shown in Table 2.4 in relation to a number of key variables within the curriculum. The table presents contrasts in relation to theories of language and learning, and in relation to objectives, syllabus, classroom activities and the roles of learners, teachers and materials. The views illustrated represent points on a continuum, rather than exclusive categories, and most teachers will move back and forth along the continuum in response to the needs of the students and the overall context in which they are teaching. The truth is that language is, at one and the same time, both a system of rule-governed structures and a system for the expression of meaning. Learning is a matter of habit formation as well as a process of activation through the deployment of communicative tasks. The challenge for the teacher, the textbook writer and the curriculum developer is to show how the rule-governed structures enable the language user to make meanings.

Table 2.4 Changing views on the nature of language and learning: Traditionalism and CLT

Teaching	Traditionalism	Communicative language
Theory of language	Language is a system of rule-governed structures hierarchically arranged.	Language is a system for the expression of meaning: primary function – interaction.
Theory of learning	Habit formation; skills are learned more effectively if oral precedes written; analogy not analysis.	Activities involving real communication; carrying out meaningful tasks and using language that is meaningful to the learner promote learning.
Objectives	Control of the structures of sound, form and order, mastery over symbols of the language; goal – native speaker mastery.	Objectives will reflect the needs of the learner; they will include functional skills as well as linguistics objectives.
Syllabus	Graded syllabus of phonology, morphology, and syntax. Contrastive analysis.	Will include some or all of the following: structures, functions, notions, themes and tasks. Ordering will be guided by learner needs.
Activities	Dialogues and drills; repetition and memorization; pattern practice.	Engage learners in communication; involve processes such as information sharing, negotiation of meaning and interaction.
Role of learner	Organisms that can be directed by skilled training techniques to produce correct responses.	Learner as negotiator, interactor, giving as well as taking.
Role of teacher	Central and active; teacher-dominated method. Provides model; controls direction and pace.	Facilitator of the communication process, needs analyst, counselor, process manager.
Role of materials	Primarily teacher oriented. Tapes and visuals; language lab often used.	Primary role of promoting communicative language use; task based, authentic materials.

We do not believe that many classrooms can be defined exclusively in terms of a particular methodology. Whether a classroom is characterized as "traditional" or "communicative" is therefore determined by the relative emphasis and degree to which the views listed in the table underpin what happens in the classroom rather than on the exclusive adherence to one set of views to the exclusion of any other. The difference lies, not in the rigid adherence to one particular approach rather than another, but in the basic orientation. Some teachers operate out of a traditional paradigm, making occasional forays into CLT, and for others it is the other way around. In the ESL and EFL classrooms we have worked in and studied in recent years, the prevailing trend has been toward CLT, although by no means exclusively so.

High- and low-structure teaching

The insight that communication was an integrated process rather than a set of discrete learning outcomes created a dilemma for language education. It meant that the destination (functioning in another language) and the route (attempting to learn the target language) moved much closer together, and, in some instances (for example, in role plays and simulations), became indistinguishable. The challenge for curriculum developers, syllabus designers, materials writers and classroom teachers revolved around decisions associated with the movements between points on the continua set out in the tables in the preceding section. Questions such as the following therefore appeared with increasing frequency in teacher-training workshops: How do I integrate "traditional" exercises, such as drills, controlled conversations and the like, with communicative tasks such as discussions, debates, role plays, etc.? How do I manage decision making and the learning process effectively in classroom sessions devoted to communicative tasks which, by definition, require me to hand over substantial amounts of decision-making power and control to the learners? How can I equip learners themselves with the skills they will need to make decisions wisely and to embrace power effectively?

For some individuals the solution lay in rejecting the changing views along with their inconvenient pedagogical implications. Others went to the opposite extreme, eschewing "traditional" solutions to their materials development and language-teaching challenges. In most contexts, however, a more balanced view prevailed.

> For some time after the rise of CLT, the status of grammar in the curriculum was rather uncertain. Some linguists maintained that it was not necessary to teach grammar, that the ability to use a second language ("knowing how") would develop automatically if the learner were required to focus on meaning in the process of using the language to communicate. In recent years, this view has come under serious challenge, and it now seems to be widely accepted that there is value in classroom tasks which require learners to focus on form. It is also accepted that grammar is an essential resource in using language communicatively.
>
> (Nunan 1989: 13)

In educational terms, a useful way of viewing this emerging dilemma in language education is in terms of high- and low-structure teaching. High-structure tasks are those in which teachers have all the power and control. Low-structure tasks are those in which power and control are devolved to the students. We have borrowed the terms "high-structure" and "low-structure" from Biggs and Telfer (1987). They suggest that the successful management of the learning process depends on teachers knowing where to locate themselves on the high-to low-structure continuum in relation to a given task. In a high-structure task, students are placed in reactive roles and accorded relatively little choice. In a low-structure context, students have many options and maximum autonomy. However, we do not equate high-structure with non-communicative and low-structure with communicative tasks. In certain communicative tasks, learners have relatively little freedom of maneuver. However, we do believe an association exists between low-structure and CLT and that the incorporation of communicative tasks with low-structure implications into the classroom increases the complexity of the decision-making process for the teacher.

We would argue that the kinds of managerial issues that arise and the sorts of decisions that teachers are required to make will be largely driven by the degree of structure implied. This concept is illustrated in Table 2.5, which provides exemplary questions relating to high- and low-structure contexts as these apply to key elements at the levels of curriculum planning, implementation, and evaluation. This schema will be referred to constantly in the pages that follow, as it is one of the key organizational frameworks underpinning the work as a whole. It allows us to deal coherently with the following key managerial questions and to demonstrate that the answers will vary according to the degree of structuring called for by the instructional goals guiding the interaction at that particular time.

What aspects of teacher talk (direct instruction, feedback, instructions, and questioning strategies) facilitate or impair effective learning?

What issues need to be taken into consideration in lesson planning and preparation?

How can the teacher most effectively exploit resources in the classroom?

What strategies exist for setting up different modes of classroom interaction, from teacher-fronted through small group, pair and individual work?

What are the implications of affective attitudes (e.g., motivation, attitude and aptitude) for the effective management of learning?

What tools, techniques, and strategies exist for the ongoing monitoring and evaluation of classroom interaction and acquisition?

(All of these questions can be explored through the investigative procedures suggested in Nunan 1990, 1992).

The curriculum in outline

Implicit in the foregoing discussion is the fact that classroom decision-making and the effective management of the learning process cannot be made without reference to the larger context within which instruction takes place. The context and environment of the learning process, including the curriculum plans that should drive the pedagogical action, are critically important here. In other words, classroom decisions cannot be made without reference to structures operating outside of the classroom, at the level of the curriculum.

Language curriculum development has been greatly influenced by changing views on the nature of teaching and learning. These changing views are reflected in the objectives and content of language programs, as well as activities, materials, and teacher/learner roles. The influence of these different views was made clear in the Table 2.4, which contrasted traditionalism with CLT.

As we can see from Table 2.5, communicative language teaching has had a major influence on language curriculum development. First, curriculum development has become much more complex. Whereas twenty or thirty years ago, the point of departure for curriculum development tended to be restricted to the identification of the learner's current level of proficiency, with the development of communicative language teaching and the insight that curricula should reflect learners' communicative needs and learning preferences,

Table 2.5 Curriculum decision-making in high-structure and low-structure contexts

Curricular elements	Management issues	
	High-structure contexts	Low-structure contexts
At the planning stage		
Course design	What does the institution tell me to teach? What are the managerial decisions entailed in the teacher's manual?	How do I design/adapt my own content/goals/tasks?
Needs analysis	How can I identify the learning preferences of my students?	How can I involve my learners in identifying and articulating their own needs?
Collegial	How can I cooperate with colleagues in course planning? How can I get the most out of staff meetings? How can staff meetings contribute to effective planning?	What opportunities exist for team teaching?
Resources	How do I manage use of set text?	How do I modify/adapt the text? How do I create my own resources? How do I design split information tasks that will be effective in my context?
At the implementation stage		
Talk/interaction	What are effective strategies for direct instruction? How do I give feedback on high-structure tasks?	What questioning strategies facilitate learner contributions to low-structure tasks? How do I give feedback in low-structure tasks? What types of teacher questions maximize student output?

Learner language	How do I correct learner errors?	How can I provide language models in small group role plays in which the principal focus is on the exchange of meanings?
Learner attitude		How do I deal with group conflicts? How do I deal with student resistance to learner initiated tasks?
Group configuration	How do I organize controlled practice? How do I manage teacher-fronted instruction effectively?	How do I set up small group learning? What strategies exist for setting communicative tasks in which students work independently?
At the evaluation stage Learner assessment	What techniques will help me to assess the achievement of my learners?	How can I help my learners develop effective techniques for self-assessment?
Self-evaluation of the learning process		
Formal evaluation		How can learners be involved in providing input to the evaluation process?

much more information about and by learners came to be incorporated into the curriculum process. The other major modification occurred with the emergence of the communicative task as a central building block within the curriculum. Instead of being designed to teach a particular lexical, phonological or morphosyntactic point, tasks were designed to reflect learners' communicative needs. Language focus exercises were developed as a second-order activity.

In summary, we can say that curriculum development represents a delicate juggling act involving the incorporation of information about the learner, about the language, and about the learning process. Language content questions include what are we teaching, why are we teaching it, and when we are teaching it. Learning process questions, which are methodological in character, include how are we arranging the learning environment. Among other things, when we focus on the learner, we must ask how well the learner has done and how well the curriculum has done in serving the needs of the learner.

We can relate these key questions to each other in terms of the central curricular elements of syllabus design, which has to do with the selection, sequencing and grading of content; methodology, which is concerned with task selection and sequencing; and assessment and evaluation, which are concerned with determining how well students have done, as well as evaluating how well the instructional process has met curricular goals. These relationships are set out schematically in Table 2.6.

Table 2.6 Key curriculum questions, procedures, and areas

Questions	Procedures	Areas
Content		
What?	Selecting	
Why?	Justifying	Syllabus design
When?	Grading	
Processes		
How?	Enacting	Methodology
When?	Sequencing	
Outcomes		
How well?	Assessing	Assessment
How effective?	Evaluating	Evaluation

One view of "curriculum" has it that curriculum processes have to do with the development of tactical plans for action. In this view, "curriculum" is taken to refer to statements about what should happen in the teaching and learning situation. According to this view, the curriculum specialist's task ends when the ink is dry on the various documents that have been produced to guide teaching and learning. We believe that this view is simplistic and naïve, that while "curriculum" includes the planning process, it also includes the processes of implementation and evaluation. These three phases are captured in Figure 2.1.

The final point we wish to make is that the language curriculum should concern itself, not only with language content goals, but also with learning process goals. Learners should be focused on the processes through which learning takes place as well as on the target language they are learning. It is our contention that learners who have developed skills in identifying their own preferred learning skills and strategies will be more effective language learners.

Phase I:	Planning (initial needs analysis, goals and objectives, content, and process)
Phase II:	Implementation (ongoing needs analysis, monitoring, action research)
Phase III:	Evaluation (assessment, self-assessment, program evaluation)

Figure 2.1 Three phases or perspectives on the curriculum process

| Curriculum goals | Language content | For example, to develop the ability to obtain goods and services in the target language |
| | Learning process | For example, to develop skills in learning how to learn |

Task

Aim   To familiarize you with some of the key tasks concerned with curriculum development and to provide an opportunity for you to relate these to your own teaching situation.

Procedure

1.   The following list contains some of the tasks that need to be carried out in the course of designing and implementing a curriculum. Study the activities and decide which of them, in relation to a context with which you are familiar, should be carried out by a teacher, a curriculum specialist, a counselor, a director of studies, etc. Write these down in the spaces provided.
2.   Select those areas for which the teacher has primary responsibility. What are some of the decisions that need to be made? Express these as questions.

Data

Interview students _____
Conduct needs analysis _____
Assign students to class groups _____
Carry out diagnostic test _____
Assess students' current level of English _____
Diagnose individual learning difficulties _____
Identify individual learning styles _____
Select and grade linguistic content (grammar, vocabulary, functions, notions) _____

Select experiential content (topics, themes, situations, settings, etc.) _____

Set out course goals _____
Write performance objectives _____
Select, adapt or develop learning tasks and materials _____
Monitor student progress _____

Assess learning outcomes _____
Evaluate language program(s) _____

In some teaching contexts, teachers will be responsible for all these tasks. In others, they will have little control. Some of the questions raised by teachers in relation to interviews, needs analysis, and assigning students to groups include the following:

—   *Student interviews* Should these be carried out before, during, or after the course has begun? Should the learners be forced to respond in the target language? How do I get information from low-proficiency learners when I don't speak their language?
—   *Needs analysis* What techniques exist for doing needs analysis? How can the resulting information be used for writing course goals and objectives? What if my learners have conflicting needs?
—   *Assigning students to groups* What criteria, other than proficiency level, can be used to assign students to groups? Is it possible to have different configurations at different times during the teaching day?

Needs analysis

In the course of designing a teaching program from scratch or modifying an existing one, it is generally desirable to collect and interpret data about the learners and the institutional context in which they learn. This information may be collected formally or informally before the course and once the course has begun. A variety of different types of information can be collected. Such information might include biographical information about the learners, data on the types of communicative tasks that learners might want or need to carry out in the target language, information on the ways in which the learners prefer to learn, and so on. A wide range of information can be collected through needs analysis procedures of various kinds, as will be seen in the sample instruments provided in this section. In the initial planning stages, the extent to which learners' subjective needs can be canvassed depends on the range and extent of learners' previous experiences. (It would be unrealistic, for example, to ask learners whether they like to learn through role play and simulations if they have never experienced such activities.)

In attempting to obtain information from learners, as well as about learners, additional limitations and constraints will apply with young learners, or with low-proficiency learners if the teacher does not speak the learners' first language and does not have the benefit of bilingual assistants or other first language resources.

Brindley (1989) suggests that there are basically three different approaches to needs analysis. He calls these the language proficiency orientation, the psychological/humanistic orientation and the specific purpose orientation. The three approaches are differentiated according to their educational rationale, the type of information collected, the method of data collection and the purposes for which the data are collected. The salient characteristics of the three approaches are set out in Table 2.7.

In learner-oriented contexts, the types of information required and the purposes to which the information will be put will vary somewhat from programs developed without reference to the learners themselves, and those for which any preliminary analysis will be largely restricted to the needs of the institution or the educational system that the curriculum is intended to serve. Within a second, rather than foreign, language context, Brindley suggests types of information and purposes that are important (see Table 2.8).

Table 2.7 Approaches to needs analysis

Language proficiency orientation	Psychological/humanistic orientation	Specific purpose orientation
Educational rationale		
Learners learn more effectively if grouped according to proficiency.	Learners learn more effectively if involved in the learning process.	Learners learn more effectively if content is relevant to their specific areas of need/interest.
Type of information		
Language proficiency/language difficulties	Attitudes, motivation, learning strategy preferences	Information on native speaker use of language in learners' target communication situation
Method of collection		
Standardized forms/tests Observation	Standardized forms Observation, interviews and surveys	Language analysis Surveys of learners' patterns of language use
Purpose		
So learners can be placed in groups of homogeneous language proficiency	So learners' individual characteristics as learners can be given due consideration	So that learners will be presented with language data relevant to their communication goals
So teachers can plan language content relevant to learners' proficiency level	So learners can be helped to become self-directing by being involved in decision making about their learning	So motivation will be enhanced by relativeness of language content

Source: After Brindley 1989: 67–69. Used by permission.

A major purpose for conducting needs analyses is to categorize and group learners. This grouping process facilitates the specification of content and learning procedures that are consonant with some aspect of the learner data that has been gathered. Figure 2.2 exemplifies some ways in which data can be used for grouping purposes.

Setting goals and objectives

In the content domain, needs analysis provides a basis for setting goals and objectives. Goal and objective setting are important tasks in most educational contexts, because they provide a rationale for selecting and integrating pedagogical tasks, as well providing a point of reference for the decision-making process. Goals are broad statements that provide general signposts for course development. The following sample goals have been extracted from a variety of second and foreign language programs. They are expressed in the broadest possible terms.

— To develop sufficient oral and written skills to obtain promotion from unskilled worker to site supervisor

— To establish and maintain social relationships through exchanging information, ideas, opinions, attitudes, feelings, and plans

Table 2.8 Types of information required in a learner-centered system

Type of information required	*Purpose*
1 Learners' life goals	So that teachers have a basis on which to determine or predict learners' language goals, communicative networks and social roles
2 Language goals, communicative networks and social roles	So learners may be placed in a group based on common social roles, and teachers may make preliminary decisions about course content appropriate to learners' social roles
3 Objective needs, patterns of language use, personal resources (including time)	So learners can be grouped according to their needs and/or interests
4 Language proficiency and language difficulties	So learners can be grouped according to their language proficiency
5 Subjective needs including learning strategy preferences, affective needs, learning activity preferences, pace of learning, attitude toward correction	So that teachers may adapt learning activities to learning strategy preferences, individual needs
6 Information about learners' attainment of objectives	So that the teacher can monitor performance and modify program accordingly
7 Information about developmental processes in second language learning, including learners' communicative strategies	So that teachers can gear language content and materials to learners' stage of development

Source: Adapted from Brindley 1984. Used by permission.

–   To develop communicative skills in order to acquire, record and use information from a variety of aural sources
–   To develop academic listening skills in order to extract key information from university lectures
–   To develop basic communicative skills in order to obtain basic goods and services as a tourist

More limited goals, couched in functional terms, can be found in teaching materials of various sorts. The following have been taken from an intermediate-level textbook.

In this book you will:
Make comparisons
Ask for and give advice
Express obligation
Talk about past experiences
Express opinions about entertainment.

(Nunan 1995a)

These goal statements are very general in nature and can encompass numerous subsidiary objectives. Most curriculum documents based on a goal and objectives approach contain a

I   Language proficiency profile
  1   Students with oral skills, but with few or no literacy skills in L1
  2   Students who belong in a new arrivals program
  3   Students who require general support in the mainstream
  4   Students with specific affective, language and communication needs
  5   Students who are approximating nativelike proficiency

(Adapted from S.A. ESL Guidelines)

II Learning strategy profile
  1   *"Concrete" learners* These learners tend to like games, pictures, films, video, using cassettes, talking in pairs and practicing English outside class.
  2   *"Analytical" learners* These learners like to study grammar, study English books, and read newspapers; they also like to study alone, find their own mistakes, and work on problems set by the teacher.
  3   *"Communicative" learners* These students like to learn by watching, listening to native speakers, talking to friends in English and watching television in English, using English out of class in shops, trains, etc., learning new words by hearing them and learning by conversations.
  4   *"Authority-oriented" learners* These learners prefer the teacher to explain everything; they also like to have their own textbook, to write everything in a notebook, to study grammar, learn by reading, and learn new words by seeing them.

(Adapted from Willing 1988)

III Learning purpose
  1   New arrivals
  2   English in the workplace
  3   English for further study
  4   English for professional employment
  5   English for access to vocational training and employment

Figure 2.2 Three alternative ways of grouping learners

limited number of goals (perhaps five or six) that provide a basis for the development of objectives. Formal performance objectives specify what learners should be able to do as a result of instruction. Formal objectives should contain a performance (which sets out what learners are to do), conditions (specifying the conditions and circumstances under which the learners should perform) and standards (setting out how well they should perform). The three objectives that follow illustrate the three components of performance, conditions, and standards.

—   Working in pairs, learners will provide enough information for their partner to draw their family tree. They will provide enough information for a three-generation family tree to be drawn.
—   Students will extract and record estimated minimum and maximum temperatures from a taped radio weather forecast. They must accurately record four of the six regions covered by the forecast.
—   While watching a videotaped conversation between two native speakers, students will

identify the various topics discussed and points at which they are changed. All topics and change points are to be identified.

The use of an objectives approach has been criticized in general education on the grounds that precise statements of what the learner should be able to do at the end of a course is somehow undemocratic and needlessly restricting on both the student and the teacher. Others argue that such precise specification greatly facilitates other steps in the design process. It forces the designer to be realistic about what learners can achieve and helps guide the selection of appropriate materials and classroom activities. It is also an essential prerequisite for devising appropriate forms of learner assessment.

Some years ago, an interesting set of specifications was developed in Australia. Called the Australian Language Levels (ALL) guidelines, these specifications were intended to be general enough to help materials writers and teachers working in a range of second and foreign languages. The ALL guidelines take as their point of departure a number of broad goals that are refined into specific goals, as shown in Table 2.9.

You can get some idea from this further example of the breadth of the goal-setting exercise. You can also see how numerous subsidiary objectives could be formulated from each of the goal statements. Interestingly, the designers of the ALL guidelines chose to move directly from goals to the specification of task or activity types without elaborating detailed sets of objectives. We also have employed this procedure in some of our work. Although we do not feel it necessary to develop formal three-part objectives for everything we wish to teach our learners, we do believe that a sample set of objectives can greatly assist in managing the learning process. They can be particularly useful in the ongoing monitoring and assessment of the learning process.

The latest manifestations of the goals and objective approach to curriculum development have appeared in competency statements that attempt to specify what learners should be able to do at different levels. The following are extracts of core competencies designed for an adult immigrant program. Once again, you can see they are formulated in terms of what the learners should be able to do as a result of instruction.

English for study

1.   Can understand the context of further education/training in Australia
2.   Can utilise a range of learning strategies relevant to further education/training contexts
   _____

3.   Can understand an oral presentation relevant to further education/training contexts
4.   Can negotiate complex/problematic spoken exchanges related to further educational/training contexts
5.   Can participate in group discussions relevant to further educational/training contexts
6.   Can deliver short oral presentations relevant to further educational/training contexts
   [. . .]

Vocational English

1.   Can understand the context of work in Australia

Table 2.9 Communication and learning-how-to-learn goals

Broad goal	Specific goals
Communication By participating in activities organized around use of the target language, learners will acquire communication skills in the target language, in order that they may widen their networks of interpersonal relations, have direct access to information and use their language skills for study, vocational and leisure-based purposes	To be able to use the target language to: — establish and maintain relationships and discuss topics of interest (e.g., through exchange of information, ideas, opinions, attitudes, feelings, experiences, plans) — participate in social interaction related to solving a problem, making arrangements, making decisions with others, and transacting to obtain goods, services, and public information — obtain information by searching for specific details in a spoken or written text and then process and use the information obtained — obtain information by listening to or reading a spoken or written text as a whole, and then process and use the information obtained — give information in spoken or written form (e.g., give a talk, write an essay or a set of instructions) — listen to, read or view, and respond personally to a stimulus (e.g., a story, play film, song, poem, picture, play)
Learning-how-to-learn Learners will be able to take a growing responsibility for the management of their own learning so that they learn how to learn, and how to learn a language	To develop: — cognitive processing skills (to enable them to understand values, attitudes and feelings to process information, and to think and respond creatively) — learning-how-to-learn skills — communication strategies (to enable them to sustain communication in the target language)

Source: Adapted from Scarino et al. 1988.

2.   Can utilise a range of learning strategies relevant to employment contexts

3.   Can understand an oral presentation relevant to workplace contexts
4.   Can negotiate complex/problematic spoken exchanges relevant to employment contexts
5.   Can participate in group discussions/meetings
6.   Can participate in casual conversations
      [. . .]

English for community access

1.   Can understand the context of welfare/community services in Australia

2.   Can utilise a range of learning strategies relevant to the local community context

_____

3.   Can understand an oral report relevant to the local community context
4.   Can negotiate complex/problematic spoken exchanges for personal business and community purposes
5.   Can participate in casual conversation

_____

[. . .]

(NSW Adult Migrant Education Service Draft Competencies)

Another useful tool is the curriculum-planning grid. Planning grids such as Figure 2.3 can be used to relate goal and objective statements with other curricular elements (such as grammar, functions, or topics). In Figure 2.3 the task or performance elements from a set of objectives are cross-referenced with settings. The grid was developed for a general English speaking course.

Tasks	Settings									
	1	2	3	4	5	6	7	8	9	10
Identify people										
Talk about past events										
Give and receive messages										
Talk about future ability										
Report what someone says										
Talk about where things are located										
Make excuses										
Express regrets										
Talk about personal qualities										
Give reasons										
Give opinions and advice										
Express references										
Make a complaint										

Key to settings
1 At work   3 Using public transport   5 On holiday   7 At the market   9 At a dinner party
2 At home   4 In bar/coffee shop   6 In a store   8 At school   10 In a government office

Figure 2.3 Planning grid for general English course

Task

Aim To apply the planning grid described in this section to your own teaching situation.

Procedure

Develop a planning grid, similar to the one in Figure 2.3, to a course of your choosing.

In this section we have tried to illustrate a range of ways in which goals and objectives can be expressed. Despite their differences, all of these goals and objectives share something in common; they all describe what learners should be able to do as a result of instruction. We believe that all language programs should take as their point of departure goals and objectives, however couched, that have been derived from an analysis of learner needs.

Summary and conclusions

The basic theme of this chapter is that a firm basis for effective classroom decision making and management must be laid well before the teacher sets foot in the classroom. It is difficult, if not impossible, to say whether many managerial decisions are either good or bad without reference to the needs of the learners or the goals and objectives of the curriculum. Because the decisions that teachers are required to make during the instructional process are driven by the nature of the program, the goals of instruction and the needs of the individual learners, we include a detailed description and discussion of these issues and procedures in the chapter. [. . .]

References

Biggs, J. and R. Telfer 1987. *The Process of Learning*. 2nd edn. Sydney: Prentice-Hall.

Brindley, G. 1984. *Needs Analysis and Objective Setting in the Adult Migrant Education Program*. Sydney: NSW Adult Migrant Education Service.

Brindley, G. 1989. *Assessing Achievement in a Learner-Centred Curriculum*. Sydney: NCELTR.

Hunkins, F. 1980. *Curriculum Development: Program Improvement*. Columbus, Ohio: Charles Merrill Publishing Co.

Legutke, M. and H. Thomas 1991. *Process and Experience in the Language Classroom*. London: Longman.

Nunan, D. 1988. *The Learner Centred Curriculum*. Cambridge: Cambridge University Press.

Nunan, D. 1989. *Designing Tasks for the Communicative Classroom*. Cambridge: Cambridge University Press.

Nunan, D. 1990. "Action research in the language classroom." In J. Richards and D. Nunan (eds.), *Second Language Teacher Education*. New York: Cambridge University Press.

Nunan, D. 1992. *Research Methods in Language Learning*. New York: Cambridge University Press.

Nunan, D. 1995a. *ATLAS: Learning-Centered Communication*. Boston: Heinle & Heinle.

Nunan, D. 1995b. Closing the gap between learning and instruction. *TESOL Quarterly*, Spring 1995.

Nunan, D. and G. Brindley. 1986. "The learner-centred curriculum in theory and practice," paper presented at the Annual TESOL Convention, Anaheim, April 1986.

Scarino, A., D. Vale, P. McKay and J. Clark. 1988. *Australian Language Levels Guidelines*. Canberra: Curriculum Development Centre.

Underhill, A. 1989. "Process in humanistic education." *English Language Teaching Journal*, 43, 250–256.

White, P. 1961. *The Tree of Man*. London: Penguin.

Willing, K. 1988. *Learning Styles in Adult Migrant Education*. Adelaide: National Curriculum Resource Centre.

Chapter 3

Michael Lewis

LEXIS IN THE SYLLABUS

SYLLABUS IN THIS CHAPTER is interpreted in what Nunan calls the 'narrow' sense – the content of the teaching programme. Willis, in *The Lexical Syllabus*, observes that an approach involves both syllabus specification and methodology, and that syllabus and methodology are not discrete options: indeed, syllabus may be specified in terms of goals, performance objectives, or other criteria such as Prabhu's procedural syllabus. Here, I am concerned with the contribution lexis may make to the specification of content. Historically, syllabuses were structural; the Communicative Approach introduced functions, and certain re-orderings. The question naturally arises as to what similar changes are called for by the Lexical Approach. The search for a **strictly** lexical syllabus is likely to be frustrating for theorist, teacher and student. Widdowson has observed that a strictly lexical syllabus would begin with one word texts each complete in itself, proceed to two word texts, and so on to ever more complex texts but where, at all times, any grammatical complexity was obligatory as the language user's meaning became increasingly complex, and **demanded** additional grammaticalisation. Even if such a syllabus were possible to devise, it is difficult to imagine it being pedagogically acceptable.

Similarly, the attempt by Cobuild to define a lexical syllabus around the most frequent **words** of the language has not, despite its fascinating theoretical base, met with widespread acceptance. Some of the reasons I perceive for this are discussed below. I emphasise that my own concern is to look at the **contribution** which lexical items of different kinds can make in determining content.

Educational syllabus

Language teaching is part of a wider whole, the education of individuals. Every learning experience should contribute to the development of mature individuals. Although educational experiences will differ in the way they contribute for every participating individual, effective educational experience should increase **curiosity, wonder and awe, confidence** and **self-worth**. In addition it should increase the individual's ability to **concentrate, appreciate, argue a case, tolerate, take responsibility** and **co-operate**.

There is in all education a hidden agenda which seeks to develop particular intellectual skills, the most important of which are involved in:

1   Identifying problems.
2   Collecting information, data and evidence.

3   Classifying data, by recognising similarity and difference.
4   Ranking, making hierarchies, separating more from less important.
5   Evaluating evidence and argument.
6   Estimating, so that the plausibility of an answer may be evaluated.
7   Taking decisions – based on complete or partial data.
8   Communicating results effectively.

It will be noted that much traditional language teaching is in direct conflict with some of these objectives. The P-P-P (present, practise, produce) paradigm, repetition, and controlled pattern practice are elements of this kind. A task-based methodology, and an O-H-E (observe, hypothesise, experiment) paradigm are in sympathy with the wider educational syllabus. This is important, for nothing which happens in the classroom should conflict with the educational ideals which the above summary expresses.

The single most distinctive feature of the Lexical Approach is that it proposes a fundamentally different attitude to the treatment of text. Firstly, it is suspicious of de-contextualised language, recognising the importance of co-text, and therefore preferring extended text or discourse. Secondly, it proposes a range of awareness-raising activities directing students' attention to the chunks of which text is composed. Texts play a role in introducing interesting content, but also act as a major linguistic resource from which students can **extract** lexical items for study, expansion, and recording in appropriate formats. A basic classroom strategy will be helping students to avoid becoming preoccupied by grammar or vocabulary, concentrating instead on different kinds of lexical item.

Syllabuses are normally thought of as listing, and perhaps sequencing, course content. In fact, three factors are important: inclusions, exclusions and sequencing.

Inclusions, exclusions and sequencing

As all teachers know, courses are invariably too short. Although a case can be made for including any language which is new for the student, a principal role for the syllabus is to provide principled ways of **including** only **maximally useful** items. What is maximally useful is not intrinsic to the language, but relates to particular courses, and even particular students. A primary distinction is between long courses – perhaps over several years in school – and short intensive courses intended to have a high surrender value. Too many courses are constructed on the implicit assumption that they are intermediate stages on the way to full language competence. Only rarely is this the case: most students will remain intermediate and this should influence the language selected for inclusion.

Within the Lexical Approach:

–   All low level courses will give students a large vocabulary, even if they are initially unable to grammaticalise it.
–   Pragmatically useful lexical items, particularly institutionalised utterances, form a significant component of all courses.
–   A balance will be maintained between (relatively rare) words carrying considerable meaning, and (relatively wide and frequent) patterns with low meaning content.

Three principal reasons may be identified for **excluding** material: it is **not identified, not valued**, or **not prioritised**. In the days of structural syllabuses, mastery of structure was regarded as synonymous with language learning; the consequent emphasis of structure within syllabuses was wholly to be expected. When the influence of pragmatics was felt in language teaching, functions became a familiar term to teachers. As a result *Would you like . . .?* was re-identified as *Offering*; its re-identification allowed it to be re-valued, and re-placed, much earlier in courses. Within the Lexical Approach different kinds of lexical item may be identified, or in relation to traditional language teaching, re-identified. Examples are treating *would* as a single word lexical item, rather than part of 'the conditional' (see below), or the recognition of fully institutionalised utterances which may be introduced and treated as unanalysed wholes contributing to, rather than derived from grammatical competence.

The tension of syllabus v language and learning

Most language syllabuses still list discrete items; this listing naturally, but misleadingly, suggests that language may be learned in a similar way, by 'accumulating entities'. Nunan (1988: 34), in his comprehensive survey *Syllabus Design*, remarks that 'there are general arguments against grammatical grading of content, whether this grading be based on traditional criteria or on more recent criteria stemming from SLA research'. And he quotes Widdowson as observing, as early as 1979:

> Inventories of functions and notions do not necessarily reflect the way languages are learned any more than the inventories of grammatical points and lexical items. This comment reflects Widdowson's claim that 'Dividing language into discrete units of whatever type misrepresents the nature of language as communication'.

The tension between language as communication and the supposed necessity for discrete item listing for language syllabuses is reflected in Willis' comment (1990: viii):

> An approach which itemises language seems to imply that items can be learned discretely, and that the language can be built up by an accretion of these items. Communicative methodology is holistic in that it relies on the ability of learners to abstract from the language to which they are exposed, in order to recreate a picture of the target language. The lexical syllabus attempts to reconcile these contradictions. It does itemise language. It itemises language minutely, resting on a large body of research into natural language. On the basis of this research it makes realistic and economical statements about what is to be learned. But the methodology associated with the lexical syllabus does not depend on itemisation.

Wilkins distinguishes between synthetic and analytical syllabuses, the former being 'a process of gradual accumulation of parts until the whole structure of language has been built up', while in the latter, Nunan (1988: 28) suggests:

> Learners are presented with chunks of language which may include structures of varying degrees of difficulty. A starting point for syllabus design is not the grammatical system of the language, but the communicative purpose for which the language is used.

Prabhu (1987: 1), describing his well-documented Bangalore Project, describes its origins:

> A strongly-felt pedagogic intuition that the development of competence in a second language requires not systematisation of language inputs or maximisation of planned practice, but rather the creation of conditions in which learners engage in an effort to cope with communication.

Prabhu, Widdowson, Nunan, Willis and indeed many others would concur with Nunan's judgement that:

> Evidence from second language acquisition research suggests that learning does not occur in a simple additive fashion.
>
> (1988: 30)

Syllabuses tend to isolate, divide and sub-divide. The tacit assumption is that macro-skills are a synthetic assembly of micro-skills; that larger units of discourse are assembled from words and structures. These assumptions are almost certainly untrue but this raises pedagogical difficulties. The implications are that we should adopt a more holistic view of language, and a task-based approach to learning, but, as Willis (1990: 129) observes:

> A shortcoming of task-based approaches is that they make it difficult to specify syllabus content, and as teachers we cannot be sure what has been learned in the course of a given language activity or a given unit.

There is a fundamental conflict between the teacher's natural desire to give clearly focused and effective lessons, and the non-linear nature of language and learning. Although there is substantial theoretical support for task-based goal-orientated syllabus specification, most teachers continue to demand much more specific linguistic objectives for each lesson. While endorsing and encouraging a methodology based on tasks and skills, rather than specifically linguistic criteria, we can identify explicitly linguistic changes which are consistent with the Lexical Approach.

Content specifying lists

One of the most influential attempts to specify content was the Threshold Level, which attempted to develop in detail the work summarised in *Notional Syllabuses*. Somewhat surprisingly, whilst claiming a primary focus on meaning, Wilkins (1976: 21) had a rather cavalier attitude to vocabulary:

> But it is therefore with the general aspects of meaning and use that the categories presented here are concerned, though they are not less significant for being general in character. This also explains why no attempt is made in this framework to account for a lexical content of learning. This is probably better approached in terms of subject-matter and situation. At the same time, lexical aspects cannot be entirely excluded since grammatical and lexical devices often interact significantly.
>
> To a certain, though limited, extent the semantico-grammatical categories themselves have applications for the lexical content . . . The lexical content of learning, therefore, can be largely derived from an analysis of the typical topics which occur in the language use of a given group.
>
> (1976: 76)

Wilkins's view is, thus, that however important vocabulary may be, it has no **defining** role to play within syllabus design.

In contrast, Willis (1990: v), developing Sinclair's ideas, regards vocabulary, and quite specifically **words**, as the key to syllabus specification:

> Sinclair advanced a number of arguments in favour of the lexical syllabus, but the underlying argument was to do with utility and with the power of the most frequent words of English. . . . We decided that word frequency would determine the content of our course.
>
> Instead of specifying an inventory of grammatical structures or a set of functions, each stage of the course would be built round a lexical syllabus. This would specify words, then meanings and the common phrases in which they were used.
>
> (1990: 15)

It will be noted that, despite the reference to 'phrases in which they occur' Sinclair and Willis largely equate the lexical syllabus with a **word-based** syllabus. Inherent in this interpretation are three problems which manifest themselves in the course described in Willis's *The Lexical Syllabus*:

1. The most frequent 'words' are frequently items previously regarded as structural and, ironically, words of low semantic content. These largely delexicalised words are highly frequent precisely because they often have several meanings, and their pattern profiles are extremely complex. Mastery of words like *to*, *with*, *have* is considerably more difficult than mastering a vocabulary item with higher meaning content: *accident*, *soot*, *slump*.

2. The word-based syllabus introduced words with both their highly frequent and much rarer meanings together. A preoccupation with the word as a unit meant infrequent meanings of highly frequent words were given preference over highly frequent meanings of rather less frequent words within the corpus. Some of these rarer meanings of high frequency words appear as of relatively low utility, and a relatively high confusion-factor for elementary students.

3. Multi-word lexical items are under-valued and under-exploited.

The Lexical Approach I propose avoids these dangers. It is specifically **not** a lexical **syllabus**, and explicitly recognises word patterns for (relatively) delexical words, collocational power for (relatively) semantically powerful words, and longer multi-word items, particularly institutionalised sentences, as requiring different, and **parallel**, pedagogical treatment.

The old structural syllabuses specifically restricted vocabulary to the level necessary to exemplify structural patterns. Ironically, Willis (1990: 74) in his word-based approach explicitly espouses the same principle: *We set out to achieve the best coverage we could with as little extraneous lexis as possible* (i.e. extraneous to the most frequent 700, 1,500 and 2,500 'words' which they selected as the basis for Parts 1, 2, 3 of their course). In contrast to their urge to restrict vocabulary at low levels, I advocate encouraging the **learning** of a comparatively large repertoire of high-meaning content nouns, adjectives and verbs. Although the words learned will inevitably be in corpus terms comparatively low-frequency, by definition they carry meaning. But words carry more meaning than grammar, and if it is communicative power which is the primary objective, increased vocabulary will play a larger contribution than additional mastery of even the most highly frequent patterns of high frequency words. There is an additional, pedagogical advantage. Willis observes that 'profiles become less complex as one moves down the frequency scale'. This means that from a naïve, student point of view the words are easier to learn, and any L2 = L1 equivalence, which students almost inevitably make, is more likely to be accurate. 'Learnability' and communicative power are at least as important in selecting words for inclusion as frequency.

Lexis contributes as a syllabus component in the following ways:

1. Certain words deserve lexical rather than grammatical treatment

These are typically high frequency, de-lexicalised items. Those items which enter into the widest range of patterns, and are thus usefully if not maximally generative, are words which themselves carry least meaning. De-lexicalised verbs — *have*, *get*, *put*, *take*, *make*, *do* — represent an important sub-category. Function words, often thought of as prepositions — *of*, *with*, *for*, *by*, are another. The modal auxiliaries, including *would*, are a third. Most importantly, *would* should be dealt with early in a course **from a lexical point of view**. *Would* was treated in structural courses as 'the conditional'; functions moved it to an earlier, but comparatively marginal, non-generative position. It deserves high priority as a one-word lexical item. Interestingly, it is one of the items which merits fullest discussion in *The Lexical Syllabus*.

2. Increased attention to the base form of lexical verbs

A preoccupation with grammar and structure has obscured the importance of the base form of the verb in English. Willis comments on courses which 'spend an inordinate amount of time on the verb phrase', that is, on the **structure** of the verb, and so-called tense formation. In fact, the simple present is about eight times as common as the present continuous in naturally occurring English and is, with the marginal inconvenience of the third person **-s**, identical with the base form. The Lexical Approach advocates the need for a large repertoire of verbs in their base or lexical form with increased attention to the highly frequent present simple.

3. De-contextualised teaching of semantically dense items

Communicative power is most rapidly increased by expanding students' vocabularies, meaning their repertoire of lexical items, but particularly simple high-content **words**. There is no need for over-elaborate contextualisation in the early stages of learning: simple identification of signification, although in no sense mastery of the word, is an appropriate and valuable basis for increased communicative power.

4. Collocations

As soon as the inadequacy of the grammar/vocabulary dichotomy is recognised, it becomes natural for collocation to assume an important syllabus generating role. This applies particularly to relatively high content nouns. When these are introduced, it should be natural to introduce **with** them verbs and adjectives which form powerful or relatively fixed collocations. The statistical evidence of corpus lexicography here clearly reveals the necessity of acknowledging both literal and metaphorical meaning. Often it is the latter which is more frequent.

5. Institutionalised utterances

Traditional grammar exercises usually include a sample sentence which provides the model for students to produce 'similar' sentences. Modern research into both grammar and learning suggests that students could usefully be offered a **group** of sentences for comprehension and reflection. These would not exemplify 'the grammar', but be pragmatically identifiable institutionalised utterances which students could **both** use immediately to increase communicative power, and as a **resource** the analysis of which would provide a basis for the gradual perception of pattern.

6. Sentence heads

These are very similar to institutionalised utterances. Sentence heads can frequently be identified and provide both an immediate increase in communicative power, and a resource to aid acquisition. These sentence heads frequently lie somewhere between grammar and function on a conventional syllabus. 'Grammar' in grammar practices frequently tried to cover all elements of the paradigm, consciously introducing first, second and third person subjects, singulars and plurals; in functional practice a single sentence head *Would you like to . . .* requires students to complete the sentence in different ways. Introspection or statistical data, however, both reveal that some combinations of, for example, a particular modal and a particular person are much more frequent than others; compare *Could you . . .* and *Could she . . .*; contrast *I might . . .* and *Might I . . .? Do you think you might . . .?* and *Do you think I might . . .?* Paradigms exemplify the **possible** sentences of English; well-chosen groups of sentence heads exemplify the **frequent** or **probable** patterns of English. Functions are all too often ungeneralisable, while sentence head groups are generalisable.

It is noticeable that the institutionalised utterances and sentence heads of spoken English are very different from those of the written language. McCarthy is only one of many to suggest that 'vocabulary work in spoken language requires separate and additional procedures from vocabulary teaching using written texts'.

7. Supra-sentential linking

Traditionally this has been practised only on a grammatical level, concerning tags, interested responses etc. In fact, supra-sentential **lexical** linking is an important cohesive device in spontaneous conversation, suggesting lexically, rather than structurally, based exercises would be more natural and more pragmatically effective. McCarthy (1991: 71) quotes data in which:

> People did not typically agree or disagree with phrases such as 'I agree' or 'I disagree' (beloved of English course book writers); rather, there seems to be a preference for simply using some sort of lexical relation between turns.

This suggestion is borne out in Willis's work, and he goes further, suggesting that much spontaneous conversation is based on joint production, in which participants contribute matching, complementary or contradictory lexical items in the development of a single unit of meaning.

Supra-sentential linking of this kind is central to spoken discourse, but quite different, and equally important features apply to the creation of coherent and cohesive written text. A central requirement of the Lexical Approach is that language material should be text and discourse, rather than sentence based. Again Willis agrees, constantly reasserting that 'only by drawing attention to occurrences in text' can learners begin to build up an adequate picture of language in use.

8. Synonyms within the existential paradigm

This is a particular example of supra-sentential linking. Observations of real data show that in spontaneous speech the ability to use alternative language items as value-synonyms, although they have different signification, is a key feature of fluency. These value-synonyms may be both individual words (*daffodils/flowers*) or fully grammaticalised utterances realising the same pragmatic function (*That has my full support. / Absolutely, I'd go along with that*).

9. 'Synopsising' words

Traditional grammar taught so-called reported speech. As discussed elsewhere, this category is wholly untypical of naturally occurring data. Most often, the speaker reports a whole **event**, rather than manipulating the words that were spoken. The 'reporter' summarises or synopsises the whole event lexically and so requires an adequate repertoire of synopsising verbs.

10. Metaphorical patterning

Metaphor is often perceived as an essentially literary device. Modern philosophical and linguistic research reveals that far from being restricted to literary language, it is intrinsic to the nature of language itself. Lakoff and Johnson (1980: 7ff), in a seminal work belonging essentially to the field of philosophy, have demonstrated convincingly that there are many concepts which cannot be discussed except in metaphorical language. They give many examples but here a single example must suffice: TIME IS MONEY.

They point out that this is an English proverb, but more than that, it is impossible to talk about time without basing the conceptualisation on the metaphor TIME IS MONEY. They developed the idea as follows (in slightly abbreviated form):

> Time is money is a metaphorical concept. It is metaphorical since we are using our everyday experiences of money, limited resources and the valuable commodities to conceptualise time. This isn't a necessary way for human beings to conceptualise time; it is tied to our culture. There are cultures where time is none of these things.

> We are adopting the practice of using the most specific metaphorical concepts, in this case time is money, to characterise the entire system.

> This is an example of the way in which metaphorical entailments can categorise a coherent system of metaphorical concepts and a corresponding coherent system of metaphorical expressions for those concepts.

They point out that in English many of the words used to describe time can also be used to describe money: *spend, invest, budget, profitably*. Here are some of their examples:

How do you spend your time these days?
I haven't enough time to spare for that.
Is it worth your while?
You don't use your time profitably.
You are wasting my time.
This gadget will save you hours.

Clearly, there is a pattern here which it is worthwhile to draw to the attention of students. Many of the words which are used to talk about money can also be used to talk about time. This is not fully generalisable, but it still constitutes a powerfully generative pattern system. The importance of Lakoff and Johnson's work is difficult to over-emphasise. It is essential reading for anyone interested in how language works.

When the Berlin wall was breached, at first a *trickle* of people came through. Later, as the gap was widened, people *flooded* through. There was a constant *stream* of people anxious to visit friends, or restore family contacts. Once the initial excitement wore off, the *flow* of people *dried up*.

The above passage represents my own observations of the language used by the B.B.C. News to report the destruction of the Berlin wall. An important metaphor is involved: crowds of people move like water. It is almost impossible to describe those events without resorting to 'water-words'. But notice, as Lakoff and Johnson constantly emphasise, metaphor highlights only at the expense of suppressing. People in movement may move like water, but they are **not** water, water does not re-establish family contacts. There is a useful linguistic pattern, but not an identification.

Editors on the Cobuild project were initially surprised at the preponderance of metaphorical usage — *torrents* are more likely to be of abuse or French than water. Lexicographic difficulties arise — if metaphorical use is more frequent than the literal, and therefore supposedly core, use should it be placed first in the dictionary? Their editors have observed, for example, the importance of plant-based metaphor in discussing abstractions such as government policy: *The problem has its roots . . .; Since the beginning of the year, we have seen a flowering. . . .*

For language teaching, the importance lies in recognising:

a   That metaphor is a part of everyday language.
b   That such metaphorical usage is patterned, often in accessible, generalisable ways.

Functions and skills

The development of communicative power will be aided by incorporating a well-balanced range of lexically derived activities in the classroom. These must reflect the different kinds of lexical item. The change, however, is a matter of emphasis not revolution. Grammar retains a place, but a reduced one; lexis plays an increased role. Language content can, however, never be wholly separated from other elements of syllabus specification. Most functional syllabuses concentrate on micro- rather than macro-functions and 'nice' rather than 'nasty' events. For many students such functions as *expressing irritation*, *expressing disbelief*, *distancing the speaker from the content of what is said*, *expressing condolence*, *telling and responding to jokes* may be at least as important as *accepting and refusing invitations politely*. In a similar way, a lexical approach suggests that the skills syllabus needs to be broadened. Two skills central to the Lexical Approach are developing the students' ability to use the dictionary as a learning resource, rather than reference work, and, most importantly of all, helping students to **identify lexical phrases** in text. This returns us to the single most powerful methodological implication, namely a different attitude to, and use of, texts.

Bibliography

Lakoff, G. and Johnson, M. *Metaphors We Live By*. Univ. of Chicago Press 1980
McCarthy, M. *Discourse Analysis for Language Teachers*. CUP 1991
Nunan, D. *Syllabus Design*. OUP 1988
Prabhu, N. S. *Second Language Pedagogy*. OUP 1987
Widdowson, H. Proper Words in Proper Places. *ELT News* No. 8. British Council Vienna July 1989
Wilkins, D. *Notional Syllabuses*. OUP 1976
Willis, D. *The Lexical Syllabus*. Collins Cobuild 1990

Chapter 4

Michael McCarthy and Ronald Carter

DESIGNING THE DISCOURSE SYLLABUS*

1 Introduction

THE ADEQUATE DESCRIPTION OF LANGUAGE is vital as a precursor of language teaching syllabuses. At the macro- and micro-level, from issues of genre down to individual grammatical and lexical choices, our findings (McCarthy and Carter 1994) have implications for how we look at the syllabus and, consequently, its content and the kinds of activities that it generates in the class. This chapter concentrates on those implications in discussing the design of the discourse syllabus.

2 The notion of 'discourse competence'

Ever since Chomsky (1965) made the distinction between **competence** and **performance**, that is what a person knows about his or her language as opposed to what can be observed from manifestations of actual use, linguists have debated just what 'competence' might mean. Chomsky was concerned with the fact that native-speakers have an underlying knowledge of what constitutes a well-formed sentence in their own language, and he set about trying to account for such knowledge. But it was not long before the notion of competence was expanded to embrace what a speaker needs to know about how a language is *used in particular situations* for effective and appropriate communication, in other words **communicative competence** (see Hymes 1971).

The notion of communicative competence has had a very powerful influence on language teaching, both in terms of methodology and the goals set by syllabus planners which learners are supposed to achieve. Thus the term **communicative syllabus** is a familiar one to most language teachers. Typically, a communicative syllabus will set out a variety of communicative abilities that the learner should be able to demonstrate at the end of a prescribed course or period of learning. One such English Language syllabus, a pioneer in its day, recommended that learners should be able to (among other things) make and receive telephone calls, handle friendly and social correspondence, make short notes to record salient information, ask questions and make comments for gleaning further information, and so on. This was the Malaysian (1976) Communicational Syllabus for Forms 4 and 5 of secondary school (see British Council 1983; 1986). The syllabus was a classic

---

* This text has been adapted.

communicative one, with no real emphasis on correctness in grammar and vocabulary, and every emphasis on the ability to communicate and achieve goals, a balance of priorities for which it came into much criticism in its own country (See Mohideen 1991). It was criticism of this swing of the pendulum away from linguistic (i.e. grammatical and lexical) competence to a preoccupation with communicative competence alone, not just in Malaysia, which led applied linguists to question whether competence could ever be seen as a monolithic concept. Might it make more sense to think of the learner developing a **set of competences**, each one essential to using language effectively, but each one separable in terms of what could be described and prescribed for the syllabus and learning programme? Thus grammatical and lexical knowledge as one of the several competences came to the fore again as an issue in language teaching. Applied linguists argued that communicative ability was a hollow notion without knowledge of the grammatical system that enabled actual realizations of communicative acts (but also vice versa; see Canale and Swain 1980). Equally, there was a return of interest in the problem of vocabulary building, without which little real communication was possible (McCarthy 1984; see also Carter and McCarthy 1988: ch. 3 for a survey of these arguments). Linguistic competence, it was argued, was a necessary, though not sufficient, condition for communicative ability. From such pressures has come what most would agree is a healthier balance between the development of competence in the language system and competence in its use, as exemplified in so-called **eclectic** syllabuses (the Swan and Walter 1984 *Cambridge English Course* is a good example), and in what Yalden (1983) calls the **proportional** syllabus, where the proportions of system-oriented knowledge and communication-oriented skills are increasingly altered in favour of the latter as the learner progresses from beginner level. The lexical syllabus (Sinclair and Renouf 1988; Willis 1990), based on a faithful description of how words are used, represents another move in the direction of integrating knowledge of the system and knowledge of use.

But other questions remain for the language teacher. If the *description* of language is incomplete without a description of the level of discourse, and if discourse-level constraints operate simultaneously with lexico-grammatical ones, then is there something akin to a **discourse competence** that can be described and articulated as a set of goals for the syllabus to aspire to? Recent debates in syllabus design have tended to assume that there is. Those linguists and applied linguists who have moved away from the idea of competence as a monolithic concept have already added to the basic notion of communicative competence subdivisions such as socio-linguistic competence and strategic competence. As Canale (1983) uses these terms, they may be briefly glossed as follows:

> *Socio-linguistic competence* an entity consisting of two sub-components: socio-cultural rules of use and rules of discourse. Socio-cultural rules are concerned with appropriacy of use with regard to such features as topic, roles, attitude and register. Rules of discourse are concerned with features of cohesion and coherence.

> *Strategic competence* verbal and non-verbal communication strategies for solving problems in communication, whether lexico-grammatical problems or problems associated with sociolinguistic appropriateness.

Among the problems facing the language teacher who tries to interpret these notional divisions and subdivisions are not least that of whether 'socio-cultural' concerns can be separated from 'discourse' and whether such notions can ever be viewed as items or entities 'to be taught', if we are faithful to the view that a syllabus is indeed a list of things to be taught and goals to be achieved. The first problem, the separation of socio-cultural features from discourse ones, is especially problematic given, as we have argued elsewhere (McCarthy and Carter 1994), that such things as register and mode are integral to the creation of discourse, not in some way 'parallel' or complementary to it. We have also sought to demonstrate that isolated lists of speech acts are insufficient to describe what speakers/ writers do and how they manage interaction over extended language events. In other words, we see the chaining together of functions or speech acts as inseparable from the creating of larger patterns and genres in discourse. By the same token, we see the realization of registers, attitudinal features and topics as inseparable from coherence and its manifestations in surface cohesion. Even more to the point, grammar and vocabulary knowledge should involve how these aspects of linguistic *form* create discourse; in other words, linguistic competence cannot be separated from discourse competence.

These views have a direct bearing on the second concern, whether things can be itemized for teaching and given socio-cultural, strategic or discourse labels and thereby allotted their rightful place in the syllabus inventory or check-list. How we analyse and classify language for our syllabus necessarily affects our methodology and what we do in the classroom.

3 Analysis and classification

Some notable writers on syllabus design follow the view that the analysis of language into its various levels and the classification of features within those levels is a feasible basis for syllabus specifications. Yalden's (1983) description of syllabus components seems implicitly to accept this with a section entitled 'A further component: discourse structure' (1983: 78), and her syllabus check-list (1983: 169–72) includes the following discourse components:

A   Cohesion and reference (based largely on Halliday and Hasan 1976)
B   Operations on text (for example extracting salient information, expanding a text)
C   Rhetorical organization (textual functions such as generalization, classification, etc)
D   Overt transactional skills in spoken discourse (for example initiating, introducing topics, closing, turn-taking).

These categories certainly represent innovative elements in syllabus specifications and are faithful to what discourse analysts have described as above-sentence features. We should note, though, that categories A and C seem to be language features, while B and D would seem to fit better under the heading of skills or strategies. This is no mere hair-splitting, and is at the heart of the process of analysis and classification that precedes specification and itemization. For instance, it could be argued that a feature such as lexical cohesion is an aspect of the language system and can thus be taught as language knowledge, just like teaching the grammatical facts about tenses or determiners. This would mean not only telling learners what the synonyms and hyponyms of a particular word or set of words are, but also demonstrating that synonymy and hyponymy *in use* are often involved in the creation of well-formed text and interactive speech (see McCarthy 1984; 1988). However, another view might be that lexical cohesion is a language universal; as such, it becomes more a matter of skill-training, practice and training in an intuitive skill in order to improve one's proficiency in its use, without any need to 'present it' as knowledge or fact. This is a crucial decision in the categorizing of syllabus components: Yalden (1983), for example, has clearly flagged features such as turn-taking and closing as 'skills', suggesting a different emphasis from that attached to cohesion and reference, while 'operations on a text' are unambiguously things we 'do' with language, rather than features which 'exist' in the language system. But separating the 'what' of the language system from the 'how' of language skills and strategic use can also be misleading: there is every reason to suppose that knowing 'what' can inform and support knowing 'how'.

Munby (1978) has a similar, though much more detailed, specification of discourse *features* (cohesion, initiating, developing the discourse, etc) mixed in with textual operations ('reading between the lines', extracting salient points, skimming and scanning the text, etc), which, among many other things, form a continuum from basic phonemic and graphemic discrimination through to macro-planning, all under the heading of 'language *skills*'. 'Discourse level units' (Munby 1978: 27) are still seen, though, as separate from language micro-functions and grammatical/lexical realizations, and discourse is a level or layer of language rather than integral to its entire operation.

Although, as we shall see, ways of implementing the notion of a discourse element in the syllabus vary considerably, there does seem to be widespread agreement that the idea of discourse cannot be ignored; syllabus templates and check-lists as offered by applied linguists such as Munby (1978) and Yalden (1983) have a discourse element built in. But we must now consider how more integrative views of discourse influence the nature of the syllabus and the teaching that evolves from it.

One problem with the views of communicative competence as implied by the syllabus specifications that we have looked at so far is that they have assumed that language use can be analysed and described as a set of components of various kinds. This assumption often creates difficulties in that the separation of components can produce a false picture of their role in creating the overall message. A good example of this is the sort of list often found in syllabus specifications of speech acts or functions, such as *promising*, *directing*, *enquiring*, *apologizing*, etc. As Candlin (1976) points out, an inventory of speech-acts of this kind 'cannot serve any more than sentences as the direct endpoint of a communicative syllabus'. Any syllabus consisting solely of such a list would fail in two directions simultaneously: it would fail to provide the learner with a clear view of the interrelated and structured nature of elements of the language *system* such as modality and mood, and it would fail to show how apologies, enquiries, promises, and so on are actually realized in interaction and as part of a *sequence* of utterances and how such realizations depended on higher-order constraints of genre. In other words, we would be guilty of dealing with (some of) 'the *components* of discourse, not with discourse itself' (Widdowson 1979: 248). Widdowson and Candlin both come at the problem from the other direction: communicative competence is not a list of learnt items, but a set of strategies or procedures 'for realizing the value of linguistic elements in contexts of use' (Widdowson 1979: 248), and, just as learners may be expected to perceive grammatical regularities in sentences, so they should be given the opportunity to interpret pragmatic clues for the attachment of value to utterances in discourse, and become themselves analysts of discourse (Candlin 1976).

One highly innovative approach to incorporating an integrative view of discourse into the syllabus is provided by Aston (1988). One of Aston's concerns is to redress the imbalance towards transactional language common in much language teaching (which we comment on in section 4) and to get to grips with the problem of creating the contexts for interactive discourse in the classroom. Aston too moves away from simply adding discourse as an extra component in the syllabus and effectively builds his syllabus around central and fundamental features of interactive discourse. For Aston (as we have argued) interactive discourse is concerned not only with illocutionary uptake (the realization of speech acts), nor just with 'cognitive convergence' (achieving shared knowledge and perlocutionary effect), but also with affective convergence (an essentially humanistic notion), with the processes of creating such convergences and with the global and local strategies negotiated in individual contexts for achieving them.

Aston recognizes the problems created by analysis and classification as the precursor of syllabus specifications: any analysis claiming to describe competence and to itemize it for a syllabus will fail to capture the fact that discourse is realized by the creative exploitation of the resources that constitute competence (Aston 1988: 163–4). In this sense, the learner can engage properly with discourse only by *doing* it. This would seem to be a strong argument in favour of the task-based approach as expounded by Prabhu (1987). In the task-based classroom, language is *used* in the process of solving preordained tasks, with the purpose of promoting and enhancing uptake and learning, rather than presented and learnt in order to be used later in exercises or outside in the real world.

Aston, however, sees many problems arising from more extreme views of the task-based approach (the extremest form of which would be the completely negotiable syllabus, with nothing preordained and everything open to negotiation among learners and teachers, which Clarke (1991) claims would be unworkable anyway). Aston seeks to build a syllabus wherein the learning process is not just left to get on with itself in unpredictable ways, but in which teaching can operate as a guidance. To this end, it is not sufficient just to specify a set of tasks for learners to undertake. For one thing, many of the task-types advocated by task-based syllabus designers fall into the same trap as the information-gap activities of communicative approaches, in that they encourage a transactional view of language at the expense of the interactional. Furthermore, simply specifying tasks ignores the fact that learners can be guided in the *procedural* knowledge (the 'how things are done' in particular speech communities) as well as the *declarative* knowledge of 'what is done', both of which are essential to the creation of coherent discourse. Aston, therefore, favours a task-based approach that does not shy away from specifying the discourse strategies that the learner will need; these will be specified in a **strategic pre-syllabus**, which he sees as a 'content-based' one (Aston 1988: 188). But even with this pre-syllabus, tasks involving the learner in creating discourse as the main syllabus are not enough. For Aston, the main syllabus is two-stranded, and the second strand involves the learner in becoming a discourse-analyst, or indeed a sort of anthropologist (1988: 184), *observing* and *deconstructing* how discourse is created.

Aston's final model therefore, looks like this:

content-based presyllabus ⟶ strategic

context-based syllabus   construction   deconstruction

(Aston 1988: 188)

Aston's view of the syllabus seems to recognize that discourse is a process rather than a product (which tends to be the view of those who see 'discourse-as-a-layer' in language use), but, sensibly, he sees the value both of an analysis and classification of discourse strategies as a precursor to selecting tasks for the classroom and of making the learner stand back a little from language and become an observer of it, though as a discourse-analyst rather than as the sentence-parser and rule-discoverer of some approaches to traditional grammar-based syllabuses.

Ours is also an integrative view, wherein the over-arching perspective of language-as-discourse will affect *every* part of the syllabus, including any conventional 'system' (lexico-grammatical) components and functional/speech-act components, however they are treated, whether as a series of layers of language, or as realizations within general specifications of discourse strategies.

4 Analysis as the precursor of tasks

Aston's programme favoured a 'pre-syllabus' oriented towards strategic issues in discourse. Specifying strategies is something that can be done in different ways and at different levels. Some syllabuses (for example ICC 1986) specify a general set of strategies, but it is also possible to conceive of a highly detailed set which translate some of the more traditionally conceived 'features' of language use into the strategic domain, and this is what we would like briefly to consider in this section. What we propose are a set of strategy-headings that can act as a sort of filter between the learning group and its need and the specification of tasks. Each heading is followed by example questions that are raised by each one and the sort of practical issues that are likely to be encountered in the detailed specification of discourse *features* that might be encountered in the subsequent tasks. We say 'likely' because we cannot always guarantee what the outcome of a task will be. It will be noted that the global set of strategy headings can subsume what has previously been seen as a separate discourse 'layer' by some syllabus designers. The most general headings are as follows.

1 Genre-related strategies

What are the media and modes that the learners will encounter?
What genres are likely to be most useful?
What patterns of interaction are most useful (e.g. narrative, problem-solution)?

2 Coherence-related strategies

What aspects of topic management, turn-taking, etc, will be involved?
What types of cohesion (e.g. stronger emphasis on across-turn lexical cohesion for interactionally oriented tasks; different types of ellipsis in different media)?

3 Politeness strategies

What aspects of face will need to be addressed?
What forms of address will be involved (e.g. pronoun systems, mood systems)?
How important will reciprocity be (e.g. very important in interactional tasks)?

4 Planning strategies

What sorts of anticipatory strategies will be useful (e.g. enumerative labelling, cataphoric uses of articles)?
Will special conditions for reference apply (e.g. anaphora across paragraph boundaries in written medium)?
What sequences of tense, aspect and voice are likely to be involved (e.g. conventions related to genre)?
What degree of *creativity* and risk-taking with language is feasible and appropriate?

5 Convergence strategies

Informational or cognitive convergence: what aspects of categories such as theme, mood and modality will be involved?

Affective convergence: what adjacency-pair types are likely (e.g. solidarity routines, problem-sharing, agreement-disagreement)?

What transaction-boundary features are likely (pitch-sequencing, markers)? What role will repetition play in creating convergence in different modes and genres? What degree of cultural convergence will be required? How will 'knowing about' language and culture assist in solving convergence problems?

6 Repair strategies

What are the risks of communicational problems or cultural misunderstandings?
Is repair likely to be largely self-repair, or more global, negotiable repairs?

Strategies invariably overlap. For example, repair strategies may involve politeness, which in itself involves cultural awareness and the problem of convergence, and so on. But given the practical exigencies of dividing the discourse process, we would argue that the strategic list represents a manageable and reasonably faithful framework for syllabus and task design. What one does with a list of strategies for a particular learner group depends on one's philosophy concerning methodology. The discourse-based approach (i.e. where we *start* with discourse as the overall driving force of our syllabus) lends itself best, we have implied, to a task-based methodology, in that, in this way, language is not atomized and treated as product, thus destroying the basic notion of discourse as engaging with language as *process* and meaning as negotiated and contextual. However, in the real world, teachers often have to work within clear and restrictive constraints where they are expected to work to explicitly stated classroom input and to achieve explicitly measurable output, in other words, syllabuses that say *what* is to be learnt and in what order.

We see no contradiction between our proposed list of discourse strategies and the subsequent specification of the syllabus in terms of a set of specific performance goals, only that we start from a different premise: that all such goals can, and should be, expressed as discourse goals rather than as lexico-grammatical or notional-functional ones. For example, we might envisage a 'learners should be able to . . .' feature including something like the following:

Ask significant favours of others in appropriate sequences involving
1 signals of opening
2 explaining the problem
3 asking
4 minimizing
5 reinforcing
6 acceding
7 thanking.

The asking of a favour is thus conceived of as a *genre* rather than as a function or speech-act, and involves not only speech-act realizations at the micro-level, but also a strategic level involving politeness strategies (face), planning (opening), convergence (reinforcing), and so on. At the lexico-grammatical interface, one could specify modality and (depending on level) use of idioms. The point is that the conventional syllabus-as-inventory view can still be meaningfully adapted to a language-as-discourse approach without just adding discourse as a layer upon the other layers. Equally, such an inventory, in our opinion, does not necessarily preclude additional use of well-chosen tasks in class that can subscribe to Aston's (1988) conditions of construction and deconstruction, nor does it necessarily preclude some sort of proportional syllabus approach such as Yalden (1983) advocates. For us, it is the analysis of language needs through a discourse perspective which is most important as a precursor to tasks and activities, whether such tasks are additional to a more conventional communicatively oriented syllabus or whether the analysis is merely a pre-syllabus for the selection of open-ended tasks that will form a whole task-based syllabus in themselves.

If analysis from a discourse point of view is to the pre-syllabus for a task-based one, then we would strongly support Aston (1988) in his view that an analysis based on *interactional* language is just as important as one based on transactional uses of language. Real data show that the two types of language use rarely occur discretely (see McCarthy and Carter 1994: 117–24; Belton 1988; McCarthy 1991: 136–7). For an interactional view of language to have an input into task design, the understanding of how natural conversation works, how speakers/writers orient towards reciprocity and convergence, how they do so using systematic resources such as lexical cohesion and how features such as topic management are realized are all central. It is here, we feel, that syllabus designers have most to learn from what discourse analysts can offer.

Designing tasks is no easy matter, and much useful literature exists which treats with more rigour than space allows us here the factors which can make or break tasks (see especially Nunan 1989). It does seem worth underlining here, however, that tasks which promote only or mainly transactional uses of language (e.g. information-gap tasks) are unlikely to engage learners in a full range of discourse strategies. Discourse strategies, we have argued, are concerned with human beings presenting a picture of themselves, not just conveying information to one another. Therefore, if 'gaps' or 'problems' are the core features of tasks which motivate their completion, then we need to build in much more than just information or 'opinion' gaps (see Aston 1988: 192–9 for a critique of information- and opinion-gap approaches). Gaps in rapport, problems of sensitivity, convergence towards acquaintance or friendship, gaps in self-image, problems of face, all of these will assume as much importance as gaps in places on a map, or gaps in agreeing on where to spend a Saturday night, the stock-in-trade of many present classroom tasks. Tasks *can* fulfil some of these interactional criteria by deliberately 'designing in' unpredictable reactions, 'difficult' participants, goals where conversational well-being is more important than informational transaction, and so on.

An example of an attempt at building into a task interactional constraints demanding politeness and convergence strategies, taken from the International Certificate Conference's teacher-training programme for teachers intending to use their discourse-strategy and task-based syllabus (ICC 1986), involves participants in a consensus activity to agree on the arrangement of furniture for a school open-day. Much of the task is transactionally oriented, culminating in leaving instructions for the school caretaker to execute the furniture plan. However, the person who role-plays the caretaker is required to take offence at the tone of the instructions and the task therefore cannot be completed until oil has been poured on troubled waters and 'affective' convergence has been achieved, even though cognitive convergence is already present in the written instructions for the furniture plan. This is only one small example, but it shows how task design can attempt to replicate a wider range of discourse conditions, and how the 'pre-syllabus' might feed into the constructional syllabus in a more controlled way, if the desire is to follow a task-based approach.

5   Conclusion

We hope that the discussion in this chapter has pointed to the following conclusion: that awareness of discourse and a willingness to take on board what a language-as-discourse view implies can only make us better and more efficient syllabus designers, task designers, dialogue-writers, materials adaptors and evaluators of everything we do and handle in the classroom. Above all, the approach we have advocated enables us to be more faithful to what language *is* and what people use it for. The moment one starts to think of language as discourse, the entire landscape changes, usually, for ever.

Bibliography

Aston, G. 1988 *Learning Comity*. Bologna: Editrice CLUEB

Belton, A. 1988 'Lexical naturalness in native and non-native discourse'. *English Language Research Journal* (ns) 2: 79–105

British Council 1983; 1986 *English Teaching Profile on Malaysia*. London: British Council

Canale, M. 1983 'From communicative competence to communicative language pedagogy'. In Richards, J. C., Schmidt, R. (eds) *Language and Communication*. London: Longman, pp. 2–27

Canale, M., Swain, M. 1980 'Theoretical bases of communicative approaches to second language teaching and testing'. *Applied Linguistics* 1: 1–47

Candlin, C. N. 1976 'Communicative language teaching and the debt to pragmatics'. In Rameh, C. (ed) *Georgetown University Round Table on Languages and Linguistics*. Washington, DC: Georgetown University Press, pp. 237–56

Carter, R. A., McCarthy, M. J. 1988 *Vocabulary and Language Teaching*. London: Longman

Chomsky, N. 1965 *Aspects of the Theory of Syntax*. Cambridge, MA: MIT Press

Clarke, D. F. 1991 'The negotiated syllabus: what is it and how is it likely to work?' *Applied Linguistics* **12** (1): 13–28

Halliday, M. A. K., Hassan, R. 1976 *Cohesion in English*. London: Longman.

Hymes, D. 1971 'On communicative competence'. In Pride, J. Homes, J. (eds) *Sociolinguistics*. 1972. Harmondsworth: Penguin, pp. 269–93

ICC (International Certificate Conference) 1986 *Foreign Languages in Adult and Continuing Education: Specifications for Stage 3 Level of the International Certificate Conference Language Certificate System*. Bonn Frankfurt: Deutscher Volkshochschul-Verband e.v.

McCarthy, M. J. 1984 'A new look at vocabulary in EFL'. *Applied Linguistics* **5** (1): 12–22

McCarthy, M. J. 1988 'Some vocabulary patterns in conversation'. In Carter, R. A., McCarthy, M. J. *Vocabulary and Language Teaching*. London: Longman, pp. 181–200

McCarthy, M. J. 1991 *Discourse Analysis for Language Teachers*. Cambridge: Cambridge University Press

McCarthy, M., Carter, R. 1994 *Language as Discourse: Perspectives for Language Teaching*. London: Longman.

Mohideen, H. 1991 'An error analysis of the written English of Malay students at pre-university level'. Unpublished PhD thesis. Cardiff: University of Wales

Munby, J. 1978 *Communicative Syllabus Design*. Cambridge: Cambridge University Press

Nunan, D. 1989 *Designing Tasks for the Communicative Classroom*. Cambridge: Cambridge University Press

Prabhu, N. 1987 *Second Language Pedagogy: a Perspective*. Oxford: Oxford University Press

Sinclair, J. McH., Renouf, A. 1988 'A lexical syllabus for language learning'. In Carter, R. A., McCarthy, M. J. *Vocabulary and Language Teaching*. London: Longman, pp. 140–60

Swan, M., Walter, C. 1984 *The Cambridge English Course*. Volume 1. Cambridge: Cambridge University Press

Widdowson, H. G. 1979 *Explorations in Applied Linguistics 1*. Oxford: Oxford University Press

Willis, D. 1990 *The Lexical Syllabus*. London: Collins

Yalden, J. 1983 *The Communicative Syllabus: Evolution, Design and Implementation*. New York: Pergamon

Chapter 5

Guy Cook

THE USES OF COMPUTERIZED LANGUAGE CORPORA: A REPLY TO RONALD CARTER

Introduction

COMPUTERIZED LANGUAGE CORPORA have inspired some of the most important insights in recent linguistics. They have shown us, for example, that actual language use is less a matter of combining abstract grammar rules with individual lexical items, and more a matter of collocation; that there are grammatically possible utterances which do not occur, and others which occur with disproportionate frequency; that in systematic descriptions of occurrences, grammar and lexis cannot be as easily separated as they have been traditionally, either in pedagogy or in linguistics. Ronald Carter is right to find such insights 'exciting', and his own work with Michael McCarthy on the CANCODE corpus has added to them. As his article (1998) illustrates very well, the grammatical constructions we find in actual conversations are not always accounted for in traditional grammars.

Clearly all these findings are important, and they do have implications for language teaching. The problem is, however, that some corpus linguists (e.g. Sinclair 1991, Stubbs 1996) overreach themselves. They talk as though the entire study of language can be replaced by the study of their collections, and as though all important insights will emerge only from automatic searches of their data and nowhere else. Clearly such solutions to the study of complex human phenomena exert a good deal of seductive power. If the traditional concern of linguistics – language in all its cultural and psychological complexity – could be replaced by a neat computer bank of data, life would be much simpler.

Yet the leap from linguistics to pedagogy is – as Carter realizes – far from straightforward. He is not one of the extremists, and his paper is, for that reason, a worthwhile and interesting contribution to language teaching. He proceeds cautiously, providing some interesting 'real' data, and pointing out significant differences between actual and textbook English. He does not say one should replace the other. In his view, materials should be influenced by, but not slaves to, corpus findings. (In this he seems to agree with the view of Summers and Rundell (1995) that pedagogic materials should be 'corpus based not corpus bound', and to disagree with the COBUILD slogan that they should be 'corpus driven' (Stubbs 1997).) This is eminently reasonable, though for that very reason not particularly radical. My problem with what Carter says is that he seems a little hesitant – or perhaps unwilling – to say where he stands. Does he reject the fundamentalist views of those linguists and language teaching theorists for whom corpus findings are the only source of truth?

My first aim in this reply is to pursue some of the shortcomings of corpus-driven approaches which I think Carter avoids confronting. I shall also consider some of the more extreme applications of corpus findings to language teaching. My argument is that there is an important difference between the hard and soft line approaches, that the former, by appearing to offer yet another easy 'scientific' solution, can do immense damage, and that we all, including Carter, would do well to consider more precisely whether we think corpus findings merely add a new dimension to earlier approaches, or replace them.

Uses and abuses of corpora

A number of false conclusions can be reached about corpora. It is often assumed, for example, that as a description of language behaviour, they are the only valid source of facts about language; the same as a description of language in the mind; provide a goal and a route for language learning. There is much in computerized corpus analysis to make us reconsider received ideas about the learning, representation, and use of language. But where pedagogy is concerned, corpus statistics say nothing about immeasurable but crucial factors such as students' and teachers' attitudes and expectations, the personal relationships between them, their own wishes, or the diversity of traditions from which they come. Consequently computer corpora – while impressive and interesting records of certain aspects of language use – can never be more than a *contribution* to our understanding of effective language teaching.

Corpus as fact

Even as a record of 'facts' computer corpora are incomplete. They contain information about production but not about reception. They say nothing about how many people have read or heard a text or utterance, or how many times.[1] Thus a memo hastily skimmed by one person and consigned to the wastepaper basket counts equally with a tabloid headline read by millions, or with a text, such as a prayer or poem, which is not only often repeated but also deeply valued. Occurrence, distribution, and importance, in other words, are not the same. This applies to whole texts, but also to shorter units. Some phrases pass unnoticed precisely because of their frequency, others strike and stay in the mind, though they may occur only once. And because different individuals notice different things, such saliency can never be included in a corpus. The same is true of a whole host of aspects of language use: metaphors, speech acts such as apologies or compliments, interactive events such as interruption or awkward uses, levels of formality. They are not 'facts' but matters of varying perception. It is a truism to observe that there is no straightforward correlation between the words people use, the intentions they had in them, and the interpretations which other people put upon them. If this were not so, there would be no disputes over the meaning of what people say.

Corpus as record

Corpora are records of language behaviour. The patterns which emerge in that behaviour do not necessarily and directly tell us how people organize and classify language in their own minds[2] and for their own use, or how language is best systematized for teaching. Linguists' analyses of these data are not necessarily users' analyses, or those which are most useful to teachers and learners. They are just one kind of fact. The ways in which grammarians and pedagogues have organized their material – in grammars, syllabuses, and dictionaries – are also facts about language. So are people's emotional beliefs that one type of language use is better than another. We should not promote some kinds of facts at the expense of others.

Corpora are only partial authorities. The cumulative language experience of an individual, though less amenable to systematic access, remains far larger and richer. Even a three hundred million word corpus is equivalent to only around three thousand books, or perhaps the language experience of a teenager. This is why our intuition (in effect our random and incomplete access to our total experience of the language) can still tell us facts about the language which cannot be evidenced by a corpus (Widdowson 1990). For example, the canonical forms of sayings and proverbs occur very rarely in corpora, though they are obviously well known by people (Aston 1995). Such omissions, however, are not merely a quantitative issue; they cannot be remedied simply by making corpora larger and larger. They are inevitable in an approach which accepts only one of the three sources of fact about language: observation; and ignores or villainizes two others: introspection and elicitation. For there are aspects of language which are known but not used. Corpus linguists are fond of observing that the commonest uses of words are not the same as their standard definitions. 'I bet', for example, is more rarely used in the sense of 'wager', and most often in the sense of 'suppose' (Sinclair 1987: xvi). But this unsurprising observation does not at all invalidate the view that 'wager' is a central prototypical meaning for many speakers to which more colloquial uses are attached. (And indeed, the 'wager' meaning is still given as the first meaning of 'bet' in the Cobuild dictionary.)

Description and prescription

But let us assume for the sake of argument that corpora are accurate records of language behaviour, that they *do* catalogue and reveal all the important 'facts' about the language. The question then arises as to whose language behaviour is accurately recorded – and the question takes on a particularly sinister significance when the corpora in question start being used not as data for descriptive linguistics, but as sources of prescription for TESOL. For the answer to the question is (as Carter seems painfully aware) that corpora are primarily records of native speakers' language behaviour. 'Real' language in effect means native-speaker English, and the only language excluded from this category (apart from the invented examples of linguists and textbook writers) is that used to and by language learners. To his credit, Carter confronts this issue, and intends to remedy it. But the proposed addition of 'a wider variety of international Englishes' will not solve the problem. This will only add other standard Englishes as spoken by their own native speakers.

And then a second question arises to which Carter explicitly refers, but does not answer. Why should the attested language use of a native-speaker community be a model for learners of English as an international language? If a certain collocation occurs frequently among British or American English speakers, must it also be used by the Japanese or the Mexicans? This is where we encounter an easy slippage from description to prescription, in effect making the former into the latter. The English which is used by one or more native-speaker communities, it is implied, ought to be the English learned for international communication.

The ready-made lexical phrases which corpora reveal to be so frequent in native speaker use are moreover – as Carter readily recognizes – very often culturally specific and loaded. In deploying such units, the foreign speaker is very likely to produce corpus-attested but contextually inappropriate language. (This is why attempts to teach set phrases are likely to be as tragicomically disastrous in lexical syllabuses as they were in functional ones.) In the terms of Hymes's (1972) four parameters of communicative competence, corpus-driven language teaching always risks stressing what is actually done at the expense of what is appropriate in a particular context.

Pedagogical issues

In an extensively quoted, and in itself excellent, essay by Pawley and Syder (1983) on native-like selection and fluency, corpus-based language teaching finds a source of inspiration, providing a potential link between the facts of language behaviour and a theory of how language is acquired and processed in the mind. Here is the claim that mature native speakers (for this is whom the essay is explicitly about) have 'hundreds of thousands' of institution-alized lexicalized or semi-lexicalized units in memory. Though many of these units can be analysed grammatically, the likelihood is, so the argument goes, that they are often produced and understood holistically. Native speakers acquire, represent, and process language in lexicalized chunks as well as grammar rules and single words.

Yet it by no means follows that foreign learners must do the same. They may not want to study language in this way; they may live within culturally diverse pedagogic traditions not compatible with this approach; they may not aspire to or need native-like English; they may not have as much time available as native-speaker children; above all, as adults with conscious learning strategies available to them, they can choose. And why should they not choose to continue viewing the language as grammar structures and slot-filling words? This may not lead to native-like English, but it may lead to communicative and expressive English. It may be learnt more quickly. And it will avoid the tedious rote learning of mundane phrases, or the bewildering refusal to teach grammar, which are the inevitable consequences of an overemphasis on 'lexical chunks'.

Yet even if appearing native-like were accepted as the goal of language learning, it would still not follow that frequency and desirability are the same. There is a hidden irony in the dogma that frequent native-like collocations are the best model to imitate. It is that even *within* the native-speaker community it is often the infrequent word or expression which is most powerful and most communicatively effective, and therefore most sought after. This is also why foreigners' speech is often expressive and striking. Both for native and non-native speakers there is an alternative goal to seeking the most usual, the most frequent or, in short, the most clichéd expression. It is the goal of rich, varied, and original language. Among native speakers it is unusual language which is valued. Should non-native speakers be treated differently?

This leads to the important point that not all types of language are equally valued, either by native speakers or foreign learners. Something is not a good model simply because it occurs frequently. A good deal of actual language use is inarticulate, impoverished, and inexpressive.[3] Inevitably, because one cannot teach everything, part of the job of teachers and course designers is to select the language use which they wish their students to emulate. Many foreign language students have strong feelings about this too. They do not want to learn just any English because it occurs in a corpus, and it is patronising to overrule them. In advocating selection and modelling of corpus data, in the use of literary rather than transcribed dialogues, and in his recognition that one of the topics in his authentic data ('straggly hair') may have a limited topic life in many classrooms, Carter seems to agree.

To be corpus driven, in short, deprives everyone (native and non-native speaker alike) of the opportunity for choice and to make their own impact on the language. Corpora are inevitably records of what has happened rather than what is happening. They present us with a *fait accompli*, a fixed product rather than an open process.

Means and ends

So corpora do not necessarily provide a goal for language learners. Yet even if they did, it would not follow that the best route to this goal is to present real language use, and to try to persuade them to emulate it straight away. Here there is a certain oddity in the corpus argument. Of course expert-speaker use of the language, and the rules which generate it, is usually more complex than that of language learners. If it were not, there would be nothing to learn. Hardly surprisingly, the description of English which emerges from corpus analysis (taking into account as it does the way in which linguistic items and structures vary across genres, social groups, and linguistic contexts) is dauntingly complex and particular. But this description cannot be presented to students all at once. The issue still remains how to simplify and stage the language presented to learners, and to simplify the rules used to explain it, in a way which will enable them to come gradually closer to native speaker use (if that is their goal). Surely the point of grammars and textbooks is that they select, idealize, and simplify the language to make it more accessible? Indeed, this seems to be Carter's view too.

For language teachers the issue remains as to what the principles for selection, idealization, and simplification should be. Here there is already a wealth of long standing ideas (dating back at least to the work of Palmer (1921) and West (1926)) concerning the relationship between the frequency with which an item occurs and the point at which it should be taught – ideas of which many corpus linguists, in their haste to advertise themselves as promulgating a totally new approach to language, seem unaware. For example, an item may be frequent but limited in range, or infrequent but useful in a wide range of contexts. Or it may be infrequent but very useful, or appropriate for some pedagogic reason. These are factors beyond mere description. Unlike many corpus linguists, Carter does show himself aware of such considerations in his conclusions. But that leaves me wondering whether his approach is such a break from tradition as he suggests.

The hard line

This brings me from Carter's views – moderate, sensible, and informed – to the more extreme, but unfortunately associated, views of language teaching based on corpus linguistics. Here is the belief that what is perceived as a linguistic revolution necessarily constitutes a pedagogic one. Very often writers are carried away by a single insight into *language*, taking it illogically to be sufficient to change *language teaching*. Thus Willis (1990) elevates frequency counts to the guiding principle for his lexical syllabus. Lewis (1993) considers the high occurrence of lexical chunks as a cue to decree (in a diatribe characterized by bombastic assertion rather than reasoned argument) that language teaching has changed forever, to be replaced by 'the way forward' (p. 196), with an ominously authoritarian definite article: his own lexical approach. 'Abstract, absolute knowledge of a system has had its day', and people who think otherwise 'are wrong' (p. 74); 'woolly mindedness in this matter leads to bad practice which has negative long term effects' (p. 167).

Such approaches are firmly in the tradition of using linguistics theory to dictate to language teaching practice. Their gross over-generalization and over-confidence are potentially damaging to good teaching practice. They invoke corpus linguistics as an unassailable authority, side-step all serious engagement in debate, and cannot take on board the kind of reservations expressed by Carter. Such corpus-driven pedagogy is a vain attempt to resuscitate a patriarchal attitude to ELT, invoking the latest linguistics theory to intimidate teachers into believing that all previous practice, all their own and their students' intuitions, all the culturally various pedagogic traditions in which they work and study, are, as Lewis would put it, 'wrong'.

Conclusion

I have contrasted throughout this reply what I see as the soft and the hard line views of the relevance of corpus findings to language teaching. In the one, we have the voice of moderation urging a limited application – 'modelling' as Carter calls it – which by virtue of its very reasonableness does not amount to anything very radical. In the other, we have the stronger view: evangelical, authoritarian, and dismissive of tradition, assuming that a little of the latest linguistics theory is all that is needed to change the course of language teaching. I believe that if Carter were to follow his arguments through to their conclusion, he too would explicitly reject, as I do, the more extreme versions both of corpus linguistics and of corpus-driven language teaching. But it is by no means clear whether he does so.

Notes

1   This point has been made by corpus linguists themselves (Francis 1979, Stubbs 1996:11), but the point is not adequately taken on board, either in corpus construction or analysis.
2   Stubbs (1996: 21) tells us that the 'deep patterning' revealed by corpus analysis is 'beyond human observation and memory'.
3   This issue is clouded by snobbish and chauvinistic claims that a particular national or sociolect is better than another. But this is not a necessary component of the notion that certain usages – literary, written, or simply eloquent and elegant ones – are more desirable models than others.

References

Aston, G. 1995. 'Corpora in language pedagogy: matching theory and practice' in G. Cook and B. Seidlhofer (eds.). *Principle and Practice in Applied Linguistics*. Oxford: Oxford University Press.

Carter, R. 1998. 'Orders of reality: CANCODE, communication, and culture'. *ELT Journal*, 52, 1, 43–56.

Francis, W. N. 1979. 'Problems of assembling and computerising large corpora' in H. Bergenholtz and B. Schader (eds.). *Empirische Textwissenschaft*. Berlin: Scriptor.

Hymes, D. 1972. 'On communicative competence' in J. B. Pride and J. Holmes (eds.). *Sociolinguistics*. Harmondsworth: Penguin.

Lewis, M. 1993. *The Lexical Approach*. Hove: Language Teaching Publications.

McCarthy, M. and Carter, R. 1994. Language as Discourse: Perspectives for Language Teaching. London: Longman.

Palmer, H. E. 1921. *The Principles of Language Study*. London: Harrap (Republished by Oxford University Press, 1964, edited by R. Mackin).

Pawley, A. and F. Syder. 1983. 'Two puzzles for linguistic theory: nativelike selection and nativelike fluency' in J. Richards and J. Schmidt (eds.). *Language and Communication*. London: Longman.

Sinclair, J. *et al.* 1987. *Collins Cobuild English Language Dictionary*. London: Collins.

Sinclair, J. M. 1991. *Corpus, Concordance, Collocation*. Oxford: Oxford University Press.

Stubbs, M. 1996. *Text and Corpus Analysis*. Oxford: Blackwell.

Stubbs, M. 1997. Review of *Using Corpora for Language Research*. *Applied Linguistics* 18/2: 240–3.

Summers, D. and M. Rundell (eds.). 1995. *Longman Dictionary of Contemporary English*. London: Longman.

West, M. P. 1926. *Learning to Read a Foreign Language*. New York: Longmans, Green.

Widdowson, H. G. 1990. 'Discourses of enquiry and conditions of relevance' in J. E. Alatis (ed). *Linguistics, Language Teaching and Language Acquisition*. Washington DC: Georgetown University Press.

Willis, D. 1990. *The Lexical Syllabus*. London: Collins.

Chapter 6

Ann Hewings and Martin Hewings

APPROACHES TO THE STUDY OF DISCIPLINARY VARIATION IN ACADEMIC WRITING: IMPLICATIONS FOR SYLLABUS DESIGN

1 Introduction

I N RECENT YEARS, SYLLABUSES for academic writing in higher education have increasingly focused on teaching students about the features of differing written genres. So, for instance, we find published material on laboratory and technical reports (for example Dudley-Evans, 1985), experimental research reports and other research papers (for example Weissberg and Buker, 1990), theses and dissertations (for example Anderson and Poole, 1994) and essays (for example Roberts, 1997). The general motivation of this approach is the need to offer appropriate descriptions and models of generic texts so that the students' ability to understand and produce them is improved. More specifically, students are taught about the textual features, both text structural and sentence-level, that are characteristic of each genre.

While this represents a valuable development from earlier approaches which treated 'academic writing' as an undifferentiated, homogeneous entity, it is important to recognise that variation is found not only from genre to genre, but also within genres. Evidence is accumulating that single genres vary over time (Bazerman, 1988; Dudley-Evans and Henderson, 1990; Selager-Meyer, 1999), vary from one cultural context to another (Taylor and Chen, 1991), and vary from discipline to discipline (Berkenkotter and Huckin, 1995; Prior, 1998).

This essay is primarily concerned with the third of these and, in particular, the methods that have been adopted for the study of disciplinary variation and the implications of findings to date for syllabus design. Knowledge of disciplinary variation is becoming especially important with the growing trend towards inter- and multi-disciplinary study in higher education so that students may be required to work within a number of disciplines which have different views on the nature of academic writing. We begin by reporting three areas of applied linguistic investigation which have explored the question of disciplinary variation in rather different ways and with rather different implications for syllabus design. First, we present Swales's approach to *genre analysis* and discuss studies of disciplinary variation based on this approach, in particular those which have explored variation in the academic research article. Second, we outline work which has examined *metadiscourse* in academic writing – that is, the part of a text which helps the reader organise, classify, evaluate and react to the propositional content (Vande Kopple, 1985) – and the way this varies in texts taken from different disciplines. Third, we report studies of one clause-level feature of text, the *grammatical subject*, that have demonstrated its significance in reflecting how writers represent data, previous research and themselves in the text, and how this varies across disciplines. A discussion of the implications of the findings of such work for academic writing syllabuses concludes the essay.

Throughout, our attention is primarily on genres produced within an academic context, either *classroom genres* – those produced by students for purposes of assessment, such as essays, dissertations and theses, laboratory and case study reports, and literature reviews – or *professional genres* – the texts by which scientists and scholars communicate with other scientists and scholars, such as conference papers, research articles, monographs, technical reports, working papers, and grant proposals.

2 Approaches to the study of disciplinary variation

2.1 Genre

Genre analysis

Within the context of English for Specific Purposes, the teaching of academic writing has been greatly influenced by the approach to genre arising from work by John Swales (for example 1981, 1984, 1990).[1] This approach considers a non-fictional genre to be:

> a recognizable communicative event characterized by a set of communicative purpose(s) identified and mutually understood by members of the professional or academic community in which it regularly occurs. Most often it is highly structured and conventionalized with constraints on allowable contributions in terms of their intent, positioning, form and functional value.
>
> (Bhatia, 1993: 13)

The primary criterion, then, by which texts are considered to be of the same genre is communicative purpose. If texts have different communicative purposes, they are likely to be of a different genre, and it is this shared communicative purpose that produces the conventionalised form of the genre and its characteristic linguistic features. The analysis of a genre for pedagogical purposes involves the identification of these regularities in text organisation and lexico-grammatical features and, in addition, an attempt to explain how they relate to the *discourse community* (Herzberg, 1986; Swales, 1990; Bizzell, 1992) within which the genre is produced. Such analysis can then be converted into syllabuses and materials that aim to teach students about text organisation and relevant language forms.

Swales's (1981, 1990) pioneering work identified a set of 'moves', and 'steps' within them, which were recurrently found in the introductions to research articles in order to contextualise an author's own research. A move is a unit which is related both to the purpose writers have and to the content they wish to communicate, while a step is a component of a move which is a more detailed option available to the writer in setting out a move (Dudley-Evans and St John, 1998: 89). Swales proposed (1990: 141) a three-move model for article introductions (modified from four in his 1981 work):

Move 1	Establishing a territory		
	Step 1	Claiming centrality	
and/or	Step 2	Making topic generalisations	
and/or	Step 3	Reviewing items of previous research	
Move 2	Establishing a niche		
	Step 1A	Counter-claiming	
or	Step 1B	Indicating a gap	
or	Step 1C	Question-raising	
or	Step 1D	Continuing a tradition	
Move 3	Occupying the niche		
	Step 1A	Outlining purposes	
or	Step 1B	Announcing present research	
	Step 2	Announcing principal findings	
	Step 3	Indicating research article structure.	

Typically, academic discourse communities are bound together by subject matter, and professional academic writing is seen as adding to the body of knowledge which is at the core of the discipline. In addition to disciplinary knowledge, the way subject matter is discussed – the genre conventions used – is also of importance. To become 'good academic writers', students need to become aware of these conventions, that is, how the textual forms and communicative functions are related to the expectations of the academic community to which they belong.

Studies of genre variation

Swales's move and step approach has been used not only to identify the characteristics of particular genres, but also to compare texts of the same genre but from different disciplines. For example, in the preliminaries to an investigation of active and passive verb forms in two astrophysics journal articles, Tarone *et al.* (1998) note that Swales's (1990) overview of the organisation of the research article as having an 'hourglass' shape is not applicable to articles in astrophysics. 'Hourglass' articles begin with a broad overview of the field, narrow the focus down to a specific area of interest which is then experimented on in some way, and conclude with a widening-out of the discussion to relate findings to broader issues relevant to the field. Astrophysics papers, however, are considered by Tarone *et al.* to have an 'inverted pyramid' construction in which the focus of the paper is gradually narrowed down, beginning with general physics, through the particular phenomena to explain, the specific physics of relevance, specific equations, to a specific solution. The reason, they argue, is that while the hourglass is a satisfactory representation of reports of experimental studies, astrophysics attends to subject matter which cannot be experimented on, so that papers in the discipline present logical arguments rather than experiments.

A number of studies have examined how sections of research articles vary across disciplines. The typical sections of research articles are an introduction, a methods section which explains the procedures undertaken (often experimental procedures in the case of scientific research articles), a report of the results of the procedures, and finally a discussion of these results and their significance. Brett's (1994) starting point is Swales's (1990: 175–6) proposal that disciplinary differences in research articles are likely to lie in methods and results sections rather than introductions and discussions. He examines results sections in research articles from sociology and observes certain communicative categories within them, such as his *Substantiation of Findings* and *Non-validation of Findings*, not previously documented as appearing in results or discussion sections (for example in Belanger, 1982; Dudley-Evans, 1989; Hopkins and Dudley-Evans, 1988; Weissberg and Buker, 1990). He relates these to the methods of quantitative sociological research in which abstract concepts such as 'ethnic identification' or 'satisfaction' are presented as numerical data. These data are then manipulated using accepted statistical techniques, and the resulting statistics interpreted to produce deductions about human behaviour. Not only are the effects on the dependent variable of the most significant independent variables discussed, but so are the effects of other variables. The second of these, Brett found, took up more space than the discussion of the most significant findings, while the effects of secondary variables are assessed as either supporting (*Substantiation of Findings*) or lessening the validity of (*Non-validation of Findings*) the main findings. As in Tarone *et al.*'s work, then, Brett suggests that the subject matter and the methodologies deployed influence the constitution of written text within the discipline.

Holmes (1997) undertakes a comparative study of the organisation of the discussion sections of articles presenting original research from the disciplines of political science, sociology and history using a Swales-type move analysis. He identifies a total of eight moves (*Background information, Statement of result, (Un)expected outcome, Reference to previous research, Explanation of unsatisfactory result, Generalisation, Recommendation,* and *Outlining parallel or subsequent developments*). In comparison with similar work on articles in the natural or hard sciences (Peng, 1987) Holmes (1997: 332) finds that discussion sections in the social sciences, as represented by political science and sociology, are less complex, employing a restricted repertoire of moves, yet are less predictable. On the other hand, social science *introductions* have been found to display *greater* complexity than those in the hard sciences (Crookes, 1986; Holmes, 1995). On the basis of such evidence, research articles in the social sciences would seem to display greater complexity and elaboration at the beginning than at the end while the reverse is the case in the hard sciences. A number of explanations for such differences might be put forward. Given the relative lack of consensus on goals and methods of research in the social sciences, there may be greater need to establish more overtly and in greater detail the parameters of research in the field. More generally, Holmes (1997: 332) proposes that the greater conventionalisation of research articles in the hard sciences is a reflection of their higher degree of *bureaucratisation*, measured 'by reference to quantitative data, collaborative authorship and external financial support' (*ibid.*). This view is supported by the observation that discussion sections in history, the least bureaucratised discipline of the three studied, have less in common with those in the hard sciences and are the least predictable.

Evidence of generic variation across disciplines is also found in 'classroom genres' in the writing of students in higher education. In a comparison of master's-level dissertations written in highway engineering and plant biology, Dudley-Evans (1993) notes particular differences in the discussion sections. In plant biology, considerable space and attention is given over to comparison of present results with previous findings reported in the literature. Thus, claims about present results and explanations of unexpected outcomes are supported with reference to previous work. In highway engineering, in contrast, emphasis is on stating present results and making recommendations based on these results, with less attention to the relationship between present results and previous research in the field. From his reading of the dissertations, Dudley-Evans' impression (1993: 145) of highway engineering is

> of a discipline in which there is not a huge amount of previous research to refer to and which sees its work in the context of practical suggestions that the practising engineer can put into operation in the field.

Such studies, then, suggest that the nature of a particular discipline, as indicated in its subject matter, its methods of investigation, the amount of previous research in the field, the level of consensus on agreed knowledge, and the degree of bureaucratization in the discipline may be reflected in its generic conventions. This has direct implications for syllabus design. It reinforces the need to move away not only from academic writing as a homogeneous entity, but also from homogeneous genres. While information on, for example, the sections of the research article may be useful as a preliminary, students also need to be made aware of the specifics of what to include, what to emphasise, and what to exclude within each section for their own particular discipline.

2.2 *Metadiscourse*

A rather different approach to the investigation of the relationship between disciplinary communities and their texts is found in studies of metadiscourse in academic writing. A distinction can be made between the *propositional* content of a text, its information or subject matter, and *metadiscourse*, that part of the text which helps the reader organise, classify, evaluate and react to the propositional content (Vande Kopple, 1985). The elements of metadiscourse have been divided (see, for example, Hyland 1999a) into those which, in the terminology of systemic functional grammar, serve a *textual* function and those which serve an *interpersonal* function. Halliday (1973: 66) describes the textual function as

> an enabling function, that of creating text . . . It is this component that enables the speaker [or writer] to organise what he is saying in such a way that it makes sense in the context and fulfils its functions as a message,

while the interpersonal function is said to include

> all that may be understood by the expression of our own personalities and personal feelings on the one hand, and forms of interaction and social interplay with other participants in the communication situation on the other hand.

Metadiscourse, therefore, allows writers not only to show how a text is organised and how different parts of the text are related, but also to express their attitude towards the subject matter of the text and towards the intended readership. Academic disciplines have conventional ways in which writers are allowed both to present their arguments and to represent themselves, and this is achieved mainly in the metadiscourse in text. It is through the study of metadiscourse in the texts of a particular disciplinary community, therefore, that the characteristics of that community can be explored. Studies of metadiscourse in academic text have looked at cultural and gender variation (Crismore *et al.*, 1993; Mauranen, 1993) and the use of metadiscourse in particular academic genres (Hyland, 1999a; Hewings, 1999). However, it is Hyland's (1999b) work on metadiscourse and disciplinary variation that is of main concern here and reported below.

In a study of fifty-six research articles taken from eight disciplines (microbiology, physics, marketing, applied linguistics, philosophy, sociology, mechanical engineering, and electrical engineering), Hyland considers variation in the writers' *stance*. Stance is part of the interpersonal component of metadiscourse and defined as

> the ways that writers project themselves into their texts to communicate their integrity, credibility, involvement, and a relationship to their subject matter and their readers.

> (1999b: 101)

It is considered to have five main components:

- *hedges* (e.g. *possible, might, perhaps, believe*), through which the writer withholds full commitment to a proposition;
- *emphatics* (e.g. *it is obvious, definitely, of course*), through which the writer emphasises the force of a proposition;
- *attitude markers*, concerned with the writer's attitude to what is said and signalled by such devices as *attitude verbs* (e.g. *I agree, we prefer*) and *sentence adverbs* (e.g. *unfortunately, hopefully*);
- *relational markers*, concerned with the writer's attempt to invoke reader participation and signalled by such devices as first *person pronouns* (e.g. *we find here, let its now turn to*) and imperatives (e.g. *consider, recall, note that*);
- *person markers*, concerned with the use of first person pronouns and possessive adjectives (e.g. *we believe, my analyses involved*) to present propositional, affective and interpersonal information.

(1999b: 103–4)

The main variation found in the use of features of stance is between 'hard' disciplines in the sciences and 'soft' disciplines in the humanities/ social sciences respectively. Overall, Hyland found some 30 per cent more features of stance in the soft discipline research articles, and he attributes this not only to disciplinary preferences in style, but also to differences in values and beliefs about knowledge and knowing across disciplines. For example, Hyland found a greater use of *hedges* in general in the soft knowledge areas. This, he suggests, is because in these areas problems are less clearly defined and thus explanations are likely to be less assured. Writers therefore, as he puts it, have to 'work harder to engage their audience and shape their arguments to the shared perspectives of the discipline' (1999b: 111).

Evidence that 'hard' disciplines have a more cohesive body of agreed knowledge than 'soft' disciplines is also provided in the observation that the hard-knowledge areas use twice as many *attributive hedges*, that is, devices such as *about, partially, approximately, generally* and so on, used to restrict the scope of the accompanying statement. He gives as an example (1999b: 110) the following extract from a research article in mechanical engineering: 'for metallurgical coal is usually met by imports from the United States while virtually all . . . .'. This kind of 'weaker hedging' is used, according to Hyland, when the writer wishes to indicate how far results diverge from a position which the disciplinary community conceives as reality. It is used less in the softer knowledge areas because there are fewer instances of agreed reality.

Hyland concludes by arguing that:

Rather than thinking of academic discourse as impersonal . . . we need to think of it as reflecting the different social practices of the disciplinary communities in constructing knowledge. Simply, some fields permit greater authorial presence than others.

(1999b: 121)

These findings can be incorporated into syllabuses for teaching academic writing through the acknowledgement of variation in the extent and type of metadiscourse in the texts of different disciplines. Students need to be helped to explore patterns of occurrence and characteristics of the discipline to which these patterns are related.

2.3 The grammatical subject

A third approach to the study of disciplinary variation has developed from the work of MacDonald (1992, 1994) on the *grammatical subject*. The subject, or grammatical subject (GS), has always been recognised as a significant component of English in both traditional and functional grammars. The typical English sentence pattern is Subject – Verb – Object, for example:

Suzanne	played	her violin
Subject	*Verb*	*Object*

and the subject is an obligatory element in all sentences with the exception of imperatives. MacDonald's rationale for focusing on the GS was that it is

> the constituent defining the topic of the sentence – that which the sentence is 'about' and which it presupposes as its point of departure.
>
> (Quirk *et al.*, 1985: 79)

Thus the GS is important for determining what a writer is writing *about* and how they represent data, previous research and themselves in their texts.

In her investigation into disciplinary differences in professional writing in the humanities and social sciences, MacDonald developed a method of classifying GSs on the basis of whether they contribute to the content of a text or whether they are more concerned with consolidating knowledge construction in a discipline – that is, the building of knowledge on foundations laid by other researchers. For some disciplines, the consolidation of knowledge is of such importance that it is reflected not only at text level but also in sentence-level choices. Analysis of the GS is used to demonstrate the rhetorical practices of such disciplines. For example, academic texts with sentences beginning 'Work by James . . .' or 'Experimental evidence . . .' are clearly building on a foundation constructed for the discipline by those within it. The GSs can thus be said to have an *epistemic* focus, one which is concerned with methods of study and the validity of knowledge claims. For other disciplines, the people, things and events that constitute the phenomena or content that are studied are foregrounded. For example, in literature studies, 'Shakespeare's plays' might well be the content or subject that is being written about, and where these words occur as the GS there is said to be a *phenomenal* focus. Within this broad two-fold division, MacDonald recognises a further disciplinary characteristic. Disciplines such as those in the humanities are more concerned with specific people, places and events, whereas those in, for example, the social sciences rely more on generalisations and abstractions. This is again reflected in the choice of GS, with a cline existing between those GSs which represent phenomena at their most specific and individualistic through to those which are most abstract.

On this basis, MacDonald (1992) has developed a classification system for GSs, a modified version of which is summarised in Table 6.1.

The value of this work for the study of disciplinary variation becomes apparent if we compare findings from psychology, history and literature (from MacDonald, 1992) and wildlife behaviour, conservation biology and legislative history (Samraj, 1995). MacDonald's data are based on an analysis of four journal-length articles in each discipline, while Samraj analysed six student papers from three different courses which formed part of a US Master's programme in environmental studies. The figures in Table 6.2 show the percentage average distribution of each of the seven classes of GSs in the texts.

Table 6.1 A classification system for the grammatical subject

Summary of grammatical subject classification

Phenomenal
Phenomenal grammatical subjects are those which deal with the material that a researcher or writer studies or writes about.

Class 1 (Particulars) contains nouns referring to specific people, places, or objects, usually named (e.g. *the USA, Stalin, Europe, the storm*).

Class 2 (Non-Specific Groups) contains generalised or grouped nouns (e.g. *large areas of the country, gullies, downland soils, the tsetse fly population*).

Class 3 (Attributes) contains the most abstract, least material nouns in the phenomenal category. They are nouns expressing properties, attributes, actions or motivations of the people or things in 1 and 2 (e.g. *agricultural practices, rainfall intensities, planning*).

Epistemic
Epistemic grammatical subjects represent the concepts, categories, abstractions or methodological tools the researcher uses to reason about the subject.

Class 4 (Research Matters) contains references to the constituents of research and the activities of researchers such as data collection and analysis, generating ideas and comparing and contrasting different theories (e.g. *the equations, the final hypothesis, it has been argued that*).

Class 5 (Researchers and Studies) contains references to published research and to writers in the field (e.g. *Pinch and Storey, 1992, I*).

Class 6 (Audience) contains subjects like the generalised *we* (but not the actual *we* which refers to authors) and *one* or *you*.

Class 7 (Discoursal) contains subjects which refer to the text itself, either in whole or in part, and rhetorical questions used to organise the discourse (e.g. *this essay, Figure 2, Why are mobile homes popular with pensioners?*).

An examination of the table shows some very large variations in the types of GSs favoured by different disciplines and the grouping of these into phenomenal or epistemic categories. Disciplines with more epistemic subjects (classes 4–7) foreground research methods, inferences and findings rather than the phenomena that are being studied or written about (classes 1–3). Some disciplines are clearly more phenomenal in their focus and some more epistemic. Psychology, for example, has a total of 62 per cent epistemic grammatical subjects, whereas literature has 84 per cent phenomenal. At the level of individual classes, legislative history and literature use more class 1 (particulars) than the other disciplines. This underlines their concern with specific people, places and objects. In contrast, psychology uses less than 1 per cent of class 1 GSs. Instead, it favours non-specific, more generalised references to phenomena as found in class 2. Most disciplines, except literature, but especially the two histories, have fairly high numbers of non-specific groups of people, places or things. Class 3 GSs are frequent in all disciplines except psychology. They are nouns which express properties, attributes, actions or motivations of the people or things in classes 1 and 2.

Hewings (1999) has used MacDonald's techniques to examine writing development among undergraduate students within the discipline of geography at a British university.

Table 6.2 Average distribution (%) of GSs in different disciplines and sub-disciplines (data from MacDonald 1992 and Samraj 1995)

GS class	Psychology	History	Literature	Wildlife behaviour[2]	Conservation biology	Legislative history
1	0.1	6	30	1	7	35
2	27	44	10	30	28	30
3	11	26	44	29	44	28
4	49	15	7	18	9	1
5	12	6	5	18	8	2
6	1	3	4	–	–	–
7	–	–	–	–	–	–

Comparing essays written by students in the first and final (third) years of their programme, she found a substantially higher proportion of phenomenal to epistemic GSs in first-year essays (76 per cent and 24 per cent respectively), while the proportion of epistemic GSs was higher in final-year essays (56 per cent phenomenal and 44 per cent epistemic). First-year essays showed a greater focus on the real-world phenomena that geography investigates, as in the following example in which GSs, all phenomenal, are underlined:

> Bus and rail are the obvious components of a mass transit system. The bus is the cheaper of the two options, but even with designated bus lanes it still adds to the problem of congestion and has a lower capacity. Rail on the other hand is much more expensive but has a higher capacity and takes travel away from the roads. There are a number of examples of mass transit systems around the world, some are highly successful others are not.

These clearly foreground the phenomena that are being studied and indicate a priority of content over rhetorical motivations. While third-year essays were also concerned with real-world phenomena, these were often displaced from the subject position by epistemic GSs, underlined in the following example:

> Experiments by Morgan et al. (1982) on 'detachment of soil particles from a sandy soil by raindrop impact in storms of 50mm/hr and 61mm/hr for 5 minutes duration showed that the rate of erosion under a cover of brussel sprouts decreased as the canopy cover increased from 0–15–25%, but erosion increased if the canopy cover increased any more and at 50% cover the erosion rate equalled that of bare soil' (Morgan 1986). Similar experiments were done on potato crops with similar findings. These results add to those of Vis which show under certain circumstances plant covers are associated with high rather than low rates of erosion mainly due to their influence on the kinetic energy of intercepted raindrops. Other experiments such as by De Ploey et al. (1976) recorded an increase in soil erosion with an increase in grass cover. . . . Morgan (1980) showed in his study on soils in Silsoe that sandy soils in Bedfordshire are ten times more erodible in summer than in winter.

On a general level, then, the model is useful for indicating certain disciplinary trends within writing. It provides a way of focusing on a particular linguistic feature and uses it to tease out aspects of the disciplinary culture which would otherwise be obscure. By this means, advice on writing can be directed more specifically to those features which reflect the underlying culture of a particular disciplinary community. GSs in successful and less successful student writing could be compared and students encouraged to classify the GSs, initially using their own criteria and later using the broad phenomenal/epistemic classification given above.

3 Implications for syllabus design

The starting point of this essay was that the recent trend towards genre-based approaches to the teaching of academic writing was a positive development when compared with those which represented a homogeneous view of academic writing, undifferentiated across genres. Indeed, in current thinking on tertiary academic literacy it is now taken almost as axiomatic that an understanding of generic conventions, particularly in terms of moves but also steps and their lexicogrammatical realisations, is essential in achieving academic success. Research is showing both how genres differ and how knowledge of one genre may be inadequate preparation for the production of another. For example, Hyland's (1999a) work on the metadiscourse of textbooks leads him to conclude that

> students need to be steered away from using textbooks as models. Too close a familiarity with the ways that textbooks address readers, organise material and present facts may mean that learners are poorly prepared when assigned research articles by their subject lecturers or ESP teachers or when asked to write argumentative prose.
> (Hyland, 1999a: 21–2)

However, in the design of syllabuses for academic writing programmes, it is necessary to recognise the lesson of the research reported in this essay: that helping students to develop a knowledge of genres is insufficient in a number of ways. First, it is important to guard against teaching genres as a set of templates to be copied unswervingly. Bazerman's (1988) investigation of the experimental article in science leads him to offer the following caution:

> the largest lesson that this study holds is not that there are simple genres that must be slavishly followed, that we must give students an appropriate set of cookie cutters for their anticipated careers, but rather that the student must understand and rethink the rhetorical choices embedded in each generic habit to master the genre.
> (Bazerman 1988: 80)

Second, it is necessary to develop students' sensitivity to the fact that genres vary, particularly across disciplines. This is increasingly important given the growing number of students in multi- or inter-disciplinary academic programmes where success is dependent both on being aware of disciplinary variation in communication practices and on developing sufficient flexibility to produce writing that reflects the predilections of a particular disciplinary community. Such flexibility is unlikely to be achieved simply by learning the preferred conventions of a discipline, but must be underpinned by a deeper understanding of how this reflects such matters as the degree of consensus within the discipline on the definition of problems and appropriate methodologies to address these problems, the amount of previous research that it is conventional to acknowledge, and the cohesiveness of the body of agreed knowledge within the discipline.

Third, we need a reassessment of 'common-core' and 'discipline-specific' components of academic writing programmes (see also Bhatia, 1999). Common-core teaching, focusing on the 'language and conventions related to the general requirements of the academic community' (Dudley-Evans, 1995), has the advantage of being addressed to students from across disciplines and is therefore efficient both in terms of the number of students taught and, often, financially. However, it has the disadvantage of being relatively insensitive to the preferred ways of writing in particular disciplines. Discipline-specific components provide this sensitivity but usually have the disadvantages of addressing smaller numbers of students, needing specially focused research and being less cost-efficient, and will often have the additional complexity of requiring the input at some stage of a subject specialist. Perhaps our goal is that of common-core teaching mediated through a disciplinary filter. While helping students develop an awareness of the general significance of certain of the characteristics of writing in particular genres – text organisational patterns, metadiscoursal features, grammatical subjects, for example – at the same time we need to provide them with the strategies for examining *how* these operate and *why* this should be so by reflecting on the subject matter, working practices, values and ideologies of the discipline or disciplines within which they are working.

Note

1   While the ESP approach to genre analysis has been particularly influential in pedagogical applications, other perspectives exist, and Hyon (1996) has identified two additional broad areas of scholarship researching non-literary genres: North American Rhetoric studies and work within Australian systemic functional linguistics (for example Martin 2000).

2   Samraj had a further category, 'miscellaneous', which is not included here. Hence the figures do not add up to 100%.

References

Anderson, J. and Poole, M. (1994) *Thesis and Assignment Writing*. 2nd edn. Brisbane, Queensland: Jacaranda Wiley.

Bazerman, C. (1988) *Shaping Written Knowledge: The Genre and Activity of the Experimental Article in Science*. Madison: University of Wisconsin Press.

Belanger, M. (1982) 'A preliminary analysis of the structure of the discussion sections in ten neuroscience journal articles' (mimeo).

Berkenkotter, C. and Huckin, T. (1995) *Genre Knowledge in Disciplinary Communication*. Hillsdale, NJ: Lawrence Erlbaum.

Bhatia, V. K. (1993) *Analysing Genre: Language Use in Professional Settings*. London: Longman.

Bhatia, V. K. (1999) 'Disciplinary variation in business English'. In M. Hewings and C. Nickerson (eds) *Business English: Research into Practice*. Harlow: Longman, 129–43.

Bizzell, P. (1992) *Academic Discourse and Critical Consciousness*. Pittsburg: University of Pittsburg Press.

Brett, P. (1994) 'A genre analysis of the results section of sociology articles'. *English for Specific Purposes* 13: 47–59.

Crismore, A., Markkanen, R. and Steffensen, M. (1993) 'Metadiscourse in persuasive writing: a study of texts written by American and Finnish university students'. *Written Communication* 10: 39–71.

Crookes, G. (1986) 'Towards a validated analysis of scientific text structure'. *Applied Linguistics* 7: 57–70.

Dudley-Evans, T. (1985) *Writing Laboratory Reports*. Melbourne: Nelson.

Dudley-Evans, T. (1989) 'Genre analysis: an investigation of the introduction and discussion sections of MSc dissertations'. In M. Coulthard (ed.) *Talking about Text*. English Language Research, University of Birmingham, Birmingham, UK, 128–45.

Dudley-Evans, T. (1993) 'Variation in communication patterns between discourse communities: the case of Highway Engineering and Plant Biology'. In G. Blue (ed.) *Language, Learning and Success: Studying through English*. London: Macmillan, 141–7.

Dudley-Evans. T. (1995) 'Common-core and specific approaches to the teaching of academic writing'. In D. Belcher and G. Braine (eds) *Academic Writing in a Second Language: Essays on Research and Pedagogy*. Norwood, NJ: Ablex.

Dudley-Evans, T. and Henderson, W. (1990) 'The organization of article introductions: evidence of change in economics writing'. In T. Dudley-Evans and W. L. Henderson (eds) *The Language of Economics: The Analysis of Economics Discourse*. London: Modern English Publications/ British Council, 67–78.

Dudley-Evans, T. and St John, M. (1998) *Developments in English for Specific Purposes: A Multi-disciplinary Approach*. Cambridge: Cambridge University Press.

Halliday, M. A. K. (1973) *Explorations in the Functions of Language*. London: Edward Arnold.

Herzberg, B. (1986) 'The politics of discourse communities'. Paper presented at Conference on College Composition and Communication, New Orleans, 1986. Cited in Bizzell, 1992.

Hewings, A. (1999) 'Disciplinary engagement in undergraduate writing: an investigation of clause-initial elements in geography essays'. Unpublished Ph.D. thesis, The University of Birmingham, UK.

Holmes, R. (1995) 'Genre analysis and the social sciences: an investigation of the introductions, background sections and discussion sections of research articles in history, political science and sociology'. Unpublished MA dissertation, University of Surrey, UK.

Holmes, R. (1997) 'Genre analysis and the social sciences: an investigation of the structure of research article discussion sections in three disciplines'. *English for Specific Purposes* 16: 321–37.

Hopkins, A. and Dudley-Evans, T. (1988) 'A genre-based investigation of the discussion sections in articles and dissertations'. *English for Specific Purposes* 7: 113–22.

Hyland, K. (1999a) 'Talking to students: metadiscourse in introductory coursebooks'. *English for Specific Purposes* 18: 3–26.

Hyland, K. (1999b) 'Disciplinary discourses: writer stance in research articles'. In C. Candlin and K. Hyland (eds) *Writing: Texts, Processes and Practices*. Harlow: Addison-Wesley-Longman, 99–121.

Hyon, S. (1996) 'Genre in three traditions: implications for ESL'. *TESOL Quarterly* 30: 693–722.

MacDonald, S. P. (1992) 'A method for analyzing sentence-level differences in disciplinary knowledge making'. *Written Communication* 9: 533–69.

MacDonald, S. P. (1994) *Professional Academic Writing in the Humanities*. Carbondale: Southern Illinois University Press.

Martin, J. R. (2001) 'Technicality and abstraction: language for the creation of specialised texts'. In A. Burns and C. Coffin (eds) *Analysing English in a Global Context*. London: Routledge.

Mauranen, A. (1993) *Cultural Differences in Academic Rhetoric: A Textlinguistic Study*. Frankfurt-am-Main: Peter Lang.

Peng, J. (1987) 'Organisational features in chemical engineering research'. *English Language Research Journal* 1: 79–116.

Prior, P. (1998) *Writing/Disciplinarity: A Sociohistoric Account of Literate Activity in the Academy*. Mahwah, NJ: Lawrence Erlbaum.

Quirk, R., Greenbaum, S., Leech, G. and Svartvik, J. (1985) *A Comprehensive Grammar of the English Language*. London: Longman.

Roberts, D. (1997) *The Student's Guide to Writing Essays*. London: Kogan Page.

Samraj, B. T. R. (1995) 'The nature of academic writing in an interdisciplinary field'. Unpublished Ph.D. thesis, University of Michigan.

Selager-Meyer, F. (1999) 'Referential behaviour in scientific writing: a diachronic study (1810–1995)'. *English for Specific Purposes* 18: 279–305.

Swales, J. (1981) *Aspects of Article Introductions*. Birmingham: The University of Aston, Language Studies Unit.

Swales, J. (1984) 'Research into the structure of introductions to journal articles and its application to the teaching of academic writing'. In R. Williams, J. Swales and J. Kirkman (eds) *Common Ground: Shared Interests in ESP and Communication Studies*. ELT Documents 117: 77–86.

Swales, J. (1990) *Genre Analysis*. Cambridge: Cambridge University Press.

Tarone, E., Dwyer, S., Gillette, S. and Icke, V. (1998) 'On the use of the passive and active voice in Astrophysics journal papers: with extensions to other languages and other fields'. *English for Specific Purposes* 17: 113–32.

Taylor, G. and Chen, T. (1991) 'Linguistic, cultural and subcultural issues in contrastive discourse analysis: Anglo-American and Chinese scientific texts'. *Applied Linguistics* 12: 319–36.

Vande Kopple, W. J. (1985) 'Some exploratory discourse on metadiscourse'. *College Composition and Communication* 36: 82–93.

Weissberg, R. and Buker, S. (1990) *Writing up Research*. Englewood Cliffs, NJ: Prentice-Hall.

PART TWO

Political and institutional constraints in curriculum development

Chapter 7

Ronald Carter

POLITICS AND KNOWLEDGE ABOUT LANGUAGE: THE LINC PROJECT

1 Introduction

THE RELATIONSHIP BETWEEN POLITICS and knowledge about language is both comprehensive and complex. In this chapter three main perspectives are offered: a brief overview of a national language education initiative in England and Wales with a particular focus on keywords in discourses about language, English and education; the place of genre theory in relation to such an initiative; some research and development questions for teaching school students *about* language.

1.1 Examining language

Here is part of a General Secondary Education paper set for 15–16-year-old pupils in Britain in the 1940s. Questions of this kind about grammar constituted between 20 and 30 per cent of the total examination paper:

Question 1

(a)   Analyse into clauses the following passage. Give the grammatical description of the clauses and show their connection with each other:

In that year (1851) when the Great Exhibition spread its hospitable glass roof high over the elms of Hyde Park, and all the world came to *admire* England's wealth, progress and enlightenment, there might *profitably* have been another 'exhibition' to show how our poor were housed and to teach the admiring visitors *some* of the dangers *that* beset the path of the vaunted new era.

(b)   State the grammatical features of the words italicized in (a).

Reference is made to such an examination exercise at the very beginning of this chapter because the views of language and of language teaching enshrined within it go right to the very centre of current debates in Britain about language teaching in the context of the new National Curriculum for English in England and Wales. The debate is characterised by different political positions and, in particular, by strenuous efforts by the British government to persuade teachers to a return to the 1940s and to the kinds of practices of language teaching illustrated by this examination paper.

What are the practices which are illustrated by this example? Why do government ministers wish to see them reinstated? What do teachers think of them? What is the view taken by linguists of such practices? Answers to such questions may begin to explain why the materials for teachers produced by the Language in the National Curriculum (henceforth, LINC) project were not only refused publication by the British government, but also became the centre of contesting views about language and education.

1.2 Views of language and language teaching

The different views of language and language teaching in respect of this representative examination paper held by government, English teachers and by linguists may be broadly summarised under three headings: (1) government views; (2) teachers' views; and (3) linguists' views.

Government views

1. The examination paper illustrates a manifest concern with measurable knowledge. A body of linguistic facts can be taught, learned by pupils and then tested. Answers are either right or wrong, the body of knowledge taught is definite and measurable, and teachers can even be assessed by how well they teach it.
2. The learning which ensues is disciplined and takes places within a clear framework. It contrasts vividly with what is felt to be the vague and undirected concern with creativity and personal expression which characterises work in many English lessons at the present time.
3. Such practices will help to guarantee correct grammar and standard English. They will remove sloppiness in expression and eradicate a climate in which errors are viewed only in relation to a process of language development and thus not always immediately corrected.

Teachers' views

Until recently, teachers' views have been regularly dominated by what are described as 'romantic' conceptions of English as a subject (see Christie, 1989; Carter, 1988). Romanticism in English teaching involves a classroom emphasis on language use which is person-centred, which stresses the capacity of the individual for originality and creativity, and a concern that strict rules and conventions may be inhibiting to pupils and, in the process, restrict their capacities for using the language. There is a particular stress on the primacy of speech, even in writing where individuals are encouraged by the teacher to find their own personal voice. During the course of the LINC project shifts in teachers' perception of formal language study were recorded, but strong resistance remains, on the above grounds, to the decontextualised study of language, to teaching practices and pedagogies which are necessarily transmissive and narrowly knowledge-based, and which allow little or no scope for an emergence of the pupil's own 'voice'.

The views of linguists

Linguists have taken a prominent role in the shaping of the National Curriculum for English in England and Wales. Most take the following main views of grammar-based teaching and testing of linguistic knowledge:

1   They point out how examination papers from the 1940s and 1950s are preoccupied with the written rather than the spoken language.
2   They point out that the analysis is invariably decontextualised since the definitions required of pupils are **formalistic**. Examinations such as those above are exercises in the naming of parts.
3   They point out that such examinations are concerned with sentences rather than texts. In fact, the text here is genuinely incidental. The focus is on a bottom-up analysis of the smallest units of language with little or no interest in eliciting from pupils how such units might combine to form larger functional meanings and effects.

Accordingly, those linguists who advised the government did not recommend a return to the 1940s and to a teaching of grammatical forms by means of decontextualised drills. But they did not reject a formal study of language. Instead, they strongly advocated programmes of study for pupils in knowledge about language (KAL), based on a wider range of analysis than grammar, and [. . .] clearly rooted in theories of language variation, both spoken and written. The government was quick to recognise that knowledge about language, based on a variety of texts, includes discussion of language in context, and that discussion of context is often necessarily social. Such an orientation served only to reinforce for the government the desirability of decontextualised drills and exercises.

2   LINC: An in-service teacher education project

LINC is designed to make the theories and descriptions of language in the new National Curriculum accessible to teachers, and to assist them with the language components of the National Curriculum for English. [. . .]

In basic outline the main project team was asked to produce study units for teachers which were to be used in in-service courses, in school-based follow-up and dissemination, and in self-study sessions. The resulting training package is therefore activity-based and open-ended. It contains many linguistically based tasks with accompanying commentaries so that teachers can work on the material in a range of contexts.

2.1 The LINC ban

The LINC project assumed political prominence when the government decided that it did not wish to publish the materials produced by the project. Neither would it allow commercial publication in spite of interest on the part of several international publishers in publishing the complete training package. Although the project was allowed to continue and although the LINC training package could be made available in photocopied form for purposes of in-service training courses, such decisions amounted to an effective ban on widespread publication and dissemination of LINC materials.

[. . .]

Debates surrounding the LINC ban centre on certain keywords. They are the same keywords which recur repeatedly at times of social and cultural change when questions of language and the nature of English as a subject are always central.

It is no semantic accident that words such as **standard**, **correct**, and **proper** are among the keywords. Debates about the state and status of the English language are rarely debates about language alone. The terms of the debate are also terms for defining social behaviour. The term **English** is synonymous with Englishness, that is, with an understanding of who the proper English are. A view of one English with a single set of rules accords with a monolingual, monocultural version of society intent on preserving an existing order in which everyone knows their place. A view which recognises Englishes as well as English and which stresses variable rules accords with a multilingual, culturally diverse version of society. Both positions include politically extreme versions. These range from a view that standard English is correct English and must be uniformly enforced in all contexts of use (with dialects extirpated) and that children not drilled in the rules of standard grammar are both deviant and disempowered (strong right-wing position) to a view that standard English is a badge of upper-class power, and that to require children to learn it is a form of social enslavement (strong leftwing position I) to a view that standard English must be taught to working-class children so that they can wrest linguistic power from those more privileged than themselves (strong left-wing position II). It is striking how political positions converge in certain respects and how the pedagogical positions are often identical.

2.2 LINC and grammar

[. . .]

In the LINC training materials there is no advocacy of a return to the decontextualised drills and exercises of the 1950s. Instead there is systematic exploration of grammatical differences between speech and writing, between standard and non-standard forms of the language, and between different varieties of English. In spite of being described in certain national newspapers as a dialect project, 97 per cent of the examples is a LINC materials are of pupils speaking, reading and writing in standard English. They also demonstrate that one of the most effective ways of learning standard English is for pupils to compare and analyse differences between their own dialects and the dialect of standard English, discussing explicitly how and when different forms are appropriate. [. . .]

Here is an example of LINC's approach to grammar taken from some local training materials. The example is based on a text in the form of a postcard delivered through the letterbox of customers of a water company.

> The following text communicates information; in this case the information concerns the interruption to water supply. Whenever instructions are given, a 'modality' enters the relationship between the writer and reader of a text. 'Modality' takes a number of different forms in English but the presence of modal verbs is particularly significant. Here are some of the main modal verbs in English:
>
> can; could; will; would; must; should; shall; may
>
> What is the function of modal verbs in the text that follows?
> What other verb forms work, in particular, to establish a relationship between the Water Company and the customers to whom it has distributed this notice?
>
> Commentary
>
> This text is in a curiously mixed mode. The Water Company has to inform its customers that repairs are unavoidable. It has to give its customers instructions which

---

Notice of interruption to supply

We are sorry to inform you that necessary mains repairs in the area may cause an interruption to your water supply between the hours overleaf.

1. Every effort will be made to keep inconvenience and the duration of the shut-off to a minimum.
2. Do not draw more water than your minimum requirements.
3. If the water does go off, do not leave taps open or flooding may result when the supply is restored.
4. You may use water from the hot water system but it must be boiled before drinking.
5. Even if the domestic hot water supply runs dry there will be no risk of damage to the system, but as a precaution keep a low fire where a back boiler is installed and turn or switch off other sources of heating the water by gas, oil or electricity.
6. Central heating systems can continue to be used at moderate temperatures.
7. The main will be flushed before the supply is restored but discolouration and or chlorine may persist for a short time. Allow your cold tap to run for a few minutes to clear this water from your service pipe.
8. Do not use your washing machine or other appliances during the discolouration.

We apologise again for any inconvenience this may cause you and request your patience and co-operation. In case of any difficulty please contact the Nottingham District Office.

Please remember neighbours who may be older or disabled – they may need your help

---

they need to follow both in their own interests and in the interests of other consumers. At the same time the company needs to reassure its customers that a more or less normal service is still available, that, in spite of the interruption to supply, the company still provides a good service and, above all, that there are no safety or health risks involved for its customers so long as they comply with the guidelines and instructions issued with the notice. It is important therefore that the company is clearly seen to be in control. This 'mixed mode' is inscribed in the different modal verbs in the texts along the following general lines:

> *Mode of reassurance/possibility*: **may** cause an interruption; **may** persist for a short time; they **may** need your help; every effort **will** be made; flooding **may** result; any inconvenience this **may** cause you.

> *Mode of control*: **must** be boiled before drinking; the main **will** be flushed; **can** continue to be used.

Notice that some modal verbs can signal possibility and control, depending on the other words which surround them as well as on the context in which they are used. For example, 'you may use water' (primarily control); 'they may need your help' (primarily possibility).

'Control' is also established through an extensive use of imperative forms of the verb which unambiguously inform us what to do and what not to do. For example:

Do not leave taps open   Do not use your washing machine
Allow your cold tap to run   Please remember neighbours

Activity

Collect examples of further texts in which you would expect modal verbs to be used quite extensively. For example,

horoscopes   school notices
weather forecasts   recipes
problem pages   legal texts

What other examples can you find? Why are modal verbs concentrated in some texts but not others?

It is one key feature of the LINC approach to grammar that teachers and pupils should, where possible, explore grammar in complete texts, in relation to social and cultural contexts and with reference both to forms and functions. It is primarily concerned with how grammar works to construct meanings in the kinds of literary texts with which many English teachers are familiar and, as in the above example, in the everyday texts we all encounter in our daily lives.

2.3 Keywords

What was effectively a ban on the publication of LINC training materials probably should have been expected. The emphasis on language variation and on language in context led to a too frequent reference to social theory and an emphasis on sociolinguistic perspectives. For governments of a particular political persuasion the word *social* is directly equitable with the word *socialist*. The training package itself was designed, it was said, in too activity-based and open a manner. The government eventually made it clear that it had preferred all along training materials which emphasised right and wrong uses of English, reinforcing such an emphasis with drills and exercises for teachers and pupils to follow, and with a printed appendix containing the correct answers to the exercises. The emphasis should be on factual knowledge which is measurable and determinable, and which can be transmitted from a position of authority rather than be discovered through activity-centred processes. A key-word here is the word **drill**. Finally, it was said that certain keywords do not appear in a sufficiently unambiguous way. In the training package words such as **correct**, **standard** and **proper** are always relativised to specific contexts and practices of teaching.

In respect of such keywords, linguists and teachers do, in fact, need to find a way of talking about language which better controls and engages with the existing public discourses, especially those of most sections of the press and media. In this connection, English teachers have to apply their knowledge about language to a major problem of communication. The very vocabulary currently available to talk about language variation offers only apparently negative or oppositional terms which play neatly into the hands of those with the most simplistic notions of language and education. Thus, to talk about *non*-standard English can be seen as a departure from standards; to talk about the dangers of absolute rules of correctness is seen as an endorsement of incorrect English or as a failure to correct pupils' work; to suggest that proper English is relative to contexts of use is itself improper. Space does not allow further exposure of these antinomies (others are traditional v. trendy; national v. unpatriotic; basic v. progressive; simple v. complex) but it is easy to trace how the generally moderate and balanced English teacher is constructed as an offender against order, decency and common sense. Rather than talk in terms of standard and non-standard English, it would be preferable to talk in terms of descriptive language such as 'general' and 'special' English.

3   LINC and genre theory

[. . .] One of the most significant recent developments is in the field of genre theory and in the teaching, in particular, of genres of writing. It is a controversial area of teaching and learning and LINC in-service training courses and materials engage in places directly with key aspects of genre theory, as developed in the United States, within the context of European text linguistics and of work in Australia within the context of systemic functional linguistics. Here is a sample of the kind of analysis undertaken in project materials within the framework of genre theory (teachers have already undertaken analysis and classification of a range of different genres of writing):

> The following piece of writing was produced by a 10-year-old girl in a junior school in England. To which 'genre' of writing might it be assigned? Which particular features of language use support your decision? Does the writing have identifiable 'stages' of generic structure?

> > Snakes are reptiles. They belong to the lizards family. Snakes have no legs but for a long time ago they had claws to help them slither along. Snakes are not slimy, they are covered in scales. The scales are just bumps on the skin. Their skin is hard and glossy. Snakes often sunbathe on rocks. This is because snakes are cold-blooded and they need the warm sun in order to heat their body up. Most snakes lives in the country. Some snakes live in trees, some live in water, but most live on land in thick, long grass.
> >   A snake will usually eat frogs, lizards, mice and even small crocodiles.
> >   (Jenny, aged 10)

> Commentary (written by a group of teachers)

> The first stage of the writing classifies the phenomenon; the second stage provides further descriptive information about the phenomenon (in this instance a snake). The genre is that of an *information report*.
>   This report is characterised by the following linguistic features: a timeless, simple present tense used to make generalisations and to convey general truths and facts (*live, sunbathe, have*). The iterative *will* (a snake 'will' usually eat) also serves in this instance to convey the sense of a general, repeated action. The writing is characterised by an absence of personal pronouns. In fact, nouns are more common than pronouns and many of the nouns are in a form (with an indefinite article 'a' or in the plural form 'snakes') which describes it as a general rather than an individualised or unique phenomenon. Many of the verbs used are also 'relational'; for example, *is, have, belong to, consist of* support a defining style of presentation.
>   The vocabulary used is neutral rather than emotive or attitudinal and this

corresponds to a report which is one of impersonal classification rather than personal observation. Such impersonality is reinforced by the use of the passive voice ('they *are covered* in scales').

[. . .]

3.1 Reactions to genre-based teaching

1. LINC teams have been convinced by the strength and depth of arguments for making the language structure of texts more visible on the grounds that genuine intervention by the teacher and consequent development in pupils' language use are not possible unless the relevant patterns of language are identified. [. . .]
2. LINC teams have accepted that a primary concern with personal shaping of experience has resulted in classrooms in which there is an over-concentration on narrative to the exclusion of other genres.
3. In a related way LINC has adopted a more inclusive view of authorship, especially in the writing classroom. It accepts the view of Pam Gilbert (1990: 70) that: 'Authorship is but one of the newest of a long line of discursive devices which serve to entrench personalist, individualist, speech-oriented theories of writing in schools.' Although such a position obscures important developmental connections between speech and writing, it establishes a basis for more impersonal writing modes, and thus a wider range of generic types of writing on which LINC has built.
4. LINC's introduction of a more genre-based approach to writing has provoked some hostility on the part of British teachers. A major concern is that such writing practices are inherently conservative and are designed to produce unreflective operatives who will be able to do no more than sustain a market economy for a conservative society. The concern of genre theorists for a wider range of writing types which are in turn closer to the requirements of the world of work is interpreted as a narrow vocationalism. What has helped to change this perception is the notion of *critical literacy*, which augments functional literacy to enable learners not only to comprehend and produce society's discourses, but also to criticise and redirect them, if necessary. As Michael Halliday (1996: 357) has put it:

   > To be literate is not only to participate in the discourse of an information society; it is also to resist it . . . it is rather perverse to think you can engage in discursive contest without engaging in the language of the discourse.

   Such work underlines that genre-based teaching is both revolutionary and reactionary.
5. British teachers have become increasingly impressed by the precise analytical work which has enabled central, prototypical features of particular genres to be identified. It is the same explicitness of analysis which has helped both pupils and teachers to develop a critical linguistic literacy.
6. LINC teams have valued the overt, explicit and retrievable arguments advanced in particular by Martin (1989) and Kress (1989) but also by others. Taking such strong, clear argumentative lines enables others to argue with or argue against in a systematic way.

3.2 Problems and issues

Work on the LINC project has also enabled teachers to identify what seem to them to be some problems with current work in genre theory, and which may suggest directions for future research and development. Such is the extent of interest in Britain in genre-based work that solutions to some of these problems are already being explored in a number of action-research projects in UK schools and teacher-training colleges. The main points of concern are stated below.

1. Existing descriptions of genre within a systemic functional tradition may have tended to neglect work in other traditions of description. There has been a concentration on the realisations of schematic and generic structure in the lexico-grammar of texts. There is now a large body of work within the traditions of text-linguistics and written discourse analysis on lexical patterning, cohesion, coherence and textual macro-structure.

2. LINC teams keep coming across texts which do not conform to any single generic structure. They are the result of mixed genres. Examples of mixed genres are arguments which make use of narrative structures, narratives which have reporting or exposition structures embedded within them, and reports which are simultaneously impersonal and personal in form, that is, they are reports which also contain personal accounts of events and specific, person-based recommendations. LINC teams would thus want to emphasise that genres are not autonomous systems, and that accounts of genre and genre teaching may be limited in their considerable potential if they become too simplistic or narrowly monologic.

    [. . .]

3. Work within the framework of Australian and British genre theory on the genre of narrative tends to be a little too simplistic overall. Because spoken narratives unfold sequentially in time, they do not normally have the characteristic embeddings, shifts in point of view, and complexities of narratorial presentation which characterise most written narratives. Within the general area of continua between spoken and written genres it is important, however, that literacy is not wholly construed as written texts.

4. Early examples within Australian work of teachers modelling genres to a whole class were perceived by LINC to be possibly over-rigid and deterministic. A common view is that there has been a tendency among some genre theorists to swing the pendulum too far in the opposite direction from romantic conceptions of learning and teaching. Research in domains of both first- and second-language teaching shows that we do learn effectively by making things our own, and by being personally involved in the processes of constructing a text. It has also been demonstrated that process-based approaches to writing, with an emphasis on ownership of the text, lead to increased motivation to use language. In a parallel way, there may be among theorists in a systemic functional tradition a tendency to overemphasise factual, impersonal genres at the expense of the personal. Accordingly, British teachers and linguists have been particularly impressed by recent work on modelling in relation to joint and individual construction which operates successfully to show writing to be both process- and product-based, and that work on genre can be integrated with more holistic approaches to language learning and development.

5. The identification of genres for description and teaching tends to be internal to the school. There is little attempt to identify the genres of writing commonly required in

the workplace. For example a report genre in a junior school is markedly different from a report genre in industrial or business work settings. Text-intrinsic accounts of genre need to take fuller cognisance of the audience, purpose and context in which particular genres operate.

6.   Encouragement to pupils to reflect on language has tended to be restricted to the patterns of language in the genre in focus. Instead, a general classroom climate needs to be established in which talking and writing about language leads to [. . .] *language awareness* – that is, general sensitivity to different styles and purposes of language use. These include differences between spoken and written language, explorations of the language of literature, the language of jokes, advertising, pop fiction, and political rhetorics, and investigations of the continua between different accents and dialects, including standard English. Such explorations are a necessary habit-forming prelude to looking more closely and analytically at the linguistic patterns which make up different genres. Analysis is not always best fostered by practising analysis of and reflection on language solely within the context of individual genres.

Several of these observations arc hardly new, and many of them have been advanced by genre theorists themselves. Teachers in Britain interested in writing development are beginning positively to embrace work on genre-theory and on genre within a functionalist perspective in particular. These observations should be viewed in a correspondingly positive light. [. . .]

4   Conclusions: the lessons of LINC

A project of the scale and complexity of LINC cannot escape criticism. It is important that the lessons of both success and failure are recorded. For example, for all their successes with teachers, LINC materials need to be further adapted in three main ways. First, materials on reading should be developed to exemplify in greater detail what a mixed methods approach to reading entails. More examples and case studies would illustrate how readers use a range of different cues and clues, syntactic and semantic, phonic and visual, in the process of learning to read. More action research would illustrate when to mix methods and when to concentrate on a single teaching procedure. Future LINC materials (or their derivatives) must also enable teachers better to analyse the linguistic differences between real books and books from graded reading schemes. Second, supplements to existing units are needed on differences between spoken and written English, particularly in relation to the teaching of punctuation, which depends crucially on the relationship between grammatical structure and the rhythms and contours of speech. More examples are also needed of how standard English varies across spoken and written modes while still remaining standard English. Third, more examples are needed to show how literary texts can stimulate enhanced knowledge about language, especially the history of the language, and how greater linguistic knowledge underpins literary appreciation.

4.1 Negative conclusions

Even if the general developments outlined above take place, they will take place against a cultural background in which both positive and negative factors are at work. The main negative factors are, first, that some teachers will continue to persist with the worst excesses of romanticism in their view of language learning and teaching. They will continue to make linguistic processes invisible and regard language only in so far as it provides a window on to content, the expression of the individual self, the world of ideas. They will continue to refuse to see forms of language as a powerful resource for creating significant domains of meaning. Second, governments may want to intervene more directly in the shaping of the English curriculum. If so, and whatever their political persuasion, governments may not want to endorse classroom language study which explores relationships between language and society, and which subjects those relationships to interrogation. They are likely to continue to be especially disturbed by classroom KAL work which encourages children to investigate such relationships independently. They may exert their powers to impose a language study which is 'neutralised' by being more decontextualised, formalist rather than functionalist in orientation, and which, above all, can be easily assessed and measured. The currently very overt demands by the British government for greater attention to phonics in the teaching of reading is but a signal of an increasing emphasis on the basics in so far as what is 'basic' often involves a decontextualised language focus.

4.2 Positive conclusions

It is a positive factor that governments are drawing attention to language, recognising it as both medium and message, mounting arguments in relation to the 'proper' study of English, attacking the positions adopted by those with a professional interest in language.

Although the battles will continue to be between those who have the power but not the knowledge, and those who have the knowledge but not the power, the very fact that governments are forced to mount explicit arguments about language is healthy both for processes of public debate and for the cause which espouses the centrality of language to the school curriculum. Increasing attention to language on the part of teachers, coupled with high degrees of enthusiasm and conviction, will lead to pupils being progressively interested in language. Increasing knowledge about language among pupils will produce within a generation a society which is likely to be less prejudiced and ignorant and more informed and articulate about matters to do with language.

Finally, a more positive view of applied linguistics emerges from projects such as the LINC project. It is a view in which teacher and linguist work more collaboratively towards common agendas. As a result, teachers become more aware of the problems of linguistic description and, in turn, linguists begin to address problems identified by teachers, rather than only those problems identified by linguists themselves. [. . .] Increasingly, all concerned with language have come to appreciate how notoriously fascinating, complex and ultimately *dangerous* language and language study are. In a project inspired by the work of Michael Halliday, the final word must be left to Halliday (Halliday, 1982):

> . . . there is a real sense in which linguistics is threatening; it's uncomfortable, and it's subversive. It's uncomfortable because it strips us of the fortifications that protect and surround some of our deepest prejudices. As long as we keep linguists at bay we can go on believing what we want to believe about language, both our own and everybody else's . . .
>
> More than any other human phenomenon, language reflects and reveals the inequalities that are enshrined in the social process. When we study language systematically . . . we see into the power structure that lies behind our everyday social relationships, the hierarchical statuses that are accorded to different groups within society . . .

Bibliography

Carter, R. (1988) 'Some pawns for Kingman: language education and English teaching', in Grunwell, P. (ed.) *Applied Linguistics in Society* 3, *British Studies in Applied Linguistics* (CILT, London) pp. 51–66.

Christie, F. (1989) *Language Education* (Oxford University Press, Oxford).

Gilbert, P. (1990) 'Authorizing disadvantage: authorship and creativity in the language classroom', in Christie, F. (ed.) *Literacy for a Changing World* (Australian Council for Educational Research, Hawthorn, Victoria), pp. 54–78.

Halliday, M. A. K. (1982) 'Linguistics in teacher education', in Carter, R. (ed.) *Linguistics and the Teacher* (Routledge, London), pp. 10–16.

Halliday, M. A. K. (1996) 'Literacy and linguistics: a functional perspective', in Hasan, R. and Williams, G. (eds) *Literacy in Society* (Longman, London), pp. 339–75.

Kress, G. (1989) *Linguistic Processes in Sociocultural Practice* (Oxford University Press, Oxford).

Martin, J. (1989) *Factual Writing* (Oxford University Press, Oxford).

Chapter 8

Gary M. Jones

BILINGUAL EDUCATION AND SYLLABUS DESIGN: TOWARDS A WORKABLE BLUEPRINT

Introduction

BRUNEI DARUSSALAM (henceforth Brunei) has a *bilingual* education system in which *two* languages, *Bahasa Melayu* and English, are used. As this paper will suggest, however, the two languages should not be regarded as independent variables or in any way as competing with one another, but as being highly inter-dependent and complementary. In Brunei, the final school leaving examination (the GCE 'O' level) has determined the syllabuses of the individual school subjects, with the result that subject syllabuses have been planned in isolation and then joined to create the school curriculum. In a bilingual system, such subject-centred planning makes little provision for the development of two languages as interlocking variables. Language development is considered in much the same way as any other 'subject': in isolation rather than as complementing other subjects and playing a key role in the child's overall cognitive as well as educational development. As I hope this paper will demonstrate, syllabus design should play a crucial role in a bilingual education system and careful consideration must be given to the timing and introduction of the various school subjects and their allotted language medium.

[. . .]

The current curriculum

The present school syllabus, as shown in Table 8.1, shifts in three steps from a predominantly Malay-medium to a predominantly English-medium system. These stage shifts, however, are abrupt rather than gradual.

At Primary 4, when the pupils are eight years old, the first and most important of the transitional steps is taken. At this time, in addition to English Language as a subject, Mathematics, Science, History and Geography are introduced and taught through English. This is a most demanding and difficult change for pupils and teachers alike. Ramirez *et al.* (1991) have noted that:

> there is some evidence that suggests that when limited English-proficient students receive most of their instruction in their home language, they should not be abruptly transferred into a program that uses only English.
>
> (Ramirez *et al.*, 1991: 40)

Table 8.1 Compulsory and examinable subjects in Brunei primary and secondary schools

English medium	Malay medium
	Lower Primary (age 5–8)
English Language	Malay Language
	Mathematics
	General Studies
	Islamic Religious Knowledge
	Physical Education
	Arts and Handicraft
	Civics
	Upper Primary (age 9–11)
English Language	Malay Language
Mathematics	Islamic Religious Knowledge
History	Physical Education
Science	Arts and Handicraft
Geography	Civics
	Lower Secondary (age 12–14)
English Language	Malay Language
Mathematics	Islamic Religious Knowledge
Science	History
Geography	
	Upper Secondary (age 15–16)
English Language	Malay Language
Mathematics	
Science/Art/Technical Subjects	
(depending on stream)	

Although some Malay continues to be used in the Bruneian system, at Primary 4 there is an abrupt change, and this occurs at a time when the pupils have only a limited proficiency in English. Not only is the number of English-medium hours greatly increased, but the increase is in some of the most cognitively demanding subjects, subjects which Cummins (1984) would characterise as precisely those that require a well-developed L2 proficiency.

BICS and CALP

Cummins (1984) has in fact distinguished between two sets of language skills: basic interpersonal communication skills (BICS) and cognitive academic language proficiency (CALP). He argues that children will be unable to cope with the school curriculum unless their cognitive academic language proficiency (CALP) is sufficiently developed. A child's language-cognitive abilities need to be sufficiently well developed to cope with the curricular processes of the classroom. This proficiency could be developed in either of the bilingual child's languages or in both simultaneously. In Cummins's (1984: 143) opinion, CALP involves some universal underlying proficiency which is shared across languages. Once acquired in one language it can be transferred to any other language. Thus, proficiency of this sort acquired in Malay could be transferred to English-medium classes and vice versa.

Cummins develops the concept of BICS and CALP in the four quadrant model which is reproduced as Figure 8.1.

	Cognitively undemanding		
(BICS)			
	A	B	
Context-embedded			Context-reduced
	C	D	
			(CALP)
	Cognitively demanding		

Figure 8.1 BICS and CALP
Source: Cummins, 1981

In the Brunei context, subjects such as Mathematics and Science, which are cognitively demanding and often context-reduced (based on abstract rather than concrete examples), would be placed in the fourth quadrant (D), while those such as Art and Physical Education, which are cognitively undemanding and generally context-embedded, would be placed in the first quadrant (A). What should be of some concern to curriculum designers in Brunei is that Cummins (1981) believes that it often takes one or two years for a child to acquire context-embedded second language fluency (the type of language that might be developed in Art or Physical Education classes), but from five to seven years to acquire context-reduced fluency (working with more abstract subjects). If this is the case, then after only three years of English Language as a subject at lower primary school, Bruneian children are unlikely to have the required English proficiency to study the type of cognitively demanding, context-reduced subjects that they are currently introduced to in Primary 4. [. . .]

Cummins's concept of BICS and CALP has been criticised for being too simplistic. Romaine (1989) argues that language skills cannot be compartmentalised as neatly as Cummins suggests and that Cummins is guilty of equating semantic development with cognitive development. It is certainly the case that not all subjects can be simply and easily placed in their respective quadrants. Science will always be cognitively demanding, but it could be taught in a context-embedded as well as a context-reduced style. The same is true of most subjects: much depends upon the style and skill of the teacher. Nevertheless, while it might be difficult to neatly place all school subjects into one of the four quadrants, Cummins's model does provide insight into why pupils working in a second language may struggle in some subjects but do well in others. Most important is that Cummins believes context-reduced, cognitively-demanding communication capability develops independently and can be promoted by either or both languages. [. . .] If knowledge is transferable across languages, then there is no need to begin the study of these academically demanding subjects at an early age through the medium of English to prepare for an English-medium examination that will be taken eight years later.

[. . .]

Threshold levels

The present assumption in Brunei is that subjects which will be examined in English at 'O' level at age 16 should be taught through the medium of English from as early an age as possible. Subjects that are eventually examined in Malay are therefore taught through the medium of Malay throughout. [. . .]

This present division of Malay-medium/English-medium subjects, especially at the primary level, is putting an unnecessary strain on pupils and the education system. Many pupils have an insufficient command of English to properly follow their new subjects, especially Mathematics and Science. The result is that many pupils are failing to acquire either sufficient subject knowledge or to improve their language skills. [. . .]

The shift to cognitively and linguistically demanding tasks at Primary 4 is at present made on the assumption that pupils have sufficient mastery of English to actually study through the medium of English (as was originally envisaged in 1951). This assumes that pupils have attained some minimum language ability or threshold. [. . .]

Although language thresholds were not discussed as such back in the 1950s, recent clarification of what they involve helps to better clarify the situation in Brunei and relate language levels there to those attained elsewhere.

Van Ek and Trim (1991) describe the threshold level in terms of the type of functions that a young European learner should be able to perform in the target language. These functions are inevitably Eurocentric, reflecting the needs of European students. They include being able to understand and use the target language as a medium of instruction and as a language of social interaction in English classes and among learners during breaks and at mealtimes; being able to report and discuss problems relating to teaching, social conditions and accommodation and also how to follow admission procedures to enter teaching institutions.

Van Ek and Trim (1991) specify the number of teaching hours that should be needed to attain the threshold level of proficiency: two to three hours per week, 35 to 40 weeks a year over two to three years. A minimum of 140 hours of teaching and a maximum of 360 hours. In Bruneian lower primary schools, prior to transfer to Primary 4 and the teaching of academically demanding subjects through the medium of English, Bruneian pupils receive approximately 262 hours teaching in and on the English language (two and a half hours per week, 35 weeks a year over three years). It should also be remembered that these Bruneian children are very young (older learners may not necessarily be better learners but they do understand the educational process and are therefore faster learners, as Singleton, 1989, has observed), that they may not have a very supportive learning environment outside school, especially for the development of English, and that English is unrelated to any of their other languages. These are conditions which must surely create greater language studying difficulties than for their European peers.

[. . .] In 1951, with selected pupils following intensive personal tuition, minimum proficiency levels were presumably considered attainable. However, the same is not true today of large mixed ability classes of children. Many pupils are failing to attain a minimum proficiency in English before the introduction of cognitively and thereby linguistically demanding English-medium subjects. It is probably the case that they are only reaching such a level when they enter Lower Secondary school, at which time they should really be functioning at an intermediary level beyond the second threshold. This level, in turn, may only be reached at the point these pupils reach upper secondary, at which time the pupils have to take their 'O' levels, which require an even higher language level.

As a result of problems beginning at primary school, pupils continue to lag behind their required level or threshold of language proficiency and the majority never really reach the language standard which their age might assume. Some evidence for this has been gathered by Lewis Larking, who tested the reading comprehension ability of Bruneian pupils in Primary 5 and 6. He found that at Primary 6, 70% of pupils were below their native-speaker equivalent grade level in English reading comprehension (28% were one year below grade level; 38% two or more years below and 4% three or more years below grade level). Interestingly, only 7% of these same pupils were below grade level in Malay reading comprehension (Larking, 1994: 58). [. . .]

Subject order: some considerations

Given the mix of primary school subjects and the various degrees of cognitive demands they make and opportunities for language interaction they offer, perhaps the easiest and most urgent changes would be to the subjects that are taught through the medium of English at upper primary and to the nature of the transition from predominantly Malay-medium to English-medium subjects.

Instead of teaching the cognitively demanding, 'context-reduced' subjects in English and the cognitively undemanding, 'context-embedded' subjects in Malay, the easiest proposal would be to switch subjects. Thus Mathematics and Science would remain Malay-medium subjects (at least, until Lower Secondary) while Art and Physical Training would be taught as English-medium subjects at the primary level. Support for retaining the teaching of Mathematics and Science in the mother tongue (at least until secondary school) can also be seen in Ramirez et al. (1991) where it is noted that students who were abruptly moved into almost exclusive instruction in English '. . . experienced a marked decrease in growth in mathematics skills over time' (Ramirez et al., 1991: 33).

To avoid the sudden increase in English-medium subjects at Primary 4, more English-medium subjects could be introduced at lower primary level. [. . .]

Art and Physical Education are not literacy but oracy and participatory activities that should not endanger the acquisition of first language literacy. Thus these two subjects could be introduced in English-medium at lower primary, together with English Language, without harming the pupils' ability to first become literate in Malay.

Age and language acquisition: some considerations

Harley (1986) and Singleton (1989) have shown that the question of age and language acquisition is complex and does not lend itself to an easy and universal answer. Most of the research supporting the 'younger is better' position does so with reference to phonological advantages, while that supporting the 'older is better' stand is on the basis of syntax and morphological measures of ability. Hamers and Blanc (1989) and others question the evidence for there being a sensitive period and a biologically determined optimal age for L2 acquisition. [. . .]

The conclusion that younger learners are at an advantage because they have more time to learn and are less likely to suffer interference from their first language matches quite closely, though for different stated reasons, the conclusions that Genesee (1987) has drawn concerning the various immersion programmes in Canada:

> Second language proficiency tends to increase the earlier immersion begins and the more second language exposure the learner has. Thus, early total immersion generally yields higher levels of second language proficiency than early partial immersion, delayed immersion, or late immersion.
>
> (Genesee, 1987: 191)

Singleton (1989) argues that many factors are involved in language acquisition and that examples of age-related research have to be analysed individually, noting the peculiarities of each study. Singleton concludes that:

> there is a fair amount of evidence suggestive of a long-term advantage for learners whose experience of the target language begins in their childhood years. . . . with

regard to short-term attainment, the picture is more confused. However, the balance of evidence does seem to indicate an initial advantage for older learners at least as far as grammatical development is concerned.

(Singleton, 1989: 122)

Despite his extensive research on the subject, Singleton remains undecided about the benefits of one approach over the other:

(1)   The available evidence does not consistently support the hypothesis that younger second language learners are globally more efficient and successful than older learners.

(2)   Nor is it possible to conclude from the evidence that older second language learners are globally more efficient and successful than younger learners.

(Singleton, 1989: 138)

Although Singleton does not favour either an early or late start, he does suggest that Cummins's BICS/CALP distinction reconciles contradictions in the evidence about age-related differences among second language learners, citing Cummins's own proposals:

the older learners, whose CALP is better developed, would acquire cognitive/academic L2 skills more rapidly than younger learners; however, this would not necessarily be the case for those aspects of L2 proficiency unrelated to CALP (i.e. L2 BICS).

(Cummins, 1979. In Singleton, 1989: 113)

This lends support to the type of subject division recommended earlier for Brunei, with the study of cognitively undemanding, context-embedded subjects preceding cognitively demanding, context-reduced subjects.

The majority of Bruneians who volunteered a reply to the question' *Are there any comments that you would like to make about Dwibahasa?'* in a national attitude questionnaire that was concluded recently suggested that more English should be introduced at an earlier age. It would be very easy to dismiss such suggestions as being uninformed and subjective, but I think that this would be wrong and a misjudgement of the respondents.

Bruneians have been exposed to a variety of school systems. There can be little doubt, however, that the Bruneians who are most at ease with the English language are those who attended English-medium mission schools at an early age. Some of these people continued their education in the mission schools while others went on to government schools. In either case, an advantage seems to have been derived from early exposure to English. Of course, an ability with English would also be dependent upon factors outside school, especially languages used in the home, and it can be assumed that many parents who sent their children to English-medium mission schools would themselves very probably use English at home. But this would not have been the case for all families. The English language ability of graduates from such schools is taken as evidence by Bruneians that early exposure to English results in better acquisition of the language. This conclusion may be subjective, but in Brunei it is accepted as self-evident and is the most commonly cited reason given by Bruneian parents who can afford it for sending their children to English-medium kindergartens.

Although research would obviously have to be undertaken to prove the point, my own impression from observations in Brunei is that as well as phonological advantages, early exposure to English also appears to result in a greater *confidence* among learners in actually using the language. Such confidence results in fewer inhibitions and a willingness to experiment with the language. At its simplest, the Bruneians who have acquired English early at mission schools are generally more confident, and therefore more at ease with the language and thus likely to use and experiment with the language, than their peers who went to government schools.

The relevance of The German Model

A well established model of bilingual education that has given consideration to the timing and sequencing of the school subjects in its system is that now referred to as 'The German Model' (Mäsch, 1993). Bilingual *Gymnasium* ('grammar') schools in Germany make a gradual transition from German to a second language, introducing the new language through a sequence of subjects that are chosen to complement each other as well as to aid both language and subject acquisition. [. . .] In sequence, the subjects chosen as vehicles for bilingualism in The German Model are: (1) Art; (2) Geography; (3) Politics (Civics); (4) History.

Art is considered to provide a concrete situational base from which to develop language skills (as well as subject ability). Geography performs a referential, information giving function and provides a relatively simple start to description. Geography is also recognised as performing a second but crucially important role in bilingual education in Germany. While some science subjects are considered to be language poor because of the specialised content of their subject-specific language (Mäsch cites Biology as an example), 'Geography alone sufficiently covers virtually all the necessary elements from the natural sciences through physical geography and geophysical phenomena, and from the application of methodological skills through its work with figures, statistics, graphs and sketches' (Mäsch, 1993: 163).

Politics (Civics) and History are included in the bilingual education system in Germany as much for integration and a better understanding of the country's European neighbours as for the language benefits of the subjects. Nevertheless, the study of politics does include a recognisable language function:

> [. . .] The aims of the course in politics suit the bilingual section: an ability to recognise different types of action and a capacity to form an opinion.
>
> (Mäsch, 1993: 163–4)

Physical Education

Physical Education is not mentioned in Mäsch's description of the German Model. However, this subject does lend itself particularly to communicative activities because it emphasises the link between language and physical movement. A physical education lecturer at the University of Brunei Darussalam has noted the link between his subject and language acquisition in Brunei. He maintains that physical education creates a language rich environment:

> [. . .] The most noticeable change in students' attitude or behaviour was a readily discernible increase in confidence . . . Emanating from this increase in confidence a noticeable improvement in fluency together with greater self-assurance whilst making statements was evident in the students' performance.
>
> (Austin, 1992: 25–6)

Revised syllabus

As an alternative to the present distribution of subjects and language media, and with due consideration to language acquisition and age as well as BICS/CALP and the threshold levels, I would suggest that compulsory and examinable subjects in Bruneian primary and secondary schools might be more appropriately distributed as shown in Table 8.2.

Table 8.2 An alternative distribution of subjects in the Bruneian education system

English medium	Malay medium
Lower Primary	
English Language	Malay Language
Arts (and Handicraft)	Mathematics
Physical Education	General Studies
	Civics
	Islamic Religious Knowledge
Upper Primary	
English Language	Malay Language
Arts (and Handicraft)	Mathematics
Physical Education	Civics
Geography	Science
	History
	Islamic Religious Knowledge
Lower Secondary	
English Language	Malay Language
Mathematics	History
Geography	Islamic Religious Knowledge
Science	
Upper Secondary	
English Language	Malay Language
Mathematics	
Science/Art/Technical Subjects	
(depending on stream)	

Physical Training and Art would join English Language as English-medium subjects in the lower primary curriculum. Geography, given the experience of the German Model, would also seem an appropriate subject to introduce at the primary level. However, rather than tax the pupils with too many English-medium subjects at once, the introduction of Geography might best be postponed until upper primary. In this revised system, History would remain a Malay-medium subject throughout (there are not the same integrative political considerations operating in Brunei that encourage the bilingual teaching of this subject in Europe) and the introduction of Science and Mathematics would be delayed until secondary school. [. . .]

The system described above is open to a number of permutations. For instance, should three subjects be introduced simultaneously from Primary 1 or would it be better to introduce them consecutively, one year at a time? Is there any advantage to be gained in switching History from Malay to English-medium? Ideally, a number of permutations might be trialled until the most appropriate model for Brunei is arrived at. Of course, this would take time and may not be feasible because of the common national examinations that have to be taken at the end of primary school. However, given the research that has been conducted into threshold levels and the timing of their acquisition, as well as considerations of context-embedded/context-reduced, cognitively demanding/cognitively undemanding subjects, then this revised model for the introduction of subjects in the Brunei education system, in one form or another, would seem more appropriate than that currently employed.

While I believe that the above would be a better system than the present distribution of subjects, there are a number of practical considerations which would impede the implementation of this proposal. As well as the problem of new examinations and syllabuses, there would also be the huge task of supplying or retraining teachers for new media of instruction. Given that providing a sufficient number of properly qualified teachers has always been a problem in Brunei, changing the language-medium of some subjects would, in the short term at least, further compound this problem. Malay-medium Art, Geography and Physical Education teachers may not be willing or able to teach in English; English-medium Mathematics, History and Science teachers may not be able to teach in Malay. Nevertheless, the introduction and redistribution of school subjects at the primary level is an issue that should eventually be addressed.

References

Austin, S. (1992) 'Language development through education'. Paper presented at a seminar in the University of Brunei Darussalam, December 1992.

Cummins, J. (1979) 'Cognitive/academic language proficiency, linguistic inter-dependence, the optimum age question and some other matters'. *Working Papers on Bilingualism* 19, 198–203.

—— (1981) 'The role of primary language development in promoting educational success for language minority students'. In The California State Department of Education (ed.) *Compendium on Bilingual–Bicultural Education*. Los Angeles: California State Department of Education.

—— (1984) *Bilingualism and Special Education: Issues in Assessment and Pedagogy*. Clevedon: Multilingual Matters.

Genesee, F. (1987) *Learning Through Two Languages*. Cambridge, MA: Newbury House.

Hamers, J. F. and Blanc, H. A. (1989) *Bilinguals and Bilingualism*. Cambridge: Cambridge University Press.

Harley, B. (1986) *Age in Second Language Acquisition*. Clevedon: Multilingual Matters.

Larking, L. (1994) 'Reading comprehension ability of Primary 5 & 6 children in Malay and English in Brunei Darussalam'. In M. L. Tickoo (ed.) *Reading and Research in Writing*. Singapore: Regional Language Centre.

Lenneberg, E. H. (1967) *Biological Foundations of Language*. New York: Wiley.

Mäsch, N. (1993) 'The German Model of bilingual education: An administrator's perspective'. In H. Baetens Beardsmore (ed.) *European Models of Bilingual Education*. Clevedon: Multilingual Matters.

Ramirez, J. D., Yuen and Ramey (1991) *Longitudinal Study of Immersion Early-exit and Late-exit Transitional Bilingual Education Programs for Language Minority Children*. Mountain View, CA: SRA Technologies.

Romaine, S. (1989) *Bilingualism*. Oxford: Basil Blackwell.

Singleton, D. (1989) *Language Acquisition: The Age Factor*. Clevedon: Multilingual Matters.

Van Ek, J. A. and Trim, J. L. M. (1991) *Threshold Level 1990*. Strasbourg: Council of Europe Press.

Chapter 9

Kimberley Brown

WORLD ENGLISHES IN TESOL PROGRAMS: AN INFUSION MODEL OF CURRICULAR INNOVATION

Introduction

IT HAS BEEN SUGGESTED (e.g. Kachru, 1988) that it is time for a paradigm shift which takes into account the changing roles and functions of English around the world in linguistic research and in language pedagogy. In spite of clearly articulated arguments and well-defined calls for applied and theoretical research in the language education community, Kachru's perspective on the role and functions of English as an international language remains a minority perspective. Even though two generations of scholars have been refining the elements of what has come to be termed the World Englishes paradigm (Kachru, 1992a), there is little evidence of its infusion into Teaching English to Speakers of Other Languages (TESOL) preparatory programs (Vavrus, 1991a).

This paper examines possible explanations for the lack of incorporation of this paradigm in TESOL preparatory programs. In an attempt to find a way to incorporate the World Englishes paradigm into TESOL programs, I will draw upon Hamnett *et al.*'s (1984) three-pronged approach to what they term 'the indigenization of social science research' (78). This paper will also explore impediments to curriculum design and teaching practice that may hamper the inclusion of the World Englishes perspective into TESOL preparatory programs.

A paradigm refers to a particular theoretic framework or perspective. The World Englishes paradigm (hereafter referred to as the WE paradigm) may be characterized by three elements (Kachru, 1988: 1):

- a belief that there is a 'repertoire of models for English'
- a belief that 'the localized innovations [in English] have pragmatic bases'
- a belief that 'the English language now belongs to all those who use it'.

Paradigm shifting and diffusion of innovation

Within meta-theory research, i.e. theories about theories, Patton (1975) explores the relationship between the context in which information is learned and the degree to which people remain attached to that information. He states: '. . . paradigms are deeply embedded in the socialization of adherents and practitioners telling them what is important, what is legitimate, what is reasonable' (1975: 9). By implication then, any process of shifting paradigms cannot be a simple process. Tollefson (1991) suggests that the intellectual belief system an individual may adhere to is often not seen as a particular set of lenses; i.e. individuals may hold to particular ideologies without even recognizing that there is something subjective about these ideologies. Thus before any shift in ideologies can come about, the first step must be to recognize and name the paradigm to which one has been intellectually socialized. [. . .]

It is possible to see the introduction of a new paradigm into the intellectual arena as similar to the diffusion of an innovation into a particular setting. In the social science literature that explores attributes of innovations, Rogers (1983) examines variables affecting the rate at which innovations are adopted. One is of particular relevance to this discussion if the WE paradigm can be considered an innovation. Rogers terms this variable 'perceived attributes of [an] innovation' (1983: 233).

The five facets of this variable are compatibility, relative advantage, complexity, trialability, and observability. Rogers suggests that compatibility of the new idea with current ideas (or paradigms) and with client needs (in this case teacher and learner needs) affects whether the new idea is adopted. An exploration of current ideas in TESOL reveals two frameworks incompatible with an underlying framework in the WE paradigm which Vavrus (1991a) terms the 'Dynamic Paradigm'. To avoid confusion, however, the term 'perspective' will be used instead of paradigm.

Much of the underlying theory in the WE paradigm belongs to what Vavrus (1991a, 1991b) calls the 'Dynamic' perspective, a framework in which non-native varieties of English are seen neither as fossil-ridden examples of interlanguages, nor as inferior examples of incorrect speech. She suggests that most language teaching frameworks may be characterized as belonging to one of two perspectives. The Deviational perspective supports the notions that all errors are due to fossilization or to learners being at various stages of interlanguage transfer. The Deficit perspective supports the notion that errors occur because learners are deficient in their command of English. Neither the Deficit nor Deviational perspectives are compatible with the Dynamic perspective. The lack of compatibility between these three perspectives thus affects the rate at which the WE paradigm may be adopted. Until educators become more aware of the reasons for adopting a WE paradigm or of the consequences of not adopting it, they may resist this innovation.

The remaining elements in Rogers' perceived attributes of innovations are relative advantage, complexity, trialability, and observability. Relative advantage refers to a perception that the new idea is better than previous ones. Complexity is self-explanatory. Rogers suggests that if an idea is seen as being too complex, it will not be adopted. Trialability refers to 'the degree to which an innovation may be experimented with on a limited basis' (1983: 231). Research suggests that if individuals can work with a new idea on a trial basis, they may be more likely to adopt it. Finally, observability refers to how visible an innovation is. If individuals are quite familiar with an idea, they are more likely to adopt it.

At the present time, the WE paradigm does not clearly possess relative advantage, compatibility, and observability. I do not believe the WE perspective is more or less complex than other perspectives. But much of the early work in World Englishes is not in a user-friendly format for classroom teacher educators. This does affect the trialability factor.

[. . .] Hamnett et al. (1984) discuss three elements that have a direct connection to expanding the presence of the WE perspective in TESOL preparatory programs. The first is *theoretic* indigenization 'in which the social scientists of a nation are involved in constructing distinctive conceptual frameworks and metatheories that reflect their own world views, social and cultural experiences, and perceived goals' (1984: 78). Within the WE perspective, theoretic indigenization would involve the creation and refinement of theory. At the present time, these parameters are well developed (see Kachru, 1992a). There does appear, however, to be a problem with access to and availability of information. This problem will be discussed more thoroughly in a later section of the paper. Another aspect of the theoretical dimension of the WE perspective is also presented by Lincoln, who looks at the politicization of the research process and suggests that at the present time 'some groups and research models [are] favored over others, with some definitions of problems more acceptable than others with avenues to funding and support clearly discriminatory' (1990: 70).

The second is *structural* indigenization, defined 'with reference to national institutional and organizational capabilities for social science knowledge [including capabilities for] educational and research institutions, a community of indigenous scholars, and locally produced social science literature' (Hamnett *et al.*, 1984: 78). Within the WE perspective, in Outer Circle countries, i.e., those countries once colonized by England or the USA and who use or have used English for intra-country purposes (Kachru, 1988), structural indigenization would involve the development of institutions which sponsor a particular type of research, the development of scholars committed to working within the WE paradigm, and the development of locally produced WE literature and empirical or qualitative studies. In Inner Circle countries, i.e. the USA, UK, Australia, New Zealand, or Canada (Kachru, 1988), the structural challenge is to support the development of young scholars from Outer Circle and also Expanding Circle countries (Kachru, 1988), i.e. those countries in which English has been taught as a foreign language, who will return home to promote structural changes in how English is taught, and to support Inner Circle scholars developing collaborative frameworks with Outer and Expanding Circle colleagues for their teaching. For example, the cooperative small group and pair work in communicative language settings is a standard concept promoted in most TESOL Methods courses. In many Outer and Expanding Circle countries, large classes and a standardized Ministry of Education curriculum which prepares students for college-level entrance exams are common. Small group or pair work may be proscribed. Having successful teachers from these large classroom settings prepare lessons on how to teach large classes, which could then be infused into current Methods courses, would help Inner Circle teachers learn from Outer and Expanding Circle colleagues.

The third element in Hamnett *et al.*'s text involves *substantive* indigenization, which is 'concerned with the content focus of the social sciences [such that] the main thrust of research and teaching in a country be toward its own society and people and their economic and political institutions' (1984: 78). Within the WE perspective, substantive indigenization would call for the development in Outer and Expanding Circle countries of their own research and teaching focus. The challenge in Inner Circle teacher preparatory programs would be to encourage Outer and Expanding Circle students to return home to conduct research on topics and with agendas that may not have been those suggested in basic research design courses. A further challenge would be to prepare Inner Circle students planning on teaching overseas to understand and appreciate the integrity of the possible alternative planning frameworks they would be working under.

Shifting paradigms in TESOL programs is a difficult task. Individuals who have completed their own professional preparation under one paradigm may not see a reason to shift. It is necessary for those scholars who have called for the paradigm shift to see themselves as change agents and to actively engage in effective promotion efforts so that teacher educators and practitioners in the field can understand the perceived attributes of the WE perspective. This promotion process may involve contributing to the development of WE theory and collaborating with colleagues in Outer and Expanding Circle countries to support the development of indigenous institutions, scholars, literature, and empirical or qualitative studies. Further, it may involve bringing to the attention of scholars in Inner Circle countries details of the current research and teaching focus of English language education programs in Outer Circle and Expanding Circle countries.

Many efforts on US campuses to 'internationalize' the curriculum have drawn upon an *infusion* model in which supplementary units on particular topics are worked into existing curricula. [. . .]

In addition to the overall difficulties with respect to any paradigm shift or curricular innovation, there are at least five other possible impediments: amount of time necessary for true diffusion of scholarship; student and instructor background schemata; text availability and level of difficulty; supporting material availability; and workshop and short-term coursework availability for Methods instructors.

Time for diffusion of scholarship

There are currently two major centers in the USA where scholars are conducting extensive research in World Englishes, at the University of Illinois at Urbana-Champaign (UIUC) and at the East-West Center (connected to the University of Hawaii at Manoa) in Honolulu. By extension, Methodology courses taught in these centers are likely to incorporate the WE perspective. A second generation of scholars who have graduated from these institutions are teaching a third generation of teachers and scholars to incorporate such a perspective in institutions from upstate New York to Indiana to California. Other scholars who have begun to publish extensively in this field have come to places like UIUC and the East-West Center for short periods of time and have returned to teaching positions throughout the world. Even in Outer Circle countries, though, it has only been recently that master's students in language education have been encouraged to conduct their research from within the WE perspective. For example, Robert Baumgardner, an expert in the field of Pakistani English, writes that in Pakistan, the first master's degree paper to look at a WE issue was presented in 1985 (personal communication).

Research being conducted around the world may not make its way into mainstream journals for three to five years after its completion. Anthologies of material published by places like the Regional English Language Centre (supported through SEAMEO) are not publicized in materials catalogues that most teachers in US TESOL programs have ready access to. When multiple copies of texts are requested from halfway around the world, many Inner Circle bookstores balk at filling orders because of currency exchange difficulties and policies which prohibit them from ordering materials from other countries.

Student and instructor background schemata

Many students entering TESOL programs have not had any prior experiences identifying paradigms and ideologies. They may not have been trained in identifying their underlying assumptions – cultural and paradigmatic, pedagogical, or personal. They arc not critical readers in the sense that they have not been asked to read material in linguistics and language education in order to categorize the ideology of the authors. One explanation for this is that much of the writing students encounter is heavily centered in what R. Paulston (1976) calls the 'equilibrium paradigm', e.g., structural-functionalist and systems theories as contrasted with theories in the 'conflict paradigm', e.g. Freirian, Marxist, or neo-Marxist theories. The rhetoric in structural-functionalist and systems theories is less readily identifiable. To ask students to consider making a paradigm shift when they cannot yet identify paradigms is problematic.

International students in TESOL programs may sometimes possess low self-esteem regarding their own language proficiency and, as Baxter (1980) points out, may never have had the chance to reflect upon and respond affirmatively to the question 'Are you a speaker of English?' To identify their own ideologies and move to a point of greater acceptance of whatever their variety of English may be comes at the expense of the amount of time necessary to absorb such a perspective.

Just as it may be difficult for students to name the ideologies and planning frameworks they work under, it may also be difficult for their teachers. Paradigm shifts cannot be made when people do not overtly identify paradigms which currently dominate the field. Both Tollefson (1991) and Phillipson (1992) deal extensively with this issue in their texts.

Text availability and level of difficulty

Three of the most popular Methods texts, Celce-Murcia (1991), Brown (1987), and Long and Richards (1987), devote one chapter or less to the concept of World Englishes. In Celce-Murcia, there is no mention at all of anything related to World Englishes. In Brown (1987), while there is reference made to Kachru, and the institutionalized versus performance varieties of English, the total number of words is less than 200. In Long and Richards (1987), one chapter by Judd defines the term 'English as an International and Intranational' language. There is no chapter dealing specifically with the concept of institutionalized versus performance varieties of English, the role of native and non-native speakers of English, or any of the points highlighted by Kachru (1992a) as being central to WE theory.

Five other concepts which need to be re-examined within traditional Methods courses if a WE perspectives is infused into the curriculum are the presentation of *instrumental* and *integrative* functions of language without introducing the *expressive* (Pride, 1979) function of language; the presentation of interlanguage continuum information and its relationship to sociolinguistic continuum information; terminology used to refer to the teaching we do; the role of native speakers in instruction in the Outer Circle (i.e. ESL countries like India, Nigeria, Malaysia, and Ghana) and the Expanding Circle (i.e. EFL countries like Japan, Germany, and Brazil); and approaches and techniques for helping students from Outer Circle countries versus students from Expanding Circle countries improve the international intelligibility of their varieties of English.

Most introductory Methods textbooks cover instrumental and integrative reasons for learning a language (Gardner and Lambert, 1972). Choosing to learn a language for the purpose of expressing one's identity or choosing to write in Filipino English or Malaysian English to express certain ways of being and knowing are not examined in traditional Methods texts. [. . .]

In units on second language acquisition, the interlanguage continuum concept which, as Vavrus (1991a) noted, is part of the Deviational perspective is usually not presented in conjunction with information which is part of the Dynamic perspective.

Terminology referring to the teaching of English still falls most consistently into the polar terms English as a Second Language (ESL) and English as a Foreign Language (EFL). Until the time when more inclusive alternative terms are used, be they 'English as an International Language' or, as Canadian colleagues have long practiced, 'English as an Additional Language', attitudes toward Inner Circle, Outer Circle, and Expanding Circle varieties of

English are not likely to change. Speakers of Outer Circle and Expanding Circle varieties of English in the program where I teach continuously remark on the lack of relevance of some material in standard Methods courses to their needs in their countries.

Regarding materials which focus exclusively on World Englishes, Görlach states 'the books published in 1982–84 make up a particularly impressive list: it is no exaggeration to say that the following ten books more or less suffice to teach a full academic course on the topic [of World Englishes]' (1991: 11). Yet one of the Kachru texts, *The Indianization of English* (1983), would not be ordered as a class text by some US college bookstores because the text is published outside the USA; and Kachru (ed.), *The Other Tongue: English Across Cultures* was out of print until just recently, and a revised edition with substantial changes has just been published (see Kachru, ed., 1992b). Another Kachru text, *The Alchemy of English* (1986), is too difficult for most undergraduate Methods students, although with study questions and referral to Richards *et al.*'s 1985 *Dictionary of Applied Linguistics*, currently also out of print, students can manage. Platt *et al.*'s *The New Englishes* (1984) as well as Pride's 1982 *New Englishes* are out of print. Görlach's 1991 volume *Englishes: Studies in Varieties of English, 1984–1988* is published by John Benjamin; one of its representatives at the 1992 American Association of Applied Linguistics meeting in Seattle commented that this publishing firm does not exhibit at international TESOL meetings as it is not worth their financial while. Teacher educators attending a key meeting in their field would thus not have access to this text to even peruse for potential course adoption. Finally, even chapters dealing with World Englishes in fine texts such as Berns (1990) have been termed 'too difficult' by some teacher educators for use with undergraduate students.

Supporting material availability

Often, instructors will assign research papers or annotated bibliographies on World Englishes topic. Over the past three years, when such assignments have been made in our Methods classes, at least one or two students per quarter have decided to research topics such as the 'Non-native English speaking teacher'. Resources such as ERIC list few references on WE. Difficulty in obtaining articles reflecting a WE perspective deters students from pursuing these topics. A cursory comparison of US library holdings via an on-line search through the Online Computer Library Center (OCLC) and Research Library Information Network (RLIN) of eight journals, six of which routinely publish articles reflecting the WE perspective and two of which sometimes publish articles in this area (*TESOL Quarterly* and *Journal of Applied Linguistics*), reveals significant differences in the number of journals available throughout the USA. In addition to the *TESOL Quarterly* and the *Journal of Applied Linguistics*, the other journals include *English Today, English Worldwide*, *World Englishes*, the *RELC Journal*, the *Indian Journal of Linguistics*, and the *Indian Journal of Applied Linguistics* (see Table 9.1).

As Table 9.1 illustrates, there is a very evident accessibility problem. Journals which consistently carry WE perspective articles are much less available to teachers and students in TESOL programs than are other journals.

This portion of the paper has examined structural impediments to infusing a WE perspective in current TESOL programs. The next portion of the paper documents why it is critically important to work to infuse a WE perspective in the Methods sequence.

Table 9.1 Journals publishing articles on World Englishes topics

Journal	Number of states	Number of institutions
TESOL Quarterly	46	384
Journal of Applied Linguistics	42	123
English Today	44	64
World Englishes	32	68
English Worldwide	26	57
RELC Journal	26	55
Indian Journal of Linguistics	11	13
Indian Journal of Applied Linguistics	9	14

Student responses in coursework

The following excerpt is from a TESL certificate student paper; the student was exposed to less than four hours of information related to World Englishes in ninety hours of Methods courses.

[Sample A]

The lack of TEFL-specific materials may be a result of a belief that most EFL teachers should themselves be non-natives [i.e. non-native speakers of English] with the result being that the majority of teaching materials are in the teachers' native languages, not English. But if a person who has learned English from a non-native then teaches EFL to yet someone else, the English of the last learner may be far removed in quality from that of a native. . . .

If however, more EFL teachers were native speakers, then more TEFL-specific materials in English would be demanded and produced. Also, the materials might be of better quality, giving the quality of EFL teaching more of a chance to improve . . .

TEFL materials oriented toward native English speakers will help them to give clear explanations of what they already know. A native speaker is better able to combine his or her inherent knowledge with the information provided in an EFL textbook to give a more comprehensive grammatical explanation. However, this is best achieved if the textbook is written with the expectation that the user will be a native.

Another benefit from having a native speaker teach English is that students get more exposure to English, especially when interacting with the teacher outside the classroom. A teacher whose native language is also the students' native language is more likely to converse with them in that language when class is not in session, whereas practice with a native English-speaking teacher outside of a stressful classroom, where performance will not be graded, can be most helpful.

The second sample was written by an individual who had completed ninety hours in a Methods course and thirty hours in a World Englishes class.

[Sample B]

As a result of the reading and thought involved in doing this paper, I now believe that as part of the shift being made in ESL/EFL teaching to accommodate needs for English as an international language rather than a language used only to communicate with native or very proficient speakers from countries where English is learned as a first language, we need to shift or perhaps, more properly, expand our views of reading. We need to extend learners' knowledge of literacy and reading rather than change it, which I believe we often implicitly if not explicitly attempt to do through our methodology and ethnocentric view as middle-class, generally white educators for a post industrial country. . . .

As a result of this paper, I have also come to realize that in my own teaching of reading, I have too heavily emphasized U.S. mainstream reading styles and strategies which may be of little use to students learning English as a world or international language, and who are most likely to read English written by writers not using discourse or newspaper styles which are predominant in the U.S.

The comments made in the first paper are geocentric, i.e., focused on Inner Circle countries' English, and reflect an attitude of linguicism. Skutnabb-Kangas and Phillipson in Phillipson (1922: 47) define linguicism as:

ideologies, structures, and practices which are used to legitimate, effectuate, and reproduce an unequal division of power and resources (both material and immaterial) between groups which are defined on the basis of language.

The comments in the second paper are much less ethnocentric and reflect an attitude of tolerance and respect for multiple varieties of English. Both individuals are leaving the same TESL certificate program. In the first case, I held an extensive conference with the student to indicate what I found problematic in many of the statements and lines of argument of the paper. I believe the conference was useful, but as the culture contact literature reveals, simply having individuals with two different perspectives meet to talk about ideas may not result in long-term attitude change. [. . .]

[. . .] It is possible for a paradigm shift to occur. However, necessary resources to facilitate such shifts need to find their way into Methods textbooks and Methods courses. Much work remains to be done at the structural and substantive levels. An infusion model of curricular revision is the most practical means to diffuse the innovation inherent in the World Englishes paradigm. The following recommendations are also key elements in promoting the diffusion of this perspective within Methods courses and without.

Recommendations

1   Language education preparatory programs must name the paradigmatic frameworks we work under.
2   We must actively combat linguicism and geocentrism, particularly institutional linguicism, characterized by structures which promote inequality.
3   We must help promote a diversity of perspectives, not only a perspective which suggests that the native speaker of an Inner Circle variety of English is the most appropriate professional language educator.
4   Professional language education organizations and their respective journals must continue to provide a forum for oral and written dialogue, e.g. within TESOL: the *TESOL Quarterly*, the *TESOL Journal*, the TESOL international conference, and the TESOL summer institute. In like manner forums should be provided with IATEFL: International Association of Teachers of English as a Foreign Language, and NAFSA: Association of International Educators.

5   Professional language education organizations should work to create a resource bank of World Englishes scholars and materials.
6   Professional language education organizations should promote mid-career professional exchange to bring World English scholars as teachers to Inner Circle teacher preparatory programs for one or two terms.
7   Professional language education organizations should support activities which help break down structural barriers to promoting an infusion model of curricular reform.
8   Publishing houses and authors of key texts in English language education programs should broaden their repertoire of citations.

References

Baxter, James (1980) 'How should I speak English? American-ly, Japanese-ly, or internationally?' *JALT Journal*, **2**, 31–61.
Berns, Margie (1990) *Contexts of Competence: Social and Cultural Considerations in Communicative Language Teaching*. New York: Plenum.
Brown, H. Douglas (1987) *Principles of Language Learning and Teaching*. 2nd edition. Englewood Cliffs, NJ: Prentice-Hall Regents.
Celce-Murcia, Marianne, ed. (1991) *Teaching English as a Second or Foreign Language*. New York: Newbury House.
Gardner, Richard and Lambert, Wallace (1972) *Attitudes and Motivation in Second Language Learning*. Rowley, MA: Newbury House.
Görlach, Manfred (1991) *Englishes: Studies in Varieties of English, 1984–1988*. Amsterdam/Philadelphia: John Benjamin.
Hamnett, Michael, Porter, Douglas, Singh, Amarjit and Kumar, Krishna (1984) *Ethics, Politics, and International Social Science Research: From Critique to Praxis*. Honolulu, Hawaii: University of Hawaii Press.
Kachru, Braj B. (1983) *The Indianization of English: The English Language in India*. New Delhi: Oxford University Press.
Kachru, Braj B. (1986) *The Alchemy of English: The Spread, Functions, and Models of Non-Native Englishes*. Oxford: Pergamon Press. (Reprinted 1990, Urbana, IL: University of Illinois Press.)
Kachru, Braj B. (1988) *ERIC/CLL News Bulletin*. September. **12**(1), 1, 3, 4, 8.
Kachru, Braj B. (1992a) 'World Englishes: approaches, issues and resources'. *Language Teaching: The International Abstracting Journal for Language Teachers and Applied Linguistics*. Cambridge University Press, January 1992: 1–14.
Kachru, Braj B., ed. (1992b) *The Other Tongue: English Across Cultures*. 2nd edition. Urbana, IL: University of Illinois Press.
Lincoln, Yvonne (1990) 'The making of a constructivist: a remembrance of transformations past'. In *The Paradigm Dialog*. Edited by Egon Guba. New York: Sage Publications, pp. 67–87.
Long, Michael and Richards, Jack, eds. (1987) *Methodology in TESOL: A Book of Readings*. New York: Newbury House.
Patton, M. (1975) *Alternative Evaluation Research Paradigms*. Grand Forks, ND: University of North Dakota Press.
Paulston, Rolland (1976) *Conflicting Theories of Social and Educational Change: A Typological Review*. Pittsburgh, PA: University Center for International Studies.
Phillipson, Robert (1992) *Linguistic Imperialism*. London: Oxford University Press.
Platt, John, Weber, Heidi and Lian, H. (1984) *The New Englishes*. London: Routledge.

Pride, John (1979) 'Communicative needs in the use and learning of English'. In *New Varieties of English: Issues and Approaches*. Edited by Jack Richards. Singapore: SEAMEO Regional Language Centre, pp. 33–72.

Pride, John, ed. (1982) *New Englishes*. Rowley, MA: Newbury House.

Richards, Jack, Platt, John and Weber, Heidi (1985) *Longman Dictionary of Applied Linguistics*. Essex, England: Longman Group Limited.

Rogers, Everett (1983) *Diffusion of Innovations*. 3rd edn. New York: The Free Press.

Tollefson, James (1991) *Planning Language, Planning Inequality*. New York: Longman Inc.

Vavrus, Frances (1991a) 'When paradigms clash: the role of institutionalized varieties in language teacher education'. *World Englishes*, **10**(2), 181–196.

Vavrus, Frances (1991b) 'Standards and models: an African perspective'. Paper presented at World Englishes colloquium; annual conference of Teachers of English to Speakers of Other Languages, New York.

Chapter 10

Numa Markee

THE DIFFUSION OF INNOVATION IN LANGUAGE TEACHING

Introduction

T HE LAST TWO DECADES IN APPLIED LINGUISTICS – which roughly coincide with the evolution of the communicative approach in language teaching – have seen the development of a number of language teaching innovations, including the notional/ functional syllabus, the process syllabus, the Natural Approach, the procedural syllabus, and task-based language teaching. All of these proposals have contributed in important ways to an understanding of theoretical issues related to designing innovative language syllabuses. But it is only rather recently that applied linguists have begun to investigate the problems associated with implementing these innovations.

Indeed, with the exception of such pioneers as White (1988), Henrichsen (1989), and a number of other writers, not many language teaching specialists have developed any familiarity with the voluminous literature that already exists in a number of disciplines on how and why innovations diffuse. This is unfortunate because, as Kennedy (1988) and Beretta (1990) demonstrate, a 'diffusion-of-innovations' perspective on syllabus design provides curriculum specialists, materials developers, and teachers with a coherent set of guiding principles for the development and implementation of language teaching innovations. Furthermore, it supplies evaluators with criteria for retrospective evaluations of the extent to which these innovations have actually been implemented. In other words, this perspective provides a unified framework for conceptualizing both the development and evaluation of innovations in language teaching. Thus, although the terminology used may at first sound exotic and unfamiliar, a diffusion-of-innovations perspective on syllabus design, for example, addresses concerns that are central to all language teaching specialists.

In contrast to applied linguistics, education already possesses a well-established tradition of innovation research and practice (Fullan 1982, Miles 1964, Nicholls 1983, Rudduck 1991), as do such disciplines as sociology (Rogers 1983), urban planning (Lambright and Flynn 1980), and language planning (Cooper 1989). Thus, a review of the issues that define innovation in the specific context of language teaching will draw on these academic specializations to develop a multi-disciplinary framework, inspired particularly by Cooper's work on innovation in language planning. The framework for this discussion consists of the following composite question: "*Who adopts what, where, when, why and how?*" (Cooper 1989), with responses to each individual component of the question. In this way, the basic issues that are of interest to practitioners may be defined. This framework should be sufficiently encompassing to account for practitioners who wish to engage in any innovation related to language education.

On defining innovation: "who"

Teachers are key players in any attempt to promote innovations in syllabus design. At the same time, other individuals will also be involved in the innovation process (Fullan 1982). The actual participants who become involved in deciding whether an innovation will be adopted vary from context to context. Whatever the specific context of implementation, however, participants tend to assume certain social roles which define their relationships with other participants. The urban planners, Lambright and Flynn (1980), have suggested that individuals relate to each other as adopters, implementers, clients, suppliers, or entrepreneurs (also known as change agents).

Kennedy (1988) suggests that, in the context of a materials project in Tunisia, ministry of education officials, deans, heads of department, and others play the role of adopters; teachers are implementers; students are clients; curriculum and materials designers are suppliers; and the expatriate curriculum expert acts as the change agent. As Kennedy points out, in practice these roles are not mutually exclusive. Indeed, it is quite likely that the same person will play different roles, sometimes simultaneously, sometimes at varying times during the course of a project. Thus, teachers may at times also be regarded as adopters; furthermore, in some cultures, they may take on the roles of change agents and suppliers. With the exception of the change agent, any of these individuals may also adopt the role of resisters who oppose an innovation. Thus, a broad range of people playing out different social roles is always involved in the design and implementation of any innovation.

"Adopts"

Adoption has been conceptualized in terms of individuals or institutions engaging in a decision-making process which may be divided into a number of different phases. Rogers (1983), a rural sociologist who is one of the leading authorities on the diffusion of innovations, suggests that there are five steps in this decision-making process. These involve potential adopters 1) gaining knowledge about an innovation, 2) being persuaded of its value, 3) making a preliminary decision to adopt the innovation, 4) implementing their decision to adopt, and 5) confirming their decision to continue using the innovation. The educator Fullan (1982) proposes a slightly different sequence of four steps which he calls initiation, implementation, continuation, and outcome.

From an evaluator's perspective, adoption may also be conceptualized in terms of "levels of implementation," a measure which specifies the depth to which any changes have occurred. Beretta (1990), for example, in his evaluation of the procedural syllabus (Prabhu 1987), uses this notion to evaluate the extent to which teachers actually implemented the task-based methodology associated with that syllabus. Lack of space precludes detailed discussion of Beretta's results, but it is noteworthy that only 47 percent of the teachers involved in implementing the procedural syllabus reached what Beretta categorized as an "adequate" level of implementation; only 13 percent reached what may be considered an "expert" level of implementation. This result shows how difficult it is to promote innovation at a fundamental level. It is salutary to remember that all innovation is a risky business and that close to three quarters of educational innovations are likely to fail over time (Adams and Chen 1981), either because they are never fully adopted or else do not survive the confirmation stage posited by Rogers (1983).

"What"

Innovation itself, as a concept, is central to the implementation and/or evaluation of new ideas and new procedures. Synthesizing what she claims are basic characteristics of innovations, Nicholls states:

> An innovation is an idea, object or practice perceived as new by an individual or individuals, which is intended to bring about improvement in relation to desired objectives, which is fundamental in nature and which is planned and deliberate (1983: 4).

However, in language teaching contexts, her definition is somewhat problematic. For the purposes of this paper, innovation will be defined as proposals for qualitative change in pedagogical materials, approaches, and values that are perceived as new by individuals who comprise a formal (language) education system.

Nicholls' idea of "newness" being a subjective matter of users' perceptions is important in language teaching contexts. This perspective correctly permits the inclusion of the Natural Approach as an innovation despite the fact that Krashen and Terrell (1983) view this approach simply as a rediscovery of the underlying principles of traditional "natural" or direct methods popular earlier in this century – suitably reformulated and updated in light of current second language acquisition research findings. While Krashen and Terrell's assessment of the absolute innovativeness of their proposals is accurate, there is no doubt that from a user's perspective, the Natural Approach was regarded as an innovation by teachers in the early 1980s. It continues to be viewed in this light by new teachers who are introduced to it for the first time today.

However, in terms of the five examples of language teaching innovations we have already identified in the introduction (the notional/functional syllabus, the process syllabus, the Natural Approach, the procedural syllabus, and task-based language teaching), the remaining components of Nicholls' definition are either too restrictive or else omit defining criteria that are important for language teaching situations. Therefore, the alternative definition given above is more appropriate to language teaching contexts. The need for this alternative definition is suggested by a critique of Nicholls with respect to the following four issues: 1) the systemic context of innovations; 2) the fundamental nature of innovations; 3) the extent to which innovations actually improve on the status quo; and 4) the extent to which innovations are necessarily deliberate and planned for.

First, the systemic context in which an innovation is implemented seems to be an important determiner of whether or not the innovation will be adopted. As Prabhu (1987) points out, the fact that a procedural syllabus was implemented in primary and secondary schools in India placed some major constraints on the project since it was decided that the procedural syllabus should not be used with students who were due to take various state matriculation exams. By omitting any specific mention of the systemic context of innovations, Nicholls lays herself open to being interpreted as saying that individuals are free to innovate as they wish. Clearly, individuals do not enjoy such a degree of freedom. This observation suggests that the relationship between individuals and systems must be considered in a definition of innovation.

Second, it is only through a modification of pedagogical values that innovation can be said to involve "fundamental" change. At the less complex levels of using new materials and approaches, teachers can adopt new practices with little or no understanding of why they are using these new materials and approaches – which hardly counts as a fundamental alteration in behavior. This limitation does not mean that such surface changes are not in any sense innovative nor that they cannot lead to deeper change later.

Furthermore, the "innovativeness" of an innovation decreases over time as it becomes institutionalized and more familiar to users. For example, notional/functional syllabuses were initially claimed to be fundamentally different from structural syllabuses because language content was organized in semantic rather than syntactic terms. However, it was soon recognized that, although notional/functional syllabuses are indeed qualitatively different from structural syllabuses, all the criteria for organizing the content of instruction in both types of syllabus (i.e., notions, functions, grammatical structures, vocabulary, etc.) are still linguistic (Long and Crookes 1992). Consequently, it is difficult to argue that the re-orientation implied by notional/functional syllabuses is fundamental in any meaningful sense of this word. Thus, it is better to define innovations in terms of qualitative change, a term which conveniently covers all three levels of innovative behavior (materials, approaches, and values).

Third, although innovations are certainly intended to improve on the status quo, it is not the case that they always do constitute an improvement on previous practice (Fullan 1982). For example, Brumfit (1981; 1984a) has sharply criticized notional/functional syllabuses as being in some instances an undesirable innovation. He argues that when these syllabuses are uncritically implemented, they deprive learners of the generative potential of grammar (i.e., the ability to use syntactic rules to create new sentences), which Brumfit regards as an indispensable resource for learning. This criticism suggests that improvement is not necessarily a defining characteristic of innovations in actual practice. Indeed, in some cases, innovations should be resisted rather than promoted because their adoption may be more harmful than beneficial.

Fourth, and finally, the notion of "deliberate planning" is problematic for language teaching in two ways. First, although the notional/functional syllabus is indeed a product of extensive planning, the only aspect of a project that can be planned is what is to be taught or tested, not what is to be learned (Brumfit 1984b). Second, it is doubtful that the articulation of the principles of the procedural syllabus, which was achieved through a process of trial and error (Prabhu 1987), can really count as an example of deliberate planning. [. . .]

"Where"

The question of where an innovation is implemented is conceived in sociocultural terms (Cooper 1989). That is, the concern is with specifying the sociocultural context of an innovation rather than its geographical location. Practitioners who wish to introduce innovative syllabuses into an educational system must recognize the potential impact (whether positive or negative) of various sociocultural constraints on their activities. For example, Markee (1986a; 1986b) identifies cultural, ideological, historical, political, economic, administrative, institutional, and sociolinguistic factors that affected the implementation of an aid-funded project in the Sudan. [. . .]

In addition, some attempts have been made to address the issue of when those sociocultural constraints should be considered in the syllabus design process (Holliday and Cooke 1982, Munby 1978; 1984). The relative importance of these constraints will vary from one context of implementation to another. [. . .] Experience suggests that these constraints cannot be accounted for in a discrete, linear fashion; rather, they will impinge on all aspects of innovative syllabus design, implementation, and evaluation.

"When"

While some adopters will implement a given innovation relatively quickly, others will need more time to carry out the same innovation. Thus, if one knows when A adopts an innovation and when B, C, or D adopt the same innovation, it is possible to specify the rate at which an innovation diffuses among a group of potential adopters and also to distinguish between different categories of adopters.

Diffusion may be expressed as the percentage of adopters who implement an innovation over a given period of time (Rogers 1983). Figure 10.1 shows a typically S-shaped diffusion curve. The lazy slope of the toe of the curve shows that adoption at first occurs very slowly; if a critical mass of approximately 25 percent of potential adopters accept the innovation, it may take off. At this point, the slope in the mid-section of the curve becomes steeper (i.e., the rate of adoption accelerates) as people "jump on the bandwagon." Finally, the curve plateaus as diffusion slows down and eventually tapers off, either because every potential adopter has adopted or else because the innovation stalls.

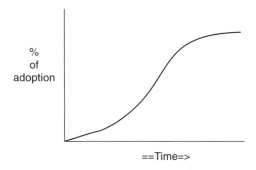

Figure 10.1 An S-shaped diffusion curve

With respect to diffusion rate, five categories of adopters have been identified (Huberman 1973, Rogers 1983). These include innovators, early adopters, early majority, late majority, and laggards; as already noted in the section entitled "Who," people who never adopt a particular innovation are known as resisters. In terms of the S-shaped diffusion curve shown in Figure 10.1, innovators and early adopters occupy the first 25 percent of the curve. Early and late majority occupy the steepest portion of the curve. Laggards occupy the last part of the curve as it flattens out to form a plateau.

This information has at least two kinds of potential applications. First, it allows program designers who introduce an innovative syllabus to focus on those teachers most receptive to the innovation. Since each category of adopter tends to be associated with personal characteristics which are either conducive or not conducive to innovation, recognition of early adopters would be important to the innovation process. Second, such data allow evaluators to determine how successfully and how quickly an innovation has spread among a group of potential adopters.

"Why"

The reasons why innovations are adopted or rejected are many and varied. The section entitled "Where" already addressed a number of the sociocultural constraints that come into play. In addition, there are individual psychological factors with respect to the persons involved, and innovations themselves possess various attributes that influence adoption.

Rogers (1983) notes that individuals with particular psychological profiles tend to display specific adoption behaviors. For example, individuals who adopt early tend to travel widely and are usually well-educated and upwardly mobile; they tend to seek out and be open to new ideas, and they tend to have a high degree of exposure to mass media. Their contacts with other people are often extensive, and they are usually able to tolerate high levels of uncertainty. Laggards, on the other hand, tend to display diametrically opposite characteristics while the people in between exhibit intermediary traits.

Finally, innovations themselves possess attributes which tend to promote or inhibit their adoption. A number of writers (Bricknell 1969, Henrichsen 1989, Kelly 1980, Levine 1980, Zaltman and Duncan 1977) have proposed different sets of attributes of innovations. The attributes proposed by Rogers (1983) are used here because they are derived from some 1,500 empirical and/or theoretical studies on innovations across disciplines and also because they are the most well-known. These attributes include the following:

- the relative advantage to potential adoptees of adopting an innovation (i.e., the costs or benefits);
- the compatibility of the innovation with previous practice (i.e., how different or similar the innovation is to what the potential adopter already uses);
- the complexity of the innovation (i.e., how difficult the innovation is to understand or use);
- the trialability of the innovation (i.e., how easy it is to try out in stages);
- and the observability of the innovation (i.e., how visible the innovation is).

"How"

In Henrichsen's (1989) account of the extent to which audiolingualism diffused in Japanese schools in the aftermath of the Second World War, he notes that several different theories exist which seek to account for how change occurs. These include equilibrium theory, evolutionary theory, conflict theory, rise and fall theory, and diffusion theory. Only the last of these is directly relevant to language teaching. Within a diffusion-of-innovations perspective, the educator Havelock (1971) distinguishes between three basic models of innovation. He labels these three the *Research, development and diffusion (RD and D) model*, the *problem-solving model*, and the *social interaction model* respectively, from which he synthesizes a hybrid *linkage model*. Similarly, the social scientists Chin and Benne (1976) identify three families of innovation strategies which they respectively call *empirical-rational*, *normative-re-educative*, and *power-coercive* strategies of innovation. These models and strategies "pair up" and have been used, mostly unconsciously, by developers of various language teaching innovations.

Empirical-rational innovation strategies assume that people are rational and will therefore be persuaded to adopt an innovation if it can be demonstrated that it is in their rational self-interest to do so. Such strategies tend to be used by people who subscribe to an RD and D model of innovation. A good example of this combination is the initial development of notional/functional syllabuses by scholars associated with the Council of Europe (Wilkins 1976).

This model is rational, systematic, and theory-based. It depends very heavily on long-term planning and involves a division of labor among teams of highly trained specialists who work on separate phases of an overall project. The planning process is basically linear (although feedback loops may be built into the framework) and assumes that the end product will be used by a passive, though rational, consumer. Planning begins with basic research, which is then followed by phases of applied research, development and testing of prototypes, mass production and packaging of the product, and finally, mass dissemination to potential users. It is assumed that the high development costs will be offset by the long-term benefits of efficiency and the anticipated high quality of the innovation (Havelock 1971).

A power-coercive innovation strategy — which involves the application of political, administrative, or economic power to resolve a problem — may also be used in conjunction with an RD and D model of innovation. This occurs when a ministry of education decides to develop and disseminate a new syllabus countrywide. A good example of this combination is the adoption of notional/functional syllabuses in primary and/or secondary schools by the Dutch and Malaysian ministries of education.

Normative-re-educative strategies are based on the assumption that users' decisions are not exclusively based on rational criteria. Rather, sociocultural and personal value systems are held to be equally important determinants of behavior. These strategies tend to be used by individuals who believe in a problem-solving model of innovation. As Havelock (1971) remarks, this is the most favored model of innovation in education, at least by writers in the United States and Britain. A good example of this combination in language teaching is the process syllabus.

The problem-solving model is based on a qualitatively quite different approach to planning from the one used in the RD and D model. More specifically, users employ action to articulate a problem and diagnose how they want to solve it. This diagnosis is followed by a search and retrieval phase in which users try to gather whatever information is relevant to their needs and which will enable them to formulate and/or select an appropriate innovation. After identifying the innovation, a process of adaptation, trial, and evaluation follows. During this time, users assess whether the solution they have devised really solves the problem that set the whole process into motion in the first place. If the users judge that the innovation is deficient or unsatisfactory in any way, the process begins again until a satisfactory solution is found (Havelock 1971).

Social interaction models of innovation often employ normative-re-educative strategies, certain elements of which underlie Kennedy's (1988) work in Tunisia. This model emphasizes the importance of social relationships as a key variable in adoption. Other factors that are stressed are noted as follows: 1) the position of potential adopters in their social network (i.e., how connected or disconnected they are from peers who might influence their decision); 2) the role of informal personal contacts as a functional mechanism for exchanging information about innovations; 3) the importance of group membership and reference-group identification as predictors of individual adoption; and 4) the typically S-shaped pattern-of-diffusion curve [. . .]. The major insight offered by this model in an educational context is the important role played by communication in promoting or inhibiting the diffusion of innovative curricula (Havelock 1971).

Finally, there are hybrid, or "linkage" models. Henrichsen points out that:

> while a [linkage perspective] allows for research and development of an innovation, it does not assume that RD and D is all that is required for successful implementation of an innovation. Furthermore, a linkage model allows for the 'dynamic' of change to be an outside force, making it appropriate for explaining directed contact change — even across cultural boundaries.
>
> (1989: 68)

Conclusion

It has been argued that the adoption of a diffusion-of-innovations perspective by practitioners is crucial to the development of language teaching theory and practice. Such a point of view provides a unified framework for conceptualizing both the development and evaluation of innovations in language teaching. In order to illustrate what issues are relevant to understanding a diffusion-of-innovations perspective on language teaching, innovation has been analyzed in terms of Cooper's (1989) question: "*Who adopts what, where, when, why, and how?*" This framework provides an appropriate set of criteria for analysis:

1   a profile of participants' socially defined roles and their adoption behaviors;
2   a definition of innovation in the context of language teaching;
3   an account of the sociocultural factors which constrain innovations;
4   a definition of diffusion;
5   an overview of the personal factors which constrain innovations, as well as the attributes of innovations which either promote or inhibit their adoption; and
6   a synopsis of various innovation models and strategies which may be used to promote change in language education.

The most important characteristic of emerging "post communicative" approaches to course design – approaches which are explicitly based on a diffusion-of-innovations perspective – is or will be their focus on two issues: 1) the extent to which teachers actually use new materials and approaches, and 2) the degree to which they actually reconstruct their pedagogical values. This shift of emphasis from design to implementation and evaluation is both desirable and also long overdue.

Bibliography

Adams, R. and D. Chen. 1981. *The process of educational innovation: An international perspective*. London: Kogan Page in association with the UNESCO Press.

Beretta, A. 1990. 'Implementation of the Bangalore project'. *Applied Linguistics*. 11. 321–37.

Brickell, H. M. 1969. 'Appraising the effects of innovation in local schools'. In R. W. Tyler (ed.) *Educational evaluation: New roles, new means*. Chicago, IL: National Society for the Study of Education. 284–304.

Brumfit, C. 1981. 'Notional syllabuses revisited: A response'. *Applied Linguistics*. 2. 90–92.

—— 1984a. Introduction. In C. Brumfit (ed.) *General English syllabus design*. Oxford: Pergamon. 1–4. [ELT Documents 118.]

—— 1984b. 'Function and structure of a state school syllabus for learners of second or foreign languages with heterogeneous needs'. In C. Brumfit (ed.) *General English syllabus design*. Oxford: Pergamon. 75–82. [ELT Documents 118.]

Chin, R. and K. D. Benne. 1976. 'General strategies for effecting changes in human systems'. In W. G. Bennis, K. D. Benne, R. Chin and K. E. Corey (eds.) *The planning of change*, 3rd ed. New York: Holt, Rinehart and Winston. 22–45.

Cooper, R. L. 1989. *Language planning and social change*. Cambridge: Cambridge University Press.

Fullan, M. 1982. *The meaning of educational change*. New York: Teachers College Press.

Havelock, R. G. 1971. 'The utilization of educational research and development'. *British Journal of Educational Technology*. 2. 84–97.

Henrichsen, L. E. (1989). *Diffusion of innovations in English language teaching: The ELEC effort in Japan, 1956–1968*. New York: Greenwood Press.

Holliday, T. and C. Cooke. 1982. 'An ecological approach to ESP'. In A. Waters (ed.) *Issues in*

ESP. Oxford: Pergamon Press. 124–143. [Lancaster Practical Papers in English Language Education 5.]

Huberman, A. M. 1973. *Understanding change in education: An introduction*. Paris: OECD.

Kelly, P. 1980. 'From innovation to adaptability: The changing perspective of curriculum development'. In M. Galton (ed.) *Curriculum change: The lessons of a decade*. Leicester: Leicester University Press. 65–80.

Kennedy, C. 1988. 'Evaluation of the management of change in ELT projects'. *Applied Linguistics*. 9(4). 329–42.

Krashen, S. and T. Terrell. 1983. *The natural approach*. New York: Pergamon.

Lambright, W. H. and P. Flynn. 1980. 'The role of local bureaucracy-centered coalitions in technology transfer to the city'. In J. A. Agnew (ed.) *Innovation research and public policy*. Syracuse, NY: Syracuse University Press. 243–282. [Syracuse Geographical Series No. 5.]

Levine, A. 1980. *Why innovation fails*. Albany, NY: State University of New York Press.

Long, M. H. and G. Crookes. 1992. 'Three approaches to task-based syllabus design'. *TESOL Quarterly*. 26.27–56.

Maley, A. 1984. 'Constraints-based syllabuses'. In J. A. S. Read (ed.) *Trends in language syllabus design*. Singapore: SEAMEO-RELC. 90–111.

Markee, N. 1986a. The importance of sociopolitical factors to communicative course design. *The ESP Journal*. 5.3–16.

—— 1986b. 'Toward an appropriate technology model of communicative course design'. *English for Specific Purposes*. 5.161–172.

Miles, M. B. 1964. 'Educational innovation: The nature of the problem'. In M. B. Miles (ed.) *Innovation in education*. New York: Teachers College Press. 1–48.

Munby, J. 1978. *Communicative syllabus design*. Cambridge: Cambridge University Press.

—— 1984. 'Communicative syllabus design: Principles and problems'. In J. A. S. Read (ed.) *Trends in language syllabus design*. Singapore: SEAMEO-RELC. 55–67.

Nicholls, A. 1983. *Managing educational innovations*. London: Allen & Unwin.

Prabhu, N. S. 1987. *Second language pedagogy*. New York: Oxford University Press.

Rogers, E. M. 1983. *The diffusion of innovations*, 3rd ed. London: Macmillan/Free Press.

Rogers, E. M. and F. Shoemaker. 1971. *Communication of innovations: A cross-cultural approach*, 2nd ed. New York: Free Press.

Rudduck, J. 1991. *Innovation and change*. Milton Keynes: Open University Press.

Swales, J. 1980. 'The educational environment and its relevance to ESP programme design'. In British Council (ed.) *ELT documents special: Projects in materials design*. London: The British Council. 61–70.

—— 1989. 'Service English programme design and opportunity cost'. In R. K. Johnson (ed.) *The second language curriculum*. Cambridge: Cambridge University Press. 79–90.

White, R. 1988. *The ELT curriculum: design, innovation and management*. Oxford: Blackwell.

Wilkins, D. A. 1976. *Notional syllabuses*. Oxford: Oxford University Press.

Zaltman, G. and R. Duncan. 1977. *Strategies for planned change*. New York: John Wiley and Sons.

Chapter 11

Zakia Sarwar

ADAPTING INDIVIDUALIZATION
TECHNIQUES FOR LARGE CLASSES

IN HIS RESEARCH FINDINGS based on responses from nonnative teachers of English from Indonesia, Japan, Nigeria, Senegal, and South Africa, Coleman (1989) lists four problems faced by teachers of large classes (100+). First, they feel self-conscious, nervous, and uncomfortable; it is indeed tiring to be the constant focus of 100+ pairs of eyes for three to four periods a day. Secondly, large classes pose disciplinary and class-management problems, in which the noise level must be kept down so as not to disturb others. Thirdly, it is difficult to evaluate the oral or written work of so many learners; teachers of large classes seem to be buried under an endless pile of homework. And lastly, teachers feel that because individual attention cannot be given, very little learning takes place.

From 1983 to 1985, as a part of my studies for a master's degree at Sydney University (Sarwar 1983–85), I designed and executed a research project entitled "Teaching English as a Foreign Language with Limited Resources." One of the aims of the research was to experiment with communicative language techniques and activities that would be effective in large classes of 100+. Communicative techniques would naturally include the broad concept of individualization. Finding effective techniques for large classes was a special concern in order to examine the teachers' popular belief that in large classes learning is nominal and the interactive approach, relying on group/pair work, is not possible.

The concept of individualization

Before outlining my research and describing the tasks and activities that encouraged individualization in my learners, I want to clarify my terms of reference for the concept of individualization. The umbrella title, *individualization*, covers "such seemingly diverse topics as one-to-one teaching, home study, individualized instruction, self-access facilities, self-directed learning, and autonomy, because they all focus on the learner as an individual" (Geddes and Sturtridge 1982). It also encompasses a learner-centred approach to language and takes special note of ethnolinguistic aspects of language learning, in which the autonomous role of the learner is coloured by their "second language self-image" and the teacher/learner roles prevalent in their sociolinguistic sphere (Riley 1988). There are also certain underlying basic assumptions regarding learning when we talk of "individualization." According to Logan (1980):

- People learn – even the same material – in different ways (this implies accepting different learning styles).
- People can learn from a variety of sources, even if the final goals are the same – implying that the instructional materials can vary.
- Direct teaching by a teacher is not essential for learning; it is only one of many possible experiences – which means that a teacher can be a facilitator instead of a preacher.
- A variety of learning activities can take place simultaneously – referring to integrative language-learning activities.
- People may have a variety of goals or objectives for learning a second language – implying that learners learn for different reasons.

Another perspective is added by Altman (1980), who clearly talks of three basic tenets that characterize individualized language teaching:

- a syllabus that meets the needs, abilities, and interests of each learner
- personalized goals, means, and expectations for learners
- teaching methods tailored to the needs of the learners

Logan's assumptions and Altman's tenets were examined for my research in general, and for the self-learning programme in particular, to determine how the concept of individualization could be exploited for large classes, where learners needed (*a*) exposure to language learning, (*b*) activities for confidence building, and (*c*) a learner-centred approach to build rapport between the teacher and the learners. Obviously, a tailor-made syllabus and teaching methodology for each learner was out of the question for my large classes of 100+. All the same, the learners were still considered to be the focal point of the learning programme, with realistic appraisal that they would all follow their own pace of learning and reach achievement levels congruent with the goals they set for themselves. It was also accepted that if Logan's five assumptions were applicable in small classes, they could very well be applied to large classes, so long as the learning programme offered the learners a variety of optional activities.

The four Rs of individualization

The working definition that emerged from these deliberations was the acceptance of Altman's "Three Rs of Individualization: *Reeducation*, *Responsibility*, and *Relevance*" (Williams and Williams 1979) – but with the addition of one more *R*, signifying *Rapport*, which can be taken for granted in one-to-one instruction or in a small class. This rapport is difficult, though just as (if not more) essential, to achieve in a large class. In the context of my research, the meaning of these four Rs of individualization are as follows.

Reeducation

This means reconstructing the role of the teacher as facilitator and the learner as the active agent in the process of learning. In the Pakistani context, this change needs to be emphasized all the more, since the teacher and the taught are both used to the lecture pattern of teaching in which the student is a passive learner as the teacher "talks" without any interaction or break for the whole teaching period.

Responsibility

This implies that learners take charge of their own learning. For the Pakistani learner this is a conceptual leap as they are used to rote learning and lack confidence in their own cognitive capabilities. It also implies the teacher's responsibility to set up clearly stated tasks that can be monitored by learners on their own and ensure the availability of self-learning materials for learners.

Relevance

As most of the glossy and readily available material is devised for the nonnative learner studying EFL in the West, we need materials relevant to our learners. Also, relevance means finding contexts of learning that are meaningful for our learners.

Rapport

A class of 100+ is a class-management challenge for any teacher. It is only through the proper rapport that an atmosphere conducive to learning can be built up. Also, "humanizing" a large class is perhaps the only way to motivate learning.

The research programme

I devised a 50-hour remedial English course that focused on reading comprehension and writing skills. It was a voluntary, non-credit course, taught for two hours three times a week, and lasting approximately eight and a half weeks. The learners (104 volunteers, who were selected on a first-come, first-served basis) agreed to stay after their regular classes for this course. They were young female adults between 16 and 20 years of age, the majority coming from a middle-class background. These students were false beginners of English, having studied it for approximately seven years. They had little or no exposure to English in their day-to-day lives except for studying it as a "subject" in the Faculty of Humanities.

While discussing the learners' expectations for the programme on the first day, it was mutually agreed that since 50 hours of class work would not be sufficient for any tangible improvement, the learners would supplement their work by following a self-monitored learning programme that included listening, reading, and writing skills. Learners were given a three-part questionnaire before and at the end of the project to evaluate their progress. The questionnaire was devised to find out (1) the learners' background, (2) their attitude towards learning English, and (3) their proficiency level in English, through a reading-comprehension check and paragraph writing.

The response – performance as well as feedback from the project group – was very encouraging. For the purposes of this article, however, I shall only focus on the steps used for putting the concept of individualization into practice. The four Rs were taken as a reference point in a two-pronged thrust: (a) individualization in large classes, and (b) individualizing learning tasks (see Figure 11.1).

Individualization in the classroom

This section deals with the last R of individualization: *rapport*. It focuses on activities that "humanized" this large class for me by helping me familiarize myself with the learners as persons. It also helped to a great extent in class management.

Voluntary learning

The 104 students who enrolled for the language project (LP) did so voluntarily. They were told that the aim of the programme was fluency rather than accuracy, and that they would be taught skills rather than prescribed textbooks. They were under no pressure to join the course – especially as it was a non-credit "unofficial" course, carried out as part of a research project. In the following years I have used the concept of voluntary learning by consulting the students at the beginning of each academic year before setting up the year's teaching programme for compulsory classes.

Background questionnaire

Learners were given an hour-long questionnaire on their first day in class. Learning about their background, attitudes, and perceived needs, as well as their proficiency level, helped me a great deal in understanding my learners. It also clarified their course expectations. The responses gave me information about the socioeconomic and ethnolinguistic community of the learners, which proved useful in organizing their group activities and outside class projects.

Grouping

On the very first day, after introducing the course, I asked the learners to form groups of three or four with their friends. As a number of activities were to use up time outside the class, we figured that it would be easier for learners to do their group tasks together in their free time in friendly groups. Forming their own groups also gave the learners more responsibility in sharing the class-management issues. Groups of four were then given a number to identify their group. They were also asked to sit together in class so they could share their group activities. Instead of moving around, we had permanent groups with a permanent seating arrangement.

Name tags

On the second day learners were requested to make name tags for themselves by writing their name and group number with a thick marker on a card measuring 3" × 4". They were to wear them as part of the class uniform throughout the duration of the course. This put a name to a face, which is otherwise impossible in a class of 104! It also made it easier for me to address everyone by their first names during activities and discussions. The magic of the first name also brought a more congenial atmosphere to the classroom, as classmates became more familiar with each other. There was definitely a better rapport between various groups as well as with me.

Profile cards

Creating profile cards proved to be a very interesting way to get to know the learners better. First, the points that were considered worth knowing about anyone were elicited in a brainstorming session and put on the blackboard. Secondly, these points were categorized and put in an order acceptable to everyone. Then students were asked to prepare their own profile cards, complete with their photograph and the details listed on the blackboard. It was announced that three prizes would be given to profile cards with good handwriting, correct spelling, and a neat, attractive presentation.

I learnt a lot about my learners' aspirations, strong points, and weak points, and having their photographs on the profile cards certainly helped me familiarize myself with their faces. The students enjoyed making these cards, too. Another advantage of having their names and addresses on their profile card was that I was able to reach my learners by mail after a sudden closing of all educational institutions (a frequent happening here!) and send them guidance on how to continue working on their own.

Lending library

As the majority of the LP learners did not have access to English books, magazines, and newspapers, I gathered from my friends and brought to the class used, simple story books, glossy magazines, and the magazine section of daily newspapers. Two or three of these were distributed to each group, who were to be (a) responsible for rotating and exchanging them with different groups, and (b) returning them to me at the end of the course. My purpose was simply to provide materials for extensive reading. I did not check to see if all the students used these, but they were film, fashion, and sports magazines, generally liked by teenage groups. I saw a brisk exchange before and after the class, so I presume a number of students did use these books and magazines. The responsibility of keeping track of these magazines gave the learners a sense of importance.

Individualizing learning tasks

I will discuss here self-learning programmes (SLP) aimed at improving students' language output as well as encouraging them to become independent learners. Training learners to monitor their own learning is as important in a large class as in a small one – in fact, more important, because in a small class, work can be supervised by the teacher, but in a large class this is virtually impossible. Hence, the best chance that a learner in a large class has is to take responsibility for his own learning. For the SLP, all the three Rs of individualization mentioned by Altman were considered. Students were given guidelines to (a) monitor their own scoring, (b) do peer correction, and (c) work independently on group projects. As a

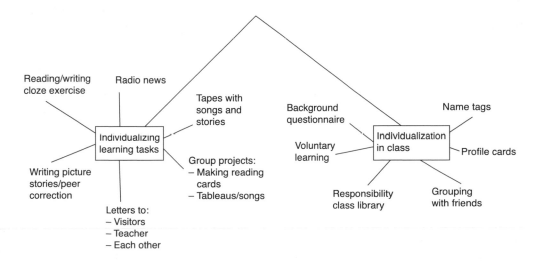

Figure 11.1 Individualization in large classes

teacher in SLP I devised materials/activities and prepared guidelines for the tasks. Except for an occasional consultation, I was not involved in the SLP after initiating it.

Most of the activities mentioned are familiar to language teachers and are used extensively in EFL classes in one form or another. Therefore, I have picked out only a few to show how they were adapted to become learner-centred for SLP.

Radio news

Students were given a sample worksheet with instructions for listening to the local radio news and filling in a grid (see Figure 11.2). This was an activity that provided exposure to real-world listening for the learners. It also helped them improve their general knowledge. Moreover, the learners could work at a time convenient to them and at their own pace, without peer and classroom pressure. Thirdly, it was a self-monitored learning task in which they were able to gauge their own progress. Beginning to listen "better" also improved their self-confidence. They were able to follow and take notes from speeches of native as well as nonnative speakers at a later stage of the language project.

- Please use your radio cassette player and keep a separate cassette for this exercise.
- Try to do this exercise once a day.

Aim: This exercise will improve your listening skills. It will also improve your note-taking skills.

Step 1
Make the following grid in your ELP workbook.

Example:	Time	Doer/person	Event	Place
	Yesterday	Prime Minister	Inaugurated conference	Karachi

Step 2
Listen to the radio news at a time convenient to you.
Tape only the headlines while listening to it.
Fill in the grid as you listen to the news. See example above.

Step 3
Put your workbook face down.
Play back the recorded news.
Fill in the portions you missed in the first listening.
Play back the recorded news again.
Check your responses and complete the grid as you play the recorded news.
Look at a newspaper to check spellings/compare facts.

Figure 11.2 Worksheet 1: radio news

Self-created cloze

Students were given guidance to improve the "look" of their written work by being given (1) handouts to improve handwriting, (2) instructions to give special attention to indentation and writing format (e.g., margin, paragraph, etc.). As an exercise for this they were asked to copy a paragraph a day from their prescribed textbooks, leaving out words, filling them in later, and then checking with the textbook again (see Figure 11.3).

- Please use your prescribed English textbook for the exercise.
- Try to write at least one paragraph every day.
- Use the attached handout as a model for your handwriting.

The aim of this exercise is to improve your

– Handwriting – Punctuation – Reading comprehension
– Grammar – Proofreading skills

Step 1
(Weeks 1 and 2)

a   Select a paragraph from your English textbook.
b   Mark or underline every 7th word.
c   Copy the passage in your best handwriting, leaving out the marked words. Draw a blank line instead.
d   Close the book. Take a break.
e   Fill in the blanks.

(Weeks 3 and 4)
Leave out every 6th word in Step 1*a*.

(Week 5 onwards)
Leave out every 5th word.

Step 2

Check your work:
    Have you put in a margin?
    Have you put in the date?
    Have you indented the paragraph?
    Does the writing look neat and tidy?

Open your textbook and check if you punctuated your work correctly.
Check your responses in the blanks.
Check the number of blanks and give yourself one mark for each correct answer.

Figure 11.3 Worksheet 2: self-created cloze

The usual practice is to give an unseen passage for cloze to teach/test comprehension or itemized grammar. But in the pilot testing of materials I discovered that my learners faced great difficulty if they were unfamiliar with the text. Copying from familiar texts made the exercise easier for them. The feedback confirms that a number of them improved in their scores with practice of this adapted version of cloze. They also became more confident when they attempted regular cloze exercises. Further, comparing their writing with the prescribed text, they got training in proofreading their own work, which highlighted their omissions and careless mistakes.

Group projects

A number of group projects were also initiated. To encourage participation, these were announced as competitions in which there would be a prize for the best entry in each of three categories: (1) picture stories (using the language of instruction, description, and narration), (2) reading cards from newspapers and magazines with comprehension questions on the back of the cards, and (3) organizing tableaus and songs for the final certificate award ceremony, which gave learners a chance to use language in real-life situations and take up a position of responsibility, while organizing the programme.

Advantages of the individualized activities

The activities described above take into consideration the underlying principles that Logan (1980) considers essential for individualization. Moreover, the four Rs – signifying Reeducation, Responsibility, Relevance, and Rapport – are also reflected in the tasks and activities described above. Their application seems to have mitigated some problems that occur because of swelling numbers of dependent, unskilled learners who lack exposure to real-world English. Using the broad concept of individualization manifested a number of advantages in these activities.

Grouping / group projects

*   gave learners a chance to make their own groups, which brought in the elements of both responsibility and choice
*   reduced the workload and made class management easier
*   gave groups of friends an opportunity to work together on projects in a nonthreatening atmosphere
*   made it possible for the weak students to learn from their peers

Name tags / profile cards

*   gave a name to a face, thus satisfying learners' basic need to be recognized as individuals
*   gave a humanistic touch to the large class
*   brought a sense of responsibility and accountability to the learners
*   developed a rapport in the class, thus making learners more motivated and positive about their learning tasks

Radio news / class library

*   provided real-world English to learners
*   gave them further responsibility, which later resulted in confidence in themselves as independent readers / listeners
*   built up managerial skills, and made the class more cohesive

Self-learning tasks

*   gave learners a chance to learn at their own pace and achieve their own goals – a great advantage in a large class
*   ensured learning for at least those who were motivated to learn

[. . .]

Implications for teaching/learning in developing countries

My research started with the basic assumption that classes in countries like Pakistan are not likely to be reduced in size in the foreseeable future. Hence, solutions have to be realistic, within the limited constraints of the present teaching/learning situation. The acceptance of this reality can help a teacher to overcome the psychological barrier that the interactive approach/activities cannot be used in large classes. This assumption led me to seek out new ways of managing the class and individualized activities.

Acceptance of reality also led to setting up realistic, measurable, short-term achievable goals, which had a reinforcing effect on the teacher and learners. What and how much can a teacher/learner achieve, given the learning conditions that prevail in large classes? A teacher obviously cannot meticulously correct a hundred papers every day. In the same way, a learner cannot learn flawless English with limited exposure to the language. Therefore, the initial target was fluency rather than accuracy, providing learners with an occasion to "use" the language in real life.

[. . .]

The broad concept of individualization and the whole structure of the project demanded a drastic change in the teacher/learner roles. Again I started with the assumption that direct teaching or lecture is only one form of learning experience (Logan 1980), and that adult students are capable of taking their learning into their own hands. The transition from learner dependence to independence was not an easy process – especially in a system of education where spoon-feeding and rote learning are common teaching/learning strategies. But the skill-based approach demanding cognitive interplay was a challenge to a number of students. It moved them towards relying on their own judgements and conclusions, so that they became gradually independent. On the other hand, as a teacher, relegating learning tasks and responsibilities to students involved an element of risk and ensuing frustrations. For a teacher used to complete control of the class, this was initially not an easy task, but the students' responses and enthusiasm lent a lot of support. In the last stages, their increased output and productivity became a reward in itself.

[. . .]

Conclusion

By incorporating individualization techniques my classroom research addressed three major ELT problems: large classes, the dependent learner, and lack of exposure to real-world English. Now what is needed most is its replication so as to evaluate the variables involved. Ideally, this replication should be done in Pakistan as well as in countries where similar teaching/learning conditions prevail. In contemplating such research, the following suggestions should be kept in view.

The basic materials and outline of the research done so far should be picked up, with adaptations and changes suitable for the age and level as well as the socio-ethnolinguistic background of the learners. The rationale behind the broad concept of individualization should be adopted as the basis of the approach used in handling large classes, and the focus of the research should be on activities and techniques that would be effective in large classes. Above all, more classroom-based research in large classes involving practicing teachers should be encouraged by institutions, organizations, and developers of syllabi and materials.

No doubt the picture of a large class of 100+ appears sad to those who have never had this experience, yet it is a condition faced by more than half the world's population of teachers and learners. Hence it is of vital importance that action research involving large classes be given high priority. [. . .]

References

Altman, H. B. 1980. Foreign language teaching: Focus on the learner. In *Language teaching: Meeting individual needs*, ed. H. B. Altman and C. V. James. New York: Pergamon.

Coleman, H. 1989. The relationship between large class research and large class teaching. Keynote paper presented at SPELT International Conference, Karachi, Pakistan.

Geddes, M. and C. Sturtridge, eds. 1982. *Individualization*. Oxford: Modern English Pub.

Hussain, A. M. and Z. Sarwar. 1989. ELT scene in Pakistan: Problems and prospects. *SPELT Newsletter, 4*, 3, p. 10.

Khamisani. 1983. English language teaching. Paper presented at University Grants Commission Conference on Teaching English as a Foreign/Second Language, Islamabad, Pakistan.

Logan, G. E. 1980. Individualized foreign language instruction: American patterns for accommodating learner differences in the classroom. In *Language teaching: Meeting individual needs*, ed. H. B. Altman and C. V. James. New York: Pergamon.

Mumtaz, A. and Z. Sarwar. 1986. Syllabus design: Theory and practice. *SPELT Seminar Report*, Karachi, Pakistan.

Riley, P. 1988. Ethnography autonomy. In *Individualization and autonomy in language learning* (ELT Documents 131), ed. A. Brooks and P. Grundy. Oxford: Modern English Pub. and British Council.

Sarwar, Z. 1983–85. Teaching English as a foreign language with limited resources. Unpublished M. Ed. research project, Sydney University, Australia.

——. 1989. The use of English in government offices. Paper presented at the International Conference on "Varieties of English in South Asia," U.G.C., Islamabad, Pakistan.

Williams, C. F. and T. L. Williams. 1979. Dealing with large classes: A course in individualized instruction. *English Teaching Forum, 17*, 1, pp. 44–45.

Chapter 12

William Savage and Graeme Storer

AN EMERGENT LANGUAGE PROGRAM FRAMEWORK: ACTIVELY INVOLVING LEARNERS IN NEEDS ANALYSIS

Introduction

WHAT DO OUR GROUP OF LEARNERS need to do with English in their work environment? What can they already do? What are the content areas which they need to talk and write about? What materials and situations do they have at work which can serve as vehicles for developing their ability to use language?

These were questions which faced us in the development of a language program for the staff of an aquaculture outreach project in the northeast of Thailand, people who had specific purposes for learning English which did not seem to consist of the sorts of information generated by needs analysis as it has come to be debated in the ESP literature. We wanted to actively involve the learners in the needs analysis and program design, but were unsure about how best to do so, despite our more than ten years' experience in ESP.

The approach which we developed evolved through a process of meeting the learners and planning and participating with them in the language program. It was after the fact that we returned to the relevant literature to place our work in the context of the ESP field specifically and language learning in general. What this paper describes is our experience working together with the learners in an emergent program. As such, it describes a piece of action research which addresses the question: "what language program framework allows for learners to be actively involved in needs analysis and program design?" The paper is organized in the same sequence as we developed the program.

I First, we describe the work situation of our learners.
II Then we discuss our initial framework for developing the program and elaborate on its three phases.
III Next, we review the language needs which were identified by the learners and how they were realized.
IV This is followed by a look at some literature relating to needs analysis and each of the four aspects of the program: working on tasks, reporting back, expanding, and evaluating.
V Finally, we will discuss implications for other learning situations and further development.

I   The AIT aquaculture outreach project

Funded by the Overseas Development Agency of the United Kingdom, the Aquaculture Outreach Project of the Asian Institute of Technology (AIT) is based in Udornthani, a major city in the resource-poor northeast. Taking an interdisciplinary research approach to freshwater aquaculture for small-scale farmers, the project's main objective is to determine aquaculture strategies which are sustainable, using inputs (feed, nutrients and materials) which are readily available. Recommendations for fish-farming practices are generated by a methodic flow of information among the project, the participating farmers and on-station research at AIT.

A delicate aspect of the project concerns the manner in which farmers are recruited and participate in the project. Thus, project staff, being from the northeast region themselves, are crucial to the project's efforts in that they are of the same culture and speak the same first dialect as the farmers. The project staff in the Udornthani main office and two sub-offices in other northeastern provinces were the group of learners for whom a language program was requested.

Our initial contact with the project's manager, a native English speaker, highlighted several general reasons to learn English. The funding agency is from an English-speaking country and the project often receives visitors from that agency and others, as well as English-speaking researchers who often stay for weeks or months at a time. Access to aquaculture research information is essential for many staff members and all the data which are collected in the field are ultimately reported in English. Finally, it seems likely that the project will be extended to other countries in the region, ideally drawing on the expertise of the Thai staff.

These reasons established the motivation for a language program but did not give much information about what needed to be learned. To that end, a one-day visit to Udornthani was arranged during which one of the two teachers met the learners to discuss with them their work-related needs. The findings from the site visit were used to set up a two-day planning workshop at the AIT campus in the northern outskirts of Bangkok. Seven representatives of the staff carried out work-related tasks alongside seven counterparts who had participated in language programs at the AIT campus. In this way, information was built up from the site visit through the planning workshop to provide the content for the 2-week intensive workshop.

II   The language program framework

One of the aims of the language program, as stated by the project manager, was to get the participants to a point where they would be able to continue to develop their English ability by themselves. That is, the conclusion of the program was not to be viewed as an end point, but as another starting point in itself. For this reason, we have avoided using "course" in our terminology as, for us, it strongly suggests a discrete end point. We also feel that a course implies a set of content which is presented in basically the same form each time it is regularly given. The content of the language program described here is unique, not only to its particular situation but also to the group of learners. Were we to go through a similar process of developing another language program at the same location, but for a different group of learners, the content would be quite different. Therefore, we will refer to the two-week phase as a workshop or simply as the two-week intensive. We view the program and its development as three-phase: the one-day site visit, two-day planning workshop and two-week intensive workshop.

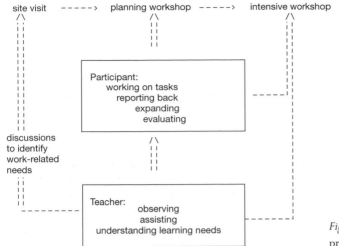

Figure 12.1 The initial language program framework

In approaching the language program, the teachers began with the framework illustrated in Figure 12.1. The role of the participant in this initial framework was to work on tasks, report back, expand and evaluate. The role of the teacher was perceived as observing, assisting and understanding the learning needs as the participants were working. Identification of needs would not be confined to one phase, but would occur throughout the program.

The one-day site visit (Udornthani)

During the site visit, one of the teachers met with the project staff. Through discussion, they were able to identify the following work-related needs:

1 EXPLAINING

    (a) The work of the project (methodology and recommendations) to visitors
    (b) Figures and graphs

2 DESCRIBING experiment results and analyzing data

3 REPORTING from farmer data collection forms

4 SPEAKING and LISTENING

5 WRITING

    (a) Monthly reports of work progress
    (b) Summaries of the monthly reports
    (c) Sub-project reports

6 READING and WRITING

    (a) Scientific project reports
    (b) Office memos
    (c) Farmer report forms

This information was inadequate in that it merely prescribed a set of content to be taught. (Should we now offer a course called "Writing Office Memos"?) It did not tell us what the learners could already do in English and what language learning concerns they thought needed to be addressed. This led us to the two-day planning workshop.

The two-day planning workshop (AIT campus)

The site visit information defined the tasks for the planning workshop when seven representatives of the project staff were paired with seven AIT campus staff. The tasks concerned writing (monthly reports, summaries of monthly reports and translating reports from Thai to English); describing and presenting information about field work, including photographs of a farmer's fish ponds; preparing captions for project extension media; and describing office procedures. The reportback saw each staff member speaking to the whole group about the task, with the partners stepping in to help out when necessary. Because the partners' work also related to aquaculture, there was a great deal of support and sharing of ideas. For some, it was their first occasion to use English to discuss their work. During the reportback session, the teachers were able to observe the participants using English and were thus better placed to comment on their needs; the participants themselves were better able to discuss their learning needs. Mr Vorapong, for example, finished his reportback by announcing "We want to write (the farmer report forms) in English." When asked why he did not do so, he began to talk about his limited vocabulary and his lack of experience in constructing sentences. That is, he began clarifying his needs for himself and for us.

On the second morning, the AIT campus staff spoke of work they had done while studying English, expanding on language learning concerns expressed by the project staff the previous afternoon. Once again, the focus of the discussions moved from simply talking about work-related needs to more specific learning concerns. For example, Mr Pirat said: "I want to use English everyday, but I [am] shy. Do you have this problem?" Mr Supong, one of the AIT partners, answered by talking about how he had overcome his shyness when he first began to learn English; he went on to explain about strategies he had developed for learning vocabulary. This widening of focus in the reportbacks meant that the teachers began to rethink their initial program framework as the teacher and participant roles as originally perceived were no longer distinct. The final afternoon was devoted to a spoken evaluation of the two-day planning workshop, during which each participant elaborated on areas they thought needed development.

The two-week intensive workshop (Udornthani)

The teachers met with the seven representatives before the intensive workshop to discuss their plans for the two weeks and to ask them to assist in the orientation. On the first morning, each of the seven representatives assumed responsibility for orienting the other seventeen staff members to the program and about what might be expected: they discussed the importance of trying to use English, of asking for help when "stuck" and the use of the first language; they talked about keeping a logbook; they spoke about developing the technical terms dictionary (an idea which had come up during the planning workshop); and they showed photographs taken during the planning workshop and explained what was happening in each one, thereby introducing the other staff members to the idea of working on tasks and reporting back.

The first task had been decided on by the teachers and the groups had been pre-formed. In the second task, though, the participants were asked to select an area from the office's weekly sub-project sheet to talk about and they were encouraged to form their own interest groups. This movement from teacher-defined tasks to tasks identified by the participants themselves was integral to the program approach. By the second week, the participants were forming their own groups and defining areas of interest to work on for the final poster session.

III Identified needs and their realization in the program

During the planning workshop, the participants and teachers were able to clarify and elaborate on the needs that had been identified during the one-day site visit. Some needs had been immaturely defined, for example, the reading and writing of farmer report forms. While the teachers understood that the report forms had to be written in English, the participants made it clear that:

Participant 1:   The quantitative data on the forms are not translated into English but are coded and then entered into the data base.

Participant 2:   The qualitative data on the forms can be in note form, not complete sentences.

After the two-week intensive, the teachers decided to trace the needs through the program and to see how they had been realized and handled through activities in the two-week intensive.

During the planning workshop, both teachers had kept detailed notes. The sessions had also been video-taped. In the two-week intensive, a daily log was kept which detailed each day's activities. The notes, the video record and the daily log served as data. In reviewing the data, the teachers looked for learning needs directly expressed by the participants; and learning needs observed by the teachers as the participants were using English. The learning needs fell into four groups:

(A)   *interacting* – includes such acts as explaining, describing and discussing, as well as the frequently mentioned listening and speaking;
(B)   *language use* – represents mechanical language abilities;
(C)   *writing and reading* – contains all references to materials to be written and read; and,
(D)   *metacognitive* – refers to comments about managing the learning process itself.

The learning needs in each of these groups and how they were realized in the two-week intensive appear in Tables 12.1–4.

IV Rethinking needs analysis

At the beginning of the paper, we asked several questions which we consider to be basic to the work done in needs analysis. Looking back on our approach, it is apparent that we have dealt in practical terms with these questions, ones still being discussed in the literature. In their approach to ESP language needs analysis, Hutchinson and Waters distinguish target needs from learning needs (1987: 53–63). In doing so, they move beyond the categorizing of linguistic features which results from instruments such as Munby's Communicative Needs Processor (1978). But what they describe as learning needs can, in fact, be seen as instructional logistics needs. For example, the learning needs relate to questions of the purpose of the course, background of the learners, types of instructional resources, and location and time of the course. When Hutchinson and Waters focus on target needs, they view learners as being short of the mark, or lacking (1987: p. 58), rather than as people who bring their own experience and expectations to a language program.

It was this neglect which prompted us to develop an approach which would more actively involve learners in the needs analysis and design of the language program. Jacobson (1986: p. 173) approached needs analysis "in terms of the strategic competence that students

Table 12.1 Interacting

Identified needs	How realized during 2-week intensive
1 Explaining	
(a) Extension material development	Interacting with visitors; reportback: description of radio station survey for extension, evaluation of extension media; "muscovy duck" video
(b) Concepts and objectives in project media	Reportback on 1st & 2nd tasks
(c) Project recommendations	Interacting with visitors; student videos; poster session: "How to get farmers to grow fat fish"
(d) Connections between various staff duties	Reportback: discussion about Khmer and Souay dialects; videos
(e) Figures and graphs	Listening posts
2 Describing	
(a) Physical features of pond systems	Poster session
(b) Procedures*	Poster session: fish fry transfer, how to deal with visitors reportback: new criteria for village selection
3. Discussing work duties	Reportback: recruitment and follow-up in one sub-office; weekly meetings; farmer visit forms
4. Interacting on the telephone	
5. Speaking and listening	Focus of all reporting back; listening posts; student videos; weekly meetings held in English; discussions of week 1 evaluation to set up week 2; defining and clarifying tasks

* These procedures arose during the 2-week intensive; one other, related to office procedure, was not addressed because of a lack of time.

need in order to successfully carry out the work required in the [university physics] lab." His task-based approach primarily involved direct observations in the lab environment in which the students were working, and interviews with the lab instructors. Including observations of what the learners actually had to do with language marked a major addition to what had typically been put forward as methods for collecting information about language learning needs, for example, with questionnaires and interviews (Mackay, 1978: p. 21). But in the end, what ensued was the delivery of a prescribed syllabus whose purpose was to fill in the gaps identified.

Widdowson's discussion of needs analysis wends its way through the inadequacy of register-based analyses to arrive at the desirability of considering "aspects of discourse" (1983: p. 85). In order to do this, he argues, we need to devise ways to engage learners in "procedural work" which will convert items of knowledge about language into "actualized

Table 12.2 Language use

Identified needs	How realized during 2-week intensive
1 Vocabulary	
(a) Improper choice (e.g. recommend for collect)	A focus of the technical terms dictionary Teacher input and some student–student correction
(b) Inadequate to complete forms	Farmer visit worksheets
(c) Avoiding circumlocution	Reportback and weekly meetings: use of media and realia
(d) Technical terms	Recording words in logbooks; contextualizing words for dictionary; farmer visit worksheets
2 Syntax	
(a) Connecting ideas	Teacher input of connectors
(b) Linking within paragraphs	
(c) Constructing sentences	Writing memos, minutes of weekly meetings and video scripts
3 Tense	As above
4 Introducing a topic in writing	Preparing for reporting back; video scripts
5 Writing clearly	Preparing for weekly meetings; recorders in meeting; minutes; video scripts; contextualizing vocabulary; explanations for dictionary and for setting up listening posts
6 Giving details	Focus of "expanding"

Table 12.3 Writing and reading

Identified needs	How realized during 2-week intensive
1 Writing	
(a) Farmer visit forms	Farmer visit worksheets
(b) Internal memos	Manager reported an increase in the number of internal memos written in English; teachers asked to check
(c) Memos to report unusual data	Did not arise
(d) Monthly reports*	
(e) Monthly report summaries*	
(f) Report outlines	Discussed with manager but not followed through
(g) Abstracts of books and articles	
2 Reading	
(a) Incoming memos	Memo from sub-office in English: discussed and rewritten at weekly meeting
(b) New sub-project tasks	Informed second task Preparation and follow-up for weekly meeting

* Note that we had intended to hold a writing workshop in the second week. This plan was abandoned as it was felt that there was just too much else going on. Writing was addressed in other areas, e.g. memos and meeting minutes, though this was only at the sentence/paragraph level.

Table 12.4 Metacognitive

Identified needs*	How realized during 2-week intensive
1 Asking others about words not understood	Examples given about how to ask for help
	Many examples of student–student and student–teacher requests for help
2 Learners assisting each other	Participants used to working as a team (a feature of way the project is set up)
	Most apparent in preparing for reporting back, meetings and poster session
3 Overcoming shyness to speak (confidence)	This was commented on by 6 of the participants in their written evaluations
4 Using L1 to explain L2	Seen in farmer visit forms and technical terms dictionary "Muscovy duck" video

* All spoken to in the orientation by the participants from the planning workshop.

communicative behavior" (1983: p. 87). Kenny's (1985) review of Widdowson's *Language Purpose and Language Use* (1983) added this:

> An analysis by the teacher of the learner's conceptual requirements in the defined field will point us in the direction of the required discourse . . . The selected discourse becomes in the lesson the object we respond to, dissect and discuss, and the communication we share. How is it conceptually organized? It is all right? What exactly is meant? Do we agree? Might we add to it? Should we elaborate this point? Can someone explain this?
>
> (1985: p. 177)

Inherent in these questions is negotiation and through such a process an understanding of learners' language needs can begin, as learners are engaged in Widdowson's "procedural work." At the same time, we are forced to consider methodological issues as being at one with finding out what learners know and what they need to know. Does the methodology allow for previously unidentified needs to be addressed or is the content of the program set in stone beforehand? Does the methodology allow for future needs to be handled by the learners "to achieve their own aims after the course is over by applying the procedures they have used in learning to the continuation of learning through language use" (Widdowson, 1983: p. 91)?

This concert of needs analysis and methodology is central to the approach presented in this paper; by engaging the learners in these concerns of program design, the learning experience is readily accessible to the participants in terms of the content and their ability to participate. Needs analyzed concurrently with the program and embedded in the methodology must be of immediate relevance. A methodology which fosters learner autonomy sustains momentum to continue learning; it becomes "a catalyst for learning" (Foley, 1991: p. 69). The validity of any approach to identify and address the language needs of learners is ultimately established by "how effectively it achieves its declared purpose of defining the content of purpose-specific language programs" (Widdowson, 1983: pp. 85–86). In the previous section, we gave examples of needs identified by the learners and how these were realized as content. Let us now turn to placing the program's aspects into a background.

Working on tasks

We depart from the types of tasks discussed in *Language Learning Tasks* (Candlin and Murphy, 1987) in one vital respect: the tasks are derived from and defined by actual work situations in which the learner needs to use English. As one of the AIT partners observed in the planning workshop, the work content can serve as the language learning content. Work-related tasks are suitable for determining learning needs because the use of tasks allows teachers to establish "the rules [the learner] is using and the systems and categories he is working with" (Corder, 1981; in Larsen-Freeman and Long, 1991: p. 41). The advantage for the learner is that it allows him to focus on what he can do, to locate his starting point.

It is important that the first task be appropriately set up so that, on reporting back, language and content are generated to allow the participants to proceed. In the case of the planning workshop, this was achieved by pairing the participants with counterparts who could advise and assist them. In fact, they were helping each other. Mr Tanin, an AIT partner, commented that although he had helped his partner with vocabulary, his partner had also explained aquaculture concepts to him.

Reporting back

Reporting back comes from the work done at the Language Center of AIT in the development of its pre-sessional master's program, Talkbase. A reportback session "involves a focus on method, a sharing of information and reciprocal curiosity about what others are doing or have done, and a first attempt at narrowing down a wide and unmotivated topic to one which is both manageable and of personal interest to the students" (Hall and Kenny, 1988: pp. 21–22). Two related points need to be emphasized here. First, method is taken to mean the way in which the task was accomplished. In our approach, because learners are dealing with work-based tasks, the method for doing the task during the language program and for doing the task for work are one and the same. Second, it follows that the topic is already of interest as it is defined by the learner and involves the attainment of a work goal. The "narrowing down" becomes a process of managing the topic within the learners' current ability level.

Expanding

An increased ability to deal with the content of the task at a more challenging level using language just beyond the current level of ability comes about through expanding what the learner has to say during a reportback. The participants' current knowledge of language use is manifested in the accomplishment of the task, upon which can be built a greater ability to report back. Problems addressed in the tasks are naturally centered on the learner who benefits from guidance, not only from the teachers but also from other learners, thus expanding the scope of the learner's task. Or put another way: "students [have] a plan for further action which might involve exploration of further sources of data, a redefinition or refinement of topic area or a search for more detailed information" (Hall and Kenny, 1988:

p. 22). This pointing toward an expanded, elaborated goal is at the level of the content of the task and reportback and language is developed to reach the next point. Thus, our understanding of expansion of language is that it occurs because of a need to discuss expanded content and not as it has been limited in Widdowson's formulation:

generalization + *clarification* + *elaboration* + *exemplification*

(Widdowson, 1978: p. 133)

A language expansion sequence such as this seems more communicatively useful when applied to the content which language is being used to transmit and not simply to the language's structural representation.

Evaluating

Evaluating is seen as "a regular and continuing process" (Rea, 1987: p. 165). The key characteristic of such evaluation is that it is integral to learning and teaching. In practice, this means that the language program participants (learners and teachers) are explicitly aware that whatever is going on is ultimately open to evaluation; they question how a given task was accomplished and how it could be improved. For example, such improvements might concern the need to develop a greater ability to talk about a certain task during a reportback session. Then the language needed can be input to the learner, from the teacher or from other learners; the outcome of that particular evaluation can be acted upon immediately. As Waters points out, the negotiation about what is required to act on a task provides an actual situation to discuss what is to be communicated and how it will be done. Participatory evaluation highlights the jobs to be done in the ESP classroom and the best means of carrying them out (Waters, 1987: pp. 7–8).

Let us now return to the language program framework in a revised form which better reflects the ideas we have forwarded and makes explicit the manner in which the program's aspects operate on each other (see Figure 12.2).

V Concluding remarks

What we have described here is the design of an emergent language program, throughout which the learners were involved in defining the content and how it would be addressed. Some will argue that the way in which we have proceeded here is singular to the situation and not transferrable. Certainly, we were helped by the fact that the aquaculture project staff were already a cohesive team before we began working with them and that they shared the same first language; and, that the two-week intensive took place on-site.

However, we wish to make explicit certain situational constraints. First, the participants were at widely different levels of ability in English, from beginners to those who were reading (and writing) research papers in aquaculture. Second, we conducted the program with a limited amount of media technology – two snappy cameras, four portable cassette players and one video camera. Third, work demands meant that some participants were called away during the two-week intensive.

We have deliberately not dealt in detail with the practical instructional features of the program because individual teachers would respond to the learners' work-related content in their own way. An area which could be developed is team teaching in an emergent program.

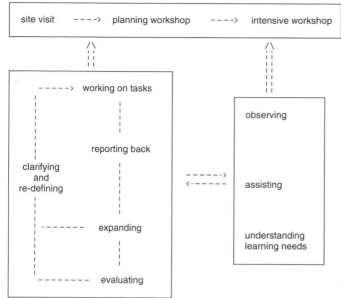

Figure 12.2 The revised language program framework

In concluding, we cite a particularly challenging passage from Clarke's discussion of the negotiated syllabus which sums up the target we would like to see reached in language programs:

> The syllabus as derived from and generated by specific groups of learners . . . will be means – rather than ends – driven insofar as the ends cannot in fact be accurately predicted. The whole discussion about "design" becomes somewhat solipsistic when it is realized that the Negotiated syllabus does not in fact exist before the learners meet with the teacher in a particular environment in order to establish its parameters. Design is therefore no longer external to, or prior to, the implementation of the syllabus and in fact becomes its most essential pedagogical component, being itself part of the learning process.
>
> (Clarke, 1991: p. 14)

References

Candlin, C. N. and Murphy, D. F. (1987) *Language Learning Tasks*. London: Prentice-Hall.

Clarke, D. (1991) "The negotiated syllabus: what is it and how is it likely to work?" *Applied Linguistics* **12**, 13–28.

Corder, S. (1981) *Error Analysis and Interlanguage*. Oxford: Oxford University Press.

Foley, J. (1991) "A psycholinguistic framework for task-based approaches to language teaching." *Applied Linguistics* **12**, 62–75.

Hall, D. and Kenny, B. (1988) "An approach to a truly communicative methodology: the AIT pre-sessional course." *English for Specific Purposes* **7**, 19–32.

Hutchinson, T. and Waters, A. (1987) *English for Specific Purposes: A Learning-Centred Approach*. Cambridge: Cambridge University Press.

Jacobson, W. H. (1986) "An assessment of the communication needs of non-native speakers of English in an undergraduate physics lab." *English for Specific Purposes* **5**, 173–87.

Kenny, B. (1985) "Review: learning purpose and language use." *The ESP Journal* **4**, 171–9.

Larsen-Freeman, D. and Long, M. (1991) *An introduction to Second Language Acquisition Research*. New York: Longman.

Mackay, R. (1978) "Identifying the nature of the learner's needs." In Mackay, R. and Mountford, A. (eds) *English for Specific Purposes*. London: Longman.

Munby, J. (1978) *Communicative Syllabus Design*. Cambridge University Press.

Rea, P. (1987) "Communicative curriculum validation: a task-based approach." In Candlin, C. N. and Murphy, D. F. (eds) *Language Learning Tasks* pp. 147–65. London: Prentice-Hall.

Waters, A. (1987) "Participatory course evaluation in ESP." *English for Specific Purposes* **7**, 3–12.

Widdowson, H. (1978) *Teaching Language as Communication*. Oxford University Press.

Widdowson, H. (1983) *Learning Purpose and Language Use*. Oxford University Press.

Chapter 13

Defeng Li

TEACHERS' PERCEIVED DIFFICULTIES IN INTRODUCING THE COMMUNICATIVE APPROACH IN SOUTH KOREA

RECENTLY, EDUCATIONAL INNOVATIONS IN L2 education have received considerable attention (Bailey, 1992; Freeman and Cazden, 1990; Kennedy, 1988; Markee, 1997; White, 1987). The literature on this topic includes studies of language curriculum development, language teaching methodology, and the process of innovation that occurs in teacher development contexts (Bailey, 1992).

Attempts to introduce communicative language teaching (CLT) into EFL contexts on EFL countries' own initiatives and through international aid projects have prompted many innovations in L2 education. In general, such innovations have had a low rate of success (Brindley and Hood, 1990), and implementing CLT worldwide has often proved difficult (Anderson, 1993; Chick, 1996; Ellis, 1994, 1996; Gonzalez, 1985; Kirkpatrick, 1984; Sano, Takahashi, and Yoneyama, 1984; Shamin, 1996; Ting, 1987; Valdes and Jhones, 1991). Difficult as it is, many EFL countries are still striving to introduce CLT in the hope that it will improve English teaching there.

Why has CLT been so difficult to implement in EFL classrooms? How appropriate is CLT for EFL contexts? I believe teachers' perceptions of the feasibility of a CLT innovation in a particular context are crucial in determining the ultimate success or failure of that innovation (Kelly, 1980; Markee, 1997). For this reason I undertook a case study of South Korean secondary school English teachers' understanding of the uptake of CLT in South Korea. As many EFL countries share some of the characteristics of English teaching in South Korea, for example, traditional teaching methods and large classes, this study has widespread implications.

CLT: one definition

CLT starts with a theory of language as communication, and its goal is to develop learners' communicative competence. Canale and Swain's (1980) definition of communicative competence is probably the best known. They identified four dimensions: grammatical, sociolinguistic, discourse, and strategic competence. This definition has undergone some modifications over the years, perhaps best captured in Bachman's (1990) schematization of what he calls *language competence*. The most significant difference between the two models is that Bachman takes a far broader view of the role of strategies than Canale and Swain do and separates strategic competence completely from what he calls *language competencies* (Bachman, 1990; North, 1997).

In CLT, meaning is paramount. Wilkins (1972) classifies meaning into notional and functional categories and views learning an L2 as acquiring the linguistic means to perform different kinds of functions. According to Larsen-Freeman (1986), the most obvious characteristic of CLT is that "almost everything that is done is done with a communicative intent" (p. 132). Teachers select learning activities according to how well they engage the students in meaningful and authentic language use rather than in the merely mechanical practice of language patterns.

Another dimension of CLT is "its learner-centered and experience-based view of second language teaching" (Richards and Rodgers, 1986, p. 69). According to CLT theory, individual learners possess unique interests, styles, needs, and goals that should be reflected in the design of instructional methods (Savignon, 1991).

CLT is characterized by

1   a focus on communicative functions;
2   a focus on meaningful tasks rather than on language *per se* (e.g., grammar or vocabulary study);
3   efforts to make tasks and language relevant to a target group of learners through an analysis of genuine, realistic situations;
4   the use of authentic, from-life materials;
5   the use of group activities; and
6   the attempt to create a secure, nonthreatening atmosphere.

I stress that the description above reflects just one definition of CLT, what Holliday (1994) terms the *weak version of CLT*. According to Holliday, the strong version is actually quite different: The focus is not on language practice but on learning about how language works in discourse. The lesson input is language data in the form of text, and *communicative* relates more to the way in which the student communicates with the text. Also, students collaborate for the purpose of helping each other solve language problems rather than for the purpose of communicating with each other. Because the aim is not to practice language forms, teachers do not need to monitor group and pair work closely, and in fact activities do not have to be carried out in groups or pairs. As long as students are communicating with rich text and producing useful hypotheses about the language, what they are doing is communicative, according to Holliday (pp. 171–172).

CLT in EFL contexts

A number of reports in the literature deal with CLT innovations in EFL contexts. Whereas some accounts have emphasized the local needs and the particular English teaching conditions in the EFL countries and the importance and success of traditional language teaching methods (Bhargava, 1986; Sampson, 1984, 1990), others have strongly advocated the adoption of CLT in EFL countries (Li, 1984; Prabhu, 1987). However, the majority of accounts have recognized the difficulties EFL countries face in adopting CLT.

Burnaby and Sun (1989) report that teachers in China found it difficult to use CLT. The constraints cited include the context of the wider curriculum, traditional teaching methods, class sizes and schedules, resources and equipment, the low status of teachers who teach communicative rather than analytical skills, and English teachers' deficiencies in oral English and sociolinguistic and strategic competence. Anderson's (1993) study of CLT in China reported such obstacles as a lack of properly trained teachers, a lack of appropriate texts and materials, students' not being accustomed to CLT, and difficulties in evaluating students taught via CLT. Based on a study that assessed the attitudes of Hong Kong educators toward using CLT in the local context, Chau and Chung (1987) report that teachers used CLT only sparingly because it required too much preparation time.

Sano et al. (1984) point out that the Japanese students they studied generally did not feel a pressing need to use English, so that the goal of communicative competence seemed too distant for them. A study conducted in Vietnam identified class size, grammar-based examinations, and lack of exposure to authentic language as constraints on using CLT (Ellis, 1994). Shamin (1996) identifies learners' resistance, among other problems, as a barrier to her attempt to introduce innovative CLT methodology in her Pakistan English classroom.

The grammar-based English language syllabus makes the English teaching situation complex and the local use of CLT challenging, according to Kirkpatrick's (1984) study of CLT in secondary schools in Singapore. Gonzalez (1985), who studied CLT in Philippine rural areas, found that English instruction there was irrelevant to the population's needs, as people there seldom used English.

In studies of CLT outside Asia, Valdes and Jhones (1991) report difficulties such as teachers' lack of proficiency in English, their traditional attitudes toward language teaching, the lack of authentic materials in a non-English-speaking environment, the need to redesign the evaluation system, and the need to adapt textbooks to meet the needs of communicative classes. Efforts to foster a communicative approach to the teaching of English in KwaZulu, South Africa, met with pervasive reluctance on the part of teachers and students to adopt the more egalitarian, decentralized ways of interacting associated with CLT (Chick, 1996).

Although these studies highlight many of the principal problems in instituting curricular innovations prompted by CLT, many of the studies take the researcher's perspective. Teachers' perceptions of innovations related to CLT remain largely unexplored.

The study

The study reported here used a case study approach to investigate Korean teachers' perceptions of the implementation of CLT.

Background: CLT in South Korea

The South Korean government has placed English learning and teaching high on its agenda to ensure that South Korea will play an active and important role in world political and economic activities. The South Korean Ministry of Education recently published a series of new policies regarding English learning and teaching. First, early in 1994 the government decided that English teaching would begin at a younger age (Grade 3 in elementary schools) starting in 1997 and began to train prospective elementary EFL teachers.

In addition, realizing that "the grammatical syllabus does not help much to develop learners' communicative competence" (Development Committee, 1992, p. 66), the government decided to introduce CLT into English teaching at the secondary school level.

In the new curricula, the goal of English teaching is "to develop the learners' communicative competence in English through meaningful drills and communicative activities, such as games, with the aid of audio-visual equipment" (Development Committee, 1992, p. 180). Students are to learn by means of authentic materials, such as newspapers, magazines, English news on the radio, and English TV programs. The curricula reflect the belief that "CLT is characterized by learner-centredness" (p. 181), and teachers are encouraged to organize materials based on students' needs.

Accompanying the release of the new curricula was the publication of a series of new textbooks. Over 10 sets of English textbooks are now available to secondary school English teachers, who are free to choose any set provided that the whole school adopts it. The new textbooks incorporate a communicative perspective and more listening and speaking materials and activities relative to the older ones.

Will the shift in the government's policy result in an improvement in students' communicative competence? Is Korea prepared to implement CLT in English instruction? To answer these questions, I investigated Korean teachers' perceptions of the difficulties in using CLT.

Design

The analysis consisted of a pilot study, a written questionnaire, and interviews. To develop an appropriate survey instrument for this study, in summer 1994 I administered a pilot survey to 21 South Korean EFL teachers studying in a teacher education program at a Canadian university. The final questionnaire included both open-ended questions and questions with fixed alternatives generated from the data collected in the pilot study (see the Appendix).

In summer 1995, the questionnaire was administered to 18 South Korean secondary school EFL teachers studying at the same Canadian university. To ensure that the participants fully understood the questions, I distributed the questionnaires at the end of a class. The participants were urged to read the questionnaire, and they asked questions for clarification. All 18 questionnaires distributed were handed back. Following the survey, I conducted in-depth interviews with 10 of the participants to explore further the teachers' back-ground, their understanding of English teaching in South Korea, and their difficulties in using CLT.

The interviews were semistructured, conducted in a systematic and consistent order but allowing me as the interviewer sufficient freedom to digress and probe far beyond the answers to the prepared and standardized questions (Berg, 1989, p. 17). The interviews were conducted in English. Although I was well aware that the teachers' imperfect English might limit the information they provided, I made certain that they were able to express their ideas fully by preparing and sending a number of questions to them ahead of time.
[. . .]

Participants

Survey participants

The participants in the formal questionnaire survey were 18 South Korean secondary school English teachers who were studying in the Korean Teacher Education Program (KTEP) at a Canadian university in the summer of 1995. [. . .]

The 9 male and 9 female participants ranged from 30 to 50 years in age, with the majority in their 30s; the average age was 36.5. Their experience in teaching English varied from 5 to 25 years, with an average of over 11 years. At the time of the study, 8 participants were teaching in middle schools, and 10 were teaching in high schools. Many had taught at both middle and high schools, as secondary school teachers in South Korea must transfer schools every 5 years; high school teachers quite commonly transfer to middle schools and vice versa. Half of the participants were teaching in rural secondary schools and half in urban settings. A representative 10 of the 18 survey participants were also given an in-depth interview.

Data analysis

Data analysis is not a simple description of the data collected but a process by which the researcher can bring interpretation to the data (Powney and Watts, 1987). The themes and coding categories in this study emerged from an examination of the data rather than being determined beforehand and imposed on the data (Bogdan and Biklen, 1992). [. . .]

Results

The South Korean teachers were interested in the methods they used in teaching English. Fourteen of the 18 participants reported that they were very concerned, and the other 4 reported that they were fairly concerned. All reported that the grammar-translation method, the audiolingual method, or a combination of the two characterized their teaching. However, 12 reported having tried CLT before attending the teacher education program in Canada and having encountered difficulties in such attempts.

The difficulties reported by the Korean teachers fall into four categories: those caused (a) by the teacher, (b) by the students, (c) by the educational system, and (d) by CLT itself. Among them, difficulties falling into the first category were mentioned most often, almost twice or three times as much as those in the other three categories (see Table 13.1).

Table 13.1 Reported difficulties in implementing CLT

Source and difficulty	No. of mentions[a]
Teacher	99
Deficiency in spoken English	18
Deficiency in strategic and sociolinguistic competence	18
Lack of training in CLT	18
Few opportunities for retraining in CLT	16
Misconceptions about CLT	15
Little time for developing materials for communicative classes	14
Students	50
Low English proficiency	18
Lack of motivation for developing communicative competence	17
Resistance to class participation	15
Educational system	61
Large classes	18
Grammar-based examinations	18
Insufficient funding	13
Lack of support	12
CLT	34
Inadequate account of EFL teaching	18
Lack of effective and efficient assessment instruments	16

[a] The number of times the research subjects referred to a theme in either the questionnaire or the interview as a constraint in using the CLT in their own context. The maximum number of mentions possible for each of the themes included within the four major categories is 18.

Difficulties caused by the teacher

[. . .]

Deficiency in spoken English

All 18 participants considered that their own deficiency in spoken English constrained them in applying CLT in their classrooms. As reported by the Korean teachers, the South Korean government wanted CLT implemented because of disappointment about students' oral proficiency in English. The government as well as the teachers hoped that CLT would help students develop better oral English. Although the teachers generally felt that they were highly proficient in English grammar, reading, and writing, they all reported that their abilities in English speaking and listening were not adequate to conduct the communicative classes necessarily involved in CLT. The following comment was typical.

1. I am good at English grammar, reading, and writing. But my oral English is very poor. Since I can't speak English well, how can I teach it to my students?
                                                          (Dong-Soon, July 31, 1995)

Surprisingly, even respondents who spoke English fluently and communicated well thought their English was "too poor to use communicative language teachings" (Jin-Kyu, July 17, 1995). Deficiency in spoken English apparently prevented some teachers from applying CLT, but for others lack of confidence was more likely to have been the reason.

Deficiency in strategic and sociolinguistic competence

All 18 participants reported that their low strategic and sociolinguistic competence in English would limit their use of CLT. As teachers' sociolinguistic and strategic competence must be much greater in a communicative classroom than in a traditional grammar-focused classroom, the participants generally felt incompetent to conduct a communicative class.

2. Students asked more questions in the class. I was happy when they asked me questions related to the English grammar. But those questions that are related to the sociolinguistic aspects of English are really hard for me. . . . In Korea, when you can't answer all of the students' questions right away, you can't be a teacher.
                                                          (Young-Cheol, July 26, 1995)

The fear of losing face because of not being able to answer students' questions all the time discouraged teachers from using CLT.

3. I once tried communicative activities with my Grade 10 kids. The kids enjoyed it. In fact I enjoyed it too, except they asked so many questions related to the English culture. They were interesting questions. Some of them I could answer, and some of them I could not. That made me very much embarrassed. . . . If your kids find that you cannot always answer their questions very confidently, you are going to lose their respect and finally lose them. In our culture, teachers are supposed to know everything and be always correct.
                                                          (Jin-Kyu, July 17, 1995)

Because of their deficiency in sociolinguistic competence in English and fear of losing the respect of their students for being unable to give prompt answers in class, teachers "chose to stick to the traditional grammar-centred, text-centred and teacher-centred methods so that [they] always had a good idea about what was going to happen in every class and made adequate preparations for it" (Dong-Soon, July 31, 1995).

Lack of training in CLT

All 18 participants named lack of training as one of the main obstacles they faced in applying CLT. As reported by the teachers, they had learned about CLT in different ways – in university methods courses, English teaching conferences, and English teaching journals – but they all agreed that they had not practiced it much.

4. Like many of us, I learned CLT when I was studying at university. But it was taught as a piece of knowledge for us to remember, not to use. I did not practice using it while at university, though I did try it a few times later when I became a teacher.
    (Eom-Mi, July 25, 1995)

5. I learned the term *CLT* at a teachers' conference. To be honest, I did not quite understand how it works.
    (Myong-Sook, July 30, 1995)

This lack of systematic training led to a sketchy and usually fragmented understanding of CLT and made it difficult for the teachers "to leave the security of the traditional methods and take the risk of trying new unfamiliar methods" (Tack-Soo, July 20, 1995).

Few opportunities for retraining in CLT

Sixteen teachers reported that few in-service opportunities for retraining in CLT were available. Most of the respondents had not had such opportunities before the teacher education program they were attending at that time. Mi-Ju expressed her frustration when asked about her in-service education.

6. This is the first time I participate in an in-service teacher education program. It took me 18 years to get such an opportunity.
    (Mi-Ju, July 28, 1995)

Even after the publication of the government's new communicative curricula, few in-service teacher education programs offered training in CLT. Without proper retraining, teachers will inevitably misunderstand some elements of CLT.

Misconceptions about CLT

Fifteen respondents referred to teachers' misconceptions about CLT as one of the principal obstacles. A typical misconception was that by concentrating on appropriateness and fluency, CLT does not teach form at all and thus totally neglects accuracy.

7. Before attending this teacher education program, I thought that communicative language teaching does not teach grammar and only teaches speaking. I did not

think that was a good way to teach our kids English. I think grammar should be part of it, at least for our kids. After all, they have to pass a lot of exams and there is a lot of grammar in them.

(Myong-Sook, July 30, 1995)

Such misunderstandings led the teachers to believe that CLT contradicted their beliefs about language learning and did not allow them to prepare students for the various exams that are critical to their future careers. For that reason, the teachers refused to accept CLT.

Little time for and expertise in material development

Fourteen teachers reported that lack of time for and lack of expertise in developing communicative materials had been constraints for them. All the English textbooks available (before the publication of the new series of textbooks accompanying the publication of the communicative curricula) had been developed under the influence of the grammar-translation and audiolingual methods, so teachers had had to write their own materials and design their own activities if they wanted to use CLT. [. . .] This problem was particularly serious for female teachers because they also had to deal with housework.

8.   I teach in a high school. I have to be at school from 8:00 in the morning to 6:30 in the afternoon. When I go home, I have to take care of my two kids. Because my husband teaches away from our home in Seoul, I have to take my kids there at weekends to see him. I really do not have time for any extra work.

(In-Ran, July 24, 1995)

Lack of expertise in designing communicative activities was also a concern among the teachers.

[. . .]

Difficulties caused by the students

[. . .]

Low English proficiency

All 18 respondents reported that one important difficulty preventing them from using CLT was their students' low English proficiency. Korean students do not start to learn English until after they enter middle school (Grade 7), and they have only four 1-hour English classes each week, making progress slow. They usually have a small English vocabulary and a limited command of English structures. Because students did not have the necessary proficiency in English, the teachers found it hard to do any oral communicative activities with them.

9.   The average secondary school students have a very small English vocabulary. They know limited number of English structures. So they have great difficulty to express themselves in English when they are assigned to do communicative activities. Gradually they lose interest in trying to speak English and become too discouraged to speak English any more.

(In-Ran, July 24, 1995)

As pointed out earlier, the Korean teachers believed that CLT necessarily involved speaking activities. Therefore, when oral activities were not possible or appeared to be difficult, the teachers became frustrated with CLT and in most cases gave it up.

10. In such activities, I often see the kids struggling to express themselves in English, only to make each other more confused. . . . I do not know whether I am doing the right thing with the kids. To be safe, I prefer to use the method I am familiar with to help the kids learn.

(Eom-Mi, July 25, 1995)

Little motivation for communicative competence

Seventeen participants identified students' lack of motivation to work on their communicative competence as a great limitation. Although an increasing number of people in South Korea have realized how important it is to be able to communicate in English rather than to know English grammar well, students in secondary schools still care much more about grammar.

11. My students know it is very important to learn to use English for communication. But since their goal is to enter the university, they prefer to work on English grammar because the National University Entrance Exam is grammar based.

(Joon-Suk, July 26, 1995)

Because grammar still plays a decisive role in all English examinations in South Korea, "teachers who teach communicative competence are not liked as well as those who teach grammar" (Mi-Ju, 28/07/95). Students complained that "they [were] not learning anything if they [did] not learn new words and grammar in a class" (Na-Yun, July 26, 1995).

Resistance to class participation

Fifteen respondents cited the students' resistance to class participation as a primary constraint in trying CLT. As students have already been in school for at least 6 years by the time they enter middle school, they have become accustomed to the traditional classroom structure, in which they sit motionless, take notes while the teacher lectures, and speak only when they are spoken to. After so many years of schooling in traditional settings, students rely on the teacher to give them information directly, making it very difficult to get the students to participate in class activities.

The inconsistencies among teachers in their expectations of students also discouraged students from participating in class activities.

12. Especially when English class is the only place where participation is encouraged, it can bring about confusion for the students as most teachers of other subjects will probably never tolerate, not saying encourage class participation.

(Jin-Kyu, July 17, 1995)

To play it safe, students usually chose to behave traditionally in English class. When students were not willing to participate in class activities, teachers saw little chance of fulfilling their goal of using CLT, rendering it pointless to adopt CLT in their class.

Difficulties caused by the educational system

[. . .]

Large classes

All 18 respondents referred to large classes as one of the principal constraints on their attempts to use CLT. In South Korea, a secondary school class usually contains 48–50 students. The teachers found it very difficult, if not entirely impossible, to use CLT with so many students in one class because they believed that oral English and close monitoring of class activities were essential in CLT.

> 13. With that number of students in one class, first of all, it is very difficult for class management if we use the communicative method. For example, when everyone starts to talk, the class can be very noisy. Teachers and students in nearby classrooms will complain about the noise in the English class. Secondly, it is not possible for the teacher to give each of them [individualized] attention as required by the communicative method. Thirdly, with so many students in one regular classroom, there is not even enough space for the students and the teacher to move around to carry out the communicative activities. Especially when the desks and stools are fixed to the floor, you cannot even move them.
>
> (Jin-Kyu, July 17, 1995)

Grammar-based examinations

Grammar-based examinations were named by all 18 respondents as another important constraint. Among the many English examinations in South Korea, the National University Entrance Examination (the English section) is the most important one because other formal and informal English examinations are modeled on it. Until 1994 it consisted mainly of grammar, reading comprehension, and translation items. Now it has an additional part called "Listening Comprehension," but its grammar-based nature has remained unchanged. Teachers, under pressure to make their students do well on such tests, often devote valuable class time to teaching test-taking skills and drilling students on multiple-choice grammar items.

> 14. This exam [the National University Entrance Examination] has had tremendous influence on the English teaching in South Korea. As soon as students start middle school, they have a clear goal in mind – to pass the National University Entrance Examination. Teachers also have a clear goal in mind – to help students succeed in the Examination. Because it only tests students' grammar knowledge and reading ability, both students and teachers are interested in grammar and reading in English classes.
>
> (Young-Cheol, July 26, 1995)

Such an attitude leaves little room for CLT for both teachers and students. As Savignon (1991) observes, many curricular innovations have been undone by a failure to make corresponding changes in evaluation.

Insufficient funding

Thirteen respondents mentioned insufficient funding as a constraint. To use CLT in teaching English, certain equipment and facilities must be in place. Extra funding is needed to obtain resource books and materials for communicative activities. When the funding is not there, using CLT is hard.

15. For example, we will need a photocopier to copy materials for students. That means we need extra money which is not always there. It's always more difficult than you plan and imagine.

(Eom-Mi, July 25, 1995)

Lack of support

Lack of support was cited by 12 respondents as a constraint. Although some of the teachers had learned about CLT in university methods courses, "applying it was yet another thing" (Dong-Soon, July 31, 1995).

16. When I had questions about what I was doing, I talked with my fellow teachers, hoping to get help from them. Often they could not help me. How I wished there was a CLT expert for questions and support.

(Joon-Suk, July 26, 1995)

Teachers also found lack of support from administration frustrating.

17. It's difficult to get help from our administrators. Particularly before the new curriculums were published the principal in my school didn't care about the method I used. He was only interested in the scores my students got in exams. Even now after the publication of the new curriculums, he still cares mostly about the students' scores.

(In-Ran, July 24, 1995)

The respondents also indicated that they seldom got support from fellow instructors teaching other subjects in the same schools.

18. Also, sometimes I needed cooperation from teachers of other subjects; but, for some reasons, they showed little interest in what I was doing.

(In-Ran, July 24, 1995)

Teachers generally found this lack of professional, administrative, and collegial support discouraging. Often they lost interest in coping with the challenges of introducing CLT in their classes.

19. This [lack of support] was extremely discouraging. It was so hard when everything was on your shoulder. Finally I had to give up CLT and return to the peaceful and easy traditional method of teaching English.

(Dong-Soon, July 31, 1995)

Difficulties caused by CLT itself

CLT's inadequate account of EFL teaching

All 18 participants reported that CLT has not given an adequate account of EFL teaching despite its initial growth in foreign language teaching in Europe. The teachers saw important differences between teaching EFL and teaching ESL. They expressed frustration at the fact that the research community, especially many Western language education researchers, has rarely differentiated EFL from ESL.

> 20. In my opinion, EFL is very different from ESL. But many people tend to confuse them and often ignore the special elements of EFL situations. I think that's why we EFL teachers usually find Western language teaching methods difficult to use.
>
> (Joon-Suk, July 26, 1995)

The significant differences that the teachers saw between EFL and ESL included the purposes of learning English, learning environments, teachers' English proficiency, and the availability of authentic English materials.
[. . .]

> 21. For example, in ESL situations, students usually have a very supportive learning environment outside school. They have many chances to hear and speak English outside class, which can reinforce what they learn in class. Besides, they have the motivation to work on oral English because they need it in their lives. In our situation, the classroom is the only place where students can hear and speak English. They do not need to use the language in their lives but only in pretended situations.
>
> (Jin-Kyu, July 17, 1995)

[. . .]

Lack of effective and efficient assessment instruments

Used to traditional discrete-point testing of grammatical knowledge, the teachers found it disconcerting that there were no prescribed, ready-made assessment tools for communicative competence and that they would have to design their own. The Korean teachers believed that one of the best ways to test students' communicative competence was to give the students oral tests. In general, they each taught four classes of approximately 48 students. Finishing even one round of individual oral tests would take a long time, and there was nobody to supervise the other students while the teacher was conducting the tests.

> 22. When you teach four classes and each has nearly 50 students, you are dealing with 200 students. If I have to do oral examinations to assess their communicative competence, it would take me dozens of days to finish just one round.
>
> (Mi-ju, July 28, 1995)

Besides, the Korean teachers generally did not support these subjective tests.

23. There is no way that my colleagues and I would use the same criteria in the test. Even I myself probably cannot use the same criteria all the time. I would probably use different criteria when I am tired after long time of testing.

(Joon-Suk, July 26, 1995)

The teachers also found it difficult to balance content and language when scoring oral exams.

24. About a year ago, for the final exam, besides the written test, I did an oral exam for the students in one of the classes I taught. Giving them a score was so difficult compared with grading the written tests. My biggest problem was how much I should assign to the content of their talk and how much to the language they used. Even before I finished the test, I knew that I used different criteria. I did not like the results of the test because they were not reliable.

(Myong-Sook, July 30, 1995)

Implications of the study

Much of what the Korean teachers said about EFL teaching in their country and about their difficulties in using CLT is common to many parts of the world. The following discussion, although it particularly addresses EFL teaching in South Korea, thus extends to other EFL countries as well.

A conflict apparently exists between what CLT demands and what the EFL situation in many countries, such as South Korea, allows. This conflict must be resolved before EFL teaching in these countries can benefit from CLT. To resolve the conflict, attention should be given to the following areas.

Educational values and attitudes

The fundamental approach to education in Korea needs to change before CLT can be successful there. The predominance of text-centered and grammar-centered practices in Korea does not provide a basis for the student-centered, fluency-focused, and problem-solving activities required by CLT. As Price (1988) points out, reform of education is not simply reform of the school system but reform of the behavior and thinking of the wider social teaching-learning process that guides moral-political ideas and behavior. Far-reaching curriculum innovation involves fundamental shifts in the values and beliefs of the individuals concerned (Brindley and Hood, 1990; Burns, 1996). If CLT is to be implemented in a previously traditional classroom, teachers, students, parents, administrators and other stakeholders must shift their conceptions of what constitutes good English teaching (Enright and McCloskey, 1985; Markee, 1997; Penner, 1995).

However; such a fundamental change takes time. "Changes in the way people think usually lag behind changes in social structure" (Ting, 1987, p. 49). Therefore South Korea and other EFL countries with similar situations should adapt rather than adopt CLT into their English teaching. Rather than simply jumping onto the CLT bandwagon by mandating its use, the government and EFL teachers of South Korea and other EFL countries should carefully study their TEFL situations and decide how CLT can best serve their needs and interests.

Reading

Because the main purpose of learning English for many people in South Korea and other EFL countries is to be able to read and translate into their mother tongue scientific, medical, and technical documents written in English, Korean teachers should continue their emphasis on developing students' reading abilities. However, instead of spending much precious time on intensive reading and grammatical analysis, teachers might introduce some ideas from CLT, such as extensive reading and reading for meaning.

Oral skills

Because the demand for people who can communicate orally in English has increased as the result of international trade and globalization, English classes should include listening and speaking activities. Teachers and administrators must be aware of the shift in societal needs and make conscious and persistent efforts to introduce more CLT into English teaching. With globalization, smaller classes, a better economy, and more competent teachers, a better understanding and acceptance of the philosophical underpinnings of the CLT are possible. South Korea and other EFL countries may then be able to use more CLT or, better still, develop their own "locally appropriate version of the communicative approach" (Tomlinson, 1990, p. 36).

Grammar

Contrary to a common misconception, CLT does not exclude the teaching of grammar. The literature abounds with arguments for including grammar instruction in L2 teaching. However, teachers must also bear in mind that the purpose of teaching grammar is to help students learn the language, and teachers must be wary of making grammar the end of their teaching. [. . .]

Students' attitudes

In introducing CLT to students who have previously studied foreign language in a traditional fashion, teachers are likely to encounter some initial reservations. Thus, teachers will need to consciously reorient students to "the basic function of the classroom, the role of the student and the nature of language" (Deckert, 1987, p. 20).

Teachers' attitudes

Teachers should have assistance and encouragement in trying out new ideas and materials. Continuing support for teachers who may need further help with CLT along the way is also important. [. . .]

Preservice teacher education

The delivery of EFL methods courses in preservice teacher education programs should change. CLT should not be lectured about but demonstrated. Novice teachers should have opportunities to get hands-on experience with and gain confidence in using CLT.

More importantly, considering the dynamic nature of EFL teaching, preservice teacher education should focus on developing student teachers' autonomy and their decision-making and problem-solving abilities as well as their ability to be reflective practitioners (Richards and Lockhart, 1994; Schön, 1983).

Local educational growth

Inasmuch as many teaching methodologies developed in the West are often difficult to introduce into EFL situations with different educational theories and realities, in the long run EFL countries may be better off developing methods in their own contexts. Rather than relying on expertise, methodology, and materials controlled and dispensed by Western ESL countries, EFL countries should strive to establish their own research contingents and encourage methods specialists and classroom teachers to develop language teaching methods that take into account the political, economic, social, and cultural factors and, most important of all, the EFL situations in their countries (Daoud, 1996; Phillipson, 1992). In this way, they will be able to devise teaching methods "appropriate to their learners, their colleagues and their societies" (Edge, 1996, p. 18).

Conclusion

Curriculum innovation involves multiple and interrelated factors that may influence it at different stages and at different levels (Shamin, 1996). "As a socially situated activity, its success is affected by ethical and systemic constraints, the personal characteristics of potential adopters, the attributes of innovations and the strategies that are used to manage change in particular contexts" (Markee, 1997, p. 41). In any attempt to improve education, teachers are central to long-lasting changes (Frymier, 1987; Fullan, 1993). How teachers as the end users of an innovation perceive its feasibility is a crucial factor in the ultimate success or failure of that innovation.

References

Anderson, J. (1993). "Is a communicative approach practical for teaching English in China? Pros and cons." *System*, 21, 471–480.

Bachman, L. F. (1990). *Fundamental considerations in language testing*. Oxford: Oxford University Press.

Bailey, M. B. (1992). "The process of innovation in language teacher education: What, why and how teachers change." In J. Flowerdew, M. Brock and S. Hsia (Eds.), *Perspectives on second language teacher education* (pp. 253–282). Hong Kong: City Polytechnic of Hong Kong.

Berg, B. L. (1989). *Qualitative research methods for the social sciences*. Boston: Allyn and Bacon.

Bhargava, R. (1986, April). *Communicative language teaching: A case of much ado about nothing*. Paper presented at the 20th Annual Meeting of the International Association of Teachers of English as a Foreign Language, Brighton, England.

Bogdan, R. and Biklen, S. K. (1992). *Qualitative research for education: An introduction to theory and methods*. London: Allyn and Bacon.

Brindley, G. and Hood, S. (1990). "Curriculum innovation in adult ESL." In G. Brindley (Ed.), *The second language curriculum in action* (pp. 232–248). Sydney, Australia: National Centre for English Language Teaching and Research.

Burnaby, B. and Sun, Y. (1989). "Chinese teachers' views of Western language teaching: Context informs paradigm." *TESOL Quarterly*, 23, 219–238.

Burns, A. (1996). "Collaborative research and curriculum change in the Australian Migrant English Program." *TESOL Quarterly*, 30, 591–598.

Canale, M. and Swain, M. (1980). "Theoretical basis of communicative approaches to second language learning and testing." *Applied Linguistics*, 1, 1–47.

Chau, L. and Chung, C. (1987). "Diploma in education graduates' attitude toward communicative language teaching." *Chinese University Education Journal*, 15(2), 45–51.

Chick, J. K. (1996). "Safe-talk; Collusion in apartheid education." In H. Coleman (Ed.), *Society and the language classroom* (pp. 21–39). Cambridge: Cambridge University Press.

Daoud, M. (1996). "English language development in Tunisia." *TESOL Quarterly*, 30, 598–605.

Deckert, G. (1987). "The communicative approach: Helping students adjust." *English Teaching Forum*, 25(3), 17–20.

Development Committee of the Sixth Curriculum for High School English. (1992). *The report on the revision of the English curriculum for high school*. Seoul, Korea: Author.

Edge, J. (1996). "Cross-cultural paradoxes in a profession of values." *TESOL Quarterly*, 30, 9–30.

Ellis, G. (1994). "The appropriateness of the communicative approach in Vietnam: An interview study in intercultural communication." Unpublished master's thesis, La Trobe University, Bundoora, Australia.

Ellis, G. (1996). "How culturally appropriate is the communicative approach?" *ELT Journal*, 50, 213–218.

Enright, D. S. and McCloskey, M. L. (1985). "Yes, talking! Organizing the classroom to promote second language acquisition." *TESOL Quarterly*, 19, 431–453.

Fotos, S. S. (1994). "Integrating grammar instruction and communicative language use through grammar consciousness-raising tasks." *TESOL Quarterly*, 28, 323–351.

Freeman, D. and Cazden, C. B. (1990). "Learning to talk like a professional: Some pragmatics of foreign language teacher training." *Pragmatics and Language Learning*, 2, 225–245.

Frymier, J. (1987). "Bureaucracy and the neutering of teachers." *Phi Delta Kappan*, 69, 9–14.

Fullan, M. (1993). *Change forces: Probing the depths of educational reform*. London: Falmer Press.

Goetz, J. P. and LeCompte, M. D. (1984). *Ethnography and qualitative design in educational research*. New York: Academic Press.

Gonzalez, A. (1985). "Communicative language teaching in the rural areas: How does one make the irrelevant relevant?" In B. K Das (Ed.), *Communicative language teaching* (pp. 84–105). Singapore: Singapore University Press.

Harvey, P. (1985). A lesson to be learned: Chinese approaches to language learning. *ELT Journal*, 39, 183–186.

Holliday, A. (1994). *Appropriate methodology and social context*. New York: Cambridge University Press.

Kelly, P. (1980). "From innovation to adaptability: The changing perspective of curriculum development." In M. Galton (Ed.), *Curriculum change: The lessons of a decade* (pp. 65–80). Leicester, England: Leicester University Press.

Kennedy, C. (1988). "Evaluation of the management of change in ELT projects." *Applied Linguistics*, 9, 329–342.

Kirkpatrick, T. A. (1984). "The role of communicative language teaching in secondary schools: With special reference to teaching in Singapore." In B. K. Das (Ed.), *Communicative language teaching* (pp. 171–191). Singapore: Singapore University Press.

Larsen-Freeman, D. (1986). *Techniques and principles in language teaching*. New York: Oxford University Press.

Lee, C. (1990). "Korean high school seniors' oral and literate comprehension and production skills in English." Unpublished doctoral dissertation, Harvard University, Boston.

Li, X. J. (1984). "In defense of the communicative approach." *ELT Journal*, 38, 2–13.

North, B. (1997). "Perspectives on language proficiency and aspects of competence." *Language Teaching*, 30(2), 93–100.

Penner, J. (1995). "Change and conflict: Introduction of the communicative approach in China." *TESL Canada Journal*, 12(2), 1–17.

Phillipson, R. (1992). *Linguistic imperialism*. Oxford: Oxford University Press.

Powney, J. and Watts, M. (1987). *Interviewing in educational research*. London: Routledge.

Prabhu, N. S. (1987). *Second language pedagogy*. Oxford: Oxford University Press.

Price, R. F. (1988). "The politics of contemporary educational reform in China." In E. B. Gumbert (Ed.), *Making the future: Politics and educational reform in the United States, England, the Soviet Union, China, and Cuba* (pp. 99–114). Atlanta: Georgia State University.

Richards, J. C. and Lockhart, C. (1994). *Reflective teaching in second language classrooms*. Cambridge: Cambridge University Press.

Sampson, G. P. (1984). "Exporting language teaching methods from Canada to China." *TESL Canada Journal*, 1(1), 19–32.

Sampson, G. P. (1990). "Teaching English literacy using Chinese strategies." *TESL Talk*, 20(1), 126–138.

Sano, M., Takahashi, M. and Yoneyama, A. (1984). "Communicative language teaching and local needs." *ELT Journal*, 38, 170–177.

Savignon, S. (1991). "Communicative language teaching: State of the art." *TESOL Quarterly*, 25, 261–277.

Savignon, S. and Berns, M. (1984). *Initiatives in communicative language teaching: A book of readings*. Reading, MA: Addison-Wesley.

Schön, D. A. (1983). *The reflective practitioner: How professionals think in action*. London: Temple Smith.

Shamin, F. (1996). "Learner resistance to innovation in classroom methodology." In H. Coleman (Ed.), *Society and the language classroom* (pp. 105–121). Cambridge: Cambridge University Press.

South Korean Ministry of Education. (1992a). *The sixth curriculum for high schools*. Seoul, Korea: Author.

South Korean Ministry of Education. (1992b). *The sixth curriculum for middle schools*. Seoul, Korea: Author.

Tilleman, H. H. (1994). Training and professional expertise: Bridging the gap between new information and pre-existing beliefs of teachers. *Teaching and Teacher Education*, 10, 601–615.

Ting, Y. R. (1987). "Foreign language teaching in China: Problems and perspectives." *Canadian and International Education*, 16, 48–61.

Tomlinson, B. (1990). "Managing change in Indonesian high schools." *ELT Journal*, 44, 25–37.

Valdes, A. I. and Jhones, A. C. (1991). "Introduction of communicative language teaching in tourism in Cuba." *TESL Canada Journal*, 8(2), 57–63.

White, R. V. (1987). "Managing innovation." *ELT Journal*, 41, 211–218.

Wilkins, D. A. (1972). *The linguistic and situational content of the common core in a unit/credit system*. Strasbourg, France: Council of Europe.

Appendix: questionnaire

Please complete the following questions as appropriate.

1 Age _____

2 Sex _____

3 How many years have you been a teacher of English? _____

4 Are you teaching in a middle school or high school?

    ☐ Middle School   ☐ High School

5 Which grade(s) are you teaching? _____

6 Are you teaching in an urban or rural middle/high school?

    ☐ Urban   ☐ Rural

7 Are you concerned about the methods you use in teaching English?

    ☐YES   ☐NO

8 What methods are you using now?

9 Have you tried Communicative Language Teaching (CLT)?

    ☐YES   ☐NO

10 Why did you or why didn't you try CLT?

11 How did you like using CLT in your classroom?

12 The following are some difficulties that other EFL teachers had in adopting CLT. Did you come across these difficulties or do you think they might be difficulties for you in adopting CLT in South Korea?

1 Teachers' deficiency in spoken English?   ☐YES ☐NO

2 Teachers' deficiency in strategic and sociolinguistic competence in English?   ☐YES ☐NO

3 Teachers' having little time to write communicative materials?   ☐YES ☐NO

4 Students' low English proficiency?   ☐YES ☐NO

5 Students' passive style of learning?   ☐YES ☐NO

6 Lack of authentic teaching materials?   ☐YES ☐NO

7 Grammar-based examinations?   ☐YES ☐NO

8 Large classes?   ☐YES ☐NO

9 The differences between EFL and ESL?   ☐YES ☐NO

PART THREE

Planning and implementing curriculum change

Chapter 14

Adrian Holliday

ACHIEVING CULTURAL CONTINUITY IN CURRICULUM INNOVATION

Introduction

IN THIS PAPER I AM GOING TO LOOK AT the issue of cultural continuity in curriculum innovation. My major point will be that a major obstacle to true cultural continuity is our own professional discourses which prevent us from seeing the real worlds of the people we work with. We therefore need to be critically aware of ourselves as cultural actors and learn how to see the people we work with in their own terms instead of in our terms.

I shall begin with the principle of cultural continuity and why it is important both in the classroom and the wider domain of the curriculum and curriculum projects. I shall then demonstrate how professional discourses create obstacles to cultural continuity, and how this might be avoided.

The principle of cultural continuity

Cultural continuity is achieved when meaningful bridges are built between the culture of the innovation and the traditional expectations of the people with whom we work. The notion of 'cultural continuity' is taken from Jacob (1996), who is interested in the way in which the teacher mediates between a 'foreign' lesson content and the 'local' orientation of her or his students. However, it can be used to refer to a broader aim which has become common in TESOL in the last ten years – to be sensitive to the cultural expectations of the 'recipients' of innovation, whether they be students or teachers encountering new teaching methodologies, or stakeholders in curriculum projects. Phillipson (1992) and Pennycook (1994) have drawn our attention to the dangers of cultural or linguistic imperialism when dominant forms of professionalism in TESOL are transported from one place to another, as has my own work on how to make classroom and curriculum project methodologies 'appropriate' to social context (Holliday, 1994). The now influential phrase, 'appropriate methodology' was introduced into TESOL by Bowers many years ago (Bowers and Widdowson, 1986). The plea for more attention to the sociopolitical environment of TESOL was made by Swales several years earlier (1980). Coleman's (1996) work on the influence of society on what happens in the classroom is a more recent part of this movement, as is recent critical thinking about how the paradigms of TESOL professionalism have been socially constructed (Beaumont and Wright, 1998). The basic idea of cultural continuity is that a particular innovation is adjusted to enable the best possible fit with a host environment (Figure 14.1). It is a two-way process in that the innovation needs to be informed by data from the host environment.

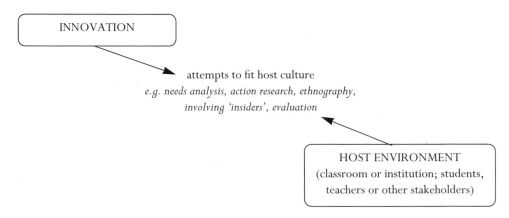

Figure 14.1 Cultural continuity

The dominant discourses of teaching

There is a strange irony here, which involves the problematic nature of learner-centredness and skills-based education. At first sight, learner-centredness and the teaching of skills would seem to support the possibility of cultural continuity in that they follow the principle that teaching should connect with the perceptions and needs of the student. Indeed, learner-centredness represents an admirable attempt in education, since the 1960s, to allow students a more interactive, participant role in the classroom. At the same time the teaching and learning of skills implied that the content of education had to be useful to the needs of the learner and the environment in which she or he was to operate.

However, with deeper analysis, various writers in education, such as Usher and Edwards (1994), following the critical sociology of Foucault, are beginning to argue that learner-centredness and skills-based education might be having the opposite effect. The 1970s and 1980s brought an increased need for accountability; and a skills-based education lent itself well to the measurement of student progress through the achievement of discrete learning objectives. The breaking down of skills into competencies was instrumental in this. The outcome is a bureaucratisation of learner-centredness. Usher and Edwards (ibid.) argue that in seeing the student in terms of a set of pre-defined, measurable competencies and skills, she or he is reduced to a learning automaton. Thus, the 'learner' at the centre of learner-centredness is no longer a real person, but a product of measurable educational technology.

Two things are going on here. First, what claims to be a sensitivity to the 'learner' – learner-centredness – has become a breaking up of the student into teachable skills. Second, the terminology with which education speaks about the 'learner' has become highly technical. Hence, learner-centredness becomes what Fairclough (1995) calls a 'technologised discourse' which appears ideologically neutral but in fact represents the bureaucratic and ideological needs, not of the 'learner', but of a particular professional group. Clark and Ivanic assert that: '"Skills" [. . .] suggests a set of neutral technologies or techniques that are somehow separate and separable from the social context. [. . .] It has led to the viewing of language and language activities as consisting of discrete, apparently manageable and "teachable" components, and so appears to facilitate teaching and learning. It implies a normative and prescriptive view of communication' (1997: 84).

This perception is being confirmed in research into the ideological basis for TESOL professionalism. Baxter (in process) has noted that in teacher training programmes, despite the liberal rhetoric of learner-centredness, the real concern is with the technology of teaching, which is presented as ideologically neutral, in which the 'learner' becomes an accessory – for the purpose of accountable professionalism.

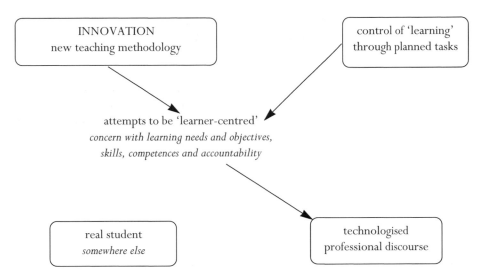

Figure 14.2 Professionally constructed image of 'the learner'

Hence, although we might claim learner-centredness, we construct an image of 'the learner' within our own powerful, technical discourse of professionalism. This is illustrated in Figure 14.2. If the innovation is a new classroom methodology claiming 'learner-centredness', the surface implication is that there will therefore be a concern with the needs of 'the learner'. However, the technologised professional discourse of learner-centredness takes attention away from the real student. Learning needs and objectives, skills and competencies serve the accountability required by the discourse rather than the real student. The outcome is a control of 'learning' through planned tasks, again, serving the technical needs of the discourse rather than the real student.

The dominant discourse of project management

I will now move on to the more macro issue of curriculum innovation and argue that a similar process is taking place. The problem here concerns the way in which the so-called recipients of curriculum innovation are perceived, accommodated and managed.

There has been much recent concern that curriculum innovation should be sensitive to the local setting. This has resulted in what has been called a more person-sensitive process approach to curriculum project management. The *process project* claims adaptation to situational needs. And in what might be called a *stakeholder-centred* approach, groups of local people are quite rightly identified as representatives of these needs; and strategies are developed to satisfy their interests and maintain their *ownership* of the innovation. Stakeholders can be broadly defined as all the people who have a stake in the innovation. Several examples of this can be seen in Hayes (1997b). In projects in Indonesia and Thailand,

Ambrose-Yeoh reports how eighty-seven secondary school teachers are consulted 'in a feasibility study', and in the resulting training:

> A generally friendly and interactive style was adopted to counter any sense of isolation. [. . .] To personalise the materials and to establish rapport with the teachers, passive language was generally avoided and there was also deliberate choice of pronouns such as 'we', 'I' and 'you' over pronouns such as 'they' or 'he' or 'she'.
>
> (1997: 89–90)

In Malta, Jarvis and Cameron (1997) monitor the changing roles of teachers as they adopt and interpret innovation. Also, Martin and Balabanis (1995) describe how in Egypt, 'working parties' are set up to involve senior representatives from USAID, the Ministry of Education and the language centre where the innovation was to take place, and negotiate consensus. Similarly, Weir and Roberts (1994) describe how 'insiders' become involved in the evaluation of the innovation process, in, for example, the establishment of 'baseline' data, and how formative evaluation becomes integrated with self-directed teacher development.

There is however a problem with this stakeholder-centred approach, similar to the problem with the learner-centred approach which I have already described. As with the classroom, there is a strange irony. As with learner-centredness, a technologised professional discourse has been created. Weir and Roberts (1994) rightly note that as the concept of formative evaluation in TESOL matures, it takes on the role of quality control. Indeed, it falls in line with the growing dominant ideology of late modern society in which everything has to be accountable to the client. Even the process project has to be commodified along with the other aspects of education and other institutional practices such as medicine noted by Usher and Edwards (1994) and Fairclough (1995). Thus, we have a professionally constructed image of the 'stakeholder', as we do of the 'learner' (Figure 14.3).

As with the technologised discourse of learner-centredness, the technologised discourse of stakeholder-centredness has an emphasis on control (right hand bubble). Here the control is situated in a proliferation of highly technical project documents, at the centre of which are the current log-frame and time-lines for resource input. Although these documents are, quite rightly, intended as the product of 'agreement' with key stakeholders, they are very

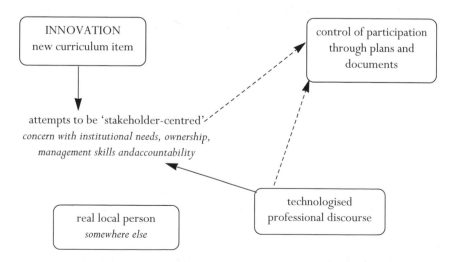

Figure 14.3 Professionally constructed image of 'the stakeholder'

much the product of the technologised discourse itself. This is very clear when stakeholders who do not belong to this discourse find them incomprehensible.

In my experience, there is an interesting puzzle here. There is often the *appearance* of agreement between the various parties with regard to project documentation. The hyperrational project discourse takes this as evidence that there is real agreement. Stakeholders coming from different discourses of their own might see the situation differently, and be prepared to go through the motions of agreement for their own ulterior motives. This type of phenomenon is well documented in Holliday (1994), where I describe the operation of informal orders and deep action within the host environment, which have stakeholders pursuing their own ends in their own ways. The following warning by Taylor against naïve notions of mutuality rings true:

> Establishment and maintenance of sustained dialogue between all those involved [. . .] [is] not easy [. . .] There are barriers and inequalities of language, culture and education, and frequently even the need for such dialogue is not recognised by either side. There is unfamiliarity on both sides with the use of common management tools for the sharing and analysis of information (from project frameworks, analysis, tables, grids and diagrams to statistical methods and computer programmes).
>
> (1997: 116–17)

Something similar was found by Smith (1991), who noted that notions of 'control', 'predictability', 'generalisation' and 'objective' were constructed differently by different parties in educational innovation in a number of scenarios.

An important extension of the discourse of stakeholder-centredness is the equally technologised discourse of evaluation, which bases itself very much on the carefully measured and verified consensus of stakeholders. If this consensus is only apparent, then the technology of evaluation cannot be as sound as it appears. According to Fairclough (1995), a political, though tacit and perhaps unconscious motive of technologised discourses in late modern societies is to create a false image of consensus as we find ourselves gradually consumed by the behavioural technicalities which they demand. As we try to get our heads around the discourse of quality control we find ourselves more and more taking part in it, especially as the discourse takes on the appearance of *inviting* us to participate in our own way. I do not somehow think that the local participants in many curriculum projects are taken in in this way. They have other discourses of their own to get on with.

Empowerment and ownership

This state of affairs throws an interesting light on the way in which the behaviour of stakeholders is perceived and constructed by the technologised discourse of stakeholder-centredness. In much of the literature on stakeholders, there is a tacit power distinction made between those parties who somehow instigate, manage, fund, design, and possess the technology of innovation, and those who do not. In TESOL projects this distinction can be expressed easily in terms of expatriate, 'native speaker' 'experts' on the one hand, and 'local' personnel on the other. This also corresponds with the 'insider-outsider' distinction, where expatriate agencies and personnel come from outside in every sense of the word, and insiders are local not only to the innovation scenario but to the country within which it takes place.

It is important to stress that I am talking here about *perceptions* created within the *discourse* of a particular innovation methodology, which constructs the reality of innovation scenarios in a particular way, rather than the *reality*. It is also important to stress that the writers of literature within the discourse might themselves be unaware of the ideological principles they are perpetuating. Fairclough (1995: 36) makes the point that people are often 'standardly unaware' of the ideological meanings which have become normalised within their own language. Clark and Ivanic (1997: 176) confirm this when they cite a study which shows that many people are often not aware of the deeper ideological meanings of what they read. Thus, it is the discourse, rather than individual actors within it, which reveals an 'us'–'them' distinction found in the literature.

Clark and Ivanic (1997) make the point that the act of writing is itself a struggle within a world where competing discourses vie for hegemony. Such a struggle can be seen in the way in which Smith (1995) writes about a key stakeholder group which falls into the local-insider category of '*counterparts*' – the people who work alongside 'expert' expatriate curriculum developers with whom there is some form of transfer to enable the innovation to continue after the 'expert' has left.

Smith suggests that it cannot be denied that there may be a power difference in many developing world locations, when the expatriate 'expert' has the 'privileges [. . .] granted to (or assumed by) the foreign guest' which enable access to budgets, key locations, events and people, and the counterpart does not, and is then expected 'to sustain project impact after the aid has been withdrawn' on 'US$25 per month' (1995: 67–8). Discussion of whether or not this is always the case involves looking more deeply at the whole relationship between insiders and outsiders; but here one can suspect that the problem might not so much be one of power *per se*, but of the nature of the technology which the counterpart is expected to carry on. Might it be that what the 'expert' is considered to be *expert* in is not sufficiently compatible, or too ethnocentric to the *discourse of stakeholder-centredness* from the outset? Smith acknowledges that a more 'humanistic approach' to project 'sustainability' must get 'closer to the ways of the recipient' and that the power required to sustain the innovation may not be something the counterpart simply does not have, but something which she or he might 'refuse to accept' (1995: 67). Here, as in so much of this literature, there is a concerted *effort* to get to grips with and understand the viewpoint of the 'local', but the outcome, the insistence that 'empowerment' of the 'local' is the answer, is still deeply rooted in the 'us'–'them' perception, in which 'they' 'don't know the technology' and are 'easily dominated'.

Although analysts do try to get under the surface at the deeper social issues, and really do try to understand the viewpoints and predicament of other parties in innovation contexts, they tend to consider large cultural factors as the overriding issue. Hence, Smith puts 'cultural' at the top of his list of 'obstacles' to empowerment. Speaking about Cambodia he suggests that local personnel:

> will have to push hard to bring about any changes. This will be difficult where culturally one defers to and is not assertive towards someone higher in the hierarchy. [. . .] Others have noted the 'cultural nature of management' [. . .] and the 'differing cultural concepts as to the appropriate roles for professionals employed in the public sector'.
>
> (1995: 71)

He continues to state the 'need for a thorough understanding by outsiders of the host culture into which the innovation is being introduced' (ibid.: 74 citing Leach). He thus alludes to the model of cultural thinking seen in Hofstede, who looks at 'the consequences of national cultural differences in the way people in a country organise themselves' and how 'organisational practices and theories are culturally dependent' (1991: xiii).

The rational, systematic nature of this national culture model fits well with the technical needs of the discourse of stakeholder-centredness, as it does with many activities, such as management, which seek to commodify human difference efficiently. Following this line of thinking, Flew sees 'counterpart training' as essentially an 'interpersonal interaction across cultures'. She quite rightly shrinks from the perception of a one-way transfer from culturally superior expatriate curriculum developer to culturally inferior counterparts as 'potentially patronising' (1995: 76) and recommends 'mutual learning between people from different cultures (1995: 81). One wonders, however, whether 'trust and esteem (1995: 78) will be sufficient to break the 'us'–'them' paradigm and stand in the way of a potentially damaging culturist process of mutual otherisation. On the one hand, one would not nowadays recommend a professional exchange of views on the basis of a sharing of gender or racial difference. On the other hand, the headings 'training' and 'empowerment' under which the exchange takes place seem to indicate the ideology of only one side.

Overall, the literature on stakeholders seems to create the 'us'–'them' distinction in a very particular way (Figure 14.4). On the one hand, 'they' are deficient, mainly in terms of the technologised discourse itself; on the other hand, they are classified as such very much in the same way, perhaps regardless of their so-called national culture. One implication here is that the major agent of difference is not the national culture at all, but the power of the technologised discourse. A colleague of mine in a project in India commented that the project created the notion of 'all Indians together'. Perhaps it is not just Indians, but anyone who does not conform to the discourse. Again, an important implication here is what does it all mean if the 'Indians' do not really want to conform to the project after all?

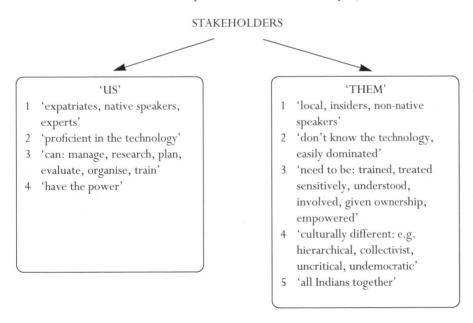

Figure 14.4 'Us' – 'them' configuration

Alternative ways of looking

There needs to be an alternative way of looking at the people we work with in innovation scenarios – in their own terms rather than ours. There is some literature developing in TESOL which begins to do this. Hayes attempts to do this as he records personal accounts of what it is like to be a teacher. Thus:

One teacher recorded her experience. 'When you speak English everybody will (say to you) "What language you do?" Other teachers (will say) "You are strange . . . you try to show off like this" '. [. . .] It is in relation to their position in society, the culture and traditions of their schools and accepted norms of behaviour within their classrooms that teachers in Thailand have to 're-interpret (INSET activities) in their own terms'.

(Hayes, 1997a: 80)

Similarly, Barmada, revisiting the curriculum project at Damascus University in which I was involved in the early 1980s, reveals an insight unnoticed by me in five years of project-motivated investigation:

But sometimes I feel as if I represent the West in the classroom and as if I were telling my students that our methods of learning and thinking are not good and should be replaced by those of the West [. . .] 'unpaid soldiers of the West'. This made my [sic] very nervous. I should pay attention to what I say in the classroom.

(1994: 175)

Understanding ourselves

Something else we need to do is to become aware of the fact that what we do as professionals is not ideologically neutral, but that it is part of a powerful, dangerous, ideological technologised discourse. We must come to terms with the fact that our discourse makes us see others in our own terms, and not in theirs. We must not be naïve to assume that technologies of investigation, evaluation, quality control and management created within our own discourses are equally meaningful to other people. We must come to terms with the fact that the bridges we build to reach other cultures might only be meaningful to our culture. The concepts of learner-centredness and stakeholder-centredness are products of our own discourses, and may not belong to the differently constructed worlds of those we wish to reach. We thus need to look deeply and critically at our own discourses before judging those of others.

Bibliography

Ambrose-Yeoh, A. (1997) 'Distance education and in-service language teacher development', in Hayes, D. (ed.) 86–89.

Barmada, W. (1994) 'Developing an institutional self-evaluation scheme in an ESP Centre in the Arab world: rationale, experimentation and evaluation', unpublished PhD thesis, Department of Linguistics, University of Leeds.

Baxter, A. (In process) 'The reproduction of professional culture through teacher education for ELT', unpublished paper, Department of Language Studies, Canterbury Christ Church University College.

Beaumont, M. and Wright, T. (1998) 'ELT and paradigm shifts: in from the cold or out on a limb', unpublished paper presented at the IATEFL conference, Manchester.

Bowers, R. and Widdowson, H. (1986) 'A debate on appropriate methodology' in Abbott, G. and Beaumont, M. (eds) The development of ELT: the Dunford Seminars 1978–1993, ELT Review, Hemel Hempstead: Prentice Hall and the British Council 141–5.

Clark, R. and Ivanic, R. (1997) The politics of writing London: Routledge.

Coleman, H. (ed.) (1996) Society and the language classroom Cambridge: Cambridge University Press.

Crooks, T. and Crewes, G. (eds) (1995) *Language and development* Bali: IALF.

Fairclough, N. (1995) *Critical discourse analysis: the critical study of language* London: Addison Wesley Longman.

Flew, A. (1995) 'Counterpart training and sustainability: effecting an exchange of skills' in Crooks, T. and Crewes, G. (eds) 76–82.

Hayes, D. (1997a) 'Articulating the context' in Hayes (ed.) 74–85.

Hayes, D. (ed.) (1997b) *In-service teacher development: international perspectives ELT Review* London: Prentice Hall.

Hofstede, G. (1991) *Cultures and organisations: software of the mind* Maidenhead: McGraw-Hill.

Holliday, A. R. (1994) *Appropriate methodology and social context* Cambridge: Cambridge University Press.

Jacob, G. (1996) 'The CDS co-ordinator', unpublished paper, Department of English, University of Pune, India.

Jarvis, J. and Cameron, L. (1997) 'Role shifting in INSET: an exploration of a primary English project' in Hayes, D. (ed.) 37–49.

Martin, W. M. and Balabanis, L. P. (1995) 'Team development in ELT projects: a case study' in Crooks, T. and Crewes, G. (eds) 16–30.

Pennycook, A. (1994) *The cultural politics of English as an international language* London: Addison Wesley Longman.

Phillipson, R. (1992) *Linguistic imperialism* Oxford: Oxford University Press.

Smith, H. (1995) 'Power and sustainability in language-related development projects' in Crooks, T. and Crewes, G. (eds) 65–75.

Smith, N. L. (1991) 'Evaluation reflections: the context of investigations in cross-cultural evaluations' in *Studies in Educational Evaluation*, 17, 3–21.

Swales, J. (1980) 'The educational environment and its relevance to ESP programme design' in *Projects in Materials Design*, ELT Documents Special. London: The British Council, 61–70.

Taylor, G. (1997) 'Management issues in INSET: a practical perspective' in Hayes, D. (ed.) 116–127.

Usher, R. and Edwards, R. (1994) *Postmodernism and education: different voices, different worlds* London: Routledge.

Weir, C. J. and Roberts, J. (1994) *Evaluation in ELT* Oxford: Blackwell.

Chapter 15

Kathleen Graves

A FRAMEWORK OF COURSE
DEVELOPMENT PROCESSES

C URRICULUM DESIGN SPECIALISTS have developed various frameworks
that break down the process of curriculum and course development into components
and subprocesses (see, for example, Dubin and Olshtain 1986; Hutchinson and Waters 1987;
Johnson 1989; Nunan 1985, 1988a, 1988b; Richards 1990; White 1988). A framework of
components is useful for several reasons: It provides an organized way of conceiving of a
complex process; it sets forth domains of inquiry for the teacher, in that each component
puts forth ideas as well as raises issues for the teacher to pursue; it provides a set of terms
currently used in talking about course development and thus a common professional
vocabulary and access to the ideas of others. The framework described here, while drawing
on the work of others, is cast in terms of my own work with teachers. It is not a framework
of equal parts: Each individual's context determines which processes need the most time
and attention. Furthermore, the processes are not necessarily sequential but may be carried
on in the planning, teaching, and replanning stages of course development.

In Table 15.1, each component is identified and rephrased in question form to clarify
its meaning.

Needs assessment

What are my students' needs? How can I assess them so that I can address them?

What is needs assessment,[1] and why does a teacher undertake it? At its most basic,
needs assessment involves finding out what the learners know and can do and what they
need to learn or do so that the course can bridge the gap (or some part of it). Thus needs
assessment involves seeking and interpreting information about one's students' needs so
that the course will address them effectively. However, how one defines a student's needs
is a complex issue open to interpretation. One way of conceptualizing needs is to distinguish
between "objective" and "subjective" needs (Richterich 1980). Brindley (1989: 70) defines
objective needs as "derivable from different kinds of factual information about learners, their
use of language in real-life communication situations as well as their current language
proficiency and language difficulties" and *subjective needs* as "the cognitive and affective needs
of the learner in the learning situation, derivable from information about affective and
cognitive factors such as personality, confidence, attitudes, learners' wants and expectations

Table 15.1 Framework components

Needs assessment: What are my students' needs? How can I assess them so that I can address them?

Determining goals and objectives: What are the purposes and intended outcomes of the course? What will my students need to do or learn to achieve these goals?

Conceptualizing content: What will be the backbone of what I teach? What will I include in my syllabus?

Selecting and developing materials and activities: How and with what will I teach the course? What is my role? What are my students' roles?

Organization of content and activities: How will I organize the content and activities? What systems will I develop?

Evaluation: How will I assess what students have learned? How will I assess the effectiveness of the course?

Consideration of resources and constraints: What are the givens of my situation?

---

with regard to the learning of English and their individual cognitive style and learning strategies."

In assessing objective needs, one can include information about students' backgrounds – country and culture, education, family, profession, age, languages spoken, and so on; students' abilities or proficiency in speaking, understanding, reading, and writing English; and students' needs with respect to how they will use or deal with English outside of the classroom. In assessing subjective needs, one can include information about students' attitudes toward the target language and culture, toward learning, and toward themselves as learners; students' expectations of themselves and of the course; students' underlying purposes – or lack thereof – in studying English; and students' preferences with respect to how they will learn.

Different students have different needs, and the information gathered through needs assessment can help a teacher make choices as to what to teach and how to teach it. For example, students who wish to attend universities in English-speaking countries will have needs related to academic tasks and academic discourse. Objective information about their prior experience in academic settings, their level of English, and their field of study can contribute to the teacher's decisions about her course. Their subjective needs may be related to concerns about adjusting to the university setting and to a new culture, their level of self-confidence, or their expectations regarding what and how they will be taught. Subjective needs are often as important as objective needs. Teachers may find that unless subjective needs are taken into account, objective needs may not be met.

Who provides information about needs? Who determines the needs? A needs assessment can include input from students as well as from the various people connected to the course, such as teachers, funders, parents, administration, and employers. In a university ESL setting, for example, information from the students' future professors regarding what the students will be expected to read, research, and present can help the teacher shape her course (Tarone and Yule 1989; see also Hewings and Hewings, p. 71 this volume). Teachers may have to work with a conception of needs determined by their institution or other party and conduct their assessment accordingly.

When does one conduct a needs assessment? Depending on one's context, needs assessment can be conducted in stage 1, the planning stage; in stage 2, the teaching stage; and also in stage 3, the replanning stage, if one determines that the assessment must be modified in some way. Teachers who have contact with their students prior to teaching the course can undertake a precourse needs assessment. In many cases, however, a formal precourse needs assessment is neither necessary nor appropriate. Some teachers are able to make fairly accurate assumptions about their students' needs with respect to the course on the basis of prior experience with the course or with those particular students. In many cases, precourse assessment is simply not feasible because the teacher does not have contact with the students until the first day of class.

Another important factor in deciding when to assess needs is the teacher's view of the purpose of needs assessment. Needs assessment can also be a teaching tool because it can help students become more aware and more purposeful in their learning. Many teachers see it as an ongoing part of teaching, on the one hand, because it may take time to establish the kind of rapport with students that allows for a clear understanding of needs and, on the other, because they view it as a teaching tool that enables them to work in partnership with their students to determine needs and ensure that the course meets those needs. Teachers who use needs assessment as an ongoing part of their classes develop activities that help students clarify and focus their needs. Such activities can include mindmapping (creating word maps based on, for example, the word *writing*) and student-generated questionnaires (Grant and Shank 1993). [. . .]

How does one conduct a needs assessment? Teachers use a variety of methods. Questionnaires are a common needs assessment tool. They can be written in English or, when appropriate and feasible, in the native language of the students. One of the challenges in designing a questionnaire is choosing questions that will be interpreted correctly and will provide the information sought, especially if one is seeking subjective data. Interviews with students and others (such as employers or professors) are another common way of finding out students' needs. Other means include observation of or, in some cases, participation in the situations in which students will use English. Teachers may obtain samples of written materials, such as manuals or textbooks, that students will have to use. Stern (1992) cautions against gathering so much data that one cannot analyze and put it to use.

Tests and interviews that measure proficiency are also a part of needs assessment because they help determine what students already know and where they are lacking. Many institutions administer proficiency tests for placement purposes. Teachers may also design in-class activities for the first days of class that measure students' proficiency in reading, writing, speaking, or listening.

Hutchinson and Waters (1987: 54) make a distinction between *target needs* ("what the learner needs to do in the target situation") and *learning needs* ("what the learner needs to do in order to learn"). Needs assessment is clearly a sensible undertaking when students have target needs – real-life language needs and a context for using the language skills gained in class, as for immigrants to an English-speaking country, students studying or planning to study in English-speaking schools, or people who use English in their work. However, even when needs are clear, as with immigrants learning to function in a new culture, they may be so general that the teacher has to find ways to assess and define them so that they can be translated into realistic goals. The challenge becomes focusing the needs assessment so as to provide adequate but not overwhelming data on which to base decisions.

In other contexts – particularly, but not only, EFL contexts – teachers face a different problem because many of their students have no target needs, no clearly anticipated use for the skills gained through study. English may be a requirement for an exit or entrance exam. It may be viewed as a subject like math or science, or it may be a social undertaking like the study of music. For these students, the notion of needs outside the classroom is tenuous. The focus of the needs assessment shifts to the learning needs or subjective needs of the students so as to increase motivation and to help students find purpose and interest in what they are doing in the course. For example, Gorsuch (1991) describes a technique for helping students in a conversation class in Japan articulate their needs and set periodic and achievable goals to meet those needs.

Issues

Needs assessment is not a value-free process. It is influenced by the teacher's view of what the course is about, the institutional constraints, and the students' perceptions of what is being asked of them. For example, one teacher of immigrants might ask them to list situations in which they use or expect to use English, with the aim of providing instruction in the language and behavior necessary to deal with those situations. Another teacher might ask the same students to articulate or enact problems they face in adjusting to the new culture, with the aim of helping them exert control over the acculturation process.

For many students, needs assessment is an unfamiliar procedure, and they may have difficulty articulating their purposes or needs. The process itself may engender uncertainty in the students, as knowing their needs is presumably the responsibility of the teacher or institution. Questions may be interpreted differently by different students or may not elicit the anticipated answers. Students' perceptions of needs may not match those of the teacher. The teacher's view of the students' needs may conflict with those of the institution.

The content and method of needs assessment should be evaluated as to appropriateness and effectiveness in achieving their purpose of identifying the needs of the students. It may take several tries to develop effective needs assessment tools. Those tools should not be viewed as "one time only" processes. Needs assessment should be viewed as an ongoing process, both in its development and in its use.

Determining goals and objectives

What are the purposes and intended outcomes of the course? What will my students need to do or learn to achieve these goals? What are goals and objectives and what is the relationship between them? Goals are general statements of the overall, long-term purposes of the course. Objectives express the specific ways in which the goals will be achieved. The goals of a course represent the destination; the objectives, the various points that chart the course toward the destination. To arrive at the destination, one must pass each of these points. [. . .]

Why set goals and objectives? Setting goals and objectives provides a sense of direction and a coherent framework for the teacher in planning her course. Breaking goals down into objectives is very much like making a map of the territory to be explored. It is a way for the teacher to conceptualize her course in terms of teachable chunks. Clear goals and objectives give the teacher a basis for determining which content and activities are appropriate for her course. They also provide a framework for evaluation of the effectiveness or worth of an activity: Did it help students achieve or make progress toward the goals and objectives? Clearly, there are many routes (objectives) to a given destination, some more circuitous than others, and the length and nature of the route will depend on one's departure point.

How does one choose appropriate goals and objectives? There is no simple answer to this question. To arrive at the goals, one asks the question, "What are the purposes and intended outcomes of the course?" The answer may be influenced by an analysis of students' needs, the policies of the institution, and the way the teacher conceptualizes content, among other factors. Stern (1992) proposes four types of goals for language learners: proficiency goals, cognitive goals, affective goals, and transfer goals. Proficiency goals include general competency, mastery of the four skills (speaking, listening, reading, and writing), or mastery of specific language behaviors. Cognitive goals include mastery of linguistic knowledge and mastery of cultural knowledge. Affective goals include achieving positive attitudes and feelings about the target language, achieving confidence as a user of the language, and achieving confidence in oneself as a learner. Transfer goals involve learning how to learn so that one can call upon learning skills gained in one situation to meet future learning challenges. Thus goals may address not only the attainment of knowledge and skills but also the development of attitude and awareness.

Goals should also be realizable. Richards (1990: 3) gives the example of a goal stated as "Students will develop favorable attitudes toward the program." He goes on to point out, "However, while this goal might represent a sincere wish on the part of teachers, it should appear as a program goal only if it is to be addressed concretely in the program."

The formulation of objectives provides the check as to whether the goals will be addressed. To arrive at objectives, one asks, "What do students need to learn or do to achieve these purposes?" One of the challenges in formulating objectives is thinking of objectives that are congruent with the goals and that are not so narrow that they enmesh the teacher in an unnecessary level of detail.

How does one state objectives? As Nunan (1988b: 60) has pointed out, "Objectives are really nothing more than a particular way of formulating or stating content and activities." Thus how one conceptualizes and states objectives depends on how one conceptualizes the content of the course. Content as knowledge might be stated as "Students will know . . .," "Students will learn the . . .," or "Students will learn that . . ." Content as skill might be stated as "Students will be able to . . .," "Students will know how to . . .," or "Students will develop the ability to . . ." Performance or behavioral objectives are most often associated with content as skill; however, this represents a narrow view as they specify terminal behavior rather than the development of skills, such as those needed to read, write, listen and speak effectively (Richards 1990). Content as attitude and awareness would be stated as "Students will be aware that . . .," "Students will develop an awareness of . . .," "Students will develop an attitude of . . .," or "Students will explore their attitudes towards . . ." Objectives stated in this way can help teachers address affective aspects of learning.

The examples given suggest what students will know, know how to do, or be aware of as a result of the course. Objectives may also be stated in terms of what students will do in the course. Saphier and Gower (1987) list five kinds of objectives, all interrelated. The first three concern what students will do; the last two, what they will have mastered.

1   *Coverage objectives* articulate what will be covered. Example: *We will cover the first five units of the course book.*

2   *Activity objectives* articulate what the students will do. Examples: *Students will write six different kinds of paragraphs. Students will do paragraph development exercises.*

3   *Involvement objectives* articulate how to maximize student involvement and interest. Examples: *Students will engage in discussions about which paragraphs they like best. Students will brainstorm lists of interesting topics to write about.*

4   *Mastery objectives* articulate what students will be able to do as a result of their time in class. Example: *Students will be able to write an interesting paragraph that contains a topic sentence and supporting details.*

5   *Critical thinking objectives* articulate which learning skills students will develop. Example: *Students will be able to determine characteristics of a good paragraph and say why they think a paragraph is good.*

Tension often exists between coverage objectives and mastery objectives because the time it takes to master skills or knowledge or to develop awareness may not correspond to the time allotted in a syllabus. This tension can create dilemmas for teachers who must cover and test the material in the syllabus yet wish to ensure that students have mastered the material prior to moving on. The tension can also put teachers at odds with their students or the institution if the teacher believes that success is achieved through demonstrated mastery but the students expect coverage to *mean* mastery.

Issues

The main issue is that many teachers do not formulate goals and objectives at all or do so only after having thought about what they will teach and how. Studies on teacher planning underscore this fact (Clark and Peterson 1986). My own work with teachers has shown that they consider the setting of goals and objectives a valuable process but one that they find difficult to articulate and organize. They feel that they must first be clear about what they are teaching and how they view the content. They report from experience that they cannot clearly formulate their goals and objectives until after they have taught the course at least once. (Returning to the map analogy, one cannot map a route until one has traveled it.) Thus for many teachers, this is not the entry point into the process of course development.

Another issue involves clarity with respect to students' needs. It is easier to set goals in situations where these needs are clear; otherwise, the goals of the course may shift and be redefined as the course progresses. Finally, goals and objectives are a statement of intent, subject to reexamination and change once the course is under way.

Conceptualizing content

What will be the backbone of what I teach? What will I include in my syllabus?

When a teacher conceptualizes content, she is figuring out which aspects of language and language learning she will include, emphasize, and integrate in her course. This is not the relatively simple process it once was. Two decades ago, language teaching was still heavily influenced by a structural view of language (Richards and Rodgers 1986). This influence resulted in a "one size fits all" approach to content and methods, meaning that, for example, an EFL teacher could use the same textbook and the same drills or pattern practice for factory workers, college students, and housewives. There was not much question about content: It was grammatical structures and vocabulary.

Much has changed in recent years in the fields of applied linguistics and language acquisition and in approaches to language teaching. The proficiency movement, the concept and various models of communicative competence, the advent of ESP (English for specific purposes), the proliferation of methods of language teaching, and the diversification of the population of English learners have all provided the teacher with many more options to consider in deciding what will be the backbone of her course (Canale 1983; Hutchinson and Waters 1987; Omaggio Hadley 1993; Richards 1990; Savignon 1983; Yalden 1987). Now the choices a teacher makes are much more context-dependent and so involve a number of factors such as who the students are, their goals and expectations in learning English, the teacher's own conception of what language is and what will best meet the students' needs, the nature of the course, and the institutional curriculum. A course for immigrants in an English-speaking country will likely stress different content than a course for high school students in their own country.

Let us look at some ways of conceptualizing and categorizing content. The boundaries between categories are permeable; they overlap conceptually and are not exclusive of each other. The teacher's challenge is to figure out which ones are appropriate for her course and how she will integrate them. They will be described and then outlined in a syllabus grid, which will be added to with each successive component. In my experience, teachers do not usually use syllabus grids to lay out the content of a course but a grid is a graphic way to illustrate possible categories.

The traditional way of conceptualizing content, which many teachers have experienced in their own learning of language, is as grammar structures, sentence patterns, and vocabulary. These aspects of language are relatively systematic and rule-governed and are often the basis of content found in textbooks. They include rules of word formation (morphology), rules of pronunciation (phonology), and grammatical structures and relationships among words at the sentence level (syntax). A syllabus grid that includes these aspects of language might look like this:

Grammar	Pronunciation	Vocabulary

For language teachers, the possibilities for what to include in a syllabus opened up with the advent of what has come to be called the communicative approach (Larsen-Freeman 1986). The work of sociolinguists such as Hymes (1972) and Halliday (1973, 1975) and of applied linguists such as Wilkins (1976) and Van Ek (1975) has helped reorient thinking about the nature of language. The communicative approach is based on ideas about language, on the one hand, and about the purposes of language learning, on the other. Language is used in a context, which determines and constrains the choices that language users make with respect to purpose, style, register, and topic. Learners must use the language and have purposes for using it. From the point of view of conceptualizing content, the communicative approach added several dimensions. First, it added the dimension of language functions, such as to apologize, to persuade, to convey information. It also added the dimension of notions, which form a continuum from general concepts such as time, space, and relationship to specific topic-related notions such as house and home, weather, and personal identification (Van Ek 1975). Language was seen as being used for communicative purposes in situations with other people, which call on the learner to pay attention to both the content of the language and its appropriateness with respect to formality, non-verbal behavior, tone, and so on. Communicative situations might include ordering food in a restaurant, buying stamps at the post office, extending an invitation to a social event. Thus we can add these categories to our syllabus grid:

Functions	Notions and topics	Communicative situations
Grammar	Pronunciation	Vocabulary

The proficiency movement and the development of proficiency guidelines have emphasized a four-skills-based approach to syllabus design (Omaggio Hadley 1993). For some teachers, these skills are a given, as students have to use some combination of speaking, listening, reading, and writing in class. However, because becoming proficient in each of these skills entails mastery of a set of subskills and processes, many teachers choose to emphasize certain skills or find ways to integrate them. For example, to become proficient in writing, a student must learn how to structure paragraphs, how to use cohesive devices, the rhetorical styles of written English, editing techniques and so on. Thus we can add the following categories to our syllabus grid:

Listening skills	Speaking skills	Reading skills	Writing skills
Functions		Notions and topics	Communicative situations
Grammar		Pronunciation	Vocabulary

The emphasis on communicative competence as based on and brought about by interaction has prompted a view of language as not just something one learns but something one *does*. Thus teachers may conceive of their syllabus in terms of what the students will do in the classroom as activities or tasks. Tasks have been variously defined. Prabhu (1987: 24) defines a task as an activity that requires learners "to arrive at an outcome from given information through some process of thought," such as deciding on an itinerary based on train timetables or composing a telegram to send to someone. Tasks have also been defined as projects in which learners work together to produce something, such as a putting together a newspaper or conducting a survey (Hutchinson 1984). Nunan (1989) proposes a task continuum, with real-world tasks at one end and pedagogic tasks at the other. Real-world tasks ask students to use language in ways that they might outside the classroom, such as listening to the radio, reading the newspaper, or using a train schedule. Pedagogic tasks are ones that would not occur outside of the classroom but help students develop skills necessary to function in that world, such as information gap activities.

The competency-based approach to syllabus design was developed in the United States in response to the influx of immigrants in the 1970s and 1980s. It is a combination of the communicative and task-based approaches and has been used in courses for teaching immigrants, who have immediate needs with respect to functioning in English in the community and in the workplace. Competencies are "task-oriented goals written in terms of behavioral objectives that include language behavior" (Center for Applied Linguistics 1983: 9). They are the language and behavior necessary to function in situations related to living in the community and finding and maintaining a job. Competencies related to living in the community have also been called *life-skills*. Those related to jobs have been called *vocational skills*. (See, for example, the California ESL Model Standards for adult education 1993.)

However one defines them, tasks can be geared to one's specific group of learners. For business personnel, tasks might include giving a business presentation or writing a report; for university students, tasks might include writing a research paper or preparing a report from notes taken at a lecture. We can add two other categories to our syllabus grid:

		Tasks and activities	Competencies
Listening skills	Speaking skills	Reading skills	Writing skills
Functions		Notions and topics	Communicative situations
Grammar		Pronunciation	Vocabulary

The role of culture in language learning is receiving increasing attention. Culture provides a broader and deeper context for how one knows or determines what is valued, appropriate, or even feasible and why. Damen (1986) calls culture the "fifth dimension of language teaching." Kramsch (1993) asserts that culture is not just a fifth skill or even an aspect of communicative competence but the underlying dimension of all one knows and does. Thus a teacher who views culture as an integral part of a syllabus might include the development of awareness of the role culture plays in human interaction, how to understand and interpret the cultural aspects of language and behavior, and the development of skills in behaving and responding in culturally appropriate ways in addition to knowledge of the target culture.

The learning of language through or in conjunction with subject matter can also be the focus of a language course. Such courses have been called *content-based* because they integrate "particular content with language teaching aims" (Brinton, Snow, and Wesche 1989). Such content may be school- or work-related for example, history, economics, or computer technology. A content-based course may teach the subject matter directly or use subject matter as the basis for language-learning lessons. Thus the target language can be both a means for and a by-product of learning the subject matter. Content-based approaches play a critical role in bilingual programs for children as well as in ESP courses and, increasingly, in EAP courses. We can add culture and content to our syllabus grid:

		Content	
Culture	Tasks and activities	Competencies	
Listening skills	Speaking skills	Reading skills	Writing skills
Functions	Notions and topics	Communicative situations	
Grammar	Pronunciation	Vocabulary	

Another major change in how teachers conceptualize content has come about because of the view that one teaches learners, not just language. The emphasis on the learner has introduced other important elements into a teacher's conception of what she will teach: the learner's affect, which includes attitudes, self-confidence, and motivation, and the learner's approach to learning, which includes both understanding and developing one's learning skills. How to improve learners' self-confidence or helping learners become aware of their attitude toward the target culture may be explicitly included in a syllabus, as may activities that help learners become aware of their strengths and overcome their weaknesses as learners. The development of definitions, taxonomies, and methods of developing learning strategies is one way in which the emphasis on helping learners become self-aware has influenced syllabus design (O'Malley and Chamot 1990; Oxford 1990).

For some teachers, enabling students to participate in determining the content of their course so that what they do in class gives them the tools to cope with and change what they will encounter outside of the classroom is the focus of their course. Thus they ask the learners to engage in participatory processes that help them understand the social context of their problems and take control of their personal and professional lives through work in the classroom (Auerbach 1993; Auerbach and Wallerstein 1987). We can now add two more categories to the syllabus grid, learning strategies and participatory processes. The completed grid is shown in Figure 15.1.

Participatory processes Examples: problem posing, experiential learning techniques	Learning strategies Examples: self-monitoring, problem identification, note taking	Content Examples: academic subjects, technical subjects
Culture Examples: culture awareness, culture behaviour, culture knowledge	Tasks and activities Examples: information gap activities, projects, skills or topic-oriented tasks such as giving a speech or making a presentation	Competencies Examples: applying for a job, renting an apartment

Listening skills Examples: listening for gist, listening for specific information, inferring topic, choosing appropriate reponse	Speaking skills Examples: turn-taking, compensating for misunderstandings, using cohesive devices	Reading skills Examples: scanning for information, skimming for gist, understanding rhetorical devices	Writing skills Examples: using appropriate rhetorical style, using cohesive devices, structuring paragraphs

Functions Examples: apologizing, disagreeing, persuading	Notions and topics Examples: time, quantity, health, personal identification	Communicative situations Examples: ordering in a restaurant, buying stamps at the post office
Grammar Examples: structures (tense, pronouns), patterns (questions)	Pronunciation Examples: segmentals (phonemes, syllables), suprasegmentals (stress, rhythm, intonation)	Vocabulary Examples: word formation (suffixes, prefixes), collocation, lexical sets

Figure 15.1 The completed syllabus grid

Issues

Teaching involves making choices. It is not possible to teach a syllabus that explicitly encompasses all the areas mentioned here so teachers must decide which categories make sense to them for a given course. The categorics also overlap, both conceptually and in the classroom. For example, pronunciation is an important part of speaking skills. Vocabulary development is a part of notions and topics. Learning strategies can be linked to specific skills. Some of the categories are vast and can be divided into several subcategories. Many readers will find that they would label or define the categories differently or that certain categories are missing. For example, some teachers conceptualize content thematically.

Teachers of courses whose content has already been specified will face different issues. They may find that the breadth of content is unrealistic for the amount of time they have to teach it or that the way content has been defined is inappropriate, in their view, for the purposes of the course. The overlapping nature of the categories may be an aid in finding ways to adapt the existing content to their vision of the course.

Selecting and developing materials and activities

How and with what will I teach the course? What is my role? What are my students' roles?

For many teachers, course development starts not with determining objectives or conceptualizing content but with ideas about the course in action. They think about material they will use, activities their students will do, techniques they will employ. They think about the way they want their students to learn and their own role in the classroom.

For many teachers, the material they use forms the backbone of the course. It is something concrete that students use, and it provides a focus for the class. Choosing material may mean development of new material when teaching a course for which there are no suitable materials, collecting a variety of materials, or adapting existing materials. Teachers consider a variety of factors in developing, choosing, or adapting materials. Two of the most important are their effectiveness in achieving the purposes of the course and their appropriateness for the students – and the teacher. Appropriateness includes student comfort and familiarity with the material, language level, interest, and relevance. Some teachers incorporate instruction in how to use unfamiliar materials as part of their course design. Feasibility and availability are also important to consider.

Developing new materials and activities for using them requires time and a clear sense of why they will be used, how, and by whom. Because of the lack of time, teachers are often constrained or prefer to adapt existing materials. Experienced teachers often develop a set of core materials and activities that they adapt each time they teach a course. The materials themselves are flexible and can be used in a number of ways, depending on the target skills or competencies. For example, newspaper articles can be used as a basis for developing reading skills, expanding vocabulary, or discussing culture. Pictures can be used as a focus for learning grammar or as a starting point for a writing assignment. Core activities are related to the way the teacher conceptualizes the content. A teacher may have a repertoire of activities for teaching pronunciation or for having students learn to understand cultural differences. For some teachers, materials and activities are integrated into a method, such as the "language experience" approach (Rigg 1989). The emphasis on proficiency and learning language in context has led many teachers to use as much authentic material as possible in their classes (Omaggio Hadley 1993). For content-based courses, authentic material is the foundation.

For teachers who are required to use a certain text, course development *is* the adaptation of the text, for the content of the text determines the content of the course. However, the text is not the course; rather, what the teacher and students do with the text constitutes the course. Textbooks are tools that can be figuratively cut up into component pieces and then rearranged to suit the needs, abilities, and interests of the students in the course. The material in a textbook can be modified to incorporate activities that will motivate students and move them beyond the constraints of the text. Das (1988: viii) points out that materials should not "pre-specify learning outcomes or attempt to control or substantially guide learning: their function is primarily to provide opportunities for learning through interaction."

The question "How will I teach?" also encompasses a teacher's approach and how she views her role and that of the learners. How much initiative will the students be expected to take, and toward what end? How will the students be asked to interact? The emphasis on learner awareness and concern for extending learning beyond the classroom have made the role of the learner a central focus of how a course is taught. Teachers design courses with activities and materials that have the students take a more active role in reflecting on their learning, determining the content of the course, and pursuing projects of interest to them. Such an approach may facilitate the search for materials in that the emphasis is not on the materials themselves but on what the students do with them.

Issues

For some teachers, the lack of materials is a challenge; for others, it is an opportunity. Developing materials requires time before, during, and after the course – for preparing, using, and modifying them, respectively. Yet having to use certain materials may produce the dilemma of coping with a text that does not meet students' needs or does not promote the teacher's view of the roles of learners and teachers. Other aspects of course development, such as needs assessment and objective setting, may help the teacher see how to adapt unsuitable materials and to what extent. Eventually, all materials are adapted or modified in some way. Even materials that have been developed by teachers for specific courses will be modified over time.

Organization of content and activities

How will I organize the content and activities? What systems will I develop?

Regardless of whether one follows a fixed sequence or adopts a more fluid approach to the order in which one teaches the content, part of course development is figuring out systems for organizing the course. Systems can focus on the lesson level (the organization of each lesson) and on the course level (the overall organization of the course). We will look first at specific considerations in sequencing material and then at considerations of the overall organization of the course.

Two general, complementary principles of sequencing are building and recycling. In deciding how to sequence material, one considers building from the simple to the complex, from more concrete to more open-ended or so that unit or activity A prepares students for unit or activity B. Building from the simple to the complex in a writing course may mean learning how to write narrative prose before developing an argumentative paper. In an introductory language course, it may mean learning the numbers 1 to 9 to use telephone numbers and then learning the numbers 10 to 60 to tell time. Building from more concrete to more open-ended in a writing course may mean that students first unscramble and discuss a sample paragraph before writing their own paragraph. In an introductory language course, it may mean talking about a family in a textbook picture using prescribed vocabulary before talking about one's own family.

Conceiving of activities as building blocks puts them in a "feeding" relation where one activity feeds into another "if it provides something that is needed for the second one . . . or the second exercise could not be done unless the first had already been completed" (Low 1989: 145). For example, in a reading unit, students predict the content from pictures or headings that accompany the text before actually reading the text. Or prior to a restaurant role-playing activity, students learn menu items and the language for ordering food.

The principle of recycling material means that students encounter previous material in new ways: in a new skill area, in a different type of activity, or with a new focus. For example, material encountered in a listening activity may be recycled in a writing exercise. Material encountered in an individual reading activity may be recycled in a role play with other students. Material about the target culture may be recycled in an activity about one's own culture. This approach to recycling material assumes that each new encounter with the material provides a challenge to students, thereby maintaining their interest and motivation. Recycling has the effect of integrating material and thus augments students' ability to use or understand it.

[. . .]

Two complementary ways to approach the overall organization of a course are as a cycle or as a matrix. Both approaches suggest a core of material to be learned and activities to be conducted within a given time frame. In the cyclical approach, a regular cycle of activities follows a consistent sequence. In a matrix approach, the teacher works with a set of possible activities for a given time frame and, as the course progresses, decides which activities to work with. For an EAP course, Blyth (1996) describes such a situation, in which she compiles a list of possible activities and materials and then decides which to use, depending on her students' interests as well as the availability of the materials.

The cycle and the matrix are not mutually exclusive; many teachers use elements of both. Certain features in a course may be predictable, augmented by other elements drawn from a matrix, depending on the situation. Teachers who work with a fixed syllabus, such as that in a textbook, may nevertheless follow a cycle in the way they work with the material. Adapting material often means approaching it as a matrix from which to select, depending on one's students. Many teachers also set up certain daily or weekly rituals. For example, some teachers begin each session with a warm-up or review. Some teachers begin each week with a student presentation or end each week with an oral feedback session. All of these methods of organization permit a teacher to give a shape to her course.

Issues

Although the order in which the content and materials are taught may be determined prior to teaching the course, it may also be determined and modified as the course progresses. For some teachers, a negotiated syllabus, in which teacher and students decide together what they will learn, is preferable. In such cases, a predetermined sequence is seen as a handicap as it does not allow teachers to take into account the particular group of students in their course. In such a course, the sequence is not determined beforehand. Rather, the teacher has a map of the possible territory and works with the students to determine where it is most useful for them to go and in what order. Where a syllabus is provided, achieving flexibility is an issue.

Evaluation

How will I assess what students have learned? How will I assess the effectiveness of the course?

For most teachers, evaluation means evaluation *within* the course; assessing students' proficiency, progress, or achievement. How proficient are students in listening? Are students improving their writing skills? Have they learned to function in English in the workplace? Teachers build in some form of student evaluation when developing a course, ranging from formal tests to informal assessments. Hughes (1989) discusses four purposes for testing: to measure proficiency, to diagnose specific strengths and weaknesses, to place students in a course or program, and to assess their achievement in a course or program. The same testing instrument may be used for more than one purpose. For example, the TOEFL test is used by graduate programs in the United States as a proficiency test, but it is sometimes used as an achievement test if students show a gain on a TOEFL posttest. However, tests are not the only means teachers have to assess their students. Teachers may structure their classroom activities so that they can assess their students while the students participate. They may use a portfolio approach, in which students put together a portfolio of their work (Fingeret 1993). They may involve their students in deciding what should be assessed and how (Hull 1991).

Evaluation in course development also includes evaluation of the course itself. Was the course effective? In what ways? Where did it fall short? Such an evaluation may not be directly linked to assessment of student progress, although student evaluation and test results can provide feedback on the effectiveness of the course. If the students do well on tests or are judged to have made progress, presumably the course has been effective. But if students do not make progress or do not demonstrate a certain level of achievement, the effectiveness of the course may be questioned. Finding where the fault lies would be one of the purposes of course evaluation and could involve having students suggest why they did not make the progress expected.

Why does one evaluate? Generally speaking, a course is evaluated to promote and improve its effectiveness. This may be an internal matter, as when the teacher is concerned with developing the best course possible, in which case the evaluation is done largely for the benefit of the students and the teacher. However, courses are also evaluated to provide documentation for policy reasons, such as continued funding or retention in the curriculum. In such cases, evaluation is an external matter, and the teacher may be required to use certain methods of evaluation or to document the effectiveness of the course in a manner prescribed by an outside party. This in turn may influence the development of the course.

What can be evaluated? Any part of the process of course development can be evaluated, including the assumptions about and analysis of students' needs or backgrounds, goals and objectives, materials and activities, means of assessing students' progress, student participation, student roles, and the teacher's role. Thus each element of the framework is itself subject to evaluation. Was the needs assessment effective? Did I seek the right input, and did it enable me to make appropriate decisions about the course? If not, why not? Were the goals and objectives appropriate and achievable? Should they be changed? Did students find the material appropriately challenging, or was it too easy or too difficult? Were the activities appropriate? Did all students participate easily? Did I find suitable ways to evaluate students' progress? Did the tests test what had been learned?

When does one evaluate? In curriculum design, a distinction is usually made between *formative evaluation*, which takes place during the development and implementation of the curriculum for purposes of modifying it as it is being developed, and *summative evaluation*, which takes place after the curriculum has been implemented, for purposes of evaluating its success and improving it for future implementation (Brown 1989). A teacher who is involved in each stage of course design can think of evaluation as an ongoing part of the entire process. Thus evaluation can occur in the planning and teaching stages of the course, after it is over, and when it is replanned and retaught.

Who evaluates? At the course level, the teacher and the students are the principal evaluators. However, administrators, funders, parents, and clients may have a role in evaluation, and their role may influence the shape or existence of the course.

How does one evaluate? A variety of ways are available. A teacher's most important means is close observation of what students do in class and how they do it. If students have great difficulty performing certain tasks, one might be wise to question the appropriateness of the objectives or the activities. Informal chats with students can often provide as much information as responses to formal questionnaires. Teachers can also provide time for students to give written or oral input regarding specific aspects of the course. For example, some teachers hold regular oral feedback sessions with their students; and others have students write in journals. The teacher's own reflection and self-questioning play an important role in evaluation.

Issues

Teachers tend to avoid extensive evaluation because they feel inadequate to a task in what they consider is the domain of "experts," for which special training in systematic analysis is necessary. Teachers must become familiar with the various purposes and types of testing, but they must also devise their own systems and areas of inquiry. As with needs assessment, teachers must experiment with different methods of evaluation and monitor the success of each so as to maximize the effectiveness of their courses.

Consideration of resources and constraints

What are the givens of my situation?

Resources and constraints are two ways of looking at the same thing. A required course book may be a constraint for one teacher and a resource for another. A class of fewer than ten students may be a resource for one teacher and a constraint for another. Though these givens may seem secondary to the processes just described, in fact they play a primary role in the development of a course because it is in considering the givens that a teacher begins to make sense of processes such as needs assessment and material selection. I have referred to this elsewhere (1996) as problematizing: defining the challenges of one's situation so that one can make decisions about what to do. In the absence of problematizing, a teacher may seek to graft solutions appropriate to another unique situation onto her situation. This became clear to me in the case of an EFL teacher who faced an extraordinary challenge: designing a conversation class for 140 students in a space meant for half as many. She felt that having examples of needs analysis questionnaires would be a key to developing her course. To me, this was an example of a teacher seeking answers from outside without having first specifically defined the challenges of her own situation. Such problematizing could eventually result in an examination of how others approached needs analysis as an aid in developing her own. Here is a sketch of one way of problematizing this teacher's situation:

- *This is a conversation class, but there are 140 students in a space that fits 70.* I need to look at ways of working within the constraints of the classroom such as ways to group or rotate students.
- *What kinds of conversations can 140 students possibly have?* I need to assess their language ability (*At what level can they carry on a conversation?*) and find out about their background and interests (*What can they have conversations about?*). How will I go about doing that? What kinds of questions should I ask them? If the assessment shows that their ability is low, I need to focus on the kind of preparation and foundation work necessary for conversations to take place.
- *How can I get them to work together to have these conversations?* Classroom management is an issue. I need to look at available materials with carefully structured activities as a means of classroom management. Or perhaps I could ask other teachers what has worked for them in this situation.
- *How can I monitor their activity?* I need to examine my role in the classroom. I also need to think about the types of monitoring and evaluation mechanisms I will use in the class.
- *What has worked in the past?* I need to think about the activities or classes in which I felt that things went well. Why did they go well? What can I take from those successes and build into this course?

These are questions that I propose. Were the teacher to go through a similar process, she might ask different ones or respond to the same ones in different ways because of her intimate knowledge of her context and her role in it. For example, how students are graded, whether there is a required text, and attendance patterns would all influence the kinds of questions she would ask. I included the question about past successes because teachers carry their experience over from one context to the next, and being able to understand what has been successful and why can provide a foundation for planning a course. In the context under discussion, the teacher had already taught the course and thus could be realistic in her expectations about what she could hope to accomplish with this group of students.

The constraints and resources of one's situation take many forms, some tangible, others not. Teachers work with or without physical and material resources such as books, technology, a classroom, and furniture. The lack of physical resources may encourage a teacher to use available resources in creative ways. The availability of technology may allow a teacher to have groups of students work independently. Time is another important consideration in designing a course. How often, how long, and over what period of time will the class meet? How much time is available to the teacher to prepare for the course and the classes? A teacher may adjust her teaching priorities according to the length of the course. The kinds of activities she designs may be affected by the amount of time she has, both in class and before class.

The institutional philosophy, policy, and curriculum are important givens. Having to work within existing curricular guidelines is both a constraint and a resource; so is having to devise one's own syllabus. The type of administrative and clerical support provided by the institution affects a teacher's choices. For example, lack of clerical support will suggest streamlining paperwork and materials. Support from the administration for innovation will encourage experimentation.

The numbers, levels, and cultural backgrounds of the students are both a constraint and a resource. For example, a large class may cause a teacher to focus on classroom management. A multilevel class may influence the teacher's selection of material or activities.

The teacher herself is the most important given. Her background, experience, and beliefs play a significant role in the choices she makes. For example, one teacher will focus on certain content because she deems it essential to successful language learning, while another will ignore the same content. A teacher who usually develops her own materials may choose to use published materials when teaching a course whose content is new to her.

The givens of a situation cover a broad range of factors and affect every decision a teacher makes. Teachers plan and teach courses not in the abstract but in the concrete of their constraints and resources. For example, an ESL teacher who teaches in an intensive English program, whose students change from one program to the next, may need to investigate the background and proficiency of her students, whereas for a high school EFL teacher, this may be a given because she knows the students. The teacher in the intensive English program might begin with a question such as "How can I find out the cultural background and needs of my students so that I can address those needs effectively in the six weeks of the course?" The high school teacher's initial question might be quite different, say, "How can I keep my students motivated in a required course?" Course development, like teaching, is not a neatly organized process but a complex one in which teachers are constantly considering multiple factors and proceeding on many fronts.

Issues

The givens of one's teaching situation, both tangible and intangible, cannot be ignored. Effecting change requires both recognizing what can be changed and accepting what cannot. The "If only . . ." syndrome (if only we had the technology, if only we had quieter classrooms, if only our students were more motivated) can obstruct change as firmly as the "Yes, but . . ." syndrome (Yes, but that will never work in my setting.) Problematizing enables a teacher to decide what she can change, what she can't, and where to start.

Conclusion

The components discussed in this chapter and summarized in Table 15.1 should serve not as a checklist for the teacher but rather as a set of tools for talking about, understanding, and directing the process of course development. Each component is contingent on every other component. For example, assessment depends on how one conceptualizes content or on how she interprets students' needs. Conceptualizing content in turn influences the course goals and objectives. Thus wherever one starts in the process, each component will eventually come into play. Each component is, in many respects, one way of working with the whole.

Note

1   The terms *needs analysis* and *needs assessment* are often used interchangeably. But as Susan Pomeroy once suggested to me, they refer to separate processes: Assessment involves obtaining data, whereas analysis involves assigning value to those data.

References

Auerbach, E. 1993. "Putting the *p* back in participatory." TESOL *Quarterly* 27 (3): 543–545.
Auerbach, E. and N. Wallerstein. 1987. *ESL for Action: Problem Posing at Work*. Reading, Mass.: Addison-Wesley.
Blyth, M. d. C. 1996. "Designing an EAP course for postgraduate students in Ecuador." In K. Graves, ed., *Teachers as Course Developers*. Cambridge: Cambridge University Press.
Brindley, G. 1989. "The role of needs analysis in adult ESL program design." In R. K. Johnson, ed., *The Second Language Curriculum*, pp. 63–78. Cambridge: Cambridge University Press.
Brinton, D. M., M. A. Snow, and M. B. Wesche. 1989. *Content-based Second Language Instruction*. Rowley, Mass.: Newbury House.
Brown, J. D. 1989. "Language program evaluation: A synthesis of existing possibilities." In R. K. Johnson, ed., *The Second Language Curriculum*, pp. 222–243. Cambridge: Cambridge University Press.
California Department of Education. 1993. *English as a Second Language Model Standards for Adult Education*. Sacramento.
Canale, M. 1983. "From communicative competence to communicative language pedagogy." In J. Richards and R. Schmidt, eds., *Language and Communication*, pp. 2–27. London: Longman.
Center for Applied Linguistics. 1983. *From the Classroom to the Workplace: Teaching ESL to Adults*. Washington, D.C.
Clark, C. and P. Peterson. 1986. "Teachers' thought processes." In M. Wittrock, ed., *Handbook of Research on Teaching*. 3rd ed., pp. 255–297. New York: Macmillan.
Damen, L. 1987. *Culture Learning: The Fifth Dimension in the Language Classroom*. Reading, Mass.: Addison-Wesley.
Das, B. K. 1988. *Materials for Language Learning and Teaching*. Singapore: SEAMEO Regional Language Centre.
Dubin, F. and E. Olshtain. 1986. *Course Design: Developing Programs and Materials for Language Learning*. New York: Cambridge University Press.
Fingeret, A. F. 1993. *It Belongs to Me: A Guide to Portfolio Assessment in Adult Education Programs*. Durham, N. C.: Literacy South.

Gorsuch, G. 1991. 'Helping students create their own learning goals." *Language Teacher* 15 (12): 3, 9.

Grant, S. and L. Shank. 1993. "Beyond questionnaires: Engaging learners in needs assessment." Presentation at the TESOL conference, Atlanta.

Graves, K. 1996. "Teachers as course developers." In K. Graves, ed., *Teachers as Course Developers*. Cambridge: Cambridge University Press.

Halliday, M. A. K. 1973. *Explorations in the Functions of Language*. London: Arnold.

———. 1975. *Learning How to Mean: Explorations in the Development of Language*. London: Arnold.

Hughes, A. 1989. *Testing for Language Teachers*. Cambridge: Cambridge University Press.

Hull, L. 1991. "Self-monitoring and self-evaluation: A guide for facilitating independent and autonomous learning." Unpublished master's thesis, School for International Training, Brattleboro, VT.

Hutchinson, T. 1984. *Project English*. Oxford: Oxford University Press.

Hutchinson, T. and A. Waters. 1987. *English for Specific Purposes: A Learning-Centered Approach*. Cambridge: Cambridge University Press.

Hymes, D. 1972. 'On communicative competence." In J. Pride and J. Holmes, eds., *Sociolinguistics*, pp. 269–293. Harmondsworth, England: Penguin.

Johnson, R. K. ed. 1989. "A decision-making framework for the coherent language curriculum." In R. K. Johnson, ed., *The Second Language Curriculum*, pp. 1–23. Cambridge: Cambridge University Press.

Kramsch, C. 1993. *Context and Culture in Language Teaching*. Oxford: Oxford University Press.

Larsen-Freeman D. 1986. *Techniques and Principles in Language Teaching*. Oxford: Oxford University Press.

Low, G. 1989. "Appropriate design: The internal organisation of course units." In R. K. Johnson, ed., *The Second Language Curriculum*, pp. 136–154. Cambridge: Cambridge University Press.

Nunan, D. 1985. *Language Teaching Course Design: Trends and Issues*. Adelaide, Australia: National Curriculum Resource Centre.

———. 1988a. *The Learner-Centred Curriculum*. Cambridge: Cambridge University Press.

———. 1988b. *Syllabus Design*. Oxford: Oxford University Press.

———. 1989. *Designing Tasks for the Communicative Classroom*. Cambridge: Cambridge University Press.

Omaggio Hadley, A. C. 1993. *Teaching Language in Context*. Boston: Heinle and Heinle.

O'Malley, J. M., and A. U. Chamot. 1990. *Learning Strategies in Second Language Acquisition*. Cambridge: Cambridge University Press.

Oxford, R. 1990. *Language Learning Strategies: What Every Teacher Should Know*. Rowley, Mass.: Newbury House.

Prabhu, N. S. 1987. *Second Language Pedagogy*. Oxford: Oxford University Press.

Richards, J. 1990. *The Language Teaching Matrix*. New York: Cambridge University Press.

Richards, J. and T. Rodgers. 1986. *Approaches and Methods in Language Teaching*. New York: Cambridge University Press.

Richterich, R. 1980. "A model for the definition of language needs of adults." In Trim, Richterich, Van Ek, and Wilkins: 31–62.

Rigg, P. 1989. "Language experience approach: Reading naturally." In *When They Don't All Speak English: Integrating the ESL Student into the Regular Classroom*. Chicago. National Council of Teachers of English.

Saphier, J. and R. Gower. 1987. *The Skillful Teacher*. Carlisle, Mass.: Research for Better Teaching.

Savignon, S. 1983. *Communicative Competence: Theory and Practice*. Reading, Mass.: Addison-Wesley.

Stern, H. H. 1992. *Issues and Options in Language Teaching*. Oxford: Oxford University Press.

Tarone, E. and G. Yule 1989. *Focus on the Language Learner*. New York: Oxford University Press.

Van Ek, J. A. 1975. *Threshold-level English*. Oxford: Pergamon Press.

White, R. V. 1988. *The ELT Curriculum: Design Innovation and Management*. Oxford: Blackwell.

Wilkins, D. A. 1976. *Notional Syllabuses*. Oxford: Oxford University Press.

Yalden, J. 1987. *The Communicative Syllabus: Evolution, Design and Implementation*. London: Prentice-Hall International.

Chapter 16

David Nunan

ACTION RESEARCH IN LANGUAGE EDUCATION

Introduction

IN THIS PAPER, I HOPE TO PROVIDE A RATIONALE for the use of action research in second and foreign language education. Questions addressed in the paper include:

What is action research in language education?
Is action research 'real' research?
What are some of the problems confronted by teachers doing action research?
What are some of the solutions to these problems?
What are the views of the teachers on the action research process?

The paper will be illustrated with data from a longitudinal action research project.

Action research: description and rationale

Until comparatively recently, the focus of concern in much of the writing on second and foreign language education was at the level of method. Methodological prescriptions were generally argued logico-deductively and prescriptions for practice were generally devoid of data. This tended to reinforce the gap between theory, research and practice, a gap which, according to van Lier, is due in part to the obstacles which prevent teachers from doing research:

> Those of us who work in teacher education know that one of the most difficult things to balance in a course is the tension between theoretical and practical aspects of the profession. . . . Theory and practice are not perceived as integral parts of a teacher's practical professional life. . . . This situation is the result of communication gaps caused by an increasingly opaque research technocracy, restrictive practices in educational institutions and bureaucracies (e.g. not validating research time, or not granting sabbaticals to teachers for professional renovation), and overburdening teachers who cannot conceive of ways of theorising and researching that come out of daily work and facilitate that daily work.
>
> (van Lier, 1992: 3)

Despite the difficulties referred to by van Lier, there is some evidence that the picture is beginning to change. The change has been prompted in part by a growing sensitivity on the part of many researchers to the complexities of the teacher's task. Practitioners, on their part, seem to have grown tired of the swings and roundabouts of pedagogic fashion, and are looking for evidence before embracing the latest trend to appear in the educational market place. This is not to suggest that a revolution has taken place, however.

> While position papers, and logico-deductive argumentation have not disappeared from the scene (and I am not suggesting for a moment that they should), they are counterbalanced by empirical approaches to inquiry. I believe that these days, when confronted by pedagogical questions and problems, researchers and teachers are more likely than was the case ten or fifteen years ago, to seek relevant data, either through their own research, or through the research of others. Research activity has increased to the point where those who favour logico-deductive solutions to pedagogic problems are beginning to argue that there is too much research.
>
> (Nunan, 1992)

An important concept underpinning action research (AR) is that of reflective practice. In his excellent book on reflective teaching, Wallace (1991) argues that reflective teaching provides a way of developing professional competence by integrating two sources of knowledge, received knowledge and experiential knowledge, with practice. Wallace's conception is captured in Figure 16.1

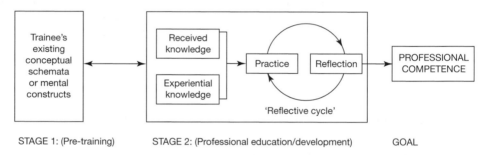

Figure 16.1 Reflective practice model of professional education/development

He links this with action research, arguing that:

> 'action research' can be attractive for two reasons:
> 1 It can have a specific and immediate outcome which can be directly related to practice in the teacher's own context.
> 2 The 'findings' of such research might be primarily specific, i.e. it is not claimed that they are necessarily of general application, and therefore the methods might be more free-ranging than those of conventional research.
> . . . 'Research' of this kind is simply an extension of the normal reflective practice of many teachers, but it is slightly more rigorous and might conceivably lead to more effective outcomes.
>
> (Wallace, 1991: 56–7)

As we can see from the selected extracts presented above, action research is justified on the grounds that it is a valuable professional development tool. It represents what I would call an 'inside out' approach to professional development. It represents a departure from the 'outside in' approach (i.e. one in which an outside 'expert' brings the 'good news' to the practitioner in the form of a one-off workshop or seminar). In contrast, the inside out approach begins with the concerns and interests of practitioners, placing them at the centre of the inquiry process. In addition to being centred in the needs and interest of practitioners, and in actively involving them in their own professional development, the inside out approach, as realised through action research, is longitudinal in that practitioners are involved in medium to long-term inquiry.

I believe that the benefits to professional development are justification enough for the development of an action research agenda. However, I believe that a further rationale for the development of such an agenda comes from the research process itself, and I shall deal with this in section three of my paper. First, however, I should like to look at the steps involved in the action research process.

Steps in the research process

The action research process is generally initiated by the identification by the practitioner of something which they find puzzling or problematic. This puzzle or problem may, in fact, have emerged from a period of observation and reflection. The second step is the collection of baseline data through a preliminary investigation which is designed to identify what is currently happening in the classroom without trying to change anything. Based on a review of the data yielded by the preliminary investigation, an hypothesis is formed. The next step is the development of some form of intervention or change to existing practice, along with a way of evaluating the effects of this change. The final step is reporting on the outcomes of the interaction, and, if necessary, planning further interventions. Two examples of the action research cycle are presented in Tables 16.1 and 16.2.

Action research and 'real' research

In the first part of this paper, I argued that action research can be justified on professional

Table 16.1 The action research cycle: an ESL example

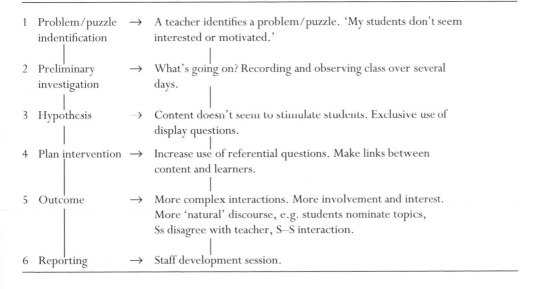

1	Problem/puzzle indentification	→	A teacher identifies a problem/puzzle. 'My students don't seem interested or motivated.'
2	Preliminary investigation	→	What's going on? Recording and observing class over several days.
3	Hypothesis	→	Content doesn't seem to stimulate students. Exclusive use of display questions.
4	Plan intervention	→	Increase use of referential questions. Make links between content and learners.
5	Outcome	→	More complex interactions. More involvement and interest. More 'natural' discourse, e.g. students nominate topics, Ss disagree with teacher, S–S interaction.
6	Reporting	→	Staff development session.

Table 16.2 The action research cycle: a foreign language example

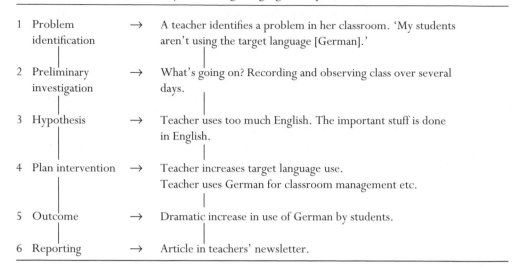

1	Problem identification	→	A teacher identifies a problem in her classroom. 'My students aren't using the target language [German].'
2	Preliminary investigation	→	What's going on? Recording and observing class over several days.
3	Hypothesis	→	Teacher uses too much English. The important stuff is done in English.
4	Plan intervention	→	Teacher increases target language use. Teacher uses German for classroom management etc.
5	Outcome	→	Dramatic increase in use of German by students.
6	Reporting	→	Article in teachers' newsletter.

development grounds. However, I believe that AR can also be justified on research grounds. In fact, I believe that there is something essentially patronising in the view that, while AR might be good for professional development, it hardly counts as research. Let us, to use a currently fashionable term, 'deconstruct' this view. First of all, what do we mean by 'research'? What is the function of research?

Elsewhere, I have defined research as 'a systematic process of inquiry consisting of three elements or components: (1) a question, problem, or hypothesis, (2) data, (3) analysis and interpretation of data' (Nunan, 1992: 3). Action research incorporates these three elements and therefore qualifies as 'real' research. For me the salient distinction between AR and other forms of research is that in AR the research process is initiated and carried out by the practitioner. As far as I am concerned, the opposition is not between action research and 'real' research, but between good research and bad research. A further characteristic, perhaps differentiating AR from other forms of practitioner research, is that it incorporates an element of intervention and change.

Fundamental to any discussion of research is a consideration of the researcher's conception of notions such as 'truth', 'objectivity', and the status of knowledge. I recently attempted to deal with the tensions of objective and subjective knowledge by suggesting that they represent two alternative ways of looking at the world:

> Two alternative conceptions of the nature of research provide a point of tension within the book. The first view is that external truths exist 'out there' somewhere. According to this view, the function of research is to uncover these truths. The second view is that truth is a negotiable commodity contingent upon the historical context within which phenomena are observed and interpreted. Further '[research] standards are subject to change in the light of practice [which] would seem to indicate that the search for a substantive universal, ahistorical methodology is futile.' (Chalmers 1990: 21) . . . This second, context-bound attitude to research entails a rather different role for the classroom practitioner than the first. If knowledge is tentative and contingent upon context, rather than absolute, then I believe that practitioners, rather than being consumers of other people's research, should adopt a research orientation to their own classrooms. There is evidence that the teacher-researcher movement is alive and

well and gathering strength. However, if the momentum which has gathered is not to falter, and if the teacher-researcher movement is not to become yet another fad, then significant numbers of teachers, graduate students, and others will need skills in planning, implementing and evaluating research.

(Nunan, 1992)

There are those who would argue that my definition of research as a systematic process of inquiry involving formulating a question, collecting relevant data, and analysing and interpreting that data is inadequate, that in order to count as research, the process should also meet the twin structures of reliability and validity. Key questions for establishing the reliability and validity of research are set out in Table 16.3.

Table 16.3 Questions for establishing the reliability and validity of a study

Type	*Key question*
Internal reliability	Would an independent researcher, on re-analysing the data, come to the same conclusion?
External reliability	Would an independent researcher, on replicating the study, come to the same conclusion?
Internal validity	Is the research design such that we can confidently claim that the outcomes are a result of the experimental treatment?
External validity	Is the research design such that we can generalise beyond the subjects under investigation to a wider population?

Source: Nunan, 1992.

While I would argue that any research needs to be reliable, the issue of validity is more problematic. If one is not trying to establish a relationship between variables, but (for example) to describe and interpret phenomena in context, does the imperative to demonstrate that one has safeguarded one's research from threats to internal validity remain? By the same token, if one is not trying to argue from samples to populations, then it would not be unreasonable to assert that external validity is irrelevant. I would argue that as most AR is not concerned with arguing from samples to populations, external validity is not at issue. (For an excellent discussion of issues to do with reliability and validity in qualitative research, see LeCompte and Goetz, 1982.)

It is popularly assumed that the purpose of research is to test theories. For example, '*That communicative language teaching is more effective than audiolingualism*.' Allwright and Bailey have pointed out that there are problems with this proposition. In the first place, some theories are untestable (for example, Krashen's attestations on 'subconscious' acquisition). Secondly, classrooms are too complex for us to control all the variables in the manner prescribed by experimental research. They propose an alternative purpose for research, namely to try and understand and deal with immediate practical problems facing teachers and learners (Allwright and Bailey, 1991). If we accept this alternative purpose, we are drawn immediately into embracing AR, because it makes no sense for an outsider to arbitrate on the practical problems facing teachers and learners. This does not mean that outsiders, such as university-based researchers, have no role to play in practitioner-based research. However, the role is one of collaboration and advice rather than direction and control.

Problems and solutions in doing action research

I would now like to reassure those who might feel that I am looking at teacher research through rose-coloured glasses. It is certainly not the case that everything is rosy in the AR garden. The principal problems identified by teachers with whom I have worked in a number of different contexts include the following:

- Lack of time
- Lack of expertise
- Lack of ongoing support
- Fear of being revealed as an incompetent teacher
- Fear of producing a public account of their research for a wider (unknown) audience

We have experimented with a number of solutions to the problems. I believe that the chances for an action research agenda to succeed will be maximised under the following conditions:

- There is someone 'on the ground' to 'own' the project.
- One or more individuals with training in research methods are available 'on tap' to provide assistance and support to teachers.
- Teachers are given paid release time from face-to-face teaching during the course of their action research.
- Collaborative focus teams are established so that teachers involved in similar areas of inquiry can support one another.
- Teachers are given adequate training in methods and techniques for identifying issues, collecting data, analysing and interpreting data, and presenting the outcomes of their research.

In order to facilitate the process, colleagues and I have developed an in-service programme. This programme was initially devised for the LIPT project (Languages Inservice Project for Teachers) in South Australia, and has been further modified and refined in Sydney, where a project has been established bringing together mainstream teachers, ESL teachers, and teachers of LOTE (Languages Other than English). In Table 16.4, I have provided a summary of the professional development programme as it currently exists.

Evaluating action research

From what has already been said, it is clear that action research is difficult, messy, problematic, and, in some cases, inconclusive. It consumes a great deal of time, and often strains the goodwill of the teachers involved, as well as those with whom they work. However, evaluative data from teachers themselves suggests that teachers who have been involved in action research are overwhelmingly in favour of it. For example, Mickan, who collected data on the reaction of outside teachers to his LIPT project, writes:

> Teachers have welcomed the articles from LIPT. They have found them particularly
> useful and relevant because they depict the complex circumstances of classroom life

in an honest and direct way. They have found them a rich source of ideas and valuable for informing their own practice. The warts and all descriptions (including failures and successes), the research techniques used, the analysis of results and the contextual detail are all elements which readers relate to and understand. As such they possess a validity which derives from the detailed narration of classroom ecology. The experiential reports give other practitioners models and ideas for their own practice. They also suggest topics and procedures for classroom investigations in different contexts.

(Mickan, 1991)

Table 16.4 The inservice programme in outline

Session 1 An introduction to classroom observation and research
a A series of reflective activities designed to get teachers thinking about their own teaching style.
b Reflecting on the teaching of others: teachers examine and critique extracts from a range of classrooms identifying those aspects of the extracts they liked and disliked.
c Identification of ideological beliefs and attitudes underlying critiques.

Between session task: teachers record and reflect on their own teaching.

Session 2 An introduction to action research
a Teachers report back on the between session task.
b Introduction to issues and methods in action research.
c Introduction to the action research process.

Between session task: teachers develop a draft action plan.

Session 3 Focus groups and action plans
a Formation of focus groups and appointment of facilitators.
b Sharing of draft action plans.
c Refining questions.

Between session task: baseline observation, focus group meetings, preliminary data collection.

Session 4 Analysing data
a Participants develop ways of analysing and making sense of their data.

Between session task: ongoing data collection and analysis, focus group meetings.

Session 5 Writing up
a Participants receive input on presenting their research.
b Development of draft reporting outlines.

Between session task: production of draft reports.

Session 6 Refining reports
Participants receive feedback on and discussion of their reports.

Session 7 Evaluation
Participants evaluate the LIPT process and provide feedback on how their involvement changed them.

An evaluation by Lewis (1992) is also favourable. She reports on a study conducted with a group of teachers of French immersion programmes in British Columbia. The focus of her research was the effect on the professional practice of the teachers of engaging in AR. She drew the following conclusions from her research.

1   Through the process of systematically implementing their own choice of action project based on the needs of the students in particular, each teacher learned more about their own theories, or frames for teaching, and modified these frames to a certain extent.

2   The frames for teaching of the participants in this study are related to the bigger questions of second language education and education in general. Practice cannot be understood thoroughly without appreciating how educational theory is expressed within teachers' frames and neither can theory be useful without recognising that what counts is how theory becomes expressed within practice.

3   The 'teacher as researcher' or 'reflection in action' approach to teacher education can be a very powerful way of facilitating change in curriculum.

In evaluating the last of the LIPT projects, we asked teachers to complete the following statements:

Action research is ....

Action research is carried out in order to ....

We also asked them to respond to the following:

1   What are the most significant things you have learned in carrying out your classroom research?

2   What questions/issues has your classroom research raised for you?

3   What further areas/ideas are you interested in pursuing?

Sample responses to the first of these probes on the most significant outcomes for the participants are set out in Appendix 1. It can be seen that these are overwhelmingly favourable, the participants choosing to focus either on the substantive content outcomes ('By collecting and analyzing data on my children, I found that they were more highly motivated than I had given them credit for'), learning process outcomes ('The active involvement of the children in the learning process facilitates learning.' 'I discovered that kids know how to learn – the project taught me to listen to them'), or reflections on the research process itself ('In working through the action research process, I discovered which methods of data collection are most suited to my research question – next time I will be better prepared as I will be more aware of what I am looking for, and will be better able to match my questions and data.'). The enthusiastic validation of learner-centred approaches to instruction, even though this was not a primary aim of most research, is also worth noting.

Finally, participants were asked to complete a checklist to indicate how their teaching had changed as a result of their involvement in the project. Results are set out in Table 16.5. It can be seen from the survey that, if self-reports are to be believed, the experience was, for most teachers, an overwhelmingly positive one.

Conclusion

In this paper, I have argued that the adoption of an action research orientation can be justified in professional development terms and research terms. Despite the bureaucratic difficulties and obstacles which are placed in the way of teachers, the elitism of a certain cadre of researchers (some of whom were once classroom teachers themselves!), and the suspicion which is sometimes directed at academics who are trying to promote a closer relationship

Table 16.5 How has your teaching changed? Complete the following: 'Since I have been doing action research, I find that when I teach I now . . .'

		More	About the same	Less
1	tend to be directive	1	14	10
2	try to use a greater variety of behaviours	16	6	0
3	praise students	15	10	0
4	criticise students	0	11	13
5	am aware of students' feelings	18	6	0
6	give directions	4	16	5
7	am conscious of my non-verbal communication	11	14	0
8	use the target language in class	19	6	0
9	am conscious of non-verbal cues of students	12	12	0
10	try to incorporate student ideas into my teaching	20	5	0
11	spend more class time talking myself	1	9	15
12	try to get my students working in groups	15	8	0
13	try to get divergent, open-ended student responses	14	10	0
14	distinguish between enthusiasm and lack of order	9	15	0
15	try to get students to participate	18	7	0

between theory, research, and practice, there is evidence that things are beginning to change. I can offer no more fitting conclusion to this paper than the following extract from the work of two of the profession's foremost advocates of the development of harmony between theory, research and practice, who have striven in their own teaching, writing and research, to enhance the status of both practitioner and researcher within language education.

> Slowly, the profession as a whole is realising that, no matter how much intellectual energy is put into the invention of new methods (or of new approaches to syllabus design, and so on), what really matters is what happens when teachers and learners get together in the classroom. . . . This shift in emphasis from concentrating on planning decisions . . . to concentrating on looking at what actually happens in the classroom, has led researchers to have much greater respect for classroom teaching. The more we look, the more we find, and the more we realise how complex the teacher's job is. And teachers, in their turn, faced at last with researchers who have at least some idea of the enormous complexity of everyday classroom life, are beginning to be more receptive to the whole research enterprise. . . . Being a good classroom teacher means being alive to what goes on in the classroom, alive to the problems of sorting out what matters, moment by moment, from what does not. And that is what classroom research is all about: gaining a better understanding of what good teachers (and learners) do instinctively as a matter of course, so that ultimately all can benefit.
>
> (Allwright and Bailey, 1991)

Appendix 1

What are the most significant things you have learned in carrying out your classroom research?

• The active involvement of the children in the learning process facilitates learning.

- Children have different learning preferences and teachers need to allow for this in their instructional practices.
- Children find it difficult to express feelings and opinions on paper.
- It is easy to 'spoon feed' children, but this leads to ineffective learning.
- Teaching problems only go away if they are recognized and tackled.
- The most important outcome for me was that I learned how to do action research. To benefit, I therefore have to do it again!
- Working with the children together (e.g. finding their thoughts/feelings and acting on them).
- In working through the action research process, I discovered which methods of data collection are most suited to my research question – next time I will be better prepared as I will be more aware of what I am looking for, and will be better able to match my questions and data.
- The process removed my tunnel vision to teaching.
- It helped me to make links with other teachers of Mandarin, as well as parents and the community.
- The process dramatically enhanced my rapport with students.
- I found that by careful, step-by-step direction of students, I was able to give them tools to manage their own learning.
- By collecting and analyzing data on my children, I found that they were more highly motivated than I had given them credit for.
- The most important outcome for me was that I discovered the children enjoy (and respond well) to being consulted about their learning and being given some say in what they learn.
- There was a negative outcome for me – I've learned not to expect children to have completed tasks or to value something just because they're important to me.
- I found that Year 7 learners still need lots of structure and guidance, even when independent skills are encouraged.
- I was disappointed. I expected too much in my initial project – book flood! Only book trickle is possible in such a short time.
- The most important discovery for me was that my students need more time and opportunities to work in groups as they need to learn to work on their own without teacher directed lessons all the time.
- The need for informed input in this process – one needs to read etc., recent research and thinking in order to maximize value of one's own research, and move beyond one's own 'blinkered' vision.
- The positive benefit of concentrating on one particular area because the attitude/ approach of openness and inquiry carries over into one's teaching in general.
- I have learned that students with a very limited knowledge of the target language are prepared to try to write more than I expected, and that in future I should try to foster this willingness in my classes.
- Contrary to my expectations, I found that the children were keen to be part of a 'project'. This led to increased motivation (maybe Hawthorne Effect?).
- I have learned that one needs to undertake classroom research. One needs to intervene – observation alone isn't a good enough indicator of how much children are learning.
- In my research, I delved into how my lessons were arranged and the effectiveness (or not) of my teaching. I looked closely at my learning strategies. It allowed me

to construct a unit that was designed for junior primary students' needs and interests and my research allowed my to construct strategies accordingly.

• I discovered that kids know how to learn – the project taught me to listen to them.

Acknowledgements

Grateful acknowledgement is made to the British Council for financial support. Figure 16.1, 'Reflective practice model of professional education development' from *Training Foreign Language Teachers: A Reflective Approach* (M. Wallace, 1991), is reproduced by kind permission of Cambridge University Press.

References

Allwright. D. and K. M. Bailey. 1991. *Focus on the Language Classroom*. Cambridge: CUP.

Chalmers, A. 1990. *Science and its Fabrication*, 21. Milton Keynes: Open University Press.

LeCompte, M. and J. Goetz. 1982. 'Problems of reliability and validity in ethnographic research.' *Review of Educational Research*, 52/1.

Lewis, C. 1992. Action research with French immersion teachers: a pilot study. Unpublished monograph, University of British Columbia: Canada.

Mickan, P. 1991. LIPT: Languages Inservice Program for Teachers Stage 3 1990. Action Research Reports Volume 6, March 1991. Adelaide: Languages and Multicultural Centre.

Nunan, D. 1992. *Research Methods in Language Learning*. Cambridge: CUP.

Van Lier, L. 1992. Not the nine o'clock linguistics class: investigating contingency grammar. Unpublished monograph, Monterey Institute for International Training, Monterey: California.

Wallace, M. 1991. *Training Foreign Language Teachers: A Reflective Approach*. Cambridge: CUP.

Chapter 17

Susan Feez

CURRICULUM EVOLUTION IN THE AUSTRALIAN ADULT MIGRANT ENGLISH PROGRAM

1 Introduction

1.1 The Adult Migrant English Program

THIS CHAPTER TRACES THE DEVELOPMENT OF curriculum and syllabus design in the Australian Adult Migrant English Program (AMEP). The AMEP is an English-language programme offered by the Australian government to all immigrants of non-English speaking background. Many people believe that the AMEP has been an important element in the successful integration of the thousands of people from diverse backgrounds who have migrated to Australia since the Second World War.

1.2 Fifty years of curriculum development

Over the fifty years of the AMEP, teachers have interpreted developments in applied linguistics in order to customise the curriculum to the needs of non-English speaking immigrants. Their interpretations have reflected their beliefs about language and language learning, both conscious and unconscious. These beliefs have shaped the way teachers in the AMEP have divided language up into chunks of content and then sequenced the content into classroom activities. Developments in applied linguistics over the last fifty years have resulted in three distinct waves of teaching approaches in the AMEP. These are:

1   structural approaches
2   learner-centred, needs-based, communicative approaches
3   text-based approaches.

2.1 Structural approaches

2.1.1 The origins of structural approaches

At the beginning of the twentieth century the learning of a foreign language in formal educational settings was limited to the privileged few. Students learnt the language by studying grammar rules and using these rules to translate literary texts, a method known as grammar-translation. As the century unfolded and more people had the opportunity or need to travel, there was a demand for approaches which taught people how to communicate in a wider range of contexts with speakers of other languages. Applied linguists in Britain and America responded to this demand in different ways. British applied linguists developed situational language teaching, while in America audiolingual methods were developed. (For an account of these developments see Howatt, 1984; Richards and Rodgers, 1986).

The AMEP looked to British situational language teaching, which linked structures 'to situations in which they could be used' (Richards and Rodgers, 1986: 35). British situational language teaching had emerged because a group of British linguists, in particular Firth and Halliday, were exploring how structure and meaning were related to context and situation (see Richards and Rodgers, 1986).

2.1.2 Structural approaches and behavioural educational psychology

Teachers using situational/structural approaches taught learners the component parts of language. They used techniques developed by behavioural psychologists to teach 'correct' language habits and accurate forms. Words and structures were taught in a fixed sequence through response, repetition and memorisation using, for example, imitation drills and substitution exercises.

2.1.3 Situational/structural approaches in the AMEP

Situational language teaching was used in the AMEP because non-English-speaking migrants needed to be able to use 'real-world' English as quickly as possible on arrival in Australia. All learners in the AMEP were taught the same dialogues in a fixed sequence from a common textbook. These dialogues were 'situated' within an everyday 'setting' such as a restaurant or a railway station. The dialogues introduced lexical items and grammatical structures which were then practised by the learners in follow-up activities. The dialogues used at the time now seem very contrived and inauthentic nevertheless, they drew learners' attention to language use in everyday settings.

The linking of structures to situation in the AMEP curriculum was an early example of the close link which continues to this day between the academic discipline of applied linguistics and the development of curriculum and expertise in the AMEP. When compared with equivalent language learning approaches of the day, the situational approach stands out for its responsiveness to the needs of learners. Through this syllabus AMEP teachers were developing expertise in linking the language learnt in the classroom and the language learners needed to use in real life. This expertise became the foundation on which future developments in AMEP curriculum were based.

Other innovations during this period now taken for granted everywhere as TESOL best practice include:

- a concern with *all* the macroskills of language – listening, speaking, reading and writing
- the use of themes and topics as a basis for course design
- classroom management strategies involving elicitation techniques, pair and group work
- presentation and practice techniques which incorporated realia, concrete and visual materials, gesture and mime
- the identification of teaching objectives in terms of what the learner should be able to do with English at the end of the course.

2.1.4 The challenge to structural approaches

Despite the innovations outlined above, the situational approach retained the following limitations:

- Language forms were learnt in isolation and in a fixed progression irrespective of the learner's needs and goals.
- Language learning was product-oriented, teacher-centred, concerned with accuracy more than fluency, and atomistic, that is, concentrating on individual isolated phrases and structures.
- Grammar and vocabulary were taught in isolation from the way language was used in real life situations (see Yalden 1987a).

2.2 Leaner-centred, needs-based communicative approaches

From the end of the 1970s the AMEP began to move away from a centralised, structural approach towards an individualised syllabus in which classroom teachers were responsible for syllabus design. Teachers constructed their syllabuses from a diverse repertoire of syllabus elements and methodologies. These can be roughly grouped according to whether they were informed by:

1 second language acquisition and progressive pedagogies
2 communicative and social theories of language and language learning.

2.2.1 Natural language learning and progressive pedagogies

Approaches which were described as more 'natural' ways of learning a language emerged after the American linguist Chomsky claimed that language use was 'not imitated behaviour but . . . created anew from underlying knowledge of abstract rules' (Richards and Rodgers, 1986: 59). Following Chomsky, second language acquisition (SLA) theorists began to describe language learning as a process in which learners actively test their emerging interpretations of the new language.

Influenced by SLA, AMEP teachers began to understand that a learner's non-standard approximation of the target language, or interlanguage, was not merely 'incorrect' but rather revealed how the learner was progressing (Corder, 1981; Selinker, 1991). AMEP teachers felt that, if language learners were in an environment rich in language input just beyond what they were able to produce themselves in a stress-free environment, they would acquire the target language unconsciously, effortlessly and fluently (Krashen, 1988).

A stress-free learning environment was achieved by drawing on the progressive pedagogies which had emerged in Western education by the end of the 1960s. Progressive pedagogies encouraged teachers to abandon their traditional authoritarian role in order to:

- develop more equal and respectful relationships with learners
- facilitate humane, interesting and interactive educational settings
- recognise and respond to the individual needs, interests and motivations of learners
- encourage learners to take responsibility for their own learning, to take risks and to discover knowledge as they need it.

AMEP teachers were especially concerned with learning principles appropriate to adults including, for example, self-directed and contract learning (Knowles, 1990). Some AMEP teachers also became interested in approaches which highlighted social justice, and political and personal freedom (for example, Freire, 1972).

By the end of the 1980s many AMEP teachers had developed the following beliefs about language learning:

- Fluency is more important than accuracy.
- Intervention in the learning process is counter-productive because it diminishes the individual's motivation, self-expression and personal development and takes responsibility for learning away from the learner.
- Learners should 'own' their learning so teachers should negotiate the curriculum with learners based on learner need.
- Classroom materials should be based on authentic language use and teachers should draw on a wide range of methodologies.

2.2.2 Hymes, Halliday, communication and discourse

Communicative and social theories of language and language learning emerged from the work of linguists who were concerned with meaning, function and social context, in particular Hymes in the United States and Halliday in the United Kingdom (see Yalden, 1987a). Hymes (1972) used the term 'communicative competence' to account for the two kinds of knowledge successful language users apply. These are:

- knowledge about language
- knowledge about the appropriate language to use in particular social contexts.

Research into the nature of communicative competence lead to the development of a range of approaches to language teaching known collectively as communicative language teaching. (See the following for accounts of these approaches: Brumfit, 1986; Richards and Rodgers, 1986; Melrose, 1991: 1–16; Yalden, 1987b). By the end of the 1980s the communicative language teaching methodologies had become the basis of the AMEP curriculum.

Meanwhile Halliday (1975; 1976; 1978) was developing a comprehensive, systematic way of describing language in terms of:

- the *meanings* people make with language
- what people *do* with language
- the *social contexts* in which language is used.

The work of Hymes and Halliday influenced the English language teaching syllabus documents prepared by the Council of Europe in the early 1970s (van Ek and Alexander, 1980). These documents were based on stretches of meaningful language with a real communicative purpose rather than on isolated sentences, grammatical structures or lexical items. Wilkins (1976) categorised these units of meaningful language in terms of two general headings:

- functions: units of meaning identified on the basis of their communicative purpose, for example *greeting*, *persuading* and *suggesting*.
- notions: the language used to express a general area of meaning such as *time*, *quantity* and *emotion*.

Increasingly AMEP teachers provided learners with opportunities to use extended chunks of language, or discourse, to achieve communicative purposes in context rather than simply providing opportunities for memorising isolated grammatical structures and vocabulary. In addition language proficiency in the AMEP began to be assessed against scales which described what learners could *do* with language at different levels in terms of extended stretches of meaningful language, as well as in terms of grammar and vocabulary (Ingram and Wiley, 1984).

As the 1980s progressed, AMEP teachers became increasingly aware of criticism being levelled at inventories of notions and functions, for example by Candlin (as cited in Melrose, 1991: 19–20) and Widdowson (1979: 248 as quoted in Yalden, 1987a: 77). These critics pointed out that, although these were lists of units of meaning rather than lists of words and structures, they remained inventories of isolated components and so were of questionable value in developing communicative competence.

2.2.3 The challenge to learner-centred, needs-based communicative approaches

By the mid-1980s, for each new class they taught, AMEP teachers were expected to:

- analyse the needs of learners (Brindley, 1984)
- negotiate language learning objectives with the learners
- use functional-notional inventories to select and sequence syllabus elements
- implement learner-centred, communicative methodologies based on self-directed learning and the development of fluency
- provide opportunities for developing the skills and strategies learners needed if they were to become effective listeners, speakers, readers and writers.

In practice the task of designing coherent courses from all these components proved to be very difficult. As teachers tried to devise situations in which the students could practise different words and structures in 'natural' contexts of use, fluency was emphasised at the expense of accuracy. Teachers tended to select and sequence syllabus elements according to their perception of what 'worked' in the classroom, forgetting that communicative practice alone would not develop communicative competence. As Hymes had pointed out from the beginning, learners also needed to develop knowledge about language.

By the end of the 1980s AMEP teachers were grappling with 'the complexities of designing individualised programs with little institutional support' (Brindley and Hood, 1990: 223–4). A consequence of this was that AMEP learners had little sense of progression or achievement (Brindley, 1985; Nunan, 1987). To overcome these difficulties, teachers requested 'non-mandatory curriculum guidelines to assist them in planning courses to meet the needs of commonly recurring learner groups' (Nunan, 1987: 59).

One commonly recurring learning group in the AMEP were 'stabilised' learners who had achieved a non-standard interlanguage which allowed them to survive in Australia. These learners, however, did not progress to more standard forms of English. Because teachers were focusing on fluency in classrooms and were trying not to intervene in language learning, learners were interacting with each other, not with the teacher. Consequently the opportunities for learners to engage with standard English were limited and their interlanguage became established as the means of communication. Non-standard forms of English limited students' opportunities in Australia, especially in further education and employment.

AMEP curriculum developers realised that it was time to revisit the idea of planned intervention in the process of language learning, but this time from the perspective of:

> an interactive model of grammar and discourse, one that demonstrates the necessity and importance of both levels of language to the language learning process and to the attainment of communicative competence.
>
> (Celce-Murcia, 1990: 146)

Developments in the wider field of English-language teaching were supporting this shift. Widdowson (1990: 164), for example, strongly challenged the 'natural' approach to language learning.

The early 1990s initiated a period of rapid social, economic and industrial change in Australia. AMEP learners needed increased levels of English-language proficiency if they were to access community services, find work or participate in further education in this changing environment. If their English-language skills were to be recognised in this environment, AMEP learners would have to demonstrate their language skills in terms of explicit outcomes of a recognised curriculum (for an account of this period, see Hagan, 1994).

The writers of the AMEP curriculum were faced with several challenges. The needs of AMEP learners in the changing social environment demanded that the AMEP curriculum comprise:

- a flexible framework to accommodate the diverse needs of learners across a wide range of teaching contexts across Australia
- a clear learning pathway
- a common language for describing learner needs and goals
- explicit statements of what learners could do at the end of each stage of the pathway, that is, explicit outcomes
- a communicative approach which reflected real-life language use in terms of discourse rather than isolated elements such as words, structures, functions or notions
- an explicit and systematic approach to the teaching of language structures and features.

To meet the challenges, the AMEP curriculum developers again turned to the work of Halliday. They began with Halliday's idea of a text being a whole unit of language use. Working with whole texts in real contexts of language use, AMEP learners would have the opportunity to develop communicative fluency as well as accuracy in terms of text structure, grammar, lexis and surface features such as pronunciation and spelling. The AMEP curriculum developers also turned to a pedagogy developed by Halliday's colleagues in Australia. This pedagogy, the genre approach, provided a model for explicit intervention in the process of language learning.

2.3 Genre-based approaches

2.3.1 Language as text

The foundation of the genre approach is the study of whole texts in context. A text is a unit of discourse (spoken or written) in which related meanings are woven together to make a unified whole which achieves a social purpose (see Halliday in Halliday and Hasan, 1985: 10). Halliday has shown that there is a systematic link between a text and the context in which it is used. Systemic functional linguists explore register variation in language; in other words they explore the way texts vary from social situation to social situation. Consider, for example, the differences between the following texts:

- a telephone bill and a legal bill
- an exchange between a parent and a child and an exchange between a teacher and a student
- a story published in a book and a story told in casual conversation.

At the same time they look for the underlying patterns in texts which remain relatively stable in order to achieve similar purposes across registers and which make texts culturally and socially meaningful.

2.3.2 The genre approach

A group of educators drawing on systemic linguistics developed a pedagogy based on the notion of 'genre'. (For more detailed accounts of the genre approach in schools, see Cope, Kalantzis, Kress and Martin, 1993; Kress, 1991; Martin, 1993; Rothery, 1996). A genre is a relatively stable pattern which recurs in texts used to achieve the same general social purpose. For example, linguists are able to describe patterns which recur when people use language to:

- build a relationship through casual conversation
- recount a series of events to share what happened with someone else
- entertain by telling a suspenseful story or an amusing anecdote
- explain how something works
- give instructions
- persuade someone to your point of view
- organise information
- make a story newsworthy for the electronic or print media.

This information is very useful to language teachers and learners because it makes learning to use language a much less hit-and-miss affair. It makes it possible to identify what people need to be able to do with language in order to be successful in education, in the community and in employment. Learners work with individual texts which exemplify different genres in order to learn:

- the overall patterns of different genres of communication
- specific language features used in examples of that genre most relevant to their individual learning needs.

Genre pedagogy is a teaching approach in which students work systematically and comprehensively with the language of texts belonging to the genres relevant to their educational goals. Genre pedagogy is usually presented to teachers in the form of a cycle of teaching and learning. (For a diagram and detailed description of the teaching-learning cycle initially used in schools, see Rothery, 1996: 101–4.)

2.3.3 A language-based theory of learning

The cycle of teaching and learning designed to teach about texts reflects Halliday's (1992: 19) view of learning as a process of 'learning to mean and to expand one's meaning potential'. Research into first language development by Halliday and his colleagues revealed language learning to be a social process (for example, Halliday, 1975; Painter, 1985; 1996). Halliday (1991) describes educational learning as an organised social process in which the construction of meaning takes place systematically.

2.3.4 Scaffolded learning

In a genre-based cycle of teaching and learning:

- what is to be learned and assessed is made explicit to students
- teacher–learner interaction is valued as much as interaction between learners.

The design of the genre-based teaching-learning cycle draws on the theories of the Russian psychologist Vygotsky (1934/1978; 1986). Vygotsky's work suggests that instruction precedes learning. Drawing on both Halliday's and Vygotsky's ideas, the genre approach is used to construct a social context in which language learning can occur. In that context:

* teachers and learners collaborate
* teachers interact with learners to guide them towards their potential level of performance
* the teacher's role is an authoritative one similar to that of an expert supporting an apprentice
* language is used interactively to mediate learning.

The genre-based cycle of teaching and learning has two key characteristics:

* scaffolding
* joint construction.

Scaffolding occurs when the teacher contributes what learners are not yet able to do alone or do not yet know. Teachers adjust, and strategically diminish, their contribution, supporting learners as they progress towards their potential level of independent performance.

Joint construction occurs when teacher and learner share the responsibility for functioning until the learner has the knowledge and skills to perform independently and with sole responsibility. (For further discussions of scaffolded learning see Gray, 1985, 1987, Gibbons, 1998.)

The genre-based teaching-learning cycle was initially developed for primary schools, but it has been adapted for ESL (see Burns, Joyce and Gollin, 1996: 88; Cornish, 1992: 17; Hammond, 1989; 1990; Hammond, Burns, Joyce, Brosnan and Gerot, 1992; Hood, Solomon and Burns, 1996; Joyce, 1992: 44). All variations of genre pedagogy, especially those designed for more advanced students and adults, provide learners with opportunities to extend and customise their knowledge about text into specific contexts which are important to their own educational or personal goals.

2.3.5 *Critical literacy*

All variations of genre pedagogy also emphasise the development in learners of a critical approach to what they are learning (see Rothery, 1996: 116–20). By making the language patterns of different types of texts more visible, genre pedagogy also makes more visible the values and worldviews embodied in those patterns. These values and worldviews are then open for discussion, negotiation, criticism and challenge (Christie, 1991: 11; Christie, 1995).

3 The Certificates in Spoken and Written English

3.1 *A national curriculum framework*

The genre approach provided the writers of the national AMEP curriculum with two key design principles:

1   a discourse-oriented unit of language around which to write generalised curriculum outcomes
2   an interactive pedagogy for intervening in and supporting language learning.

The writers of the curriculum used these principles to develop a curriculum framework called the Certificates in Spoken and Written English (CSWE). This framework was written in terms of a pathway of language outcomes organised across four levels:

1   Beginner
2   Post-beginner
3   Intermediate
4   Advanced.

The CSWE language outcomes are written in terms of genres to make the language descriptions general enough to be a common language for planning courses and monitoring and assessing learner progress across the AMEP. At the same time Halliday's language model allows teachers to use the notion of register to customise the very general genre descriptions of the framework in order to meet the specific language-learning needs of individual AMEP learners.

3.2 From curriculum to syllabus

3.2.1 Defining terms

The writers of the CSWE differentiated between two levels of English-language provision, one general, the curriculum level, and the other specific, the syllabus level.

3.2.2 General outcomes: the curriculum level

The CSWE is written at the general level of curriculum. Learners work through the CSWE pathway at a pace related to their educational background. As they move from level to level, they work in increasingly specialised contexts, from a general learning context at beginner and post-beginner level to more specialised contexts related to employment, further study or community access at the intermediate and advanced levels.

The discourse-oriented learning outcomes are written in terms of very general genre categories, for example, description, recount, instructions or information text. These categories are then linked to a macroskill – listening, speaking, reading or writing – in order to describe what a learner should be able to do with language at the end of a course of study at that level, for example:

•   Can demonstrate understanding of a spoken information text
•   Can tell a recount
•   Can read written instructions
•   Can write a description.

The outcomes are grouped into language-learning domains:

•   listening and speaking
•   reading
•   writing.

This organisation makes it possible to break the curriculum into smaller modules for students who need intensive work in listening and speaking or reading and writing where one of these areas lags behind the other. The complete learning pathway is illustrated in Figure 17.1.

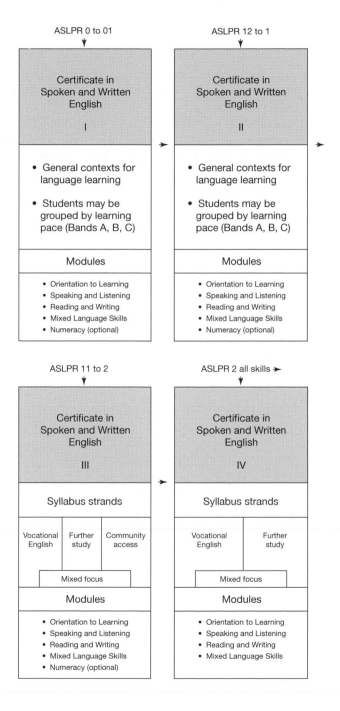

Figure 17.1 Certificates in Spoken and Written English: curriculum structure

1	Can undertake the roles and responsibilities of a learner in a formal learning environment
2	Can use a range of learning strategies and resources
3	Can demonstrate understanding of a spoken information text
4	Can provide personally relevant information using spoken language
5	Can request information/goods using spoken language
6	Can tell a short recount
7	Can read social sight signs
8	Can read simple written instructions
9	Can read a short information text
10	Can read a short narrative/recount
11	Can complete a simple formatted text
12	Can write a short description
13	Can write a short recount

Figure 17.2 Outcomes for Certificate I in Spoken and Written English

The way curriculum outcomes are organised into domains within a level is illustrated by the list of outcomes for Certificate I in Spoken and Written English, the beginners' level, in Figure 17.2.

Each outcome is written in terms of a generalised text type, or genre. The key language features of each text type are written as elements of the outcome. Performance criteria for assessment are based on the elements. Thus the performance criteria for each outcome draw on what the genre approach tells us about the predictable language features of that type of text. The elements, and their related performance criteria, are organised, using Halliday's language model, into:

- features relating to the structure and texture of whole texts
- lexical and grammatical features
- phonological or graphological features.

(For overviews of the stratified systemic functional language model see Eggins, 1994: 1–24; Feez, 1998: 8; for an introduction to functional grammar see Butt, Fahey, Feez, Spinks and Yallop, 2000).

The number and complexity of the performance criteria for each outcome depend on the learner's level. The range within which students will be assessed against those criteria, and an evidence guide, is also indicated for each outcome.

Figure 17.3 shows an example of a writing outcome for Certificate 1, the beginner level. Because the outcomes of the CSWE are explicit, learners studying within the framework know what is expected of them at any point in the learner pathway. They are also able to map their own progress. In addition, teachers working within the AMEP, and in other contexts where the CSWE is used, share a common framework for course design and for assessment.

Elements	Performance criteria	Range statements	Evidence guide
Discourse structure			**Sample task**
1 can use appropriate staging	• uses appropriate staging, i.e. beginning, middle and end (orientation, sequence of events and optional reorientation)	• at least five clauses with correct past tense forms	• Learners recount sequence of past events, for example excursion, weekend activities
2 can use conjunctions	• joins simple clauses with conjunctions, for example 'and', 'then', 'because'	• uses at least one conjunction	
		• familiar/relevant topic	
Grammar and vocabulary		• recourse to dictionary	
3 can use vocabulary appropriate to topic	• uses vocabulary appropriate to topic	• may include a few grammatical, punctuation and spelling errors, but errors should not interfere with meaning or dominate text	
4 can construct simple clauses	• constructs simple clauses		
5 can construct simple noun groups	• constructs simple noun groups and uses adjectives, for example 'I had a good weekend', 'My weekend was good'	• may redraft	
6 can use action verbs in the past tense	• uses action verbs in the past tense		
7 can use personal pronouns	• uses personal pronouns as required		
8 can express time and/or location	• indicates time or location as required, for example by using adverbs and/or prepositional phrases		

Graphology

It is assumed that:

• there may be inaccuracies in letter formation, spelling and punctuation
• teaching programmes will pay attention to graphological features

In CSWE I the punctuation focus will be on capital letters, full stops and question marks.

Figure 17.3 Competency 13: Can write a short recount

3.2.3 Specific objectives: the syllabus level

The general CSWE framework is common to all AMEP programmes. Teachers report learner achievement at the end of a course against the performance criteria of the common framework. The design of individual courses of study, however, is carried out at the level of the syllabus. At this level teachers address the needs of specific groups of learners.

Course objectives are statements about what is planned for a particular course of study. They bridge the gap between the general outcomes and a specific learning context. Course objectives are a distillation of an analysis of learners' needs and goals and other variables of the learning context.

To design a systematic plan of course content customised to the learners in their class, teachers work through the following steps:

1   Analysing learner need and set specific course objectives, including language-learning objectives related to the immediate contexts where learners need to use English.
2   Linking the specific objectives to the general curriculum outcomes, identifying the immediate contexts in which learners will be using texts belonging to the genre of that outcome.
3   Identifying and selecting what needs to be learnt to meet the course objectives.
4   Sequence the syllabus elements into an effective progression of teaching and learning.
5   Planning how to monitor learner progress during the course and assess learner achievement at the end of the course against the specific course objectives.
6   Planning how to report learner achievement against the general curriculum outcomes.

3.2.4 From curriculum to syllabus: from genre to register

We have already seen that language outcomes in the CSWE framework are based on generalised text patterns, or genres. To customise the general curriculum outcome to a specific course, teachers identify the immediate context of use in which these text patterns will be used. In other words they identify the register or variety of language learners will be working with.

For the selected context of use, teachers identify the social activities and topics which relate to the chosen situation of use (the field), as well as the role of those involved in the situation (the tenor). The CSWE outcomes are already written in terms of whether the texts will be spoken or written, that is, the role language is playing in the situation (mode). For contexts of use relevant to specific students, teachers may need to refine the mode description of some outcomes. For example, they may need to teach a particular spoken text in the context of using the telephone rather than speaking face-to-face. (For more detailed introductions to Halliday's model of register see Eggins, 1994: 49–80 and Feez, 1998: 75–81).

If at the level of curriculum, learners are working towards the general outcome Can write a short recount (CSWE I, Competency 13), they might work with texts such as the following:

* a recount of an excursion to a place of interest (field) for a class book (mode) being prepared for visitors to the teaching centre on open day (tenor)
* a recount of a traffic accident (field) onto an insurance form (mode) as part of a claim to an insurance company (tenor)
* a recount of a mishap with an electrical appliance (field) in a letter of complaint (mode) to a manufacturer (tenor)

- a recount of a visit to a tourist destination (field) on a postcard (mode) to a friend (tenor).

If learners are preparing for employment, they might work with this text:

- a recount of an incident (field) on a shift hand-over report (mode) for the foreman (tenor).

Learners could produce any of these texts at the end of a cycle of teaching and learning to meet the requirements of the competency.

3.2.5 Language features

The elements and performance criteria of each CSWE outcome are listed in two categories of language features:

- discourse structure, which relates to the recognisable parts of the genre pattern and the way clauses are linked to construct a cohesive, unified text
- grammar and vocabulary.

As learners work with specific texts, the elements and performance criteria of the outcome guide what they learn about the structural, grammatical, lexical and phonological or graphological language features of texts of that type. Each element is addressed within the specific context of situation in which the learners are learning to write the text type.

3.2.6 Units of work

The process of syllabus design also involves linking the different types of texts being taught in the course into related units of work. For example, a unit of work on writing a text belonging to the genre of recount at CSWE Level 1 can be linked to units of work on spoken accounts and written descriptions. These units of work might be based on related contexts of use or students might be shown how to transfer what they have learnt to completely new contexts of use.

3.2.7 Assessment

The approach to assessment which underpins the CSWE is described by Macken and Slade (1993: 205–6, 207) in the following way:

> an effective language assessment program must be linguistically principled, explicit, criterion-referenced, and must inform different types of assessment, including diagnostic, formative and summative assessment. . . . Shared criteria based on a sound knowledge of language and its varieties will enable teachers to reflect on the strengths and to diagnose weaknesses in the texts produced by their students.

The general curriculum outcomes of the CSWE provide general statements and related performance criteria against which all AMEP teachers can assess learner achievement within a common framework. Specific course objectives provide a syllabus-level focus for assessment of individual learner progress. Teachers can use the data collected at both levels to evaluate their course design.

Instead of grading and ranking learners against vague notions of general language proficiency, assessment within the CSWE framework enables learners to demonstrate, against the explicit criteria of the curriculum and syllabus, what they have learnt during their course.

3.3 Text-based syllabus design

Texts, these stretches of unified, meaningful and purposeful natural language, are the core component of a text-based syllabus. Each text is a single instance of language use in a particular context of situation. Texts, however, draw on predictable generic text patterns, or genres, which relate to social purposes and the broader cultural context. Syllabus elements and syllabus design principles focus on the use of whole texts in context.

3.3.1 Syllabus elements

The key elements of a text-based syllabus in the context of the CSWE are:

*   *texts*, identified according to the type, or genre, they belong to, and therefore, to the curriculum outcome to which they relate
*   *topics*, organised according to whether they relate to community access, employment or further study
*   *language features*, related to the text type of the text in which they are used
*   *skills and strategies*, organised according to situation/register, especially macroskill
*   *activities and tasks*, including teaching activities and assessment activities, which determine the materials and resources required.

Figure 17.4 is an outline for a unit of work on casual conversation to illustrate how syllabus elements have been selected to customise a general curriculum outcome to the needs of a specific group of learners.

3.3.2 Design principles

A text-based syllabus is what Ur (1996: 178) describes as a 'mixed or multi-strand' syllabus. It combines different syllabus elements – such as topics, texts, structures, lexis, skills and strategies – 'in order to be maximally comprehensive' (Ur, 1996: 178). In summary, a text-based syllabus is a mixed syllabus in which the organising principle is the study of whole texts in context. In the context of the CSWE, course objectives, and therefore learner need, determine the selection of syllabus elements. These elements are then incorporated into a text-based cycle of teaching and learning.

3.3.3 From syllabus to methodology: a text-based cycle of teaching and learning

Genre pedagogy, and its interactive cycle of teaching and learning, provides teachers with a framework for selecting, organising and sequencing the comprehensive mix of text-based syllabus elements in a principled way, supporting learners as they gradually move to increasingly independent language use.

The process of sequencing syllabus elements, that is, *what* is to be taught, involves teachers in deciding *how* to teach them; in other words, it involves teachers in choosing a methodology. The text-based methodology designed to support learners working towards CSWE outcomes is represented graphically in Figure 17.4.

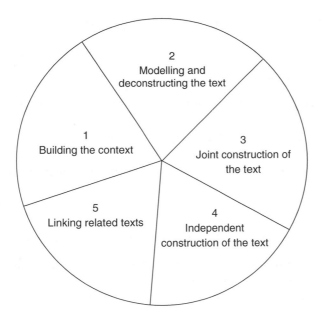

Figure 17.4 Methodology to support learners working towards CSWE outcomes
Source: Feez with Joyce, 1998:28, adapted from Callaghan and Rothery, 1988; Cornish, 1992; Green, 1992

This methodology is built around five phases of classroom interaction adapted from the original genre-based cycle of teaching and learning (Rothery, 1996).

Phase 1: Building context

Context-building is a critical phase for second-language learners. In this phase learners experience and explore the social context of the target text type, building cultural knowledge and the knowledge of the immediate context of use. Once this knowledge is shared between teacher and learners it can become the foundation of subsequent language learning. Typical context-building activities are brainstorming; listening and talking to others; guided reading of relevant material; viewing realia, pictures or video; taking part in role-plays and discussions, cross-cultural comparisons, guided research or field trips.

For example, to build the context for filling out an insurance claim, students might engage in the following activities:

- viewing a television advertisement for a car insurance company
- build up vocabulary lists
- research information about insurance written in their first language to identify key words and concepts they need to understand in English
- meet and interview, in English or in their first language, people who have played different roles in the context of car insurance in Australia
- complete a table comparing the nature of car insurance in their country of origin and in Australia
- survey the different types of texts which they may be called on to use in the context of car insurance in Australia.

Phase 2: Modelling and deconstructing text

Phase 2 is teacher-directed. Learners are introduced to model texts belonging to the target genre in the context they explored in Phase 1. Learners use the model texts to study the structure and language features of the text type. This is the phase in which second-language learners learn the grammar of the target language, but in the context of purposeful language use.

For example, activities relevant to writing recounts at beginner level would focus on the structure of simple declarative clauses with past simple tense forms of action verbs, as well as the use of conjunctions and prepositional phrases to sequence the clauses in time. Students would also learn the structure of noun groups. Many traditional ELT grammar activities can be effectively used during this phase, although, in the context of Halliday's grammar, learners' attention is always drawn to meaning as well as form.

Phase 3: Joint construction

During this phase the teacher begins to hand over responsibility to the learners. The learners contribute to the construction of a text belonging to the target text type with the teacher acting as guide, and if necessary, scribe. Teacher and learners discuss and negotiate the meanings they are making as they go.

Phase 4: Independent construction

During this phase the scaffolding is taken away and learners research the context and work with their own texts independently, consulting with other learners and the teacher only as needed. Achievement assessment is carried out at this stage of the cycle.

Phase 5: Making links to related texts

At the end of the cycle, links are made to related text types, so learners have the opportunity to recycle what they have learnt in other contexts of use, comparing and contrasting different texts and their uses and effectiveness. Some learners may be ready to adapt the text type they have learnt to control to a specific purpose, adjusting the stages and the language features as needed.

3.3.4 Meeting the needs of different learners

Whenever necessary the teaching-learning cycle is modified to suit the needs of different learners. Learners can enter at any phase of the cycle, returning to an earlier phase for review as needed or skipping phases if they are not ready or if they do not need them. In most adult ESL classes the context-building phase is essential. Some beginning learners with minimal formal learning in their first language, however, may not go beyond the joint construction phase for some more challenging text types. In contrast, many tertiary-educated adult learners with sophisticated study skills find the joint construction phase unnecessary.

3.3.5 A language teaching repertoire

A characteristic of the teaching-learning cycle which makes it so valuable to AMEP teachers is that it allows them to draw on a variety of tasks, activities, classroom management styles and assessment procedures. Teachers in the AMEP draw on a second-language teaching repertoire which has been built up over fifty years. Text-based syllabus design makes it possible for teachers to select, modify and locate a variety of methods in a principled and strategic way. In other words, they select from the language-teaching repertoire methods which make it possible to build the type of classroom interaction required by the different phases of the cycle.

4 Conclusion

Overall the AMEP has benefited greatly from basing its new curriculum on genre pedagogy. AMEP learners now can track their progress against general descriptions of English text patterns while, at the same time, learning to customise their own texts to meet the demands of their immediate situations. Learners can consciously build the cultural and linguistic knowledge which will help them make the most of the new community they are entering. The CSWE is a framework within which teachers plan courses and map learning pathways.

To support curriculum change in the AMEP, classroom materials and resources modelling a text-based approach to syllabus design have been published (for example Brown and Cornish, 1997; Clemens and Crawford, 1994; Cornish, 1992; Delaruelle, 1998; Feez, 1998; Joyce, 1992; NSW AMES writing team, 1997). Professional development has included extensive training in educational linguistics, course design and assessment. Since the implementation of the new curriculum framework, there has also been an ongoing cycle of national classroom-based collaborative action research. The action research model provides teachers with a useful technique for reflecting on and renovating classroom practice (see Burns and Hood, 1995; 1997; 1998; Burns and Joyce, 1999).

Genre pedagogy, like language pedagogy generally, is evolving and changing. The way teachers in the AMEP are working with the pedagogy is also changing as different teachers interpret it in different ways. When teachers first applied genre pedagogy, many super-imposed structural approaches onto the generic descriptions of text structure and language features. This resulted in teachers teaching text patterns as fixed rules and forms rather than in terms of meaning and function. It also resulted in some teachers feeling that they had to abandon the learner-centred methods developed as part of needs-based, communicative approaches and return to teacher-centred classrooms. As teachers have adapted to the new curriculum environment, gaining knowledge, skill and confidence and adjusting their beliefs about language and language learning, they are increasingly integrating the best of situational, learner-centred and communicative approaches into a text-based framework. Teachers are also beginning to identify which aspects of the text-based approach need reviewing or developing.

The AMEP is currently experiencing a period of rapid change. Changing political and economic ideologies are moving the AMEP away from being a stable, unified, public-sector programme to a more fragmented market-oriented programme. It remains to be seen whether this new orientation will be able to deliver a service of comparable quality. It certainly is not clear whether the new environment will continue to support the principled development of AMEP curriculum and expertise in tandem with developments in the field of applied linguistics.

While the future for migrant education in Australia is unclear, it is clear that text-based approaches provide language educators with a strong foundation for further developments in language teaching. The key elements of this foundation are:

- an understanding of what constitutes a whole unit of language in the context of its use

- a methodology for providing learners with experience of whole units of language use in context while they are still only able to manage language fragments.

From this foundation, language educators have the opportunity to develop increasingly effective ways of teaching explicitly and systematically about text, grammar and lexis in order to make it possible for learners to build skills in spoken and written English which they would not be able to develop on their own.

References

Brindley, G. (1984) 'The role of needs analysis in adult ESL programme design'. In R. K. Johnson (ed.) *The Second Language Curriculum*, Cambridge: Cambridge University Press.

Brindley, G. (1985) *The Assessment of Second Language Proficiency: Issues and Approaches*, Adelaide: NCRC.

Brindley, G. and Hood, S. (1990) 'Curriculum innovation in adult ESL'. In G. Brindley (ed.) *The Second Language Curriculum in Action*, Sydney: NCELTR.

Brown, K. and Cornish, S. (1997) *Beach Street 1: An English Course for Adults*, Sydney: NSW AMES.

Brumfit, C. (ed.) (1986) *The Practice of Communicative Teaching*, Oxford: Pergamon Press.

Burns, A. and Hood, S. (eds) (1995) *Teachers' Voices: Exploring Course Design in a Changing Curriculum*, Sydney: NCELTR.

Burns, A. and Hood, S. (eds) (1997) *Teachers' Voices 2: Teaching Disparate Learner Groups*, Sydney: NCELTR.

Burns, A. and Hood, S. (eds) (1998) *Teachers' Voices 3: Teaching Critical Literacy*, Sydney: NCELTR.

Burns, A. and Joyce, H. (eds) (1999) *Teachers' Voices 4: Staying Learner-centred in a Competency-based Curriculum*, Sydney: NCELTR.

Burns, A., Joyce, H. and Gollin, S. (1996) *'I See what you Mean': Using Spoken Discourse in the Classroom: A Handbook for Teachers*, Sydney: NCELTR.

Butt, D., Fahey, R., Feez, S., Spinks, S. and Yallop, C. (2000) *Understanding Functional Grammar: An Explorer's Guide*, 2nd edn, Sydney: NCELTR.

Celce-Murcia, M. (1990) 'Discourse analysis and grammar instruction', *Annual Review of Applied Linguistics* 11: 135–51.

Christie, F. (1990) 'The changing face of literacy'. In F. Christie (ed.) *Literacy for a Changing World*, Melbourne: The Australian Council for Educational Research.

Christie, F. (ed.) (1991) *Teaching Critical Social Literacy: A Project of National Significance on the Preservice Preparation of Teachers for Teaching English Literacy*. A report submitted to the Federal Minister of Employment, Education and Training, Canberra.

Christie, F. (1995) 'Genre-based approaches to teaching literacy'. In M. L. Tickoo (ed.) *Reading and Writing: Theory into Practice*, Singapore: SEAMEO Regional Language Centre.

Clemens, J. and Crawford, J. (1994) *Words will Travel: An Integrated Communicative English Language Program for Intermediate Level Learners*, Marrickville, NSW: ELS.

Cope, B., Kalantzis, M., Kress, G. and Martin, J. (1993) 'Bibliographical essay: developing the theory and practice of genre-based literacy'. In B. Cope and M. Kalantzis (eds) *The Powers of Literacy: A Genre Approach to Teaching Writing*, London: The Falmer Press.

Corder, S. Pit (1981) *Error Analysis and Interlanguage*, Oxford: Oxford University Press.

Cornish, S. (1992) *Curriculum Guidelines*, Sydney: NSW AMES.

Delaruelle, S. (1998) *Beach Street 2: An English Course for Adults*, Sydney: NSW AMES.

Eggins, S. (1994) *An Introduction to Systemic Functional Linguistics*, London: Pinter.

Ek, J. van and Alexander, L. G. (1980) *Threshold Level English*, Oxford: Pergamon Press.

Feez, S. with Joyce, H. (1998) *Text-based Syllabus Design*, Sydney: NCELTR.

Freire, P. (1972) *Pedagogy of the Oppressed*, Harmondsworth: Penguin.

Gibbons, P. (1998) 'Classroom talk and the learning of new registers in a second language'. *Language and Education* 12 (2): 99–118.

Gray, B. (1985) 'Helping children become language learners in the classroom'. Paper given at the Annual Conference of the Meanjin Reading Council, Brisbane, May 1983, in M. Christie (ed.) *Aboriginal Perspectives on Experience and Learning: The Role of Language in Aboriginal Education*, Geelong, Victoria: Deakin University Press.

Gray, B. (1987) 'How natural is "natural" language teaching – employing wholistic methodology in the classroom' *The Australian Journal of Early Childhood* 12 (4): 3–19.

Green, J. (1992) *Making the Links*. Melbourne: AMES Victoria.

Hagan P. (1994) 'Competency-based curriculum: the NSW AMES experience', *Prospect: A Journal of Australian TESOL* 9 (2): 30–40, Sydney: NCELTR.

Halliday, M. A. K. (1975) *Learning How to Mean: Explorations in the Development of Language*, London: Edward Arnold.

Halliday, M. A. K. (1976) *System and Function in Language*. London: Oxford University Press.

Halliday, M. A. K. (1978) *Language as a Social Semiotic*, London: Edward Arnold.

Halliday, M. A. K. (1991) 'The notion of "context" in language education', in T. Le and M. McCausland, *Language Interaction and Development: Proceedings of the International Conference, Vietnam, 1991*, Launceston: University of Tasmania.

Halliday, M. A. K. (1992) 'Towards a language-based theory of learning'. Paper prepared for the Phonetic Society of Japan in the context of the Symposium on Language Acquisition Tokyo 3, October 1992.

Halliday, M. A. K. and Hasan, R. (1985) *Language, Context and Text: Aspects of Language in a Social Semiotic Perspective*, Geelong, Victoria: Deakin University Press.

Hammond, J. (1989) 'The NCELTR literacy project', *Prospect: A Journal of Australian TESOL* 5(1): 23–30, Sydney: NCELTR.

Hammond, J. (1990) 'Teacher expertise and learner responsibility in literacy development'. In *Prospect: A Journal of Australian TESOL* 5(3): 39–51, Sydney: NCELTR.

Hammond, J., Burns, A., Joyce, H., Brosnan, D. and Gerot, L. (1992) *English for Social Purposes*, Sydney: NCELTR.

Hood, S., Solomon, N. and Burns, A. (1996) *Focus on reading*, Sydney: NCELTR.

Howatt, A. (1984) *A History of English Language teaching*, Oxford: Oxford University Press.

Hymes, D. (1972) 'On communicative competence'. In J. B. Pride and J. Holmes (eds) *Sociolinguistics*, Harmondsworth: Penguin, pp. 269–93.

Ingram, D. and Wiley, E. (1984) *Australian Second Language Proficiency Ratings*, Canberra: Australian Government Printing Service.

Joyce, H. (1992) *Workplace Texts in the Language Classroom*, Sydney: NSW AMES.

Knowles, M. (1990) *The Adult Learner – A Neglected Species*, Houston: Gulf.

Krashen, S. (1988) *Second Language Acquisition and Second Language learning*. New York: Prentice-Hall.

Kress, G. (1991) 'Texture and meaning'. In *Working with Genre*, Papers from the 1989 Conference, University of Technology, Sydney, Sydney: Common Ground.

Macken, M. and Slade, D. (1993) 'Assessment: a foundation for effective learning in the school context'. In B. Cope and M. Kalantzis (eds) *The Powers of Literacy: A Genre Approach to the Teaching of Writing*, London: Falmer Press.

Martin, J. R. (1993) 'Genre and literacy – modelling context in educational linguistics. *Annual Review of Applied Linguistics* 13, 14–172.

Melrose, R. (1991) *The Communicative Syllabus: A Systemic-functional Approach to Language teaching*, London: Pinter.

NSW AMES writing team (1997) *Wanyarri: Indigenous Australia in the ESL Classroom*, Sydney: NSW AMES.

Nunan, D. (1987) *The Teacher as Curriculum Developer*, Sydney: NCELTR.

Painter, C. (1985) *Learning the Mother Tongue*, Geelong, Victoria: Deakin University Press.

Painter, C. (1996) 'The development of language as a resource for thinking: a linguistic view of learning'. In R. Hasan and G. Williams (eds) *Literacy in Society*, London: Longman.

Richards, J. C. and Rodgers, T. S. (1986) *Approaches and Methods in Language Teaching: A Description and Analysis*, Cambridge: Cambridge University Press.

Rothery, J. (1996) 'Making changes: developing an educational linguistics'. In R. Hasan and G. Williams (eds) *Literacy in Society*, London: Longman.

Selinker, L. (1991) *Rediscovering Interlanguage*, London: Longman.

Ur, P. (1996) *A Course in Language Teaching: Practice and Theory*, Cambridge: Cambridge University Press.

Vygotsky, L. S. (1934/1978) *Mind in Society: The Development of Higher Psychological Processes*, Cambridge: Cambridge University Press.

Vygotsky, L. S. (1986) *Thought and Language*, revised and edited by A. Kozulin, Cambridge, MA: MIT Press.

Widdowson, H. (1990) *Aspects of Language Teaching*, Oxford: Oxford University Press.

Wilkins, D. (1976) *Notional Syllabuses*, Oxford: Oxford University Press.

Yalden, J. (1987a) *Principles of Course Design for Language Teaching*, New York: Cambridge University Press.

Yalden, J. (1987b) *The Communicative Syllabus: Evolution, Design and Implementation*, London: Prentice-Hall.

Chapter 18

David R. Hall

MATERIALS PRODUCTION: THEORY AND PRACTICE

Introduction: learning a language

BEFORE PLANNING OR WRITING MATERIALS for language teaching, there is one crucial question we need to ask ourselves. The question should be the first item on the agenda at the first planning meeting. The question is this: *How do we think people learn language?*

Nobody knows how we learn language. Of course, there are plenty of theories around. Many people make a distinction between first language learning and second or foreign language learning. Others distinguish clearly between "learning" a language and "acquiring" a language. There is a further distinction between "learning to speak", "learning to understand spoken language", "learning to read", and "learning to write", with some thinking that these are similar processes, others that they are different but related processes, and still others thinking that they involve completely unrelated skills. Some think that we learn by studying and internalising rules, others that we learn by repeated practice of common patterns, yet others that we learn by memorising words and collocations, by simulating real situations, by negotiating, by hearing and reading things we can understand [. . .] The list is long.

No-one knows how we learn language, so the words *we think* in the original question are very important. What is our own opinion? What can the writing team agree on? It is our view of how we learn language that will underpin everything else that we do in planning and writing our materials. There are, of course, other important considerations, some of which will be mentioned here, and there are always constraints – the straitjacket of a centralised syllabus, the need for pupils to pass public examinations, the lack of library resources, a cultural preference for the teacher being the holder of all knowledge, the need for an orderly and industriously quiet classroom, and so on. But these should not govern what we must do. They should be accepted as features of the context in which we attempt to do what we think is the right thing to do.

In the second section of this chapter, I will put forward some of my own beliefs about language learning and teaching, suggesting criteria by which materials might be evaluated. The discussion is conducted under four headings: the need to communicate; the need for long-term goals; the need for authenticity; and the need for student-centredness. In the third and final section, I will examine materials from projects in which I have been involved and evaluate them in the light of the criteria.

Theory

The need to communicate

There are three things about language learning that are fairly obvious and uncontroversial, but which are not often enough stated together. First, just about everyone learns to communicate fluently in at least one language. This is normally the L1 or mother tongue. Second, very few people learn to communicate fluently in a new language learned entirely in formal language classes. Third, most people who learn to communicate fluently in a language which is not their L1 do so by spending a lot of time in situations where they have to use the language for some real communicative purpose.

The conclusion I draw from these three facts is that the need to communicate is at the heart of learning a language. If we want our pupils or students to learn English, we must put them in situations where they need to communicate in English. For real communication to take place, there are three conditions:

1   We must have something that we want to communicate.
2   We must have someone to communicate with.
3   We must have some interest in the outcome of the communication.

In most language-teaching materials, and in most language-teaching classrooms, these three conditions do not exist. It is, of course, unrealistic to expect that they could exist all the time. A secondary school class of forty pupils and their teacher cannot all have the need to communicate in a foreign language for their own purposes all the time. Nevertheless, given the lack of success of conventional classroom teaching, it is perhaps worth making the attempt to approximate as closely as possible to the three conditions.

The need for long-term goals

In devising a syllabus, materials or methodology for a language-teaching program, it has always been necessary to conduct some sort of needs analysis. This tends to concentrate on aspects of language structure, language function, situational features, technical content, or behavioural outcomes (competencies).

We should, however, look at the longer-term needs of students. The language-teacher operates within fairly tight limitations. What, in observable terms, can be achieved in a program of one school year when you see the students three times a week and they never have to use the target language outside those three hours? By the end of the year, the students may be able to perform more or less satisfactorily in a formal test, but only the really exceptional will have progressed to anything approaching fluency. No matter what exciting methodology you use, the results are always going to be disappointing.

It is only in the longer term that some students will experience the need to communicate in the target language and will have the chance to become fluent. In looking at needs, perhaps we should look more closely at this longer term. If we are going to help our students succeed in learning a language, we must prepare them for the opportunities which will come outside the classroom. In other words, we must teach them how to learn. By 'teaching how to learn', I do not mean to refer to learning in classroom settings, where considerable work has been done on learning styles and their applicability to the language class (Hawkey, 1982; Willing, 1989), but rather to the ability to take advantage of any opportunity to learn outside the classroom.

If a teacher is to provide students with the tools to learn language outside the classroom, the main aim has to be to give students confidence in their ability to communicate despite difficulties, to the point where they can: (a) initiate communicative events, and (b) persist with the attempted communication even when it becomes difficult. The use of gestures, facial expressions, rewordings, questions, guesswork, and approximations is a crucial part of such communication, and the ability to use such strategies becomes an essential feature, in my view, of student needs.

I believe that in a natural setting, people learn language by having to communicate something that they do not know how to say. While more elegant or more accurate or more verbal ways of expressing the point may be developed as similar situations are repeated, the real initial learning takes place when a solution has to be found to the problem of not knowing how to communicate something. It is the long-term goal of our language teaching to provide our students with the confidence and ability to do this.

The need for authenticity

In the light of the above assumptions about language learning and the long-term needs of language learners, the question of the use of authentic materials can be refocused. It is not, primarily, the materials themselves which have to be authentic. It is, rather, the response to the materials – what is done with them – that should be authentic.

Many materials are impeccably authentic, by which I mean that they are 'found' materials originally written for some other purpose than language teaching. But because they deal with topics from the students' particular specialisation, they often deal with topics which are already very familiar to students. The reading of such materials becomes merely an exercise, not involving an authentic need for reading – it is neither the seeking of specifically needed information nor the exploration of a new topic. in many cases, it is nothing more than the reading of a text for the purposes of being tested on it through various forms of comprehension tasks and linguistic manipulation.

An authentic response depends on the existence of an authentic need. In the classroom context, this need may only be an approximation and may be artificially created. It can be helped, in ESP materials, by close cooperation with the content teacher, so that the ESP materials complement and support what is happening in the content class. At the very least, an authentic response dictates the addressing of content rather than form, and discussion for clarification or expansion rather than for the mere checking of understanding. (I am not saying that teachers should not check understanding. Checking can be done just as easily and is more natural during genuinely communicative events.)

Kenny (1989) classifies student response to content into three categories:

* the empirical
* the interpretational
* the socially validated.

By 'empirical' is meant the addressing of the content as a context-free, isolated entity. The empirical response involves working out the meaning of a text within the boundaries of the text. The language teacher's typical tools of comprehension questions, structure manipulation exercises, summaries, vocabulary explanation, and mode-switching (e.g., text to table, graph to text) all stay firmly at the empirical level of response.

An 'interpretational' response addresses the meaning of a text in relation to the individual. It involves assimilating new knowledge into the structure of information in the individual's head. Learning styles are obviously important in this area, as they relate to the way in which knowledge and experience are stored and retrieved. The content is examined in relation to existing knowledge structures and belief systems. Traditional essays ("Compare and contrast the views of *x* and *y*") might include interpretational responses to a number of texts, as might examination of parallels and contradictions between different texts.

The 'socially validated' response involves exposing the individual's response to a text to group evaluation. In other words, it is not enough to assimilate new knowledge individually. The understanding of a text and the validity of that understanding need to be tested through group interaction, and the interpretation defended in a process of critical scrutiny. Public presentation of ideas through poster sessions, debates, presentations, and so on, is an opportunity for socially validated responses. In this context, the opportunity for cross-disciplinary communication in ESP classes with a heterogeneous student population should be seen as an advantage rather than a disadvantage (Hall, 1994).

To put these three categories of response another way: the empirical has a single dimension – the content; the interpretational has two dimensions – the content and the individual; while the socially validated adds a third dimension – that of society, represented in the classroom by the group. Combining the need for authentic response with the need for developing confidence to initiate and persist with communication, we can see that it is desirable to aim for a socially validated response to materials in class. It is also clear that most materials used in the language-teaching classroom approach neither social validation nor the prerequisites for communication. What sometimes looks like a social validation activity is often no more than an exercise in which real beliefs are not explored, the content being dictated by either the teacher or the materials. An example of this might be where a student is given notes on arguments for better public transport and asked to "role-play", by giving a presentation as a lobbyist to a group of other students playing the role of policy-makers.

The need for student-centredness

The language classroom may be thought of as having three components – the teacher, the learners, and the materials. Traditionally, all of the actual content of the class, i.e., what is talked about, comes from the teacher or the materials. The potential for learners to participate in generating materials has long been neglected. I would suggest that students themselves are in a unique position to look for relevant resource materials. They know what their own needs and interests are.

The process of learners searching for materials and then bringing the materials back to class where they are presented to other students involves more than simple selection. The process changes student status from passive receivers of information to active accountability (see Kenny, 1993). Their selection of materials not only has to be presented, it has to be defended. Where only teachers and textbooks have previously been exposed to comments about the repetitiveness, irrelevance, tedium, interest, variety, or pertinence of the lesson, now everyone becomes accountable.

I do not mean by this that ready-made or teacher-prepared materials and the teacher have no place. But materials writers might give more thought to the use they can make of student inventiveness and energy, and the advantages of allowing student participation in resource generation. It is possible to build opportunities for this into your materials: not everything has to be specified in advance. You do not have to be operating in a resource-rich environment to do this. Even beginning learners in an environment with few samples of target language use can be involved in content-generation, e.g., Clayton et al., 1993, Kenny and Laszewski, 1993.

Sample materials

I have been involved in a number of materials and curriculum development projects. I will here illustrate four of them and give an example of representative classroom activity from each, analysing the activity in terms of the above discussion.

A notional-structural approach

The development of the materials which became the "Nucleus: English for Science and Technology" series arose out of the demands of the teaching situation in the early seventies at the University of Tabriz in northern Iran. Teachers and students alike were unmotivated by the general English textbooks then in use and wanted something more relevant to the actual purposes to which students were going to put their English.

The new materials were arranged under chapter headings labelled with scientific "concepts" such as Measurement, Description and Process (Bates, 1978; Dudley-Evans et al., 1976), in a similar way to a Notional Syllabus (Wilkins, 1976). There is no doubt that the materials were very innovative in a number of ways, but it is also clear that the ostensibly notion-based framework for the syllabus disguised an underlying structural approach using pattern practice and traditional guided writing techniques. The series proved to be very popular when it was released commercially, and the syllabus framework was widely imitated, both in other commercially produced textbooks and, more significantly, in hundreds of individual materials-writing projects in different institutions around the world as ESP became the catchword of the late 70s and early 80s. Here is a representative exercise.

A quadratic equation has two solutions, called roots. If the factors of a quadratic equation can be found easily, then we can find the roots by factorising.

Example: Factorisation of $x^2 + x - 12 = 0$ gives $(x - 3)(x + 4) = 0$.

The roots of the equation are therefore 3 and -4.

Now make similar sentences about the following:

a) $x^2 + 7x + 10 = 0$
b) $x^2 - 9x + 18 = 0$
c) $x^2 - 100 = 0$
d) $x^2 + 5x - 6 = 0$

(Hall, 1980: 51–52)

In terms of expected student response, it is clear that there is nothing here beyond the empirical level. The student may be motivated by the partial relevance of the subject-matter, but there are no demands made on student inventiveness and nothing is contributed by the student. All language production is controlled entirely by the textbook, to the extent that conceptually correct answers that are not in conformity with the prescriptiveness of the textbook author are deemed to be incorrect. In terms of the prerequisites for communication, this text would only provoke authentic communication if students disagreed on some aspect of the content and the teacher allowed the discussion to go beyond the demands of the text. The view of language learning is essentially behaviourist – that learning takes place through exposure to language patterns.

A communicative approach

The University of Malaya Spoken English Project of the early 80s (Hall, 1985; Khong, 1984), set up with British Council help, used the Munby 'communicative' needs analysis approach (Munby, 1978), and was perhaps the only major project to attempt to do so with any rigour. A major problem in the project was that the first 18 months of the 3-year project were devoted to discussion of needs analysis and theoretical considerations, with the predictable result that by the time it came to actually writing, the team members were so entrenched in different antagonistic theoretical positions that consensus writing had become almost impossible. Despite the warnings in this chapter to consider theoretical positions seriously before planning materials, writing should not be delayed too long. The acts of writing and trialing cannot be delayed until a fully worked out theoretical position has been established. In fact, the development of theory and practice go hand in hand. See Figures 18.1 and 18.2 for a representative example.

1 You are looking for a scholarship to study overseas.
  Complete this table with the details of the scholarship you would like to get.

Amount per month	
Duration	
Subject of study	
Country	
Extra allowances	

2 You have some accommodation to rent.
  Fill in this table with the details of the accommodation you can offer.

Nature of accommodation	
Number of rooms	
Rent	
Facilities	
Location	
Conditions	

Figure 18.1 Worksheet 1: student A only

1 You are looking for accommodation to rent.
  Complete this table with details of the accommodation you would like.

Nature of accommodation	
Number of rooms	
Rent	
Facilities	
Location	

2 You have a scholarship to offer.
  Fill in the table with the details of the scholarship.

Amount per month	
Duration	
Subject of study	
Country	
Conditions	

Figure 18.2 Worksheet 2: student B only

No linguistic structure is prescribed in the example given, although the materials did in fact include a language support section in each unit in an attempt to anticipate the language needs of the activity. One consequence of using the Munby approach was that often more time was devoted to setting up a situation than actually doing the activity. It was not unknown for a couple of pages of input to produce only a line or two of linguistic output.

The above exercise is fairly typical of the sort of information gap exercise frequently found in 'communicative' textbooks. Despite an outward appearance of social validation (opinions have to be exchanged), roles are assigned, and content relatively tightly controlled. The exercise does not have the three prerequisites for genuine communication. The content is not the student's own – the role-play attempts to create ownership artificially – and in the end it is a matter of indifference to the student whether the outcome of the financial negotiations is advantageous or not. The student is not *engagé*, is not involved to the extent of having a personal stake in the outcome.

A genre-based approach

The approach to reading and writing technical texts developed at the Asian Institute of Technology in Thailand in the mid-80s can be classified as a genre-based approach (Hall et al., 1986) in that it attempts to analyse text in terms of the typical discourse features and language functions to be found in different kinds of technical writing, particularly those relating to the research article and the student dissertation. Unlike the approach taken by Australian genre-based theorists (Derewianka, 1991; Martin, 1993), it does not attempt to assign grammatical features to particular functions. It aims, rather, to provide analytical tools to students so that they can approach reading in a critical way, transferring this skill to a critical reading of their own writing. Here is an example of an activity, chosen more because it is short than because it is representative. A more representative sample would stretch to many pages and normally involve the analysis of part of a text in the context of a whole article or thesis.

Predict how the following extracts might continue. All extracts are taken from the journal "Solar Energy Materials", Vol. 19, 1 and 2, 1989.

In fig. 6 the dependence of the optical transmission and sheet resistance on the annealing time at 620°C for two different coatings are shown. The behavior of transmission T and sheet resistance R at this temperature in the investigated time interval is different for different stabilizer materials. For Ni (see fig. 6) we observed at the beginning an increase of the transmission and a decrease of the sheet resistivity. After two minutes, _____

_____

_____

Two different unconstrained optimization approaches were implemented to evaluate layer thicknesses and Ag optical constants. In one approach all unknowns (three thicknesses and 36 pairs of n and k) were evaluated simultaneously using the Marguardt algorithm [12, 13]. The merit function, F, was the following:

$$F = \Sigma \, [(\psi_i^{exp} - \psi_i^{cal})^2 + (\Delta_i^{exp} - \Delta_i^{cal})^2]/m,$$

where the subscript i denotes ith measurement, the superscripts exp and cal refer to the experimental and calculated values, respectively, and m is the number of measurements. We will call this the "one shell" approach. _____

_____

_____

Fig 4a shows that in the case of thick coatings (60 C/dm^2 and more) the well known emission characteristics of intermediately absorbing dielectric media are obtained. The dashed curves were calculated with the optical functions of fig. 3 and agree satisfactorily with the emittance measurements.

_____

_____

_____

This is a small part of a unit for students of Energy Technology on sequencing. It concentrates on using linguistic and contextual clues for efficient reading. Students discuss possible completions to the extracts in small groups, so that there is a limited degree of genuine interaction, provided that the texts are ones that are of real interest to the students. In terms of the criteria for communication and response to text, this third example seems to me to be approaching authenticity within the constraints of the classroom. In particular, the analysis of text very often involved discussion of the intention of the authors and a critical examination of their arguments, often extending to students' own knowledge and hence involving social validation.

As the course developed, we began to rely less and less on published texts and to get students to bring their own work to class. This appeared to be even more motivating, given that the aims of the Information-Structuring course were to help students develop their own writing for immediate deployment in assignments and a research-based thesis. In this way, the course also fulfilled the criterion that it should provide students with the tools to continue improvement after the course. Nevertheless, some of the tasks in the course still looked like exercises designed for practice rather than the occasion for genuine involvement, and it is worth noting that the course for which these materials were originally developed at AIT has itself now evolved into something which integrates language and other skills with the initial stages of carrying out research and writing a thesis.

A student-generated, experiential approach

The 'Talkbase' approach, also developed at the Asian Institute of Technology in the 80s, (Hall, 1994; Hall and Kenny, 1988; Hall and Kenny, 1995), was devised for an intensive, full-time course. No detailed timetable or content is specified. Only a general syllabus outline is given, based on a repeated pattern of Plan, Do, Report Back, Evaluate, and Plan Again. Students carry out a major piece of independent work during the course, using all the resources of the immediate environment including teachers and other students. Work proceeds through a series of report-back sessions in various modes – poster sessions, presentations, individual consultations, interviews, and so on.

The course, unfortunately for the purposes of this chapter, does not use teaching materials as such, so representative examples are difficult to find. The syllabus is a set of procedures rather than a set of materials or a set of linguistic, functional, behavioural or situational categories. However, a description of the first week of operation may help to give an idea of what the course is like.

On the first morning of the course, the only teacher-provided "material" of the first week is given to students. This consists of a slip of paper, on which are written the words:

> Welcome to the Talkbase course. We would now like you to leave the classroom and to come back again this afternoon ready to talk for a few minutes about X.

'X' is a single word or a phrase chosen by the teacher. Examples are: Drying; Unexpected Outcomes; Autonomy; Water; Technology; Saving.

First presentations by students are normally short and not particularly coherent, but they are discussed by the teacher and all the other students, normally in groups. At the end of this, students have to plan again, informed now by feedback from others and by their experience of what others have done. They then go off and report back a second time. On the third occasion, they report in writing, and writing is passed around among the group for comments. As the first week develops, students begin to find personal meanings in their "word" and gradually the very wide area covered by the original word is delimited to a topic which is of personal interest to the student.

As the course develops, and students begin to analyse published and unpublished academic discourse produced by others, both form of presentation and organisation of content improve markedly, and communication within the classroom, as well as outside it, becomes committed and almost totally student-dominated. Except at a very few places, such as the example from the first day of the first week, texts (recorded interviews, journal articles, etc.) are found and brought to class by the students themselves, so that course content is generated by students, not by teachers.

Students find themselves engaged in research in their own field of study, research which many of them will go on to develop further as part of their Master's or Doctoral dissertation. They struggle to communicate their research not only to others in the class who share their technical specialisation, but also to those who need more detailed background information. At the end of the course, students' sense of achievement at being able to present complex technical information to various different audiences gives them precisely that confidence mentioned in the section of this paper on "The need to communicate" to initiate communication and to persist with it when there are difficulties.

In terms of the prerequisites for communication, they are all present: there is a genuine commitment to communicate, there is a genuine audience, and students care about whether they have made their point. It is interesting to watch the effect that this has on weaker students, who in many language classes would never open their mouths unless forced to by the teacher. In this course, the desire to take the floor and to make a point does not depend on linguistic ability or a forceful personality; it depends on having something to say. In terms of Kenny's three categories of interaction with text, activities fall clearly into the social validation category. Students present their work, their ideas and their opinions for public scrutiny.

Concluding remarks

The principles and opinions given in this chapter are based on personal experience and reflect my own development as a teacher and materials writer. The 'social validation' of my values has ultimately been through presentations in journal articles and conference presentations, but initially they have been discussed in the hothouse context of materials and curriculum development teams and tested in actual use in the classroom.

For materials writers, it is worth bearing this in mind. You do not write to conform to somebody else's model. You look at other people's models and you read current theory, but in the end your materials and the writing of the materials will not be the simple passive implementation of someone else's ideas. They will be developed in the interaction between the writers, the teachers and the students. They will contribute to the sum total of materials writing experience. Both your own and other people's beliefs about effective language learning will be modified and enriched by your experiences.

References

Bates, M. 1978. "Writing 'Nucleus'". *English for Specific Purposes*, ed. by R. MacKay and A. Mountford, 78–96. London: Longman.

Clayton, T., Shaw, J., Le, T. T. M., Nhan, C. H. and Pham, T. 1993. "Discovering resources in Ho Chi Minh City: preparing the ground". *Language Programs in Development Projects*, ed. by W. Savage, 331–341. Bangkok: Asian Institute of Technology.

Derewianka, B.1991. *Exploring How Texts Work*. Newtown, NSW: Primary English Teaching Association.

Dudley-Evans, A., Shettlesworth, C. and Phillips, M. 1976. "The ESP materials of the University of Azarabadegan, Tabriz, Iran". *Teaching English for Science and Technology*, ed. by J. C. Richards, 163–197. Singapore: SEAMEO Regional Language Centre.

Hall, D. 1994. "The advantages for the LSP teacher of having different specialisations in the same class". *The Practice of LSP: Perspectives, Programmes and Projects*, ed. by R. Khoo, 209–217. Singapore: SEAMEO Regional Language Centre.

Hall, D. and Kenny, B. 1988. "An approach to a truly communicative methodology". *English for Specific Purposes* 7: 19–32.

Hall, D. and Kenny, B. 1995. "Evolution of a language centre: pursuing autonomy in a collegial context". *Spreading English: ELT Projects in International Development*, ed. by A. Pincas, 26–42. *Review of English Language Teaching* 5, 2. Hemel Hempstead: Phoenix ELT.

Hall, D., Hawkey, R., Kenny, B. and Storer, G. 1986. "Patterns of thought in scientific writing: a course in information structuring for engineering students". *English for Specific Purposes* 5: 147–160.

Hawkey, R. 1982. "An investigation of interrelationships between cognitive/affective and social factors and learning". Unpublished PhD thesis, University of London.

Kenny, B. 1989. "Content and language learning". Paper presented at the Fifth International ILE Seminar, Hong Kong.

Kenny, B. 1993. "Investigative research: how it changes learner status". *TESOL Quarterly* 27: 217–232.

Kenny, B, and Laszewski, M. 1993. "Doing Talkbase with Lao technicians". *Language Programs in Development Projects*, ed. by W. Savage, 181–192. Bangkok: Asian Institute of Technology.

Martin, J. R. 1993 "Life as a noun: arresting the universe in science and humanities". *Writing Science*, ed. by M. A. K. Halliday and J. R. Martin, 221–267. London: The Falmer Press.

Wilkins, D. A. 1976. *Notional Syllabuses*. Oxford: Oxford University Press.

Willing, K. 1989. *Teaching How to Learn*. Sydney: NCELTR Publications.

Chapter 19

Simon Sergeant

CALL INNOVATION IN THE ELT CURRICULUM

Introduction

THE COMPLEXITY OF INFORMATION TECHNOLOGY (IT) innovation and the speed of diffusion and technological advance seem to have left the English language teaching profession searching for ways of integrating IT usefully into the curriculum. While there seems to be little doubt of the potential of IT, it is difficult to specify the nature of the new learning opportunities. Papert (1987) and Perkins (1985) highlight the fact that there is much still to be discovered about the place of computer-assisted learning (CAL) in education, and this is still the case today. This article does not claim to produce answers, but I hope it will contribute to awareness of the problem. The aims of the article are:

- to examine the nature of CALL (computer-assisted language learning) innovation and its potential as a force for curricular change with examples drawn from my work in a language centre in Singapore;
- to investigate reasons for the shortfall between the potential of CALL and actual use, and discuss reasons why CALL opportunities are not taken;
- to indicate strategies by which a change agent may add value to a CALL facility.

Computers in commerce and industry are associated with higher efficiency. This assumption has been carried into the educational arena, and into language teaching in particular, with varying degrees of success. CALL as a discipline is establishing a research base after several years' local trial and error supported by anecdote. However, research is often carried out under ideal conditions which are only partially realizable within the constraints of everyday use. These local constraints are informed by attitudes of the major stakeholders in CALL: managers (usually non-users), CALL personnel (initial users), and teachers and students (end-users). Students, who are the recipients of CALL, are the least consulted during the decision-making process. They are also the ones who are most disadvantaged if CALL is not effectively implemented.

The full potential of integrating computers into the ELT curriculum has not yet been reached and their use is still limited. CALL is treated as a separate entity and bolted on to the existing curriculum. I will suggest in this article that due to the additional complexity of the computer medium compared with normal classroom activities, a high standard of teacher expertise is essential. Without this expertise not much useful learning takes place and CALL becomes a form of 'electronic baby-sitting'.

Background

CALL facilities have been available at my teaching institution for many years, starting with an exploratory project to investigate the pedagogic value of microcomputers in the ELT classroom. Since then, informal evaluation based on the observation of teachers and students using computers, positive comments in student questionnaires and informal discussions all suggest that on the whole, despite a small number of negative reactions from students, using computers to learn English can be enjoyable as well as educational.

CALL facilities have grown so that computers feature throughout our course structure. The main computer room houses a network of computers. Students usually work in pairs or groups of three. Timetabling is flexible. Slots are booked, usually a week in advance by teachers when they feel their class would most benefit. On a 100-hour full-time course, a student may spend ten hours using the computer. In terms of a quantitative evaluation, CALL in our centre has had an extremely high adoption rate. Over a ten-year period there have been between 300 000 and 350 000 half-hour lessons booked. The actual time students spend in front of a computer and the high degree of adoption by teaching staff is an important visible sign of success, especially as use is discretionary, but it conceals the important dimension of quality, which I shall return to later.

Teachers are trained in a number of ways. Each teacher has a short induction giving them a broad overview of CALL and how to use the most popular programs. The teacher is then supported by written information which offers more detailed help. A CALL co-ordinator (CC) is on hand to respond to questions as they arise, while more experienced teachers pass on their expertise. A special four-day training course, the CALL Teacher Education Course (CALLTEC), was also designed. CALLTEC aims to give teachers the theory and practical experience necessary for effective CALL use and materials development.

The fascination of the computer as machine

The introduction of computers into the culture of language learning is a complex change. When we think of CALL, the first impression is of the computer itself, apparently doing something sophisticated with students peering intently at the screen. Then we may reflect that the apparent sophistication is a stitched-together product of people and systems with their inherent flaws. Less obvious is the enthusiast working late behind the scenes trying to ensure that the stitches are not obvious and that the thing does not suddenly get out of control, by making the hardware, software, pedagogy, communications and infrastructure robust. We then need to add the reactions of the users and managers: enthusiastic, accepting, indifferent, cynical, nervous or rejecting. Finally, we step back and look at the whole picture, and reflect on how all these interacting elements constitute a new sub-culture of language learning.

It is clear that, together with a fascination for computers, many students rank acquisition of computing skills alongside the acquisition of English language as essential for survival in the modern world. Given the holding power of the computer, it is hardly surprising that we tend to foreground the computer and computer applications, when we should concentrate more on the interaction between the technology and the culture of learning. Papert (1987) calls this tendency technocentrism – making an object the centre of our attention. Technocentrism is endemic in CALL research and evaluation as well as in the way teachers, students and managers perceive computers in education. It often leads to the assumption that having provided the opportunity to use computers, learning happens by itself.

The ecology of CALL innovation

CALL, like any classroom innovation, takes place at many levels. 'The first important thing is that change is systemic, that is to say it takes place in an environment which consists of a number of interrelating systems' (Kennedy 1988).

Kennedy employs a 'wheels within wheels' diagram in which classroom innovation forms the centre of the wheel, and institutional, educational, administrative, political and cultural levels form progressively outer circles. Chin and Benne (1976: 33) discuss the problems of introducing new 'thing' technologies (for example, audio-visual devices, television, computers) into school situations:

> As attempts are made to introduce these new thing technologies into school situations, the change problem shifts to the human problems of dealing with the resistance, anxieties. threats to morale, conflicts, disrupted interpersonal communications and so on, which prospective changes in patterns of practice evoke in the people affected by the change.

Paisey (in White 1988: 116) reminds us that

> . . . it is people who inhabit an institution, and an organisation consists of networks of relationships between people acting and reacting on each other – thus organisations contain rational as well as non-rational elements . . . Most crucially, an educational organisation is operated by the persons who are themselves the instruments of change. Without their willingness and participation, there will be no change.

These writers give some idea of the dynamics of introducing 'thing' technologies into interacting systems and subsystems, although they fall short of providing a detailed model of the curriculum in a state of flux.

Innovation or change?

White (1988) defines innovation as 'a deliberate effort, perceived as new and intended to bring about improvement'. It is distinguished from change, which is any difference between Time 1 and Time 2. Delano et al. (1994) define innovation more narrowly for the ESL context in terms of change, development, novelty and improvement. An innovation in a second language teaching programme is an informed change in an underlying philosophy of language teaching/learning, brought about by direct experience, research findings, or other means, resulting in an adaptation of pedagogic practices such that instruction is better able to promote language learning.

Kemmis et al. (1997) make a distinction between minimal and maximal curriculum innovation. Minimal innovation occurs when there is a change in the way a particular aspect of the syllabus is presented to students. The course will be altered to accommodate the new idea. Maximal innovation would be evident in a massive reorientation of a course influenced by the CALL aspect of the course.

First order and second order innovation

Perkins (1985) sheds light on the way in which innovations are minimally adopted in education. He distinguishes between first and second order 'fingertip effects' of information processing technology. First order fingertip effects are the obvious differences an innovation makes, the immediate advantage put at one's fingertips, such as being able to converse with friends overseas (telecommunications), or easier typing (the word processor). Second order fingertip effects are the deeper repercussions of the innovation. The use of the word processor for instance puts a powerful tool at the fingertips of the L2 student of writing. The ability to create and manipulate text easily to move, insert, copy or delete blocks before deciding how the completed document will appear, liberates the writer from linear constraints and from the chore of rewriting in long-hand.

The 'opportunities get taken' hypothesis (Perkins ibid.) suggests optimistically that students will recognize the opportunity of large-scale editing. The deeper, second order effects involving a restructuring of the cognitive skills underlying the writing process will be 'soaked up' by assigning writing tasks on the word processor. In other words, the opportunity does the teaching by itself. However, Perkins claims, 'Most typically . . . the opportunities are not taken.'

The nature of missed opportunities

Something will always be learned when a student engages in a CALL activity but this may not be even at Perkins' first order level. Opportunities for the deeper second level learning may also be missed. Consider the results of a survey of perceived program use among full-time students on a 100-hour intensive general English course. At the end of the course 200 students were asked which programs they had used and to estimate how many times they had used them. The results are shown in Figure 19.1.

One of Perkins' criteria for transfer of learning is a variety of wide-ranging practice. This is not occurring since almost 57 percent of perceived CALL use is accounted for by two programs: Storyboard[1] and Gapmaster.[2] Teachers are not exploring different programs. The popularity of Storyboard and Gapmaster may be accounted for by the ease of entering texts into the programs, or 'authoring'. To author Storyboard, teachers type in a text (author the program) and save it. The same applies to Gapmaster. Teachers place the words they want to blank out in square brackets. The texts used are usually extracts from student textbooks or grammar/vocabulary practice books.

Another way of getting closer to the nature of missed opportunities is to relate the level of actual program use to types of learning generated by CALL. Kemmis et al. (1997) distinguish five learning styles for CAL, which Phillips (1985) uses to map the types of learning naturally arising from a particular program type. These are recognition, recall, comprehension, experimental and constructive understanding. In the first style, the student is required merely to recognize previously presented language forms. In the second, the student is required to reproduce previously acquired knowledge. Neither recognition nor recall involve the active construction of new knowledge. The third type, comprehension, involves a more active role and entails the ability to operate on a body of content and transform it in some way. Experimental learning may involve the active exploration of a simulation. Language production is less constrained by on-screen text. Constructive understanding involves using the computer as a tool to discover new language.

The most common use of Storyboard is for students to retrieve a text which they have previously encountered in their textbook. Storyboard contains a 'cheat' feature which means

Program	Student half-hours	%	Mode*
Storyboard	1266	38.3	Instructional/conjectural
Gapmaster	614	18.6	Instructional
Word processing	577	17.5	Emancipatory
Vocab Games	322	9.8	Instructional
Testmaster	150	4.5	Instructional
Grammar Games	116	3.5	Instructional
Clarity Grammar	94	2.8	Instructional
Pinpoint	49	1.5	Instructional/conjectural
Fast Food	35	1.1	Revelatory
Wordstore	34	1.0	Instructional
FCE Exercises	22	0.7	Instructional
Matchmaster	13	0.4	Instructional
London Adventure	10	0.3	Revelatory

* Instructional: learners recall what has been taught
  Revelatory: learners take part in a relatively structured learning situation, e.g. a simulation
  Conjectural: learners engage in tasks with open-ended, unpredictable solutions
  Emancipatory: learners engage in authentic, real activities

Figure 19.1 Perceived program use

that at any time a student may see the entire text again without a penalty. The same applies to individual words. Both these strategies are used by students to reduce learning load. Though teachers intend this activity to improve comprehension, the type of learning arising from this activity is usually at the level of recognition or recall. Copying a text verbatim may help students to remember words or syntactic structures, spelling may improve, and it is probably more fun than copying a text using pen and paper.

If they work on a Storyboard activity collaboratively, students may learn something from the language they use to complete the text. though research on the nature of talk generated in front of CALL programs summarized by Nicholls (1992) and Nicholls' own research on Storyboard in particular suggest that conversational spin-off is limited. The discourse produced is impoverished in terms of lexical and syntactic variety, with many single word utterances and repetitions of screen text, and it is of limited pedagogical value.

Gapmaster is most frequently used in the drill-and-practice mode. An exercise from a grammar textbook is typed in, for instance to practise question tags. The outcome is fixed and non-negotiable. The facility of the program to accept more than one correct answer requires more effort by a teacher to author the alternatives (enter the text required) and is often not used. The off-screen interaction is limited and the learning is at the level of recognition or recall.

The problem of opportunities for learning not being taken deepens when the mode of the CALL experience is considered (Figure 19.1). CALL in the instructional mode accounts for 81 percent of total use, whereas CALL in the revelatory mode accounts for 1.4 percent. Word processing accounts for the total use of CALL in the emancipatory mode at 17.5 percent. CALL in the instructional mode involves no negotiation of outcome. The aim of activities is for the student to produce text which has been pre-determined before the activity began. They involve the manipulation of language in ways which do not involve any exchange of meaning. Transformation exercises and controlled pattern practice are activities which involve the production of language but not the use of language (Willis 1990). This approach is therefore at odds with current communicative language teaching methodology which asserts that people learn a language best by using the language to achieve real meanings and outcomes. Underwood (1984) comments that CALL in this mode tries to simulate what the teacher does in the classroom – to be exact, the least interesting things. It tends to be authoritarian, evaluative and overly structured. The shortfall between the potential learning opportunities that could be realized and the reality of the way programs are frequently underused is obvious.

Summary of the problem

Teachers with a low level of CALL expertise are less likely to be aware of the range of opportunities offered by authoring and using well designed CALL activities, though some novices make up for this by being enthusiastic and creative because they do not have preconceived ideas. During a four-hour lesson, migrating to the computer room is a welcome change of scene which tends to give the teacher and students a break from each other. Once a task has been set, the teacher can take a more passive role, offering guidance only when required, sometimes not at all. Teachers take a technocentric viewpoint and assume that the minimal task imposed by the program, whether gap filling, test reconstruction, or interacting at a basic level with a simulation, constitutes a worthwhile task.

Each time teachers use a new CALL activity, it represents a micro-innovation. Teachers will usually make a cost/benefit calculation based on how much benefit their classes will receive from half an hour in front of the computer offset against the amount of effort and risk involved. The effort teachers need to put into learning a new program and training their students to take part in an activity will be calculated. The risk of failure is an important part of the calculation, based on perception of the reliability of the hardware and the complexity of the program. The more complex a program is, the more a teacher will fear the failure of the activity due to someone pressing the wrong key or entering part of the program that the teacher has not yet discovered. A number of personal failures, for example with word processing, may discourage a teacher from using valuable activities, and staffroom anecdotes about such experiences will discourage other teachers. As a consequence, the safer, less complex activities tend to be favoured by the majority.

Certain factors militate against the use of more time-consuming integrated activities such as simulations, which involve the class and the teacher in learning how to use a program that has less repeat value than a text reconstruction activity. This type of program involves more preparation and time in terms of pre-CALL and post-CALL activities in the classroom. There is the need to complete the textbook material prescribed for the lesson, which is especially the case where classes are shared by more than one teacher, so 'extra' activities, which are less obviously related to course content, may be less used. There is, therefore, a danger of over-using a small number of programs and requiring students to use the same program (with different texts) repeatedly.

A similar cost benefit calculation applies to the creation of materials. Certain programs such as Storyboard are easy to author (enter text) and highly productive in terms of the ratio of authoring time and effort to the amount of student use. Storyboard has a consistent history of almost 100 percent reliable use, so there are few lost lessons. Under conditions of teacher ownership, materials are written into courses using these easily mastered packages which produce as much student 'busyness' as possible for the least effort in materials writing or lesson preparation.

Most materials exist only as texts. They are supplementary to the textbook materials. They are easily authored materials written into courses, so that a particular unit in a textbook may be supplemented with a text reconstruction activity, a vocabulary activity and/or a gap-filling activity. They are written into the teacher's notes, and become institutionalized, fixed supplementary elements for a particular course. The syllabus then becomes resistant to more integrated activities in emancipatory or revelatory modes, such as word processing or simulations. At this stage it is difficult to alter the materials or introduce a wider variety of programs.

The preponderance of CALL materials in the instructional mode (see Figure 19.1) reflects the nature of the wider syllabus, primarily derived from textbooks with a structural/functional ordering of items. In the wider syllabus these structures and functions are supplemented with further materials of the same nature. A number of communicative activities are also available, but are considered secondary to the process of teaching the subject matter of the syllabus. This is also reflected in the balance of CALL materials. The prevalence of the supplementary use of CALL tends to define the normal level of CALL use, which is the typical level of adoption of the majority of teachers.

CALL implementation strategies

CALL expertise is a complex skill which can be acquired by various means. In an ideal situation, the CC (CALL co-ordinator) gains expertise by studying the field intensively, by talking to other practitioners and by everyday observation and practice. A selection of these skills are simplified and transferred to teachers through in-service training in various forms and through dealing with everyday problems and queries. A similar selection, simplification and transfer of skills takes place between teacher and students.

The CC, in his/her efforts to ensure effective CALL lessons, is in the position of co-ordinating the interaction of two highly complex systems: networked computers and the staff within the organization (see Appendix below). To ensure adoption, the CC can therefore work at the 'thing' level or at the 'person' level. Working at the 'thing' level leads to ease of access for all users: students, teachers and materials writers. Working at the 'person' level involves creating and maintaining a flow of information between all stakeholders within the institution, both users (students and teachers) and non-users (managers, technical staff, administrative staff – see Appendix).

On a day-to-day basis, the CC makes decisions about the most effective line of work, whether to focus activity from the bottom-up of the system (e.g. materials development. writing clear instructions/documentation) or from the top-down (e.g. teacher training, maintaining the goodwill of the management). Everyday priorities usually involve the bottom-up approach, dealing with problems as they arise, working under the assumption that if things are running smoothly, the goodwill of the management is assured. Improvements made to the system, materials and instructions are permanent, whereas training and retraining is a constant requirement for new staff or for those requiring updating. Most of the time it is more profitable to focus on permanent improvements. For example, something can be made easier for teachers to use, perhaps simplifying a procedure by a single key press, or writing clearer instructions. If this is multiplied by 40 staff or 2000 student users, it means that far less training is required.

The full implementation of CALL is a lengthy process. Five years were needed in our centre for the institutionalization of a minimal level of CALL: to set up system structures, to source software, to provide instructions to teachers, to author high quality materials and weave them into the structure of courses. Eight years were required before our centre achieved the standard of implementation and expertise required to generate a teacher training course such as CALLTEC.

Summary of value-adding activities

The summary in the Appendix to this article illustrates the ways in which a teacher with responsibility for CALL may add value to a CALL facility by working with managers, teachers and students either at the thing (system) level or at the person level.

Where only a small amount of non-teaching time is made available, the main focus of activity tends to shift away from teacher training to other considerations which, while they are more mundane, are the sine qua non of CALL: trouble shooting, software acquisition and installation, timetabling, maintenance of materials (printing, cataloguing, deletion, file backup) and therefore the level of use decreases in scope and quality. The provision of more time allows the CC to focus on value-adding activities which are less concerned with the day-to-day running of the facility such as teacher training, developing interesting materials, evaluation and self-education.

Conclusion

With insufficient management, the level of CALL use is likely to decline. The change agent, in this case the CALL co-ordinator (CC), is central to the process of ensuring that CALL operates smoothly. The CC deals with practical problems, and ensures that the innovation is at least minimally implemented. The CC can minimize problems faced by users of CALL by 'adding value' to the system at various levels. On a larger scale, the actions of the CC are pivotal to the process of significant curriculum change. These actions are responsible for facilitating conscious learning opportunities by ensuring that CALL learning exists, and that managers, teachers and students recognize these opportunities and take them.

To create and maintain the CALL facility in good working order requires a professional change agent: the CALL co-ordinator (CC) or a team of professionals with a high degree of expertise in CALL. They can interpret CALL use in terms of current methodology, define, create and maintain high quality learning structures and communicate their potentials to managers and users simply and effectively. The CC is responsible for the creation and maintenance of a student learning niche within the curriculum. Ideally, therefore, the expertise of the CC as change agent should include at least a rudimentary appreciation of how CALL is embedded in the curriculum and how to manage the innovation.

In this article, I have explored the nature of day-to-day CALL value-adding activity within the context of the CALL facility where I work. I put forward possible strategies for dealing with problems arising from the institutionalization of a minimal level of CALL use. The resolution of these problems is seen as a precondition for maximal benefit to the ELT curriculum.

Appendix: value-adding activities

1 Working with non-users (managers)

Influencing
Influencing the private evaluation of CALL by managers, on the level of finance and hardware/software.

Technical matters
Reassuring managers that the technical performance of the system is robust and reliable.

Materials development
Encouraging managers to have an active interest and investment in materials development for CALL.

Teacher training
Encouraging the management to initiate and develop various forms of teacher training.

Communications
Improving the information flow between CALL personnel and managers.

Evaluation
Evaluation by managers of CALL on the level of consumer satisfaction, observable organizational change and flow of communication.

2 Working with users (teachers and students)

Working at the system level
Designing and programming the system to make it reliable and transparent to use, and identifying the need for new hardware.

Software evaluation and acquisition
Initiating the purchase or design of new software and submitting it to materials writers for evaluation.

Guiding CALL use
Administering the timetable. Writing instructions and manuals to support CALL use. Cataloguing and publishing materials in a form that teachers find useful when planning lessons.

Materials development
Writing materials and model lessons and supporting teachers who are authoring courseware.

Teacher training
Initiating and developing teacher training, ranging from presentations and workshops to responding to the day-to-day questions of individual teachers. Training may be either in the use of existing activities or in the creation of materials.

Evaluation
Evaluating the level of CALL use and the contribution CALL can make to different courses.

Influencing
Changing the way teachers think about CALL. This level is the private domain of the teacher, concerned with how teachers relate to CALL and the way CALL is integrated into a lesson at the planning stage.

Notes

1   In Storyboard, students have to reassemble a text which has been deleted from the screen.
2   Gapmaster is a form of cloze procedure, with students filling in missing words in a text.

References and bibliography

Brumfit, C., Philips, M. and Skehan, P. (eds) 1985 'Computers in English Language Teaching: A View from the Classroom'. In *British Council Occasional Papers* no. 122 (British Council/Pergamon)

Chin, R. and Benne, K. D. 1976 'General strategies for effecting changes in human systems'. In Bennis, W. G., Benne, K. D., Chin, R. and Corey, K. D. (eds.) 1976 *The Planning of Change* (Holt, Rinehart and Winston, New York)

Delano, L., Riley, L. and Crookes, G. 1994 'The meaning of innovation for ESL teachers'. In *System* vol. 22 no. 4 (Pergamon)

Kemmis, S., Atkin, R. and Wright, E. 1997 'How do students learn?' (Occasional Paper no. 5, CARE, University of East Anglia)

Kennedy, C. 1988 'Evaluation of ELT projects'. In *Applied Linguistics* vol. 9 no. 4: 329–42 (OUP)

Nicholls, L. 1992 'Computers as a stimulus for talk: the nature of talk generated by pairs of students using Storyboard'. In *ON-CALL* vol. 9 no. 2: 19–29 (University of Queensland, Australia)

Papert, S. 1987 'Computer criticism vs. technocratic thinking'. In *Educational Research* 17: 22–30 (NFER, Routledge)

Perkins, D. N. 1985 'The fingertip effect: how information-processing technology shapes thinking'. In *Educational Research* 14: 11–16 (NFER, Routledge)

Phillips, M. 1985 'Logical possibilities and classroom scenarios for the development of CALL'. In Brumfit, C., Phillips, M. and Skehan, P. (eds.) 1985

Underwood, J. H. 1984 *Linguistics, Computers and the Language Teacher: a Communicative Approach* (Newbury House)

White, R. 1988 *The ELT Curriculum: Design, Innovation and Management* (Blackwell)

Willis, D. 1990 *The Lexical Syllabus* (Collins)

PART FOUR

Evaluating curriculum change

Chapter 20

Pauline Rea-Dickins and Kevin Germaine

PURPOSES FOR EVALUATION

1 Introduction

A NUMBER OF DIFFERENT PURPOSES for evaluation can be identified. They can be divided into two broad categories:

1   general purposes
2   specific, topic-related purposes.

The main general purposes are examined first.

2 General evaluation purposes

Evaluation may be undertaken for three principal reasons:

1   accountability
2   curriculum development and betterment
3   self-development: teachers and other language teaching professionals.

Evaluation for purposes of accountability

Evaluation for purposes of accountability is mainly concerned with determining whether there has been value for money, in other words whether something has been both effective and efficient. The main aim is to report on a product and give an evaluative judgement, whether something is intrinsically a 'good thing' or not. Generally the information derived from evaluation for purposes of accountability is not used in any major way to improve the functioning of the curriculum or classroom practice. Rather it informs decisions as to whether something is to continue or be discontinued. If, for example, sponsors or heads of institutions are not satisfied with the implementation of a particular project, then cuts may be made. Thus, if a particular reading scheme is introduced, evaluated a year later, and then judged to be ineffective, it is highly likely that a school will discontinue supporting this venture.

Evaluations of this type are largely, although not exclusively, the domain of policy makers or providers of resources. There is a close link between power and evaluation for accountability. There are other points to notice. Usually, such evaluations are carried out after an innovation has been running for some time, or at the end of a project. This type of evaluation, known as *summative evaluation*, has also tended to involve testing and measure-ment, and analyses of the statistical significance of results obtained. It has focused on the overall outcomes, i.e. end product of an innovation, and has consistently failed to take into account teachers' evaluative comments. Summative evaluations are limited by their focus on outcomes at the end of an educational innovation.

Evaluation for purposes of curriculum development

Teachers have a key role to play in the curriculum renewal and development process. The ideas of Stenhouse (1975) were pivotal in placing classroom practice at the forefront of curriculum enquiries:

> From the first set of trials it was learned that information coming from children's test results was tentative and not readily usable for guiding rewriting without being supplemented by other data. The results played a useful part in confirming that the general approach of the materials was effective in promoting achievement of its stated objectives, and the development of tests also had side-benefits for the production of Units. But for indicating changes which would make the Units more effective they were of much less use than information from other sources . . .
>
> Whilst it could not be said that the test information was without value for this Project, it can be said that where resources are limited and it is necessary to concentrate upon gathering information to give the greatest return on money, time and human energy, then the choice would be for teachers' reports and direct observations in the classroom and not for tests of short-term changes in children's behaviour.
>
> (Harlen 1973: 91–92 cited in Stenhouse 1975)

Evaluation for curriculum development purposes will involve information from teachers and other relevant ELT professionals. It is important in the management of evaluation to include all relevant parties. From this it follows that teachers have major contributions to make in the evaluation of classrooms. It is the teacher, rather than the 'tester' or the evaluation 'expert', who has most information about specific classroom contexts. This information may be reported at various times and in various forms, for example as responses to questionnaires, interviews, records, or diary keeping. It may be largely descriptive and qualitative, and need not entail tests, measurements, and inferences about curriculum quality from statistical data. In contrast to summative evaluation for purposes of accountability, evaluations intended to improve the curriculum will gather information from different people over a period of time. This is known as *formative evaluation*. Such evaluations are ongoing and monitor developments by identifying the strengths and weaknesses of all aspects of teaching and learning. As opposed to merely passing an evaluative judgement on the end product of a teaching programme (summative evaluation), formative evaluation is designed to provide information that may be used as the basis for future planning and action. It is formative since it aims to strengthen and improve the curriculum.

Evaluation for purposes of teacher self-development

A third and major role that evaluation has to play is in formalizing and extending a teacher's knowledge about teaching and learning in classrooms. This is sometimes referred to as *illuminative evaluation* (Parlett and Hamilton 1987) because it involves raising the consciousness of teachers and other ELT practitioners as to what actually happens (as opposed to what is supposed to happen) in the language teaching classroom. This type of evaluation is also developmental and formative.

Evaluation of this kind is definitely not concerned with measurement. Through awareness-raising activities, teachers are involved in describing and better understanding their own contexts with a view to improving the teaching and learning process. Such evaluations are both illuminative and formative in purpose. They focus more on the process, and less on the product, of teaching and learning and have a major role to play in teacher self-development.

Summary

In this section we have examined the general purposes for evaluation (accountability, curriculum development, and teacher self-development). Accountability is usually linked with summative evaluation while curriculum development and teacher self-development are better informed by evaluation as a formative process.

[. . .]

3 Specific topic-related purposes for evaluation

In this section, we examine ways in which evaluation is important to classroom teachers and how their awareness can be raised by evaluation activities. We are concerned with formative and illuminative evaluation, associated with curriculum development and teacher self-development.

What is meant by the *environment* of the classroom since it is this that provides the focus for our evaluations? The environment is made up of many things including the social organization of the classroom, the textbooks, the mode(s) of teacher presentation, and the resources available to the teacher. Thus, when we ask the question 'Do our teaching and learning programmes work?' (i.e. are they effective?), we need to identify clearly the focus of our question. Are we interested in evaluating the classroom organization, aspects of teacher presentation, or is the focus on the textbook or the way we teach grammar? The evaluator has to be clear as to what is being examined.

Key factors are that:

1   evaluation is not restricted to the testing of learners' abilities
2   more than just the end product is important when evaluating a learning programme
3   there are different conditions that may explain, or contribute towards an explanation of, why a programme is successful or not
4   other information, related to a range of different aspects of the teaching and learning process, should be included in an evaluation of the curriculum, to complement data typically derived from a test analysis of learner performance.

In other words, the varied processes of teaching are as important as the outcome of learning, and in order to improve learning outcomes, there is a need to examine more closely those conditions that may contribute to successful language learning. What is needed is a detailed examination of the environment created by the teacher and learners to promote effective language learning. Evaluation is the means by which we can gain a better understanding of what is effective, what is less effective, and what appears to be of no use at all. In order to do this, evaluation must focus on both the means and the product of the learning process.

4 Materials

Before analysing the extent to which given teaching and learning materials are suitable, there are preliminary questions to address. The materials selected for classroom use can be defined in a number of ways.

What do materials mean for you?

1   Do you refer exclusively to textbooks, or do you include teachers' guides, teaching manuals, supplementary units, readers, audio and visual materials, etc?
2   Do you make a distinction between materials designed specifically for first and second language teaching, and also between those targeted specifically for use in school and materials that are non-pedagogic but authentic?
3   Do you include materials produced by the teachers and the learners?

The role of materials within your teaching and learning context

1   What role(s) are they expected to play?
2   What goal(s) are they expected to achieve?

How are the materials to be used?

1   Are they to be used as the sole source and resource for teaching?
2   Are they one of several available resources?

There has been a tendency for overreliance on classroom teaching materials, with unrealistic expectations made of them. However, the effectiveness of teaching and learning is not explained solely in terms of how good or bad the learning materials are. As Allwright (1981) suggests, materials are only *part* of the co-operative management of language learning. It is also crucial not to overemphasize the importance of learning materials.

Evaluation of classroom learning materials

The first way in which materials may be evaluated is in terms of how well they reflect the principles by which they have been written. In the case of class textbooks, the evaluation criteria will be those used when deciding which book is best for your teaching context. When it comes to teacher-made materials a specification, i.e. a list of criteria against which to evaluate the materials, is indicated at the outset – or accumulated during the process of materials writing – and is thus 'known' to the teacher. In both cases, we are referring to the theoretical worth of the materials.

Examining the materials as they stand, that is without reference to their actual use in the classroom, gives us no information about how these materials actually work with a class. This distinction between the theoretical (i.e. construct validity) and empirical value of materials has been explored by Breen (1989), who distinguishes three phases in the evaluation of materials: materials-as-workplan, materials-in-process, and outcomes from materials.

We can generalize from the notion of 'tasks' to the notion of teaching and learning materials in the following manner. 'Materials-as-workplan' refers to the theoretical value of materials, taking up the range of points covered in comprehensive checklist. But, as Breen (1989: 189) states:

Workplans can only provide opportunities for change in knowledge and capability and for successful outcomes in relatively unpredictable and broad measure.

This brings us to an evaluation of 'Materials-in-process'. This stage generates information about the ways in which learners and teachers actually use and respond to materials, thus providing indicators as to whether the materials are 'successful' or not. The 'outcomes from materials' represent the relative achievements of learners.

Who evaluates the materials is the final point to be considered here. Low (1987) comments on the range of individuals connected with a language learning course and examines both the nature and purpose of the evaluations they are likely to make. For Low, ten different perspectives on materials evaluation could be offered:

The Learner
The Parent
The Teacher
The Head or College Principal
The Teacher Trainer
The Curriculum Committee Member
The Inspector
The Educational Researcher
The Publisher
The Materials Designer

(Low 1987)

By examining the role(s) of these participating groups in the materials evaluation process, Low (1987) shows how each group will have different interests and different questions to be answered. For example, a materials writer might carry out a formative evaluation designed to indicate whether the texts are appropriate to the target learners, and then make the necessary changes. A parent, on the other hand, might only be interested in examination results, which implies a summative assessment of learner performance.

On the premise that 'teachers may benefit greatly in the evaluation, design and use of materials by engaging the help and views of learners', Breen and Candlin suggest ways in which learners may participate in the evaluation of materials.

On the procedures for working with tasks and activities in the classroom
What do you find are the most useful ways to learn a new language?
What are the best kinds of language learning tasks and activities? What are the reasons for your choice?
What can a teacher do which would help you most when you are learning a new language?
What can other learners in the class do which would help you most when you are learning a new language?
What is your favourite kind of language lesson?
What are the reasons for your choice?
What are the good things and the bad things about learning a language in a classroom?
What can materials best provide you with to help you learn a new language?
What are the best kinds of language learning materials?
What do they look like? Why do you think they're best?

What is good and not so good about the materials you are working with now? What do you think is missing from them?
What changes would you make to them?

(Breen and Candlin 1987: 27)

As with most inventories of this kind, the questions can be reformulated to make them more relevant to individual contexts. It is important to recognize the different and relevant contributions to materials evaluation. As Low (1987: 27) maintains: 'the evaluation of a language learning programme, or the materials used to teach it, involves more viewpoints than that of the "independent" outside observer'.

Summary

In evaluating materials it is necessary to examine the ways in which teaching and learning materials are sensitive to the language learning process. Evaluation criteria should relate not only to the aims and contents of language learning, but also, and importantly, to the procedures for working with texts and performing tasks in the classroom. It is necessary to analyse learner outcomes, but not to the exclusion of evaluating other aspects of the teaching and learning process. From this we may conclude that a comprehensive evaluation of our teaching and learning materials will entail a theoretical (i.e. workplan) and empirical (i.e. process) analysis of materials, the data from which will be augmented with details of learner outcomes. The importance of observational data, derived from an analysis of materials in use, should not be undervalued.

5 Teachers and teaching

Purposes for classroom observation

Evaluation is a crucial part of teaching, but how is it done well? Testing knowledge of theory is not enough to judge effective teaching. We need to observe teachers in action using their knowledge in the real setting of the classroom. Classroom observation gives us the opportunity to see teachers putting theory into practice: it shows us what teachers *do* rather than what they know.

Grading teachers

Your own teaching context will influence your view on the purposes of classroom observation. The experience of many teachers suggests that it is primarily summative in purpose, inextricably bound up with reporting a grade, accountability, and judgemental statements.

The focus when grading teachers using a checklist is mainly on the product of teaching and learning, for example, 'ability to establish rapport', 'suitability of materials and methods', 'use of aids'. Also, the checklist is used by an external observer. Typically, teachers are visited by inspectors who check their class records and lesson plans, observe a lesson, and then comment on the lessons using a checklist as a guide. Sometimes this evaluation is carried out without much participation by the teacher who is actually being observed.

[. . .]

Teacher development

Using observation merely to grade teachers, for example, with a view to promotion, is extremely limiting. It is important to use observation to provide information that teachers can use as a basis for future action. Here we refer to the formative value of classroom observation where the feedback from evaluation will be used to further develop or improve an aspect of classroom practice, or as part of curriculum betterment or teacher self-development. Consider this following way of evaluating teacher performance:

> The classroom assessment process should consist of three stages:
> 1 pre-lesson material
> 2 the lesson
> 3 the trainee's post-lesson evaluation
>
> 1 The pre-lesson material includes:
>   (a) information about the class: descriptive and evaluative
>   (b) the scheme of work and the place of the assessed lesson in it
>   (c) the lesson plan (normally accepted form)
>
> 2 The lesson; attention to the following:
>   (a) classroom personality   (d) what is being sought
>   (b) classroom management   (e) how it is being sought
>   (c) awareness of learners   (f) what the learner is doing
>
> The above should be gone into in detail.
>
> 3 Post-lesson evaluation; written self-assessment on:
>   (a) the lesson plan
>   (b) the major headings on the assessment schedule
>   (c) any additional relevant points
>
> (James 1983)

In this approach not only is the teacher formally included at stage 3 by means of a written self-assessment, but also there is an attempt to examine the process or teaching and learning. The category 'what the learner is doing' could highlight, for example, the nature of the interaction (teacher to learner, learner to learner, learner to teacher) or the type of writing that the learners are doing: copying from the blackboard, filling in a gapped passage, reordering words and sentences). An item on a checklist which focuses on 'how', i.e. what the teacher is doing, can also identify a wealth of information about the teacher and teaching, for example, 'What are the different question types that the teacher uses?' 'How are visual aids used at the different stages (presentation, practice, or production) of the lesson?' Checklist items such as these focus attention on details of the teaching and learning process and provide information that is useful in terms of modifying and improving classroom practice. It is, therefore, an example of formative teaching evaluation.

Peer teaching is an alternative method of evaluating teachers in training. Here trainees 'teach' a lesson to their colleagues. Tutor and learner observers look out for specific points in the teaching practice. Feedback can come both from the trainer and fellow learners. Another way is using microteaching. In its simplest form a trainee teaches a group of learners for a short period of time, for example, fifteen minutes covering a specific topic or skill (apologizing, reading for specific information, etc.). Again, peers and/or a trainer observe this performance and comment on it using a checklist as a guide.

The observation involved in the above practices can be used for improving the teachers' techniques, monitoring their progress, and counselling them on relevant aspects of their teaching. However, in many cases, they are primarily geared towards training and grading, in other words, used to determine whether the training institution will qualify a teacher, the syllabus is being covered, the teacher uses the appropriate methodology, and so on. Additionally, not only is the observation largely controlled by someone other than the classroom teacher, but checklists may reflect an external observer's judgement on what is effective teaching. There is a need to consider ways in which teachers themselves may become more involved in the process of evaluation.

Teacher self-development

A more participant-orientated evaluation through observation is important in raising teachers' awareness, a key feature of the teacher development process. Taking microteaching as an example, we can consider ways in which evaluation may be made more illuminative, collaborative, and useful in terms of teacher self-development. The process can be examined at three levels: self-evaluation, peer evaluation, and collaborative group work. We shall examine these in detail.

Teacher self-evaluation

Self-evaluation is simply the practice of teachers reflecting on what has taken place in the lesson with a view to improving their performance. It can be very informal, for example in the form of brief notes written immediately after the lesson. Or it can be part of a written (such as the class record) or oral report on the lesson itself. Alternatively, a checklist can be used. One of the advantages of self-evaluation inventories is that they can be designed by individual teachers to suit their own teaching contexts. They are relatively simple to use and yet potentially they can provide a wealth of information about teachers, their teaching, and their learners.

Peer evaluation

Peer evaluation can be incorporated into microteaching where several trainees are present during the lesson or where they share the same microteaching session. Here it is important for there to be some means of encouraging open and constructively critical discussion.

Now, consider the following procedure (adapted from James 1983) which may involve both teacher self-evaluation and peer evaluation.

1   The teachers prepare an open profile of themselves as teachers. It is in the form of a sort of self-presentation which can precede the feedback session at the end of the microteaching.

2   Statements such as the following would make up a teacher's own professional principles:

I always correct learner errors.
I do not allow learners to use their first language.

I teach the rules of grammar to help learners use the language.

I never ask a learner to use language which has not been previously presented and practised.

I always use authentic materials as a basis for teaching.

I make certain that a large proportion of the learners' time is spent in group work.

I never ask learners to read aloud to the rest of the class.

I always mark learners' written work.

I believe that learner errors are the result of first language interference.

I try to exercise a strong personality in the classroom.

I adapt my teaching to suit what the learners say they want.

3   For each of these statements, the teachers in discussion groups indicate whether they agree or disagree. If there is disagreement then they are asked to rewrite the statement to reflect what they think.

Note that this self-evaluation checklist [. . .] does not presuppose any external observer. Nonetheless, in microteaching it can be used by both peers and tutors to discuss what constitutes elements of good teaching practice. Because peer evaluation is collaborative in approach, the teachers being observed might themselves suggest areas of their teaching that they feel need to be improved and ask their colleagues to concentrate on these.

At this point evaluation has moved away from the narrow summative functions of evaluation for grading purposes and has taken on illuminative and support functions and become formative in purpose.

Collaborative group work

This is a further extension of peer-evaluation where the focus of the evaluation is agreed on beforehand by the group. More control is in the hands of the peer group but it requires good leadership skills. Collaborative group work can offer an additional opportunity to evaluate the trainer and the programme.

Kouraogo (1987), in an article about Burkina Faso, discusses the junction of teachers' self-help groups which can form the basis of a collaborative national teacher organisation.

Kouraogo suggests that groups could meet on a monthly basis and discuss the practical problems that teachers have. At a later date, these small groups and their discussion topics could be brought together in a national conference. One of the purposes of these self-help groups is that they may not only help teachers resolve practical problems, but may also encourage and support teachers in difficult circumstances.

Summary

We have moved from the narrow perspective of grading teacher performance to an evaluation of teachers and teaching which can provide information of practical use to teachers for the development of their teaching. Evaluation through observation is useful at all stages of a teacher's career to improve the quality of teaching for the benefit of the learners. It may be a gradual process which is initially prompted by an external observer but later moves towards self-evaluation. Since teachers may find themselves in a situation where there is little or no in-service training, evaluation can be the means to understanding their own teaching better, improving their performance, and adapting to the changing needs of the classroom. Evaluation in this broad sense is an important part of teacher education which teachers can use throughout their careers.

[. . .]

Bibiliography

Allwright, D. 1981. 'What do we need materials for?' *English Language Teaching Journal* 36/1: 6–9.

Breen, M. 1989. 'The evaluation cycle for language learning tasks.' In: R. K. Johnson (ed.): *The Second Language Curriculum*. Cambridge: Cambridge University Press, 1989.

Breen, M. P. and C. N. Candlin. 1987. 'Which materials?: a consumer's and designer's guide.' In: L. E. Sheldon (ed.): *ELT Textbooks and Materials: Problems in Evaluation and Development*. ELT Documents. London: Modern English Publications/British Council, 1987.

James, G. 1983. *Teacher Assessment 2: Report of the Second Exeter Seminar*. Exeter: Language Centre, University of Exeter.

Kouraogo, P. 1987. 'Curriculum renewal and INSET in difficult circumstances.' *English Language Teaching Journal* 41/3: 171–8.

Low, G. 1987. 'The need for a multi-perspective approach to the evaluation of foreign language teaching materials.' *Evaluation and Research in Education* 1/1.

Parlett, M. and D. Hamilton. 1987. 'Evaluation as illumination: a new approach to the study of innovatory programmes.' In: R. Murphy and H. Torrance (eds.): *Evaluating Education: Issues and Methods*. London: Harper and Row, 1987.

Stenhouse, L. 1975. *An Introduction to Curriculum Research and Development*. London: Heinemann Educational.

Chapter 21

David R. Carless

A CASE STUDY OF CURRICULUM IMPLEMENTATION IN HONG KONG

1 Introduction

CURRICULUM INNOVATION is both a highly complex phenomenon (Fullan, 1993; Markee, 1997) and one that requires further research and investigation (Markee, 1993; Stoller, 1994). To date there is insufficient information on the process of curriculum implementation: the extent to which teachers carry out innovations as intended by the developers, how they go about moulding the innovation to their own context, the strategies that they use during the implementation process and how their pupils respond to the innovation. Within the Hong Kong context, as elsewhere, it is common for curriculum innovations to result in a facade of change, but with little noticeable impact on what goes on in the classroom (Morris, 1992, 1995).

The study described in this paper sought to explore the process of the implementation of Hong Kong's Target-Oriented Curriculum (TOC) initiative through a multiple case study research design. In order to facilitate detailed discussion, this article will focus on one of the case study teachers who seemed to be particularly successful in implementing the innovation. A picture of the process of curriculum implementation will be developed mainly through the analysis of qualitative data, comprising classroom observation and interviews. The aim of this analysis is to verify and develop elements of the theory of curriculum innovation through exploring TOC implementation in the specific context of a well-qualified teacher, positively oriented towards the innovation.

The paper will begin with a brief review of selected factors affecting the implementation of curriculum innovations. This will be followed by a short discussion of the main elements of TOC. A description of the research methodology and its rationale prepares the way for the main body of the paper containing a presentation and discussion of relevant data from the study, including lesson transcripts and interview extracts. Implications for primary ELT, teacher education and curriculum innovation are discussed.

2 Review of selected factors affecting the implementation of innovations

The literature on the management of change (e.g. Fullan, 1991; Markee, 1997) indicates a number of different factors that may affect the implementation or non-implementation of curriculum innovations. This section will briefly discuss just three factors that seem particularly relevant to the case study discussed in this paper, namely teacher attitudes, teacher training and teachers' understanding of the innovation.

Teachers' attitudes obviously affect their behaviour in the classroom. Their attitudes tend to be derived from their own experiences as learners, their training, their teaching experience, their interaction with colleagues and the values and norms of the society in which they work. When teachers' attitudes are congruent with the innovation, then they are likely to be positively disposed towards its implementation. However, teachers who are initially enthusiastic about an innovation may easily become disillusioned if there is a lack of support for the innovation, such as inadequate resourcing or negative sentiments from the principal or colleagues.

If the innovation is incompatible with teachers' existing attitudes, resistance to change is likely to occur (Waugh and Punch, 1987). Within ELT, for example, there are a number of recent reviews of largely unsuccessful attempts to implement learner-centred communicative curricula amongst teachers whose background and experience tends towards more traditional teacher-centred methods. In some form this scenario has been documented in China (Hui, 1997; Penner, 1995), Egypt (Holliday, 1994), Greece (Karavas-Doukas, 1995), and Oman (Harrison, 1996). [. . .]

Teacher training and support are crucial issues in the preparation of teachers to implement a new curriculum [. . .]. Verspoor (1989), in a study of change in developing countries, suggests four elements needed for successful teacher training to support innovation:

- permanent and locally available in-service training, e.g. through a cascading model;
- establishment of effective systems for supervision and support of teachers;
- adjustment of the content of teacher training to the teachers' own level of knowledge and experience; and
- encouragement of teacher motivation and commitment, e.g. through improved working conditions or opportunities for professional development.

Training therefore needs to be ongoing and developmental rather than piecemeal (Brindley and Hood, 1990). Teachers need both on- and off-site training; the former to relate the innovation to the realities of the specific school context, the latter to permit the opportunity to reflect on the meaning of the innovation away from the pressures of daily routines. [. . .]

If teachers are to implement an innovation successfully, it is essential that they have a thorough understanding of the principles and practice of the proposed change. It is desirable that they understand both the theoretical underpinnings and classroom applications of the innovation, but it is the latter that tends to prove most essential, especially in contexts where teachers are not well-trained and/or lack sound subject knowledge. Fullan (1991, p. 199) warns us of a cardinal fact of social change, that "people will always misinterpret and misunderstand some aspect of the purpose or practice of something that is new to them." For example, Karavas-Doukas (1995), in an investigation of a communicative syllabus being introduced in Greek secondary schools, found that teachers exhibited incomplete understanding of the innovation they were charged with implementing and that these misconceptions contributed to negative perceptions of the innovation.

Dissemination of innovation from curriculum developers or change agents is often insufficient to achieve understanding amongst potential implementers. Instead, what is often needed is the negotiation of meaning between developers and teachers, so that a shared vision of the implications of the change can be developed. Understanding can be further consolidated by the generation of specific classroom teaching procedures for the innovation along with resource materials that can be used without adaptation in the target classrooms. Allied to on-site classroom support discussed earlier, these strategies seem to be promising methods in minimising the problem of misconceptions about innovations.

3 Nature of TOC

A TOC cross-circular framework was developed by a research and development team, and outlined in Clark et al. (1994). Initially TOC was to be implemented in the three core primary school subjects of Chinese, Mathematics and English, with subsequent introduction of other subjects and also extension into secondary schools. The implementation schedule for TOC is an incremental one, starting in Primary 1 classes who proceed through the school using TOC. Hitherto, schools have been given some flexibility in the pace and extent of implementation.

In summary, TOC is made up of three main conceptual elements: targets, tasks and task-based assessment. The learning targets provide a common direction for learning for all schools in Hong Kong and facilitate the planning of schemes of work or text-books and the evaluation of progress towards the targets. "Tasks" are purposeful and contextualised learning activities through which pupils progress towards the targets. Criterion-referenced assessment is used to assess pupil progress towards the targets and enables information to be recorded and reported to relevant parties, such as parents. This alignment of targets, tasks and assessment forms an integrated curriculum framework, linking teaching, learning and assessment in a recursive way.

A major premise of TOC is that pupils should be actively involved in their own learning and in the construction and development of knowledge and ideas. TOC postulates that students learn through five fundamental, intertwining ways of learning: communicating through receiving and sharing meaning, inquiring through questioning or testing hypotheses, conceptualising through organising knowledge and identifying patterns, reasoning through logical argument and by deducing or inferring conclusions and problem-solving, including identifying, justifying and evaluating solutions. TOC also proposes that more attention should be paid to the individual learning needs of different pupils, so that variations in pupil learning styles, speeds and abilities can be better catered for.

TOC is, to a large extent, congruent with "international good practice", based on current knowledge about how children learn, and with respect to ELT, TOC has much in common with communicative methodologies. It is, however, innovative within the Hong Kong context where teacher-centred, whole-class teaching styles predominate and teachers tend to emphasise the transmission of information and knowledge. "It is a tradition of the education system in Hong Kong that didactic teaching is a superior mode because of constraints of public examinations and unwillingness of teachers to change" (Wong, 1996, p. 92).

4 Research methodology and rationale

The study involved case studies of three English teachers, in different schools, implementing TOC over a 6-month period in their own Primary 1 or Primary 2 classrooms, with pupils aged 6–7 years old. The case study approach seems particularly suitable to investigate a curriculum innovation because, as indicated earlier, relatively little is known about how innovations are or are not implemented in the classroom context. Case studies enable information to be collected from a number of sources and over a period of time. The approach enables the development of an understanding of the phenomenon from the teacher's view. This teacher perspective is crucial because teachers are the key element in the implementation process, in that they are the individuals who will implement faithfully, reinvent or reject an innovation.

The central focus of the study was to explore the nature of curriculum innovation through analysing the process of TOC implementation in the classroom. The research questions that guided the study focused mainly on the following issues:

- the teachers' attitudes towards English teaching and towards TOC;
- the teachers' familiarity with TOC principles, the extent to which they believed that they were carrying them out, whether they were actually implementing TOC principles and the strategies that they were using; and
- the extent and nature of change and development in the teachers during the period of the study.

Data collection methods used for the study comprised classroom observation, focused interviews and an attitude scale. Classroom observations were conducted for 5–6 consecutive English lessons for each teacher in three separate cycles during the school year, totalling 15–18 audio-taped observations per teacher. I took the role of a participant observer and was willing to take part in lessons; for example, I tried to encourage, assist or monitor pupils during individual, pair or group activities. Both quantitative data in terms of a tailor-made classroom observation schedule and qualitative data in terms of lesson transcriptions and field notes were collected. This "compatibilist" stance (Lynch, 1996) or mixed-method approach aimed to facilitate triangulation through the use of both numerical and non-numerical data.

A 26-item attitude scale was developed to measure the orientation of respondents to ELT and TOC. Thirteen of the items (numbers 3, 5, 7, 9, 10, 11, 12, 13, 14, 17, 18, 20 and 24) implied a broadly positive orientation towards TOC and related principles, the other items indicated a broadly negative orientation. The attitude scale was administered to the case study teachers prior to the classroom observation period and again 6 months later at its conclusion. It was also administered to a wider sample of primary English teachers.

A series of five semi-structured interviews were conducted with each of the three teachers. A baseline interview, prior to the commencement of classroom observation, collected relevant background information about the teacher and the school. Post-observation interviews, carried out at the end of each cycle of observations, focused primarily on the lessons that had just been observed. Summative interviews were conducted in order to probe into some of the main issues, arising from the classroom observations and the ongoing data analysis. All interviews were transcribed verbatim by the researcher.

For reasons of space, this paper will focus principally on qualitative data from the classroom observations and interviews.

5 Background to the teacher and the school

The teacher involved in this case study, referred to as Carol Lee (a pseudonym), had 4 years' teaching experience at the commencement of this study. She has completed a teaching certificate as an English major from the Hong Kong Institute of Education, the main provider of pre-service teacher education in Hong Kong. She also holds a B.Ed. degree from a British university and is currently studying for an M.Ed. at the Open University of Hong Kong. She is very well-qualified academically in comparison with the majority of Hong Kong primary teachers. In fact, a recent survey indicates that only 3% of English teachers are graduates and 55% of English teachers are not subject trained (Education Department, 1996). At the time of the research, it was the third year that she had taught in her current school. She is the panel chair (similar to a head of department) for the subject of English and also the TOC coordinator in her school.

Her school is situated in Kowloon, one of the major urban areas in Hong Kong. The school is a bi-sessional one, meaning that there are two sessions, a morning one and an afternoon one that co-exist more or less independently in the same premises. Carol works in the afternoon session. This section has seven timetabled lessons of 35 min each between 1.00 pm and 5.40 pm. Seven lessons per week are allocated to the subject of English. During the period of the research, she carried out TOC with a Primary 1 class of 26 pupils aged mainly 6 years old.

The principal of the school is supportive of Carol and allows her a high degree of autonomy, both as the TOC coordinator and the panel chair for English. His own attitude to TOC is characterised by Carol as one of acquiescence rather than enthusiasm. In her opinion, the reason for TOC implementation in the afternoon session was mainly to follow the lead of the morning session rather than through a proactive desire to introduce TOC.

6 Findings and discussion

This main body of the paper will consider data from the three sources mentioned earlier, namely classroom observation, interviews and the attitude scale. [. . .]

6.1 Classroom data

In order to provide a flavour of how this teacher carries out TOC in her classroom, the lesson transcript shown in Table 21.1 provides excerpts from one of the lessons observed in the first cycle of observation. The target language structures for the lesson were, "Who is this?" "This is + names of family members."

Although the methodology of this lesson may seem relatively typical of international ELT practice, in comparison with the traditional norms prevalent in Hong Kong primary schools, it represents an innovative approach consistent with TOC principles. The mingling activity part of the lesson (see lines 29–40) exemplifies a number of key TOC features. The pupils are actively involved in using the target language and are carrying out a TOC language learning task. The open-ended nature of the activity caters for learner difficulties and the pupils can respond at their own level both in terms of quality and quantity of utterance. In terms of the five fundamental intertwining ways of learning, pupils are principally involved in communicating and inquiring, with elements of reasoning and problem-solving involved in the identification of family members in the photos. Taken as a whole, this lesson therefore seemed to indicate that Carol was able to put into practice a number of the main features of TOC, a finding corroborated by subsequent observational data not included in this paper.

With respect to ELT, we can see in this extract a number of features that have been indicated by Ellis (1988) as likely to facilitate second language development.

Table 21.1 Excerpt from a lesson transcript

Line No.

---

1   *(She takes out an attractive enlarged photo of her family)*
     T: Look at me *(points to herself)*. I am Miss Lee. My name is Miss Lee. I am
     Miss Lee. My name is Miss Lee. And this *(points to the photo)* is my family.
     And this is my family. Miss Lee's family. This is my family. Who is this
5   *(points)*? Who is this? Who is this?
     L1: This is Miss Lee.
     L2: This is Miss Lee.
     L3: This is Miss Lee.
     T: This is me *(points)*. I am Miss Lee. This is my family. This is my father
10   *(points)*. This is my mother *(points)*. And I have two sisters. They are my
     sisters *(points)*. This is my sister *(points)*. Her name is Celine. Her name is
     Celine. This is my sister *(points)*. Her name is Stella. Her name is Stella.
     This is my father *(points)*. This is my father. He is a man. He. He is my
     father. His name is Pui. His name is Pui. HIS. His name is Pui.
15   *(Then she recaps and reminds pupils of the names and then asks them questions*
     about the names and relationships of her family members. She then asks them to take
     out their family photos; many of them make comments in Cantonese, presumably
     excuses / apologies; she tells pupils with no photos to take out their handbooks, which
     have photos in them. She takes one pupil photo as an example.)
20   T: Look. Who's this *(points)*? Who's this? This is . . .
     L4: Irene.
     L5: This is Irene.
     T: Good. This is Irene. Her name is Irene. Okay, this is Irene.
     LLL: This is Irene.
25   T: Her name is Irene.
     LLL: Her name is Irene.
     T: And this one *(points)*, who's this?
     (Further demonstration and practice)
     T: Stand up. Stand up. Now I want you to get with [*sic*] your photo or your
30   handbook *(uses gesture)*. You can walk around and then look at the others,
     'What's this?' and then you can answer, you can answer okay now try, get
     your book and get your photos ready. *(Some get out of their seats.)* Yes, go
     around *(uses gesture)*. . . . .
     (Pupils leave their seats and move towards the front of the class)
35   Irene, you can ask Tommy. Or Heidi you can ask Kitty. . . . . . .
     Okay come out. Come here children. Come here children.
     (Pupils stand near the front of the class, at first they are led by the teacher to ask the
     target questions and answer them, but after some initial prompting and
     encouragement, more independent pupil participation develops. The researcher also
40   *joins in which encourages further communication in the target language.)*

Transcription conventions: T = teacher; L1, L2 etc = identified learner; *LLL* = whole class choral; *(in italics)* = commentary; . . . = pause; CAPITALISATION = emphasis.

- the target language serves as the medium as well as the focus of instruction;
- the input is rich in directives;
- there is an adherence to the "here and now" principle;
- students seem to be converting input into intake: and
- in the activity stage, learners have some independent control over the propositional content: they have some choice over what is said and there is some information gap between speaker and listener.

Noteworthy is the quantity of comprehensible input to which the pupils are being exposed and the use of techniques such as repetition (e.g. lines 2–5), short simple sentences (e.g. lines 10–14) and visual support (e.g. use of the photo) to facilitate pupil understanding. Interview data indicates that the teacher is aware of Krashen's (1987) distinction between acquisition and learning and that she believes that acquisition is the most favourable route for pupil language learning. "For primary school students, I think acquisition is important for them. I believe that it's much more easy for them to acquire a language rather than learn a language" (baseline interview, p. 9). In other words, she has a clear rationale for using the target language so as to facilitate language acquisition among the pupils.

It is suggested that the task-based approach of TOC puts a greater onus on teachers' language proficiency than more restricted form-focused textbook exercises. Carol's fluent and confident use of English seems to play a greater role in the choice of language medium than the pupils' own limited knowledge of the language. In other words, she is able to maintain English medium during the lessons mainly because of her own high overall proficiency and her ability to use clear, simply English supported by pointing or gestures. This contrasts with a view, commonly expressed by Hong Kong primary teachers, that they need to use Cantonese or mixed code because of the low level of language skills of the pupils. Carol explains the benefits of using the target language as follows:

> If they can try to listen to English more, it is easier for them to learn a language. I think it's strange if you learn, for example, French in a Chinese way with Chinese as a teaching medium as that's why pupils like to go overseas to learn a language. I think it's a kind of acquisition and I have to give them an environment that English is the first language instead of Chinese.
>
> (summative interview, p. 1)

6.2 Interview data

Having looked briefly at an example of how Carol carries out TOC in the classroom, I will now proceed to discuss a number of themes from the interview data. The extracts discussed here relate to her attitude towards TOC, her understanding of TOC, the role of the principal, change implementation, teacher support and teacher reflection.

6.2.1 Attitude towards TOC

Her actions in the classroom, her statements in interviews and her attitude scale responses all indicate that Carol has a positive attitude towards TOC and associated principles. For example, in the interviews she describes her attitudes towards TOC as "positive" or "more than positive but I can't say very positive."

Initial analysis of the attitude scale responses shows that she has a more positive orientation to principles congruent with TOC than a wider sample of primary school English teachers. The following are the statements that she either strongly agreed with or strongly disagreed with in both parallel administrations of the attitude scale used for the study. These provide a sample of her attitudes.

She strongly agreed with the following statements on both administrations of the scale:

Item No.	Statement
3	Making errors is a natural part of the learning process
7	The main role of the teacher is to facilitate learning amongst pupils
9	Pupils learn most when they are actively involved
10	It is important to give pupils the opportunity to learn at their own pace
11	Pupils learn through constructing their own grammar rules
13	It is important for pupils to create their own sentences
14	It is important for pupils to use a communicative approach to teaching
24	The teacher would take into account pupils' needs and interests

She strongly disagreed with Item 22 of the attitude scale, on both administrations.

Item No.	Statement
22	Under TOC pupils will be less motivated than before

Overall, her expressed attitudes seem to be congruent with the constructivist view of learning espoused in the TOC framework (Clark et al., 1994, p. 15) and those linked to communicative and/or task-based approaches to ELT. Interview data indicates that her attitudes seem to derive mainly from her English language learning experiences as a school student, her pre-service training and her experience of "language immersion" when studying in the UK as an adult.

6.2.2 Understanding of TOC

The first four interviews all asked respondents to summarise their understanding of the main principle of TOC. Carol put different emphases on different aspects of TOC at various times, but in general demonstrated a reasonable, though not full, understanding of TOC, despite confessing to some confusion about the differences between TOC tasks and associated terms, such as activities, exercises or worksheets. The following sample answer is quoted to illustrate elements of her conception of TOC:

> I think we should try to motivate them, try to increase their interest in learning, not just copying. I think put the knowledge in use is quite important in TOC. I think in TOC it should be more lively, not just a classroom situation, not just learn this but know that it is useful and they can use it and they know that it is useful for the whole life, I think that is TOC.
>
> (post-observation interview three, p. 7)

Although she has not used TOC terminology directly, she has touched on a number of TOC elements, for example, active involvement of pupils (first two sentences), task ("knowledge in use"), real-life context ("not just a classroom situation"). Understanding of the principles and practice of a curriculum innovation tend to evolve over time and it is to be expected that Carol will develop her interpretation of TOC further as she continues to gain experience with it.

6.2.3 The role of the principal

Instructional leadership, staff development, the building of collaborative cultures, academic, administrative and resource support are some of the main means by which principals can facilitate change. In Carol's case the principal is supportive and willing to permit her a high degree of autonomy. It is not clear the extent to which this is an informed management strategy or is indicative of a reluctance to be directly involved with TOC, a "wait and see" attitude prevalent amongst principals according to Morris et al. (1996). Carol acknowledges the supportiveness and flexibility of her principal:

> Even he thinks we shouldn't do that [implement TOC] but once we started, he gives a full support to me and if I want to take some courses he always mentions that I shouldn't worry about missing lessons. He thinks that it is good for me to take some courses and he always asked me to encourage my colleagues to go out and take some courses. He doesn't control what I did, I can do it however I like.
>
> (baseline interview, p. 5)

This laissez-faire style is in contrast with more authoritarian leadership styles commonly perceived to be found amongst many Hong Kong principals. In Carol's case, it seems to be effective as she has the confidence and ability to benefit from the autonomy granted by her principal.

6.2.4 TOC and change

Change is often best effected gradually and as indicated by Clark et al. (1994) in the TOC curriculum framework there should be flexibility over time-scales, with the development and implementation of TOC being aligned with the readiness of teachers and schools. As Carol comments:

> Maybe it's too rushed for the school to run the TOC class, we have to adapt it and change bit by bit. First of all, we have changed the time for each lesson, change the format of teaching, before we just adapt the whole TOC, the TOC matter because we have to change the assessment task, the format of assessment, the format of report card, too many things at a go, so I don't think it is a good way to change the curriculum.
>
> (baseline interview, p. 16)

On the other hand, the implementation of TOC seems also to have brought some benefit to Carol. As indicated by Morris et al. (1996) in their report on a major TOC research project, innovation can be used by principals or teachers as a vehicle for countering inertia and legitimising attempts to improve. The introduction of TOC provides teachers with a rationale for more active and innovative teaching approaches. Carol expresses it in the following way:

> Because it is TOC I can do a lot of activities and prepare a lot of things. I have an excuse, because it is TOC class so I can make it different from the other class. If everybody is doing a traditional class, maybe if I do it in a different way then the others may say, "why do you have to do so many things? We don't do it so if we compare with you, it seems that we are lazier than you," so because it's TOC class, it's a kind of excuse or reason why I change my way of teaching.
>
> (summative interview, p. 7)

In other words, the TOC initiative provides a theoretical and administrative backing for Carol to carry out the kind of learner-centred activities that she would like to carry out anyway. This enables her to teach in her preferred way, yet with less risk of facing negative peer pressure from her more traditional-minded colleagues.

6.2.5 Teacher-researcher collaboration

As mentioned earlier, school-based support is an essential component of inservice teacher education provision for innovations (Verspoor, 1989). This support can take different forms, for example, the collaboration between a teacher and a teacher educator researcher as described in this paper was mutually enriching. From my angle, I have developed new understandings of the primary classroom and of TOC, and in my own teacher education classes, I now frequently use examples from Carol's class to exemplify points that I am making. From the teacher's point of view, Carol comments as follows:

> You make my class a real English class, you make the classroom really English. You make me get used to having somebody watching my lesson, so now I don't care if anybody comes into my classroom and watches how I teach, and I have confidence in my teaching and you have given me a lot of advice in the whole year, thank you very much. I think I've improved in some parts.
>
> (summative interview, p. 10)

It is also suggested that the process of being interviewed plays a role in clarifying a teacher's understanding of the innovation by prompting thought and discussion about relevant issues.

6.2.6 Teacher reflection and development

At various points in the interviews, Carol shows her open-mindedness and interest in finding out more about teaching as a means for professional improvement. She comments on the value of peer observation in the following extract:

> I think going to another classroom to watch how the others teach is important. I think it's good because now I am doing the assignment [M.Ed. assignment] and I have to go into the classroom to watch the students. Even though I watch the students, I can watch how the teachers teach, I think I really learn a lot of things, many many things. I think my teaching skill is quite good already but I find I can learn some more even newer things. So, I believe that if teachers like to watch each other, I think the others can give you some comments so you can improve and also improve by watching how the others teach . . . but I think it is difficult because a lot of teachers don't like other people to come in their classroom and watch how they teach.
>
> (summative interview, p. 5)

Other responses also show an interest and ability in identifying and beginning to reflect on relevant teaching issues. Reflection and the ongoing consideration of alternative teaching strategies is one of a number of factors identified by Hopkins and Stern (1996) as being characteristic of effective teachers. The following extracts show evidence of Carol developing a reflective orientation to her teaching:

I think under the condition of TOC brighter students become brighter and brighter but the weaker students are still very weak and I am still puzzling about this problem.

(baseline interview, p. 17)

. . . sometimes I find that they enjoy doing those activities but how much did they really learn? I just wonder.

(post-observation interview 2, p. 1)

[. . .]

7 Conclusion

This paper tried to show how a well-qualified English teacher has responded to a curriculum innovation. Reference has been made to her attitude towards the innovation, her understanding of the innovation, her classroom teaching, her professional development and interview comments on a number of issues relevant to the change process. The analysis is of a case study, so extrapolating the findings is not possible but it is suggested that the discussion has raised a number of issues that may have wider implications.

It has been indicated that despite the challenges associated with successful curriculum innovation, this teacher's initial experiences with TOC have been largely positive. A number of her characteristics have assisted her:

* her academic and professional training;
* her high standard of English proficiency;
* her positive attitudes towards teaching and towards the innovation; and
* her desire for further self-improvement and professional development.

This discussion is not meant to imply that curriculum innovation can only be fostered by teachers who have the above characteristics, but it is fair to say that such teachers are probably in a favourable position. Therefore, general governmental initiatives that upgrade the professionalism of teachers, in addition to being desirable in their own right, do help to provide a climate conducive to the development of curriculum reform. Such initiatives are part of a long-term enhancement of primary education in Hong Kong (Education Commission, 1992) of which TOC is one component. This reinforces Stenhouse's venerable dictum that there is no curriculum development without teacher development.

In addition to these wider initiatives, support for teachers at the classroom level plays a significant role in facilitating the implementation of innovations. In this case, the supportiveness of the principal and fruitful collaboration between the teacher and an external teacher educator/researcher seemed to encourage a capable teacher in carrying out the innovation. In other cases, proactive involvement from principals or senior colleagues and/or advisory visits from inspectors, teacher trainers or experienced teachers may be needed to facilitate implementation. Support and encouragement, in one form or another, are an essential prerequisite for successful classroom implementation of a curriculum innovation.

References

Brindley, G., Hood, S., 1990. "Curriculum innovation in adult ESL." In G. Brindley (Ed.). *The Second Language Curriculum in Action*. NCELTR, Sydney.

Clark, J., Scarino, A., Brownell, J., 1994. *Improving the Quality of Learning: A Framework for Target-Oriented Curriculum Renewal in Hong Kong*. Institute of Language in Education, Hong Kong.

Education Commission, 1992. Report No 5: The teaching profession. Government Printer, Hong Kong.

Education Department, 1996. *Teacher Survey*. Education Department, Hong Kong.

Ellis, R., 1988. *Classroom Second Language Development*. Prentice-Hall, London.

Fullan, M., 1991. *The New Meaning of Educational Change*. Teachers College Press, New York.

Fullan, M., 1993. *Change Forces: Probing the Depths of Educational Reform*. Falmer Press, London.

Harrison, I., 1996. "Look who's talking now: listening to voices in curriculum renewal." In: K. Bailey, D. Nunan, (Eds.). *Voices from the Language Classroom*. Cambridge University Press, Cambridge, pp. 283–303.

Holliday, A., 1994. *Appropriate Methodology and Social Context*. Cambridge University Press, Cambridge.

Hopkins, D., Stern, D., 1996. "Quality teachers, quality schools: international perspectives and policy implications." *Teaching and Teacher Education* 12(5), 501–517.

Hui, L., 1997. "New bottles, old wine: communicative language teaching in China." *English Teaching Forum* 35(4), 38–41.

Karavas-Doukas, E., 1995. "Teacher identified factors affecting the implementation of a curriculum innovation in Greek public secondary schools." *Language, Culture and Curriculum* 8(1), 53–68.

Krashen, S., 1987. *Principles and Practice in Second Language Acquisition*. Prentice-Hall, Englewood Cliffs, NJ.

Lynch, B., 1996. *Language Program Evaluation: Theory and Practice*. Cambridge University Press, Cambridge.

Markee, N., 1993. "The diffusion of innovation in language teaching." *Annual Review of Applied Linguistics* 13, 229–243. See also chapter 10 of this volume.

Markee, N., 1997. *Managing Curricular Innovation*. Cambridge University Press, Cambridge.

Morris, P., 1992. *Curriculum Development in Hong Kong*. Education Papers 7. Faculty of Education, Hong Kong University, Hong Kong.

Morris, P., 1995. *The Hong Kong School Curriculum*. Hong Kong University Press, Hong Kong.

Morris, P. and 12 associates, 1996. *Target-Oriented Curriculum Evaluation Project: Interim Report*. Faculty of Education, University of Hong Kong, Hong Kong.

Penner, J., 1995. "Change and conflict: introduction of the communicative approach in China." *TESL Canada Journal* 12(2), 1–17.

Stoller, F., 1994. "The diffusion of innovations in intensive ESL programs." *Applied Linguistics* 15(3), 300–327.

Verspoor, A., 1989. *Pathways to Change: Improving the Quality of Education in Developing Countries*. World Bank, Washington DC.

Waugh, R., Punch, K., 1987. "Teacher receptivity to systemwide change in the implementation stage." *Review of Educational Research* 57(3), 237–254.

Wong, Y. F., 1996. "To investigate the understanding of principals and teachers of the key features of the Target-Oriented Curriculum (TOC) and their perceptions of its impact on their teaching." Unpublished master's thesis, University of Hong Kong.

Chapter 22

Joan Lesikin

DETERMINING SOCIAL PROMINENCE: A METHODOLOGY FOR UNCOVERING GENDER BIAS IN ESL TEXTBOOKS

[. . .]

Introduction

T HE MOST SIGNIFICANT INFLUENCE on an individual's role is "the social
prescriptions and behavior of others," according to Thomas and Biddle (1979, p. 4).
The female and male characters in ESL textbooks have the potential to serve as those *others*
– sources of social prescriptions and behaviors for ESL students. According to some studies
(e.g., Cole, Hill, and Dayley, 1983; Bem and Bem, 1973), same-gender role models provide
stronger role identification for some people than models of a different gender. Thus, for
example, female characters in texts are stronger role models for some women than they
are for some men. Any one depiction of a female or male, however, may be inconsequential;
it is a particular bias sustained over time and through repetition which has a cumulative
effect.

Because of their ubiquitous presence in our schooling, educational texts may have just
that effect. Content analysis of textbooks in a variety of educational subjects (e.g., social
studies, Sleeter and Grant, 1991; science, Powell and Garcia, 1988; teacher education,
Sadker, 1981; children's readers, Weitzman and Rizzo, 1974; ESL, Porreca, 1984) has shown
them to contain gender bias. And we know that teachers in a variety of educational subjects
use textbooks about seventy percent of the time (Komoski, 1985); ESL teachers are probably
no exception.

The potential influence of gendered role models may have particular weight in ESL in
higher education. For many ESL college students, ESL textbooks may be their first encounter
with the American educational system. ESL textbooks especially may have a more profound
effect than textbooks used subsequently in a college student's academic career.

ESL text materials attempt ideological neutrality in order to appeal to a broad and often
censorious educational market. Real and imagined pressures have often led writers and
publishers to substitute or eliminate topics deemed objectionable to various constituencies
(Tanner, 1988). Text materials published for second language learning in particular present
language in ways that reinforce the sense of ideological neutrality. These texts are typically

filled both with extended discourse in narratives or essays and with individual sentences in lists. Language items may be presented with little if any surrounding context, devoid of its history of usage, and with little background given to make sense of it. Yet ideological knowledge in texts informs meaning, according to critical linguists such as Hodge, Kress, and Fairclough (Fairclough, 1989; Kress and Hodge, 1979) whose theory of social semiotics links language with power. External social forces influence a writer's choice of language. Thus, the meanings and structures of language in a textbook – or any other writing – reflect ideology. Feminist critical analysis, an outgrowth of critical analysis, focuses on the semantic and structural properties of language in order to examine ideas and assumptions about gender. Feminist content analysis, on the other hand, is grounded in a semantic and lexical linguistic tradition in the social sciences. Feminist researchers use both these general and sometimes overlapping perspectives.

The methodology I present below allows for the analysis of text materials containing both extended discourse, where ideology may be more apparent, and context-reduced sentences, where ideology may be less apparent, as can be found in many ESL text materials. The approach, related to feminist critical analysis, analyzes language at the structural/meaning level and seems to be less inferential than analyses that only count occurrences of language elements.

Methods of analyzing gender bias in texts

Researchers have examined gender bias by quantifying language items – in the content analysis tradition and by interpreting language content – more in the critical analysis tradition, or by combining methodologies that encompass these perspectives. Recently, Macaulay and Brice (1997) reported the results of two studies that show widespread gender bias and stereotyping in the example sentences of syntax textbooks. Using a combination of methodologies, they looked at grammatical function, thematic role, and lexical choice, based on the works of Jackendoff (1972), Dillon (1977), and Cowper (1992). Using another methodology to examine ESL textbooks, Porreca (1984) found widespread bias primarily by quantifying language items. Her study focused on omission, firstness, occupational visibility, nouns, masculine generic constructions, and adjectives.

The methodology I propose both interprets language content and quantifies language items. Similar to Mills's methodology (1995), grounded in Halliday but dealing only with extended discourse, the present methodology can also be applied to context-reduced, sentence-level items. It is advantageous because it gets at meaning that may be hidden due to the presentation of context-reduced language. The methodology can be used alone or in conjunction with other methodologies, such as those in Porreca's study, in order to triangulate findings. If different methods have similar results, we can be more certain that the findings are robust and not influenced by our methodology (Firestone, 1987).

A variety of approaches may be needed to account for the inherent contradictions in texts. For example, in examining the middle chapter of *Developing Reading Skills: Intermediate* (Markstein and Hirasawa, 1981), this researcher (Lesikin, 1994) found less than half as many females named as males (40:100) yet a greater quantity of female-specific nouns and pronouns (100:84). At the same time the two structural analyses, based on Halliday, presented below, showed that females and males are equally represented in terms of social prominence.

Analyzing gender bias as social prominence in texts

The methodology is based on M. A. K. Halliday's examination of the functions of language, specifically his concept of participant roles of nouns and pronouns and the division of theme and rheme from the Prague School of Linguistics and reconstituted by Halliday (1985). I use these concepts to determine the relative social prominence of females and males in written texts.

Theme, rheme, and last stressed element

According to Quirk and Greenbaum (1973), "the theme is the most important part of a clause from the point of view of its presentation of a message in sequence" (p. 412). Theme is the psychological subject. It is the first element in a clause (with the exception of initial adverbs) "which serves as the point of departure of the message; it is that with which the clause is concerned" (Halliday, 1985, p. 38). Rheme is the remaining part of the message, which develops the theme. The last stressed element of a clause is also important. The person or persons occurring as the last stressed element bear the information focus of the clause and, like the person or persons in theme position, have communicative prominence (Quirk and Greenbaum, p. 412).

From communicative prominence to social prominence

A character in the position of theme or as last stressed element in a clause is the person in a position of communicative prominence. It is the person who is the center of conversation, the topic in writing, or the information focus until another person is introduced or focused on or the communication or text ends. People who are centers of conversations, topics of writing, or the information focus would seem to have more social prominence than people who are not. We communicate about people who in some way interest us or are important to us; those who are not of interest are not the focus. Thus people can be perceived as having different degrees of social prominence by the degree of interest shown them.

Similarly, in a written text such as a textbook, if characters of one gender (represented by gender-specific nouns or pronouns) occur more frequently in the position of communicative prominence – as theme or last stressed element – an underlying message to readers is that one gender has higher social prominence than the other. They most likely present a stronger, more alluring role model than those characters in rheme position.

Participant functions

The division of gender-specific nouns and pronouns in clauses into theme, rheme, and last stressed element does not specify what those role models potentially are. A noun or pronoun in a clause also has a participant role in terms of the ideational function of the clause, which helps us to get at the ideological message. Since themes and last stressed elements are the most prominent and could be more influential roles for students than those roles embedded in rheme, I examine their participant functions.

According to Halliday, the ideational function of a clause is how it represents experience in terms of meaning. The role of a noun or pronoun in a clause is how it participates in the process of a particular experience expressed by that clause. Thus the noun or pronoun also has a participant role in terms of this ideational function.

The participant roles can be divided into two groups (see Table 22.1). In Group I, the functions include doing, acting, sensing, saying, attributing, and relating. Those in Group II are the complements of the participants in Group I. Group I participants take a more active role experientially than those in Group II, where the role of *actor* is defined as the most active and direct participant in an experience.

Table 22.1 Participant roles of nouns and pronouns

Group I	Group II
Actor	Recipient, Client, Goal
Behaver	Beneficiary
Sayer	Receiver, Target
Sensor	Phenomenon
Token	Value

Procedure

The procedural steps to apply this methodology are:

1   Collect all clauses in the "unmarked" form (those that are not questions and/or negations), containing at least one gender-specific noun or pronoun (e.g., *Anne is here* or *They waited for Bob to come*).[1]
2   Categorize these clauses by gender and by theme/rheme distinction. Simultaneously examine each clause to see if it contains a last stressed gender-specific noun or pronoun in the same clause signaling a competitive focus of new information. If it does, note the gender-specific focus. Eliminate themes or rhemes which have both female and male nouns or pronouns (e.g., *Anne and John are here* or *Either Jane or Bob left*) since co-occurring forms offset each other.
3   Tabulate the number of themes, rhemes, and last stressed elements according to gender, and compare the number of themes and last stressed elements to the number of rhemes, by gender.
4   To determine the roles of those gender-specific nouns and pronouns labeled as theme and last stressed element, re-examine them in terms of participant functions.
5   Tabulate the themes and last stressed elements by participant function and gender.
6   Lastly, incorporate into the results the quantity of themes and last stressed elements compared to quantity of rhemes.

Findings

Theme and rheme

I applied this methodology to a single chapter in each of several textbooks developed for the ESL academic market. I will discuss the findings from one of the textbooks, *Grammar in Use* (Murphy, 1989), to demonstrate the application of the methodology.

Out of 55 gender-specific nouns and pronouns in clauses, 44 are theme, as in *Ann* in *Ann telephoned someone* (p. 94). Of these, the ratio of females (n = 15) to males (n = 29) is 52:100 (34% to 66%). Eleven gender-specific nouns and pronouns in clauses are rhemes, as in *him* in *you want him to get some stamps* (p. 101). Of these, the ratio of females (n = 3) to males (n = 8) is 38:100 (27% to 73%). In addition, seven gender-specific nouns as rhemes are the last stressed elements in seven of the clauses, as in *Tom* in *I've just seen Tom* (p. 98). Of these, the ratio of females (n = 2) to males (n = 5) is 40:100 (29% to 71%). As theme and rheme (including the last stressed element) of a clause, female nouns and pronouns are present on average 33% compared to 67% for male nouns and pronouns (n = 37) or the ratio of 49:100 (see Table 22.2).

Table 22.2 Grammar in Use: frequency of gender-specific nouns and pronouns as theme and rheme in "unmarked" clauses

	Female		Male		Total	Ratio
	N	%	N	%	N	F to M
Theme	15	34	29	66	44	52:100
Rheme	3	27	8	73	11	38:100
Total	18	33	37	67	55	49:100

Note: Theme = psychological subject of a clause; rheme = noun or pronoun developing the subject including last stressed element bearing information focus.

As theme and as the last stressed element (n = 51) – the prominent forms in terms of meaning – 17 are females and 34 are males (33% to 67%) or a ratio of 50:100. (See Table 22.3.) Thus males dominate the positions of communicative prominence in clauses in this chapter by double the number of females. The total number of female to male nouns and pronouns in the chapter is more equitable: 44% to 56%.

Table 22.3 Grammar in Use: frequency of gender-specific nouns and pronouns as theme and last stressed element in "unmarked" clauses

	Female		Male		Total	Ratio
	N	%	N	%	N	F to M
Theme	15	34	29	66	44	52:100
Element	2	29	5	71	7	40:100
Total	17	33	34	67	51	50:100

Note: Theme = psychological subject of a clause; element = last stressed element in a clause bearing information focus.

Participant roles

By examining those gender-specific nouns and pronouns in theme position in the same clauses to determine their participant roles, I found that they (n = 44) function in five participant roles (see Table 22.4). That is, they are actors, sensers, tokens, sayers, and behavers. The 15 females occupy four of the roles while the males occupy five. Males outnumber females in all roles except that of senser, where females (n = 4) are present twice as often as males (n = 2). However, males (n = 11) are actors, the strongest participant role, more than three times as often as females (n = 3) or the ratio of 27:100. In addition, there are more than twice the number of males (n = 10) than females (n = 4) as sayers or the ratio of 40:100. The roles of actor and sayer have the greatest number of nouns and pronouns. Females (n = 4) and males (n = 5) are most evenly matched in the role of token, the second largest role, in the ratio of 80:100.

Table 22.4 *Grammar in Use*: frequency of participant roles of gender-specific nouns and pronouns in "unmarked" clauses

	Female		Male		Total	Ratio
Roles	N	%	N	%	N	F to M
Actor	3	21	11	79	14	27:100
Senser	4	67	2	33	6	100: 50
Token	4	44	5	56	9	80:100
Sayer	4	29	10	71	14	40:100
Behaver	0	00	1	100	1	0:100
Total	17	33	34	67	51	50:100

Note: Actor = a doer; senser = a person feeling, thinking or seeing; token = a person having an attribute or relation to another; sayer = a verbalizer; behaver = a person exhibiting physiological or psychological behavior.

Summary of findings and implications

Males dominate the positions of communicative prominence (100:50) in *Grammar in Use*. At the same time, males are actors, the strongest participant role, more than three times as often as females and dominate four of the five roles in theme position in clauses, with an overall presence more than twice that of females. Males are primarily presented as actors and sayers, suggesting males as the doers and verbalizers. Females outnumber males as sensers, suggesting females as feeling, thinking, and seeing individuals. Both are fairly evenly divided as tokens expressing having an attribute or relation to another. While the comparable frequency of females and males varies and males occupy the two strongest roles, all the roles presented for both females and males are active experientially.

The greater quantity of males in the position of communicative prominence and in the participant roles in clauses in the chapter suggests that the males presented have greater social prominence and therefore more power than the females. The greater number of male nouns and pronouns in clauses in general reinforces these findings of dominance. The findings also suggest that fairly traditional, stereotypical roles are presented for each gender (the males as actors and sayers; the females as sensers).

Grammar in Use is one of the largest selling textbooks to the academic ESL market, based on the opinions of ten marketing experts in publishing and distributing ESL textbooks (Lesikin, 1995). The textbook may influence how our students view their own social power relative to that of others as they sort out a new gendered identity in the acculturation process. Language learners are "constantly organizing and reorganizing a sense of who they are and how they relate to the social world. They are, in other words, engaged in identity construction and negotiation" (Norton, 1997, p. 410). As part of the acculturation process, ESL students' new identities are shaped in part by what they read in our classes. When the texts they read reflect biased assumptions about gender, the texts may transmit these biases, often reinforcing the lower prestige and power ascribed to females.

To my knowledge, no research has been done on the effects of gender bias in ESL textbooks. Studies on gender and language have suggested that gender bias and sexual stereotyping in written texts and pictures and sexist behavior in classrooms have deleterious effects for American females. These effects include feelings of exclusion, devaluation, alienation, and lowered self-expectations. (See, for example, McArthur and Eisen, 1976; Montemayor, 1975; MacKay, 1979; and Todd-Mancillas, 1981.) Macaulay and Brice (1997) report on several empirical studies in education suggesting that "the stereotyping of mathematics as a male domain negatively affects females students' attitudes toward, performance in, and perceived proficiency in the subject" and that graduate students (females most especially) who perceived gender-biased behavior in their classes were negatively affected; in some cases they withdrew from the discipline or graduate program (pp. 820–821).

The results of these studies suggest that our female ESL students, like American females, may also construct less powerful and prestigious identities than their male counterparts from similar sources. The undervaluing of women potentially adds to the female language learner's sense of alienation and worthlessness, making adjustments more problematic and perhaps slower than for her male counterpart.

Conclusion

In conclusion, I would like to offer some recommendations for countering the gender bias that may be present in ESL textbooks and elaborate on the reasons for classroom teachers to discuss – even focus on – gender issues with students. Teachers might begin by citing perceived instances of gender bias in the ESL class's textbook.

By discussing what we as teachers perceive as gender bias, we may find that students have different perceptions and views from our own. Discussion might lead to reflective writing or to students interviewing Americans or friends and family members on specific topics raised about gendered roles, behaviors, stereotypes, or expectations. Students may also create alternative texts as language learning activities. For example, students might take a published text containing generic masculine forms (e.g., he, mankind) and rewrite the text using more inclusive language. A subsequent activity could have students applying this new knowledge to their own writing. We can also counter the gender bias by supplementing the material with more evenly represented text in instances where we are comfortable with other aspects of the textbook or cannot change the textbook for programmatic reasons. Finally, we can write to publishers or speak to their representatives at professional conferences to make them aware of our discoveries of gender bias in their materials and our distaste for these biases.

In bringing gender bias in ESL textbooks to our students' attention, we immediately raise gendered behavior and roles as issues in their own acculturation process. Behavior and role assumptions and expectations are changing, not only in the US mainstream culture but in the students' cultures as well. Students may be aware of these forces of change in their own cultures but may not be aware of them in the US. As their teachers, we help our students explore, sort out, and construct their new roles and identities in the new culture by making the unconscious conscious.

Knowledge of gender bias in educational texts and in other aspects of schooling, such as perceived academic strengths and differential conduct and expectations of teachers in relation to female and male students, may help students reflect on their prior school experiences, consider their present behaviors with teachers and students, and make knowledgeable decisions about their future educational goals. In constructing new identities, issues of gender also seem highly relevant to our students' familial, social, and occupational realities and expectations.

Issues of gender impact on our students' lives in their gendered roles as family members and in their expectations of family life in the US. What will be the household division of labor? Who will care for aging parents? Who will contribute to family support? What are the expectations for daughters and sons regarding work, education, family, religious or cultural customs?

Gender roles and behaviors also frame our students' social lives. As young adults in a new culture, they may now, as never before, consider choices in gendered social roles and behaviors. Dating and courting customs may undergo change in the new culture; our ESL students are ripe for exploring options, their benefits, and drawbacks. Who do I date? How do I arrange it? Do I tell my parents? Do I submit to their expectations?

As college students considering career options, our ESL students may also want to explore gender issues in the US workplace. Topics such as child care options, sexual harassment, perspectives on parental leave, work-related stereotyping, and career opportunities can provide information and reflection on students' future participation as gendered workers in the US.

Our students knew the expected gendered behaviors and options in their own cultures, but now in the US, they probably do not. Issues of gender have relevance for our students and can provide valuable information and insights as they learn English and create new identities.

Note

1   Eliminating clauses containing questions and/or negations may exclude some data but makes the analyses of the participant roles that follow more straightforward.

References

Bem, S. L., and Bem, D. L. (1973). "Does sex-biased job advertising 'aid and abet' sex discrimination?" *Journal of Applied Social Psychology*, 3 (1), 6–18.

Cole, D., Hill, L, and Dayley, L. (1983). "Do masculine pronouns used generically lead to thoughts of men?" *Sex Roles*, 9, 737–750.

Cowper, E. A. (1992). *A concise introduction to syntactic theory*. Chicago: University of Chicago Press.

Dillon, G. L. (1977). *Introduction to contemporary linguistic semantics*. Englewood Cliffs, NJ: Prentice-Hall.

Fairclough, N. (1989). *Language and power*. New York: Longman.

Firestone, W. A. (1987). "Meaning in method: The rhetoric of quantitative and qualitative research." *Educational Researcher*, 16 (7), 16–21.

Halliday, M. A. K. (1985). *An introduction to functional grammar*. London: Edward Arnold.

Jackendoff, R. (1972). *Semantic interpretation in generative grammar*. Cambridge, MA: MIT Press.

Komoski, P. K. (1985). "Instructional materials will not improve until we change the system." *Educational Leadership*, 42, 31–37.

Kress, G. and Hodge, B. (1979). *Language as ideology*. London: Routledge and Kegan Paul.

Lesikin, J. (1994, October). "Contradictory findings in text analysis: A focus on gender." Paper presented at the Applied Linguistics Symposium, NYS TESOL, New York, NY.

Lesikin, J. (1995). *ESOL textbooks and the social power of ESOL student: Procedures for analyzing the potential influences of textbook characteristics*. Unpublished dissertation, Columbia University Teachers College, New York.

McArthur, L., and Eisen, S. (1976). "Achievements of male and female storybook characters as detriments of achievement behavior by boys and girls." *Journal of Personality and Social Psychology*, 33, 467–473.

Macaulay, M., and Brice, C. (1997). "Don't touch my projectile: Gender bias and stereotyping in syntactic examples." *Language Journal of the Linguistic Society of America*, 73, 798–825.

MacKay, D. G. (1979). "Language, thought, and social attitudes." In H. Giles, W. P. Robinson, and P. M. Smith (Eds.), *Language: Social psychological perspectives* (pp. 89–96). New York: Pergamon Press, 1980.

Markstein, L., and Hirasawa, L. (1981). *Developing reading skills: Intermediate*. New York: Newbury House.

Mills, S. (1995). *Feminist stylistics*. London: Routledge.

Montemayor, R. (1975). "Sexism in children's books and elementary teaching materials." In A. P. Nilsen, H. Bosmajian, H. L. Gershuny, and J. P. Stanley (Eds.), *Sexism and language* (pp. 161-179). Urbana, IL: National Council of Teachers of English.

Murphy, R. (1989). *Grammar in use: Reference and practice for intermediate students of English*. New York: Cambridge University Press.

Norton, B. (1997). "Language, identity, and the ownership of English." *TESOL Quarterly*, 31, 409–429.

Porreca, K. L. (1984). "Sexism in current ESL textbooks." *TESOL Quarterly*, 18, 705–724.

Powell, R. R., and Garcia, J. (1988). "What research says . . . about stereotypes." *Science and Children*, 25: 21–23.

Quirk, R., and Greenbaum, S. (1973). *A concise grammar of contemporary English*. Fort Worth, TX: Harcourt Brace Jovanovich College.

Sadker, M. (1981). "Diversity, pluralism, and textbooks." In J. Y. Cole and T. G. Sticht (Eds.), *The textbook in American society* (pp. 41–42). Washington, DC: Library of Congress (ERIC Document Reproduction Service No. ED 225 185).

Sleeter, C. E., and Grant, C. A. (1991). "Race, class, gender, and disability in current textbooks." In M. W. Apple and L. K. Christian-Smith (Eds.), *The politics of the textbook* (pp. 78–110). New York: Routledge.

Tanner, D. (1988). "The textbook controversies." In L. N. Tanner (Ed.), *Critical issues in curriculum* (pp. 122–147). Chicago, IL: NSSE.

Thomas, E. J., and Biddle, B. J. (1979). "The nature and history of role theory." In E. J. Thomas and B. J. Biddle (Eds.), *Role theory: Concepts and research* (pp. 3–19). Huntington, New York: Robert E. Krieger.

Todd-Mancillas, W. R. (1981). "Masculine generics = sexist language: A review of literature and implications for speech communication professionals." *Communication Quarterly*, Spring, 107–115.

Weitzman, L. J., and Rizzo, D. (1974). "Images of males and females in elementary school textbooks." New York: National Organization for Women's Legal Defense and Educational Fund.

Index